REINTERPRETING THE

# BANANA REPUBLIC

# REINTERPRETING THE

## REGION AND STATE IN

# BANANA REPUBLIC

## HONDURAS, 1870–1972

Darío A. Euraque



THE UNIVERSITY OF NORTH CAROLINA PRESS *Chapel Hill & London*

Manufactured in the United States of America

The paper in this book meets the guidelines for permanence and durability of the Committee on Production Guidelines for Book Longevity of the Council on Library Resources.

Library of Congress Cataloging-in-Publication Data

Euraque, Darío A.
Reinterpreting the Banana Republic: region and state in Honduras, 1870–1972 / Darío A. Euraque.
p. cm.
Based in part on the author's doctoral dissertation, University of Wisconsin–Madison.
Includes bibliographical references (p. ) and index.
ISBN 0-8078-2298-1 (cloth: alk. paper).
ISBN 0-8078-4604-x (pbk.: alk. paper)
1. Honduras—Politics and government—1933–1982.
2. Honduras— Politics and government—1838–1933.
3. Honduras—Armed Forces—Political activity—20th century.
4. Civil-military relations—Honduras—History—20th century.
I. Title.
F1508.E87 1996
972.8305—dc20 96-6234
CIP

00 99 98 97 96 5 4 3 2 1

FOR JORGE ZAVALA EURAQUE,

DISAPPEARED IN 1981

## CONTENTS

## TABLES

# MAPS AND FIGURE

## MAPS



## FIGURE

# ACKNOWLEDGMENTS

Many people and institutions in the United States and Honduras supported my research for this volume and contributed to my intellectual development. The Tinker Foundation funded a summer of research in Honduras in 1984. In 1986 and 1987 the Fulbright Doctoral Research Abroad Program funded the examination of archives in Honduras, Washington, D.C., and New York City. The University of Wisconsin's Advanced Opportunity Fellowship Program financed much of my work in Madison between 1982 and 1990.

During that time in Madison I enjoyed the intellectual sustenance of many scholars, especially Steve J. Stern, Florencia E. Mallon, and Thomas E. Skidmore (now at Brown University). I am particularly grateful that each of these scholars believed that Honduras deserved a wide-ranging reappraisal and that a small country in Central America little known in the "historiography" merited a study of this magnitude.

Equally deserving of my gratitude is Professor Michael Fleet of Marquette University, Milwaukee, where I studied history and philosophy from 1978 to 1982. Professor Fleet's courses on the politics of Latin America stimulated a reconsideration of my academic priorities. He knows what I mean by that. Moreover, Professor Fleet aroused my interest in graduate studies at the University of Wisconsin-Madison, and he passionately encouraged my curiosity about something called "Latin American Studies."

The understanding of many friends and young scholars supported the final production of this book. Special people include Luis Suárez, David Stemper, Gloria Almeyda, Luis García, James Krippner-Martínez, Judith Allen, Joel

Wolfe, Olivia Martínez-Krippner, Carlos Coronel, and Gardenia Vidal. But another person deserves specific mention: Luis A. Figueroa. We became friends in 1982, and he introduced me to Puerto Rico as a Latin American reality beyond the colonization that that nation has suffered for too long. Discussions with Luis and later Zaira Rivera encouraged me to see in the Honduran North Coast aspects of a Caribbean culture that stimulated questions that now enrich this book. I treasure their friendship.

After 1990 various other scholars and individuals played central roles in making this book possible. First, Robert G. Williams of Guilford College believed in the potential of this work from the outset. We established a scholarly exchange that has traversed his commentary on various drafts, as well as my appraisal of his 1994 book on coffee and the evolution of the state in Central America. I can say much the same about Lowell Gudmundson, of Mount Holyoke College, whose support extends back to the earliest versions. David Perry nurtured this book's potential from the beginning. Stevie Champion copyedited the "final" manuscript and made it a better book.

The sources for this volume can be found in many libraries and archives in the United States and Honduras. The interlibrary loan staffs of the University of Wisconsin, Northern Illinois University, and Trinity College deserve great praise for all the rare documents and books they retrieved from many institutions in the United States. Since 1990 Pat Bunker, Linda McKinney, Mary Curry, all associated with Trinity College's library, have retrieved even the most obscure materials on Honduran history found across the United States.

Also important in this respect has been the support of Steve Peterson, director of the Trinity College Library. His willingness to purchase almost the entire microfilm collection of U.S. State Department Records on Honduras allowed me to comfortably peruse hundreds of valuable documents that few Hondurans ever chance to read when researching their tortured history. Here I should also thank the young research assistants at Trinity who over the years have helped me sift through thousands of the microfilmed documents. Special recognition goes to Deborah McBride, Dora Castro, Anthony Cirelli, and William Daley. Finally, Barbara Furbish and Kate Erskine read final versions of the book, corrected grammatical problems, and provided assistance with some conceptual issues.

Besides the microfilm, Trinity College has been most generous in acquiring many important monographs. Doris Kammradt, the library's Collection Development Librarian, deserves credit for ensuring a steady stream of books for the library. Equally central to my work, Jan Cohn, dean of the faculty at Trinity during most of the post–1990 research for this volume, supported the purchase of microfilms and covered photocopy costs. I also thank Jan for supporting the Spanish translation of this study. This allowed me to write the book in English while simultaneously preparing a version for the Honduran public. Elaine Garrahy in the dean's office facilitated the paperwork and the accounting of the funds in Hartford and Honduras.

A person deserving special recognition at Trinity is the indefatigable Mrs. Gigi St. Peter, the office administrator of the History Department. Mrs. St. Peter oversaw the assistance offered by the chairs of my department, Borden Painter and Gene Leach, in making this book possible. What is more, on my arrival at the college she welcomed me warmly and has maintained that demeanor despite the countless demands that I have made on her time in and outside the office, not just in Hartford. In many ways she knows this book better than many people at Trinity. I hope that she reads the final product and that the many tables and statistical data no longer provoke panic and momentary madness.

In Honduras many people helped me get access to libraries and archives rarely used for studies of this kind. Lic. Dionisio Sánchez of San Pedro Sula introduced me to the bureaucracy of the Registro Mercantil de Cortés, an archive critical to the first half of this book. Oscar Salazar Méndez and his friends helped in accessing documentation never before seen in San Pedro Sula's Municipal Archives. Oscar and Doña Moncha also provided an inviting home in which to study and rest in San Pedro Sula before and after 1990.

I never would have met Oscar without the help of Lic. Aníbal Delgado Fiallos. Lic. Delgado Fiallos, amid death threats during the late and repressive 1980s, provided entrée to the private papers of Don Amílcar Gómez Robelo. In a similar vein I thank Don Pompeyo Melara, who first allowed me access to the papers of Ing. Rafael López Padilla and later entrusted me with the collection until I someday pass it on myself. Also in San Pedro Sula, the poet José Antonio Funes deserves my thanks, for he faithfully forwarded newspaper articles, books, and even *asientos* (photocopied documents) from the Registro Mercantil de Cortés long after 1987.

The Municipal Archives in San Pedro Sula are now under the supervision of Lic. Eliseo Fajardo Madrid. He was not there in 1986–87, but since 1993 Fajardo Madrid has transformed the old musty archives into one of the best depositories of historical documents in Honduras (only the new archives and library of the Banco Central de Honduras are better organized).

Another key person in San Pedro Sula who has earned my gratitude is Don Gabriel A. Mejía. Though he may disagree with much that I say here, he understands that our friendship is imbued with intellectual honesty. The same goes for Doña Daisy Fasquelle de Pastor, who answered very personal questions regarding the life of Dr. Rodolfo Pastor Zelaya, a figure crucial to this history.

Finally, I thank all the interviewees in San Pedro Sula and in Tegucigalpa for information critical to my understanding of the politics of the 1960s. Their special insights and details enrich this book.

In Tegucigalpa many people contributed to my search for documents before and after 1990. Don Julio Ponce (now deceased) of the National Archives in Tegucigalpa helped in so many ways in 1986 and 1987 that I cannot list them all here. The same is true of Don Juan Pablo Rosales of the National Library. In 1986–87 Doña Marta Reina Argueta of the Honduran Central Bank's library provided special documents and literary conversations as well. The current staff of the library of the Banco Central de Honduras also helped. Doña Carmen Fiallos and the staff of the Finance Ministry Archives unearthed *Memorias* rarely examined before.

In 1987 Dr. Nelson Avila's connections with the bureaucracy of the Economics Ministry helped in ways only he knows. Moreover, Dr. Avila's sense of humor and warmth were as important as his intellectual support. Other scholars who should be recognized here include Leticia de Oyuela, Rafael del Cid, Hugo Noé Pino, Roger Isaula, Ramón Oquelí, Mario Felipe Castillo, Laura C. Gálvez, Marielos Chaverri, Mario R. Argueta, Antonio Murga Frassinetti, Mario Posas, Marvin A. Barahona, Kenneth Finney, Gary Kuhn, Kathleen Bruhn, Steve C. Ropp, David Kaimowitz, Thomas Schoonover, Michael Niemann, Carol Barrett, and John V. Cotter.

Mario R. Argueta deserves special recognition because he is the only Honduran historian who read and critiqued an English version of this book. Marvin A. Barahona, one of Honduras's best young historians, read a Spanish account of the manuscript and offered criticism that improved this version. Michael Niemann's computer expertise not only assisted in producing Figure 1 in this book, but he was also helpful in solving this or that computer problem. Carol Barrett and John V. Cotter, able cartographers each, were central to the production of first versions of the maps used in the book. Finally, I am grateful to Christopher Lutz and Mr. Cotter of *Mesoamérica* for the use of the maps that appeared first in that journal in 1993.

Now to family matters. My family in Honduras and my adopted family in Chicago deserve thanks for understanding why sometimes I could not "be there." I also cannot finish these lengthy acknowledgments without recognizing Polly Moran's role in the collective effort behind the production of this book. Her warmth and sensitivity amid many travails and joys—in Madison, Tegucigalpa, San Pedro Sula, Chicago, and Hartford—cannot be expressed in a few sentences. I hope she knows what our life together means not only in the context of the labor behind this book but also in other more important *obras*. Someday Katalina Teresa Euraque Moran will understand as well.

# INTRODUCTION

"Hondurans joke that their country is so poor it can't even afford an oligarchy." This joke, almost an adage now, enjoys wide currency among scholars and commentators who study Honduras.[1] In a lengthy economic history of nineteenth-century Honduras, José Francisco Guevara-Escudero stated, "the Honduran super-rich . . . when compared to that of other Central American nations appear to be quite modest and with limited influence." Moreover, the poverty of elite Hondurans has assumed a peculiarity that has distinguished the country from its counterparts in Central America since the colonial period.[2]

On the other hand, in this discourse the nature of "an oligarchy" is connected to more than the Aristotelian notion of a form of government in which power is exercised by the few. Rather, an oligarchy in the Central American context has been associated with economic elites whose political power has depended on their monopoly of the countries' economic resources, usually land, and, since the last century, land cultivated with crops that are exported—beginning with coffee and bananas after the 1870s. In this scenario, the quip about Honduras's historic and current poverty and the absence of an oligarchy also implies that coffee and banana cultivation never served as the extensive basis of even landed oligarchic government. It is not surprising, then, that William S. Stokes in the 1940s felt comfortable arguing, in a now classic study, that Honduras's structure of land tenure could "in time be the basis for the development of a kind of rural, agrarian democracy."[3]

The character of Honduran poverty and its relationship to land tenure, as well as its social and political implications, have always distinguished the country's position in Central American history generally. In fact, a conceptual consensus exists in studies of modern Central American history. That concensus is that the region cannot be understood unless its economic, social, and political processes are linked to an "1870s–1930s" conjuncture. Some studies extend the twentieth-century limit of the period to the early 1940s.[4]

Understanding this conjuncture involves characterizing how each country in the region became integrated into an industrializing world market via vibrant agroexports, especially coffee and bananas. Significant explanations of the intraregional variation of the 1980s "Central American crisis" usually connect its origins with the 1870s–1930s period. Such interpretations focus on various issues: the historical relations between agrarian structures, state formation and policy making, and the resulting political systems and the collective and mobilizing capacities of dominant classes in the face of militant, revolutionary challenges in the 1970s.

The Honduran position in the Central American crisis is often distinguished in the following way. Unlike its dictatorial counterparts elsewhere in the region, the argument goes, the Honduran military in the 1970s actually allowed for relatively substantial agrarian reform. This ameliorated rural conflict by channeling peasant militancy into a state-sponsored reformist project that then staved off more revolutionary undertakings that could have exploded in the 1980s. In fact, Honduran peasants received more land from this process, even during its downturn after 1975, than during any other period since the first agrarian reform laws passed in 1962.

How has Honduran military populism and its relative autonomy from "agrarian bourgeois" interests and the country's "oligarchy" been explained? The military populism and the agrarian bourgeoisie's defensive position of the 1970s are usually traced to the 1870s–1930s period. In effect, understanding the potential of Honduran military populism and its autonomy from oligarchic interests implies an appreciation of the specific process of Honduras's integration into the world economy via banana exports at the turn of this century. Explaining the 1970s in Honduras requires focusing on the relationship between the agrarian structures that consolidated between the late 1870s and the 1930s and the effects of those structures on class formation and the struggles over the political system and the state.

This argument assumes common elements. A key element involves a thesis first offered by Edelberto Torres-Rivas in the late 1960s.[5] Torres-Rivas linked political instability in the first three decades of the century to the specific way that the country's elites and foreign capital maneuvered Honduras's integration into the world economy through banana exports. The historical record seemed to show that in Honduras foreign capital monopolized the banana industry to such an extent that the landed elites, unlike their counterparts in the region, failed to secure even minimal control over the cultivation, processing, and export of the country's only product capable of securing meaningful foreign exchange in the world market.

As a result, between the 1870s and 1930s the political class comprising the local elite emerged not from an export-based landed "oligarchy" but instead, in a radically chaotic way, from the civil-military struggles associated with presidential elections. In the 1970s Héctor Pérez Brignoli refined Torres-Rivas's early insights with some new research.[6] In the 1980s various scholars linked the 1970s military populist project with the earlier "absent Honduran oligarchy" hypothesis offered by Torres-Rivas.[7]

Discussions of "the absent" Honduran oligarchy have continued despite little or no systematic research on the issue.[8] In fact, in the late 1980s Torres-Rivas's initial theory of a nonexistent oligarchy received further elaboration in the continuing work of Pérez Brignoli and his collaborator, Ciro F. S. Cardoso. During the last decade Torres-Rivas and Pérez Brignoli have continued to refine their positions as each scholar has further conceptualized capitalist development in Central America as a whole. But the historiography of national political development has been limited to one or two works.[9]

This study is an avowedly historical analysis that aims to change this by offering a different interpretation of modern Honduran history. Its concerns, however, transcend the Honduran and Central American context. First, the analysis contributes to filling the historiographical gap in regional studies that explore connections between state formation, civil society, and national political development in Latin America as a whole. Second, by focusing on the Honduran North Coast, this work is situated in a broader literature that explores what William Roseberry has called "noncentral regions" in Latin American history.[10]

The analysis presented here offers a reinterpretation of the relationship between the North Coast banana enclave, overall social formation and politics, and the evolution of the Honduran state.[11] The traditional historiography has often dismissed the region's social and political importance for twentieth-century Honduran history by emphasizing the overwhelming economic power of the banana companies and the absence of an oligarchy.[12] Unfortunately, that perspective primarily addresses only what was not there.

This study does not disregard that point. However, it looks very closely at the capitalists and workers of the region as subjects of their own history and rather than as mere appendages of the banana companies; that is, it considers more than simply the effects of the oppressive power of banana imperialism. In doing so, the book shows that the North Coast developed a liberal and

Map 1. Honduras in Middle America (adapted from original by Carol Barrett, Cartographics St. Paul, © 1987)

defiant social and political culture that cut across class lines and that served as the basis for distinguishing Honduras in twentieth-century Central American history, and whose legacies affected the character of the crisis of the 1980s.[13]

The story begins with an examination of the economic and social era of the 1870s–1930s and tries to explain how the subsequent history of the Honduran

North Coast, as an area with its own unique history, is critical to understanding the military populism of the 1970s, its relative autonomy from agrarian bourgeois interests, and the consequent possibility of agrarian reform. More specifically, the narrative centers around the economic, social, and political life of the North Coast's most important city, San Pedro Sula, once a tiny banana town, today the country's industrial center.

The reformism of the 1970s, its ideology and the people and leaders who projected it, emerged from the long history in and near San Pedro Sula and the Department of Cortés (see Map 1). Chapter 1 discusses how the establishment of the banana economy affected state and class formation in the context of national development. It also addresses a critical problem in Central American historiography of the nineteenth century: why did coffee not become the major export in Honduras, as it did in the other countries in the region? This chapter offers an answer that is distinct from those in the existing literature, which emphasize geography, poor transportation, and market disadvantages.[14]

Chapter 2 outlines the commercial and industrial structures that developed in the Department of Cortés between the 1870s and the 1940s. Accumulation processes in Cortés and their relationship to other areas of the North Coast are contrasted with those of the interior, with close attention to modernization of the infrastructure, especially railroads. The chapter ends with an analysis of the structure of the local economy and by differentiating foreign investments from Honduran investments. The important years from the 1870s to the 1940s, Chapter 2 shows, were distinguished by a unique process of capitalist modernization linked to various banana companies—in particular, the Cuyamel Fruit Company, in the Sula Valley, a business sold to the United Fruit Company in 1929. Two crucial implications of these instances of imperial accumulation are considered: first, the strength of the Honduran state in the 1920s and its relationship to the political and cultural integrity of Honduras as a "nation" before the 1930s crisis; and second, the uniqueness of a reformist political culture in the North Coast generally. The economic structure of the local elite is also examined, especially the rise of Arab merchant capital and its relationship to this political culture.

The major task of Chapter 3 is to characterize the national politics of Honduras between 1876 and 1945. How did Honduras's integration into the world economy affect elite class formation, Honduran politics, the nature of individual political leadership, the country's political parties, and the nature of the political system per se. This examination provides necessary background to the different kind of politics that surfaced in the 1950s and 1960s, especially because of the economic development of San Pedro Sula.

Chapter 4 outlines Honduras's political history between 1945 and 1957. The political narrative is preceded by a discussion of the economy after World

War II and its affect on class structure, as well as the modernization of state institutions, including the military, particularly under the administrations of Juan Manuel Gálvez (1949–54) and Julio Lozano Díaz (1954–56) and in the context of the coup of 1956. Traditionally, the 1956 coup has been understood primarily as a function of a general postwar military professionalization and "the reformist inclinations of the urban middle class."[15] This study complicates that perspective by viewing the coup and its aftermath from the vantage point of North Coast history; in short, it links the coup's origins to civilian personalities closely associated with capitalist development on the North Coast.

Chapter 4 pays close attention to the presidential elections of 1948 and 1954, the general strike of 1954, and the eventual rise of the Liberal Party—from exile in the late 1940s to presidential empowerment via the Constituent Assembly of 1957. These events serve as a backdrop to the very different politics of the 1960s, especially during the presidency of Ramón Villeda Morales (1957–63).

Chapter 5 outlines Honduras's economic integration into the Central American Common Market from the late 1950s to the early 1960s. It demonstrates the importance of the technocrats' control over macroeconomic policy, especially industrial policy, during this period. Also evident is the close historical relationship between San Pedro Sula capitalists, local and international financial markets, and the emergence of joint ventures in the manufacturing sector with new multinational corporations. The chapter likewise details the structural differentiation between factory-based manufacturing in San Pedro Sula and Tegucigalpa. Discussed in this context are the new organization and activism of San Pedro Sula capitalists, in particular their efforts to create a national bourgeoisie and their use of *La Prensa*, their own newspaper, in this and other struggles.

After World War II San Pedro Sula became the country's most important nexus of labor's political activism, long before local capitalists contributed to the new politics of the late 1950s.[16] Why? How did this come about? Why is this history relevant to the broader argument? Chapter 6 explores these questions. It explores the timid labor legislation introduced by the Gálvez administration after 1949 and the reaction in San Pedro Sula culminating in the general strike of 1954. That strike not only redefined state-labor relations but also became crucial to Villeda Morales's adherence to a new politics after 1958.[17] It merits analysis not only because of its centrality to modern Honduran history but also because it further differentiates modern Honduran history, including state-military relations, within Central America, and especially because of the resulting unique relationship between Honduran labor, a militant peasant movement, and the military of the mid-1970s. In short, the

1954 strike, yet to be systematically studied, here is assigned the kind of importance for national political development attributed to labor history elsewhere in Latin America.[18]

Chapter 7 considers the origins and outcomes of the military coup of 1963, and it carries forward the political narrative from 1958. In this context President Villeda Morales's liberalism is linked with the general aspirations of San Pedro Sula capitalists as a whole, while also examining the unique institutional connections between economic development policy and technocrats who enjoyed ties with San Pedro Sula interests. The 1963 coup is placed in the context of a changing regional situation—particularly as a result of the Cuban Revolution and John F. Kennedy's Alliance for Progress—and within the machinations between the modernizing military and a National Party on the verge of political extinction. The chapter ends with the reaction of the San Pedro Sula leadership to the ouster of its president as one basis for a militancy assumed in the mid-1960s.

The last two chapters analyze the rise and temporary fall of progressive capitalists in San Pedro Sula from the middle 1960s to the early 1970s. Chapter 8 argues that the earlier process served to promote the military reformism of the later period. It shows how political elites within the San Pedro Sula bourgeoisie finally confronted *caudillo* politics and military dictatorship, as well as the conformity of organized capitalists in Tegucigalpa.[19] It then appraises the class politics of the leaders of the San Pedro Sula bourgeoisie, mainly between 1965 and 1968.

Chapter 8 gives special attention to three critical issues: (1) the efforts by San Pedro Sula liberals, those closely associated with the leadership of the local bourgeoisie, to guide the Liberal Party under an ideology of a post–Villeda Morales "democratic left," (2) the attempts by the San Pedro Sula bourgeoisie to transform the problems of the Central American Common Market into the basis for a confrontation with the regime of General Oswaldo López Arellano in 1968, and (3) the incorporation of militant North Coast labor into the struggles first spearheaded by San Pedro Sula capitalists.

The Salvadoran-Honduran war of 1969 emerged as a watershed not only for Honduran civil society as a whole, but also for the political relations between San Pedro Sula capitalists, labor, and the regime of López Arellano (1965–71). Chapter 9 describes the various agendas for reform presented in the war's aftermath by different organized sectors of capital and labor. Emphasis is placed on the intraclass conflict within organized management, with the San Pedro Sula capitalists still ahead in the struggle but now incapable of controlling caudillo politics, the traditional political parties, the armed forces, or the newly militant peasant movement.

In a conclusion, the book assesses the implications of the military coup of 4 December 1972 and Honduran military reformism, its connection with the Central American crisis of the 1980s, and the evolution of the Honduran state and civil society prior to the 1970s. Incorporated in the historical analysis is a critique of the most recent and incisive monograph exploring "how Honduras escaped revolutionary violence" in the 1980s.[20]

## ABBREVIATIONS USED IN THE TEXT

| | |
|---|---|
| ACASH | Asociación Campesina Social Cristiana de Honduras |
| AGAS | Asociación de Ganaderos y Agricultores Sula |
| AID | Agency for International Development |
| ANACH | Asociación Nacional de Campesinos de Honduras |
| ANDI | Asociación Nacional de Industriales de Honduras |
| APL | Association of Professional Liberals |
| BCH | Banco Central de Honduras |
| BCIE | Bank for Central American Economic Integration |
| BNF | Banco Nacional de Fomento |
| CACM | Central American Common Market |
| CCA | Cámara de Comercio de Atlántida (La Ceiba) |
| CCE | Consejo Central Ejecutivo |
| CCH | Cámara de Comercio de Honduras (Tegucigalpa) |
| CCIC | Cámara de Comercio e Industrias de Cortés (San Pedro Sula) |
| CCIT | Cámara de Comercio e Industrias de Tegucigalpa |
| CCUC | Comite Central de Unificación Campesina |
| CEHSA | Cervecería Hondureña, S.A. |
| CEMSA | Cementos de Honduras, S.A. |
| CEUSA | Cervecería Unión, S.A. (San Pedro Sula) |
| CIA | U.S. Central Intelligence Agency |
| CIC | Compañía Industrial Ceibeña |
| CNE | Consejo Nacional de Economía |
| COEHMSA | Compañía Embotelladora Hondureña, S.A. |
| COHEP | Consejo Hondureño de la Empresa Privada |
| CONSUPLANE | Consejo Superior de Planificación Económica |
| CTH | Confederación de Trabajadores de Honduras |
| DFI | direct foreign investment |
| DPAGR | Documentos Privados del Ingeniero Don Amílcar Gómez Robelo (1944–48) |
| DPRLP | Documentos Privados del Ingeniero Don Rafael López Padilla (1923–62) |

| | |
|---|---|
| EAP | economically active population |
| ECLA | Economic Commission for Latin America |
| FDH | Frente Democrático Hondureño |
| FDRH | Frente Democrático Revolucionario Hondureño |
| FECESITLIH | Federación Central de Sindicatos de Trabajadores Libres de Honduras |
| FENACH | Federación Nacional de Campesinos de Honduras |
| FENAGH | Federación Nacional de Agricultores y Ganaderos de Honduras |
| FESITRANH | Federación Sindical de Trabajadores Norteños de Honduras |
| FICENSA | Financiera Hondureña, S.A. |
| FOH | Federación Obrera Hondureña |
| FSH | Federación Sindical Hondureña |
| GDP | gross domestic product |
| IDB | Inter-American Development Bank |
| IIAA | Institute for Inter-American Affairs |
| IMF | International Monetary Fund |
| INA | Instituto Nacional Agrario |
| IOL | International Office of Labor |
| OAS | Organization of American States |
| OIAA | Office of the Coordinator of Inter-American Affairs |
| ORIT | Inter-American Regional Labor Organization |
| PCH | Partido Comunista de Honduras |
| PDR | Partido Democrático Revolucionario (San Pedro Sula) |
| PDRH | Partido Democrático Revolucionario de Honduras |
| PINU | Partido de Innovación y Unidad |
| RMC | Registro Mercantil de Cortés |
| SITRATERCO | Sindicato de Trabajadores de la Tela Railroad Co. |
| UNAH | Universidad Nacional Autónoma de Honduras |

# REINTERPRETING THE
# BANANA REPUBLIC

# 1

## THE HONDURAN REFORMA: THE STATE, ECONOMIC STRUCTURE, AND CLASS FORMATION, 1870S–1940S

"Nations," Eric J. Hobsbawm has argued, "do not make states and nationalisms but the other way around."[1] In Honduras the formation of the modern state as the basis of nation building began in the 1820s, but the process did not assume strength until well after the 1870s. Numerous problems confronted nation builders after independence in 1821. Most of these difficulties originated in the colonial period and only intensified between the 1820s and the 1870s. Honduras emerged from this period with a specific economic structure whose connections to the world economy affected the country's different geographic regions rather distinctively. The Honduran North Coast slowly accumulated a social and political prominence intimately associated with the peculiarities of the region's geography and class structure.

In the 1820s the Honduran population amounted to about 130,000, of which an estimated 60,000 were indigenous inhabitants recovering from their demographic collapse in the sixteenth century (see Table 1.1). Then, the indigenous population amounted to about 800,000. The *negro*, *mulato*, *pardo*, and *zambo* populations of Honduras seem not to have been large, and most apparently lived on the North Coast.[2]

During the colonial period Honduras remained a province of the Captaincy General of Guatemala, itself administered by Mexico. Contemporary Central America emerged as a formally unified nation in the 1820s. In 1821 creoles of the Captaincy General declared their independence from Spain, frankly acknowledging that they took the step to "prevent the dreadful consequences resulting in case Independence was proclaimed by the people themselves."[3]

Table 1.1. Estimated Population of San Pedro Sula, Tegucigalpa, Honduras, Mexico, and Central and South America, Selected Years, 1800–1950

| City, Country, or Region | Year | | | |
|---|---|---|---|---|
| | 1800 | 1850 | 1900 | 1950 |
| San Pedro Sula | 500 | 600 | 7,182 | 54,268 |
| Tegucigalpa | 5,431 | 12,058 | 23,503 | 99,948 |
| Honduras | 128,353 | 350,000 | 543,841 | 1,368,605 |
| Mexico | 6,000,000 | 7,662,000 | 13,607,000 | 26,640,000 |
| Central America* | 1,110,000 | 1,967,000 | 3,341,000 | 8,317,000 |
| South America* | 4,800,000 | 18,001,000 | 40,043,000 | 57,843,000 |

*Sources:* Pastor Fasquelle, *Biografía*, pp. 13, 142; Dirección General de Estadística y Censos, *Honduras: Histórica-Geográfica*, pp. 115, 323; Guevara-Escudero, "Nineteenth-Century Honduras," pp. 84, 166, 178, 183; Sánchez-Albornoz, "The Population of Colonial Spanish America," p. 34, and "The Population of Latin America," p. 122; Furtado, *Economic Development of Latin America*, p. 12.

*Central America excludes Belize and Panama. South America includes all the present officially Spanish speaking countries of the mainland continent. San Pedro Sula's figures for 1800, 1850, and 1900 are for 1801, 1860, and 1901 respectively. Tegucigalpa's figures for 1800 and 1850 are for 1801 and 1855 respectively. Central America's figure for 1800 includes Panama and the state of Chiapas, in Mexico.

## NATION BUILDING BEFORE THE 1870S

Nation-state building in Honduras became a chaotic process. From 1821 to 1838 Honduras remained a province of a Central American nation, a nation for which creole leaders, as in the rest of postcolonial Latin America, tried desperately to establish and consolidate a state that might actually give this new nation a reality beyond the paper on which it was outlined.[4] Between the 1830s and 1870s Honduran governments remained very unstable, constantly oppressed by civil wars and military movements and threats, thus incapable of consolidating a central state. In fact, from the 1820s to 1876, chief executives averaged only about 6.5 months in power.[5] The nature and intensity of these conflicts originated in the late colonial period.

Between the 1770s and the 1820s Honduran creoles enjoyed three basic sources of wealth: a tobacco factory near the provincial capital of Comayagua, silver ores exploited near Tegucigalpa, and the domestic cattle market. Unfortunately, these exports collapsed early in the nineteenth century. The dynamic behind growth and stagnation in the late eighteenth century lay with the

European demand for Salvadoran and Guatemalan indigo. Cash from indigo stimulated the other economies. But from the 1790s to the early 1800s war in Europe interrupted indigo marketing, and, worse, locusts attacked the crop itself. Moreover, indigo exports from Venezuela and indigo imports to England from Bengal further damaged indigo's role vis-à-vis the Central American economy.[6] Civil wars during the 1820s and 1830s aggravated the collapse.

These problems did not disappear with independence. Indeed, "the new nation was born in debt." In 1821 the treasury recognized outstanding obligations amounting to over four million pesos, a sum that increased to about five million after independence from Mexico. Soon more loans were assumed. In 1825 Central American federal governments contracted loans in British financial markets.[7] By 1826 the first loan succumbed to a British stock market collapse, and the Central American government was saddled with debts largely for expenses, commissions, government salaries, and cash advances. The collapsing regional economies and civil wars did not help in obtaining resources to pay the bills that accumulated into the 1860s, long after 1838, when Honduras separated from the Central American Federation.

The Honduran economy before the 1870s could little afford to sustain a strong, centralizing state. During this period three commodities alternated as Honduras's most profitable exports: cattle, hardwoods, and mineral products, mainly silver and gold. Exports of cattle, hardwoods, and mineral products beyond Central America stimulated commercial growth in certain areas of the territory and during given periods: cattle to the Caribbean, especially to Cuba (1850s–80s); hardwoods to Great Britain via Belize (1840s–70s); and gold (1830s–40s) and especially silver (1850s–70s) to England and the United States.[8]

Yet fiscal revenues from these exports never energized the state. The fact is that economic relations connecting Honduras and world markets from the 1830s to the 1870s did not sustain a state capable of producing the "nation" imagined by elite Hondurans. A different history occurred between the 1870s and 1940s.

## Liberal Reform in Honduras

In July 1877 U.S. Consul Frank E. Frye, stationed on the North Coast of Honduras, informed the U.S. Department of State that the recently empowered liberal Marco Aurelio Soto seemed determined to carry out a "thorough regeneration of the country." Soto and his followers received military support from the Guatemalan liberal general Justo Rufino Barrios, and on that basis Honduran liberals set out to incorporate the country into a newly vibrant world economy and imagine a new nation. Consul Frye did not misunderstand Soto's objectives. Earlier, in October 1876, Ramón Rosa, Soto's cousin and closest adviser, had promised a "radical change in the way of seeing, representing, and serving the rights and interests of the nation."[9]

The new regime confronted the questions of nation-state formation directly.[10] In a speech to Congress in 1877, Soto described reforms that emphasized commercial agriculture as the major economic sector on which to base the country's "regeneration," but he did not mention banana cultivation as a priority. Legislation that April only offered incentives for commercializing agriculture generally. In the mid-1870s banana markets seemed unimportant. Coastal regions did not yet report major profits in banana cultivation. Soto and Rosa imposed new duties only on the thriving Bay Island commerce in 1879. Authorities taxed only banana exports in 1893, when the Department of Cortés was finally created. However, local regional authorities saw a different situation. In 1898 San Pedro Sula, the North Coast's leading town at the time, made banana cultivation its official patrimony.[11]

In the early 1880s Soto and Rosa concentrated on reforms necessary to create a state that might support commercial agriculture as a whole, especially road construction. But a financial crisis throughout this period prevented investment in a national road-building program. The *carretera del norte* from Tegucigalpa to San Pedro Sula reached its halfway point only in 1918.[12]

Authorities paralleled road development with efforts to refurbish fifty-seven miles of railroad that extended from the port of Puerto Cortés to San Pedro Sula, both in the Department of Cortés. Soto hoped to use this "Interoceanic Railroad" to integrate the region's economic development and secure revenues to pay a massive foreign debt assumed in order to build these few miles. Negotiations concerning the railroad dated back to the 1850s. U.S. investors and Honduran governments projected a railroad that might cross Honduras, pass through Tegucigalpa, and end in a Pacific port in the Bay of Fonseca. Between 1867 and 1870 Honduran governments negotiated loans in French and British financial markets, but the project failed utterly.[13]

Corruption in Honduras and in Europe reached impressive proportions. Little of the negotiated funds made it to Honduras. Contractors built the fifty-seven miles available to Soto in the 1870s, and the loans continued to accumulate. In 1888 "one observer calculated the debt at twelve million pounds" while also noting that at "prevailing land values, Honduras could not repay such a debt by selling its entire national territory." Honduran and British officials did not sign an agreement resolving the matter until the mid-1920s. Honduras finished paying the debt in 1953.[14]

In 1876 Soto reclaimed the railroad and operated it for his government's benefit. In 1879, short on funds and personnel, he granted U.S. investors an exclusive ninety-nine-year concessionary contract to develop the railroad, build ports, obtain land, exploit mines, and deal with the debt claimed by the

British. The venture faltered and a notorious legacy was established. By the 1890s the Cortés Interoceanic Railroad fell under the control of Washington S. Valentine, a U.S. mining tycoon operating near Tegucigalpa.[15]

## Silver and Bananas: Prelude to the Fate of Coffee

Did Soto and Rosa's incentives to export lumber and cattle provide the basis for the wealth of a Honduran oligarchy? What about tobacco and sugar?[16] What happened to coffee, the prime export elsewhere in Central America and the inspiration for liberal reformers in Honduras? Rosa's dream never materialized, and late in life he was keenly aware of the impediments. By the late 1880s silver, owned primarily by foreign companies, became the major export originating in Honduras, mostly in the interior. Mining companies rarely located on the North Coast.[17]

Direct foreign investment in Honduras between the 1870s and 1890 was small, and it did not grow much even in the first decade of this century. In 1897 and again in 1908 the U.S. DFI amounted to only $2 million. It soared during the next two decades, amounting to $9.5 million in 1914 and $18.4 million in 1919.[18] These investments went mostly into the banana exporting industry controlled by U.S. capital. First, however, foreign investors took control of the most important mineral exporting companies, a critical issue often marginalized in discussions of the so-called Banana Republic.

The most profitable companies, especially Washington S. Valentine's New York and Honduras Rosario Mining Company in silver, exploited mines near Tegucigalpa, within a southeastern radius of ten to sixty miles from the city. The economic significance of this foreign investment remained limited to that area, where laborers for the mining companies rarely exceeded 1,500 workers even in the 1940s. In the 1910s and 1920s the annual employment by foreign banana companies often amounted to ten or fifteen times employment by the mining industry of the interior.

Tegucigalpa's population increased from about 12,000 in 1881 to about 24,000 by 1901. But the consequences for cementing the process of state formation on a national scale was minimal. Despite a "boom" recorded after the early 1880s, the import and export dollar values registered in 1900 only equaled the figures registered in 1880. Data for Honduran mineral exports for this period show that export values remained stable but limited, with the value of banana exports quickly surpassing that of mineral exports by the early 1900s, particularly after the 1910s.[19]

It is evident that state revenues did not secure any tax base from even the few companies that eventually initiated mineral exploitation or from those that actually profited greatly, particularly the New York and Honduras Rosario Mining Company. By executive decree and by concessions, companies did not pay import duties on mining machinery, nor did they pay taxes on mineral exports.[20] Also, most of the influential companies generally avoided paying municipal taxes, either by manipulating or cajoling local authorities or by obtaining privileges through executive decrees from Tegucigalpa.[21]

Government officials thus excluded a significant tax base with which to complement general import duties and the rum monopoly—this despite the fact that silver exports from Honduras outdistanced silver exports from anywhere else in Central America, and despite the fact that the value of bullion production of the New York and Honduras Rosario Company alone increased 1,500 percent between 1882 and 1916. The tax exemption status persisted in the 1920s, 1930s, and 1940s, even while silver often ranged between 10 and 25 percent of total exports, second only to bananas.[22]

In 1918 the Honduran government imposed a small emergency tax on bananas exported by the major foreign companies.[23] It then faced an immediate revenue crisis caused by slack import duties resulting from obstructed trade during World War I. Because the concessionary system had long excluded the mining enclave as a revenue base, only the rum monopoly could perhaps complement import duties. By this time deficit spending, supported by domestic loans, became a difficult policy to follow, as internal credit capacity remained largely tied to the import-export business. How did this come about?

The mining enclave did not contribute greatly to the process of state formation, but its lack of economic dynamism prevented foreign financiers from directly menacing the integrity and authority of the Honduran state. Not that the mining interests did not try to control the early banana industry. Washington S. Valentine took charge of the Interoceanic Railroad through a concessionary contract in 1890.[24] By the 1910s Valentine's exploits to secure privileges had earned him the title of "King of Honduras" in New York City's financial circles.[25] His reign did not continue much longer, however, for he died in early 1920.

Valentine controlled the Cortés railroad until 1912. His hold over the railroad must have brought him great profits. From the mid-1880s on, banana exports captured at least a one-quarter share of the total value of exports. The transportation of bananas offered him considerable returns, even if U.S. interests in the La Ceiba area, in the Department of Atlántida, cultivated and exported more bananas than Puerto Cortés. In the early 1920s the different enterprises engaged in the export of bananas became the Standard Fruit Company, itself owner of the region's most prominent bank, the Banco Atlántida. By the late 1920s, banana exports from the North Coast consistently captured more than 60 percent of total exports.[26]

In Cortés, foreign-financed railroad construction separate from the existing railroad began during the years 1902–5. A U.S. concession holder built five miles of a line from Cuyamel to Veracruz, located in a coastal area five miles west of Puerto Cortés, near the Guatemalan border (see Map 2). William F. Streich rented 5,000 hectares of land on both sides of the Cuyamel River and imported agricultural machinery duty-free. In exchange, he paid the state a differential rent for cultivated and uncultivated land. When Streich's profits did not meet his expectations, he sold the rights and his old Cuyamel Company to Samuel Zemurray, who paid for them with United Fruit Company funds. By 1907 the United Fruit Company sold its shares to Zemurray. In 1910 Zemurray continued to finance the railroad westward; in 1911 his lines probably amounted to a little over ten miles.[27]

In 1911, then, Valentine still controlled the Cortés railroad, but Zemurray's lines were the most promising, new modernizing force in the region. By most measures, Zemurray's presence already implied a new potential for the radical transformation of the area, representing the beginning of an empire, in effect, the first step in what a United Fruit Company public relations executive later called "the conquest of Honduras."[28]

Indeed, in 1911 Zemurray financed the overthrow of President Miguel Dávila, mainly by distributing $100,000 to Dávila's opponent, General Manuel Bonilla. Bonilla's successor, Francisco Bertrand (1913–19), lavished concessions on Zemurray.[29] These usually gave the banana companies duty-free import privileges and the right to build and control docks, electric power facilities, sanitary infrastructure or to simply rent land. In New York City Zemurray was probably now crowned the new King of Honduras.[30]

Of the fifty-seven concessions of all kinds to the major banana companies or their predecessors from 1900 to 1930, thirty-seven were granted between 1910 and 1920; half of the remaining concessions were given after 1920 and half before 1910.[31] This process extended the concessionary system first encouraged during the Reforma (1877–83) period and consolidated during the formation of the mining enclave in the 1880s. The consequences for the Honduran state's finances were tragic.

The nexus to the world economy established between the 1870s and 1930s rarely produced consistent and expansive state revenues that might have provided the material base on which to strengthen and refine the government apparatuses designed in the 1870s and early 1880s. From 1900 to 1945 the rum monopoly, as a single revenue producer, continued to place second among the sources of state revenue. On the other hand, potentially expansive import-export duties were a casualty of the concessionary system that surfaced as a legacy of the Reforma period.[32]

In 1937 Pedro Rovelo Landa compared budgeted and actual government revenues from 1927 to 1935 and revenues lost because of concessionary ex-

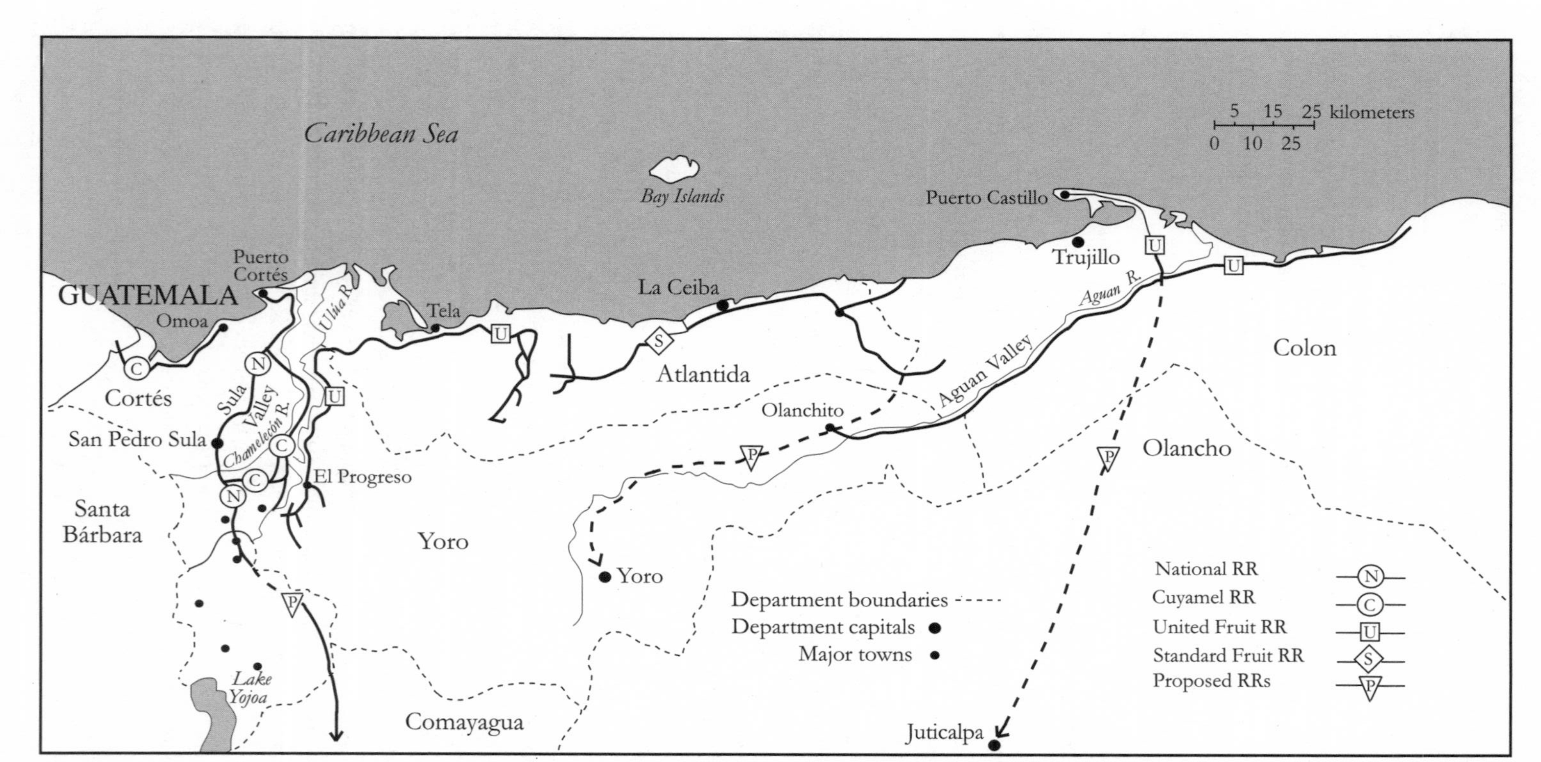


Map 2. North Coast of Honduras, 1925 (adapted from original by Carol Barrett, Cartographics St. Paul, © 1990)

emptions. He offered dramatic and sad statistics. During the eight-year period the Honduran state had failed to collect an average of slightly over $8 million per year as a result of the exemptions. During the same period the state managed to collect an average of only slightly over $5.5 million annually![33]

## THE FATE OF COFFEE: A HYPOTHESIS

Before the 1950s Honduran coffee exports never achieved the status acquired by coffee elsewhere in Central America, and until recently the reasons why have not been systematically addressed. Too often this fact has been attributed to general difficulties such as poor soil, low population densities, uninviting geography, and consequent transportation difficulties.[34]

Robert G. Williams's new research on the relationship between agrarian structures in the nineteenth century, state formation, and the character of national governments in Central America in the twentieth century is the most current and systematic work that addresses this question.[35] According to Williams, the different intraregional political cultures and government structures existing in the 1970s, on the eve of the Central American crisis, exhibited "patterns of governance" founded during the "moment of construction of Central American states," that is, when "coffee townships" became politically dominant (1840s–1900).

Williams also argues that local elites and patriarchs frustrated by the "limits of accumulation" within the coffee township boundaries eventually coordinated cross-regional politics against, presumably after the 1870s, the precoffee national governments, largely legacies of the late colonial period. He notes that a key to this process was the use of police and the military to enforce labor discipline as well as institutionalizing violent, elitist, and exclusivist "patterns of governance," especially in Guatemala, El Salvador, and Nicaragua. Therefore, political cultures and government structures that had developed between the 1840s and 1900 persisted despite agroexport diversification and even limited industrialization.

More specifically, Williams contends that the precise relationships and timing of land, labor, and capital inputs prior to elite cross-regional coffee township alliances served as the differentiating bases for the path dependence of political institutions in the given countries of Central America. His more detailed analysis here is a critical contribution—namely, the notion that "coffee patriarchs," again in the context of local variations of land, labor, and capital, used the municipal power of coffee townships as a first step toward eventual national power, that is, by 1900. He calls this "nation building from the bottom-up." This occurred in El Salvador, Guatemala, Nicaragua, and Costa Rica, although Costa Rica's coffee townships and patriarchs established patterns of governance that were different from those in the other three countries.

Williams, however, does not reduce the resultant character of the states to different relationships of land, labor, and capital as they developed between the 1840s and 1900. He recognizes that each country contained "pockets of coffee production" with "highly distinct structural arrangements," regardless of the prominence of certain coffee townships. In short, he asks: "With so many different models [of land tenure and labor relations in coffee production] to choose from, why did states end up favoring one over the others? In particular, why did the governments of Guatemala, El Salvador, and Nicaragua enact national land, labor, and capital laws that reinforced the large plantation model, while the national government of Costa Rica encouraged the formation of family-sized farms in the coffee districts?"[36]

The answer, he says, is, "The adoption of national policies that favored large plantations was reinforced by the existence of a potential Indian labor force. Because of the power of Indian community structures, coffee growers needed a strong counterforce to help them pry labor and land from those communities."[37] Thus, Costa Rican governments, lacking the "Indian problem," as others have called it, and enjoying a formidable agricultural frontier, could promote family-size farms in the coffee districts. Ultimately, this led to a more open political system in Costa Rica and a state less repressive and dependent on its coffee oligarchy.

The situation in Honduras was different. "Unlike the other countries," Williams suggests, "Honduras did not develop a national class of coffee growers capable of building a national state." What is more, "without an active class of agricultural entrepreneurs to push the reforms from below, the actions of the Liberal state scarcely penetrated beyond the capital city." Finally, "although legislation was passed giving the facade of a liberal, secular state, the Honduran government continued the colonial tradition of living off concessions to *aguardiente* producers and foreign companies." In the end, "in Honduras a national coffee elite did not emerge to influence the formation of the national state during the late nineteenth and early twentieth centuries."[38]

This does not mean, Williams argues, that Honduras remained totally marginal to the regionwide effort to produce coffee and that somehow the country lacked coffee elites and even important coffee townships. "Capitalist agriculture penetrated the Honduran coffee economy during the nineteenth century, but it did best in areas that had already been carved out for haciendas." Furthermore, "most of the land suitable for coffee . . . was located in areas previously dominated by peasant agriculture," including the richest coffee areas, Santa Bárbara and Comayagua. And because the "national state was unable (and, perhaps, unwilling at times) to intervene on their behalf, capitalists investing in coffee had to go through local institutions to gain access to land."[39]

Although it is not clear how it happened, "the exception in Honduras [to this pattern]," according to Williams, "was in the [southern] department of Choluteca, where capitalist agriculture preceded the introduction of coffee, and the more commercialized townships privatized the surrounding lands."[40] However, while "in southern Honduras, merchants and landowners had sufficient clout in the commercial township of Choluteca to secure the land at higher elevation suitable for coffee . . . , they did not have colleagues in a similar position in other towns to form a lobbying force at a national level." Thus, in stark contrast to the other countries in Central America, "Honduras retained a state that lived off concessions, [and] the government was run by a succession of generals and lawyers, and only one president, Luis Bográn (1883–91), became a coffee planter in 1892."[41]

This interesting analysis leaves open the critical question about why the bottom-up state building theory he posits for the other countries in Central America may not apply to Honduras. Williams notes, for example, that "the empirical focus on coffee alone . . . prevents this study from uncovering the forces that did shape the evolution of the Honduran state"; in other words, Honduras was "incapable" or at times "unwilling" to intervene on behalf of "capitalists investing in coffee" in places like Santa Bárbara and Comayagua.

In Williams's view, in order to apply his theory of state formation to Honduras, "one would have to examine the municipal records of commercial townships located in zones other than the peasant-dominated coffee areas." In fact, he suggests, "it would be interesting to see to what extent local elites in the North Coast, cattle barons in Olancho, and mining officials or merchants in the major mining centers played a positive role in the development of national state institutions in Tegucigalpa, using their local townships as a springboard for national action."[42]

This study addresses Williams's suggestion by drawing on research in the San Pedro Sula region of the North Coast during the crucial era between the early 1870s and 1900, that is, before foreign companies directly invested in railroads and land for banana cultivation and exportation. The new research also responds to his contention that the weak concessionary state in Honduras originated "in the colonial era [when] functionaries of the state . . . enrich[ed] themselves by granting mining and timber concessions to foreign enterprises."[43] In short, this work offers another reading of why Santa Bárbara and Comayagua elites, coffee or otherwise, may not have even considered potential alliances with their counterparts in Choluteca.

First, let us examine the concession enjoyed by Washington S. Valentine for the Interoceanic Railroad between the 1890s and 1912. What was this mining tycoon based in Tegucigalpa transporting for almost two decades?—mostly bananas, a product providing a small export tax to a state deeply indebted to British bondholders since the 1870s. This fact is significant in light of Williams's recognition that "Honduras was the last of the Central American countries to embrace the coffee boom and the last to have a commercial bank [the Banco de Honduras]." Moreover, he indicates that "even after 1888 when the first Honduran bank was chartered, long-term lending to agriculture (including coffee) was impeded by the durability of a peasant-based land tenure system."[44]

Consider an alternative approach to the problem caused by the lack of "long-term lending to agriculture," that is, that the "durability of a peasant-based land tenure system," even in the coffee-rich areas of Santa Bárbara and Comayagua, does not explain why the Banco de Honduras "failed" to offer long-term credit to coffee cultivators. It remained an issue, but the main difficulty turned on the role of the silver boom and its relationship to the founders of the bank itself. For starters, most of the founding members of the Banco de Honduras had a commercial interest in the mining boom, both as shareholders in major companies and as ministers in the Reforma state.[45]

Therefore, "long-term lending to agriculture" and the "durability of a peasant-based land tenure system" were not necessarily connected. The bankers associated with the mining boom from 1880 to 1900, including President Luis Bográn (1883–91), who owned shares in Honduras's first private bank, were not interested in "long-term lending to agriculture." In fact, Bográn, unlike Soto, argues one scholar, "actively supported the *ejidal* system," distributing communal lands at a time when the opposite was taking place in El Salvador and Guatemala. There, coffee-promoting executives were slowly attacking communal properties.[46]

In Honduras, the Reforma presidents profited immensely from mining and commerce, including Marco Aurelio Soto, who was a major shareholder in the New York and Honduras Rosario Mining Company. Indeed, one of his sons married a daughter of Washington S. Valentine.[47] In short, the "durability of a peasant-based land tenure system" did not represent an "impediment" because in the 1880s and 1890s the bankers and the liberal reformers effectively abandoned the coffee option.

The issue can be explored from a different angle by emphasizing other facts: the second most important bank in twentieth-century Honduras after the Tegucigalpa-based Banco de Honduras has been the Banco Atlántida, established in 1913 by the Vaccaro Brothers banana company, the predecessor of the Standard Fruit Company. After its founding and development on the North Coast, its offices were transferred to Tegucigalpa. Of course, Banco Atlántida's presence on the North Coast in 1913 was the result of a rapidly expanding banana export economy that took off after the 1870s and paralleled the mining boom.

Seriously regarding the emerging role of banana cultivation by Hondurans between the 1870s and 1900 in the context of Williams's argument does not overemphasize world system forces to the detriment of local conditions, pre-coffee or otherwise. It merely underscores the fact that the North Coast's most prominent landed families emigrated to that area from Santa Bárbara and Comayagua, and that the process intensified precisely during the decades when the state in Tegucigalpa began promoting export agriculture generally and not just coffee.

The point here is that the reason why elites began abandoning two of the most important coffee-growing regions in Honduras for the North Coast in the 1880s and 1890s had less to do with "impediments" they may have confronted when considering the coffee option. The problem, again, was not the "durability of a peasant-based land tenure system." Rather, the commercial and even landed elite had more to gain from relatively easy access to the banana lands and commercial opportunities than they did in the case of coffee. Over the long term, Honduras did not establish a coffee oligarchy and its attendant ultra-authoritarian, exclusivist state; instead, the North Coast became a frontier region with a distinct economic and political culture.

So where does this leave Honduras in Williams's overall argument? First, his contention that state building in Honduras did not follow the "coffee township to national stage scenario" evidenced elsewhere in Central America between the 1840s and 1900 is correct. However, given the country's mining and banana economies, can he still say, "it was not until the 1930s under Tiburcio Carías Andino (1933–1948) that national level institutions [in Honduras] reached down through departmental and municipal governments, giving greater coherence and effectiveness to national policies in Honduras"?[48] Paradoxically, maybe he can.

If this was the case, the process was possible not only because of Carías's relations with the monopolistic banana companies in the 1920s and early 1930s, but also because of the broader associations that developed between nation-state building and the banana economy between the 1880s and the 1920s. Nonetheless, the origins of a different "path dependence" of Honduras's political institutions in this scenario are still situated in "pre-coffee" local conditions as they responded to changes in the world system, that is, the demand for bananas and silver. Whatever the complete answer, the fact is that by the 1920s and 1930s the Honduran North Coast emerged as a distinct economic region that harbored a social evolution quite different from the Honduran interior, particularly when contrasted to regions like Choluteca.

## Demography and Class Structure: Regional Variations

The Cortés Chamber of Industry and Commerce reported in December 1950 that the Department of Cortés, fifty-seven years after its creation in 1893,

Table 1.2. Demographic Growth in Honduras, by Region and Department, Selected Years, 1801–1945

| Region | 1801 | 1855 | 1887 | 1910 | 1945 |
|---|---|---|---|---|---|
| Western | | | | | |
| Comayagua | 13,845 | 50,000 | 16,739 | 26,339 | 60,452 |
| La Paz (1869) | — | — | 18,000 | 28,764 | 48,351 |
| Intibucá (1883) | — | — | 17,942 | 27,285 | 54,882 |
| Santa Bárbara | 9,054 | 42,000 | 32,634 | 39,064 | 87,814 |
| Copán (1869) | — | — | 36,634 | 40,282 | 87,631 |
| Cortés (1893) | — | — | — | 23,559 | 100,054 |
| Lempira | 40,103 | 65,000 | 27,816 | 49,955 | 81,182 |
| Ocotepeque (1906) | — | — | — | — | 28,190 |
| Subtotal | 63,002 | 157,000 | 149,765 | 235,248 | 548,556 |
| Central | | | | | |
| F. Morazán | 25,948 | 55,000 | 60,170 | 81,844 | 173,938 |
| El Paraíso (1869) | — | — | 18,057 | 42,118 | 73,597 |
| Choluteca | 17,308 | 20,000 | 43,588 | 45,817 | 96,559 |
| Valle (1893) | — | — | — | 30,479 | 58,737 |
| Yoro | 14,392 | 18,000 | 13,996 | 18,926 | 78,359 |
| I. Bahía (1892) | — | — | 2,825 | 4,893 | 7,314 |
| Atlántida (1902) | — | — | — | 11,372 | 50,413 |
| Subtotal | 57,648 | 93,000 | 138,636 | 235,449 | 538,917 |
| Eastern | | | | | |
| Olancho | 7,703 | 52,000 | 31,132 | 43,368 | 68,113 |
| Colón (1881) | — | — | 11,474 | 11,191 | 27,802 |
| Subtotal | 7,703 | 52,000 | 42,600 | 54,559 | 88,915 |
| Total | 128,353 | 302,000 | 334,742 | 525,256 | 1,176,388 |

*Sources:* The data for 1801, 1855, 1887, and 1910 for all departments except the Islas de la Bahía are from Guevara-Escudero, "Nineteenth-Century Honduras," p. 92. The data for the Islas de la Bahía and the 1945 data for all departments are from Dirección General de Estadística y Censos, *Honduras: Histórica-Geográfica*, various pages.

provided more than 30 percent of total central state revenues and that San Pedro Sula thus required national attention because with "its revenues it contributed to the resolution of the vital problems of the rest of the country." The municipal authorities had made similar claims a few days earlier. By this time, the North Coast, especially San Pedro Sula, was enjoying a postdepression economic resurgence that consolidated the position of importance it had acquired between the 1880s and the 1940s.[49]

Table 1.3. Demographic Growth on the North Coast, by Major Departments and Cities, Selected Years, 1901–1950

| | Year | | | | | |
|---|---|---|---|---|---|---|
| Department/City | 1901 | 1910 | 1926 | 1930 | 1940 | 1950 |
| Cortés | 21,801 | 23,559 | 44,278 | 58,273 | 87,269 | 125,728 |
| San Pedro Sula | 7,182 | 7,820 | 17,030 | 24,425 | 40,396 | 54,248 |
| Atlántida | 8,797 | 11,372 | 31,964 | 32,506 | 43,862 | 63,582 |
| La Ceiba | 3,379 | 2,954 | 12,136 | 13,073 | 15,124 | 20,949 |
| Yoro | 19,988 | 18,926 | 32,683 | 42,555 | 63,339 | 98,700 |
| El Progreso | 749 | 1,156 | 6,583 | 10,920 | 15,720 | 25,430 |
| Colón | 13,791 | 11,191 | 19,891 | 31,787 | 30,644 | 35,465 |
| Trujillo | 4,040 | — | 6,040 | 8,865 | 8,313 | 13,125 |

*Source:* Dirección General de Estadística y Censos, *Honduras: Histórica-Geográfica*, pp. 181, 323, 357, 385.

By the late 1940s the North Coast, as the engine of economic recovery, had also become the locus of a major demographic transformation. The departments of the North Coast, most of which were established after 1890, came to account for a significant percentage of Honduras's overall population increase recorded during the transition from the nineteenth to the twentieth centuries.[50] Table 1.2 provides comparative data on demographic growth for Honduras by region and department. After the 1920s the departments of the North Coast—Cortés, Atlántida, Colón, Yoro, Gracias a Dios (part of Colón until 1957), and the Islas de la Bahía—in effect became a new region whose cohesion depended on the banana nexus to the world economy.

Another important demographic change accompanied the broader population changes: settlements on the North Coast recast the urbanization hierarchy that dominated village and town life in Honduras prior to the 1880s. The process occurred slowly, as even in 1910 only "16.9 percent of the nation's population lived in cities of more than 1,000 inhabitants, while the rest lived in more rural settings."[51] Table 1.3 shows that the demographic upsurge in the departments and important cities of the North Coast really began after the mid-1910s and took off especially after the 1920s, in great part as a result of a massive immigration from the interior.

Also, by the 1930s and 1940s the North Coast had become Honduras's most urbanized area, despite the fact that its departments did not account for the largest percentages of the country's population (see Table 1.4). In 1930 the North Coast accounted for about 20 percent of the Honduran population, as well as for about 42 percent of the total population living in cities of 2,000 or

Table 1.4. Regional Growth as a Percentage of Total Population, 1930, 1940, and 1950

| Region/Departments | 1930 | 1940 | 1950 |
|---|---|---|---|
| | Percentage of Total Population | | |
| North Coastal<br>Cortés, Atlántida,<br>Yoro, Colón, I. Bahía | 19.9 | 20.9 | 24.2 |
| South Coastal<br>Valle, Choluteca | 12.8 | 12.8 | 12.6 |
| Western Highlands<br>Santa Bárbara, Copán | 14.9 | 14.7 | 14.0 |
| Southwestern Highlands<br>Ocotepeque, Intibucá,<br>La Paz, Lempira | 21.1 | 20.4 | 18.1 |
| Central Highlands<br>Comayagua, El Paraíso,<br>F. Morazán, Olancho | 31.2 | 31.2 | 31.0 |
| | Percentage of Total Population in Places of 2,000 or More | | |
| North Coastal | 42.2 | 37.8 | 38.2 |
| South Coastal | 5.4 | 10.2 | 8.2 |
| Western Highlands | 11.4 | 9.7 | 9.2 |
| Southwestern Highlands | 5.9 | 3.8 | 3.4 |
| Central Highlands | 35.1 | 38.5 | 41.0 |

*Source:* Gibson, "A Demographic Analysis of Urbanization," p. 186.

more people. Scholars of Latin American urbanization choose the range between 2,000 and 3,000 inhabitants for settlements classified as "urban" because they are capable of sustaining a health center, a gasoline station, a secondary school, a cinema, a restaurant, and an auto repair shop.[52] Although not every Honduran city with 2,000 or more inhabitants possessed all of these amenities, the largest surely did.

Therefore, it is safe to assume that North Coast urbanization had important social implications for intraregional differences relating to occupational structures, literacy levels, and ultimately modes of life among elites and nonelites. Moreover, as Table 1.4 shows, the transition to the mid-twentieth century produced a restructuring of geographic regions when compared with those Francisco Guevara-Escudero identified for the nineteenth century (see Table 1.2).

Mapping the geography of the Honduran class structure between the 1870s and the 1940s is problematic.[53] In the twentieth century census reports do not

Table 1.5. Estimated Number of Workers in Major Export Industries and Factory Manufacturing in Urban Centers, Selected Decades, 1880s–1940s

| | Major Export Industry | | Factory Manufacturing in Urban Center | | |
|---|---|---|---|---|---|
| Decade | Bananas | Mining | Tegucigalpa | San Pedro Sula | La Ceiba |
| 1880s | — | 2,000 | — | — | — |
| 1910s | 2,480 | 2,000 | 233 | 47 | 37 |
| 1920s | 16,600 | 1,500 | — | 210 | 126 |
| 1930s | 17,381 | 1,051 | 871 | 397 | 411 |
| 1940s | 32,877 | 1,000 | 2,645 | 795 | 830 |

*Sources:* As complete industrial census data for Honduras only became available after 1950, the figures on factory manufacturing and banana plantation labor presented here draw on many reports published in the *Memorias* of the Ministry of Development. However, because the data for the 1910s and 1920s are very uneven, a particular methodology was used to arrive at the estimates in this table. The data on mining also come from many sources that required special analysis. For a full explanation, see Euraque, "Modernity, Economic Power," app. I, pp. 61–63.

list occupations until 1930, so employment data on factory-based production, for example, are difficult to come by. And because industrial censuses are not available for the pre–1950 period, estimates of factory- and artisan-based manufacturing employment for the 1930s and 1940s are tentative (see Table 1.5). When compared with the data available for the 1950s, however, estimates here generally coincide with trends in the structural and growth rates of the economy, manufacturing share of gross domestic product, types of goods produced in the manufacturing process, either artisan or factory-based, and location of manufacturing establishments, mostly in Tegucigalpa, San Pedro Sula, and La Ceiba.

Data published by the Ministry of Development in the 1930s, 1940s, and early 1950s also show that manufacturing concerns remained almost entirely in the consumer goods sector, with few companies employing more than five workers, the base number that defined a "factory" after 1950.[54] Similarly, the industrial censuses of the 1950s indicate that more than 75 percent of value added in manufacturing production occurred in the case of consumer goods, with intermediate and capital goods production generally remaining between 5 and 14 percent of total value added and most of this established late in the decade.[55]

Data on banana and mining company employment has been easier to lo-

Table 1.6. Distribution of Professional and Artisan Classes, by Department, 1927–1928

| Department | Professionals | | Artisans | |
|---|---|---|---|---|
| | Number | % of Total | Number | % of Total |
| F. Morazán | 359 | 37 | 2,812 | 40 |
| Cortés | 195 | 20 | 748 | 11 |
| Santa Bárbara | 60 | 6 | 457 | 7 |
| Comayagua | 57 | 6 | 247 | 4 |
| Olancho | 41 | 5 | 205 | 3 |
| Choluteca | 41 | 5 | 306 | 4 |
| Copán | 36 | 4 | 456 | 7 |
| Colón | 34 | 4 | 138 | 2 |
| El Paraíso | 29 | 3 | 539 | 8 |
| Ocotepeque | 23 | 2 | 221 | 3 |
| Valle | 19 | 2 | 310 | 5 |
| Yoro | 18 | 2 | 242 | 4 |
| La Paz | 18 | 2 | 142 | 2 |
| Lempira | 17 | 2 | 267 | 4 |
| Intibucá | 13 | 1 | 223 | 3 |
| I. Bahía | — | — | — | — |
| Atlántida | — | — | — | — |
| Total | 960 | 100+ | 7,313 | 100+ |

*Source:* Ministerio de Fomento, "Cuadro Que Demuestra el Número de Profesionales de la República, 1927 a 1928" and "Cuadro Que Demuestra el Número de Artesanos de la República, 1927 a 1928," *Memoria de Fomento, Obras Públicas, Agricultura y Trabajo, 1927–1928* (1929), n.p.

cate, and its geographic distribution, of course, is readily available. Table 1.5 provides, based on tentative but suggestive data, a comparative look at the very unequal distribution of the Honduran labor force employed in capitalist agriculture and manufacturing. Consider as well how banana company employment rebounded after the 1940s, and how disproportionate was that upsurge when compared with factory-based employment.

Honduran artisans and professional classes, usually located in urban centers, paralleled the geographic distribution of capitalist employment. Data from the 1920s connote a distinct occupational and class structure more clearly documented after 1930. According to Table 1.6, based on a Ministry of Development report of 1929, indicate that Honduras's professional class—doctors, lawyers, engineers, dentists, and accountants—was already generally distributed in the North Coast departments, especially Cortés. Of the interior

Table 1.7. Percentage of Honduras's Economically Active Population in the Secondary Sector, by Department, 1930, 1940, and 1950

| Department | 1930 | 1940 | 1950 |
|---|---|---|---|
| Cortés | 12.6 | 11.8 | 17.5 |
| Atlántida | 18.6 | 8.4 | 14.6 |
| Copán | 10.2 | 7.0 | 10.9 |
| Colón | 12.1 | 4.9 | 10.8 |
| Yoro | 6.2 | 7.5 | 7.2 |
| I. Bahía | 6.2 | 15.9 | 11.8 |
| Subtotal | 37.1 | 48.5 | 61.9 |
| F. Morazán | 13.9 | 16.3 | 19.3 |
| La Paz | 6.3 | 3.2 | 15.3 |
| Comayagua | 8.4 | 5.4 | 9.4 |
| Santa Bárbara | 22.5 | 15.5 | 9.1 |
| Ocotepeque | 8.9 | 3.8 | 8.3 |
| Valle | 6.9 | 5.0 | 8.9 |
| Choluteca | 7.0 | 4.7 | 7.6 |
| El Paraíso | 5.1 | 3.2 | 7.8 |
| Olancho | 10.8 | 8.1 | 7.6 |
| Intibucá | 6.0 | 2.1 | 6.7 |
| Lempira | 6.5 | 5.9 | 5.5 |
| Subtotal | 62.9 | 51.5 | 38.1 |

*Source:* David F. Ross, "Economic Development of Honduras," p. 195.

departments, only Morazán, seat of the country's capital, rivaled this occupational concentration.

The geographic distribution of the Honduran artisan class, as reported in the Ministry of Development report of 1929, does not show a clear-cut geographic distribution of the professional class. Unfortunately, Atlántida and Islas de la Bahía did not submit reports, for the inclusion of their information would probably have placed the North Coast in the lead of this category as well. Data from the censuses of 1930, 1940, and 1950 generally support, albeit indirectly, the 1929 evidence and the stated assumption regarding the artisan class.

Table 1.7 shows the percentage of the "secondary sector" of the economically active population of the country's various departments. The secondary sector of the EAP includes mining, construction, manufacturing, public works, gas, electricity, and so forth. Because, according to the 1950 industrial census, 98 percent of the manufacturing enterprises occupied five or less workers, it is reasonable to conclude that most of the EAP's secondary sector consisted of artisans. Therefore, it is likely that the North Coast departments also accounted for the greatest percentages of artisans receiving incomes, especially after the 1940s.

Although the preceding data are somewhat limited by their regional focus, it is safe to assume that the urban locus of the class structure outlined tended to be the major population centers within each department. Thus, between the 1880s and the late 1940s, demographic and class structure transformations accompanying Reforma legislation and its aftermath produced a distinct regional variation that centered around major urban centers of the North Coast. In the process, San Pedro Sula was transformed from a small, dispersed village, to use the language of urban sociologists, into a complex urban center in the heart of similar transformations throughout the North Coast.

# SAN PEDRO SULA'S CAPITAL AND LABOR:

## STRUCTURE AND ORGANIZATION, 1870S–1940S

In 1536 Pedro de Alvarado, founder of San Pedro Sula and lieutenant of Hernan Cortés, was engaged in a brutal war with various indigenous chiefdoms in the Sula Valley, today part of the Department of Cortés, in the Honduran northwest (see Map 3).[1] The struggles of the 1530s in the Sula Valley demonstrated that the locals continued to desperately defend environmental entrepôts that had sustained their ancestors for thousands of years. In the twentieth century, the Sula Valley has again become a major center of wealth. From San Pedro Sula, the Sula Valley extends for about sixty miles north to the Caribbean Sea and for about thirty miles south to the beginning of mountains that separate this tropical lowland valley from the fertile, highland plain of Comayagua, the colonial and immediate postcolonial capital of the country. (Tegucigalpa became the capital of Honduras in 1880.)

The peoples occupying the Sula Valley, around fifty thousand before the Spanish invasion, enjoyed the fertility of one of Honduras's three major river systems—a system fed by the Chamelecón and Ulúa Rivers.[2] The Ulúa River, flowing north, receives water from various smaller waterways, but especially from the Humuya River, which drains the plain of Comayagua. The Chamelecón, on the other hand, originates in the mountains that separate Honduras and Guatemala in the northwest. It then flows eastward into the Sula Valley and, paralleling the Ulúa River, turns northward for about sixty miles and into the Caribbean Sea.[3] In the 1520s these waterways remained crowded from commerce with outposts of Mayan and Aztec traders and agents.

About thirty-five years before the wars of the 1530s, Christopher Columbus

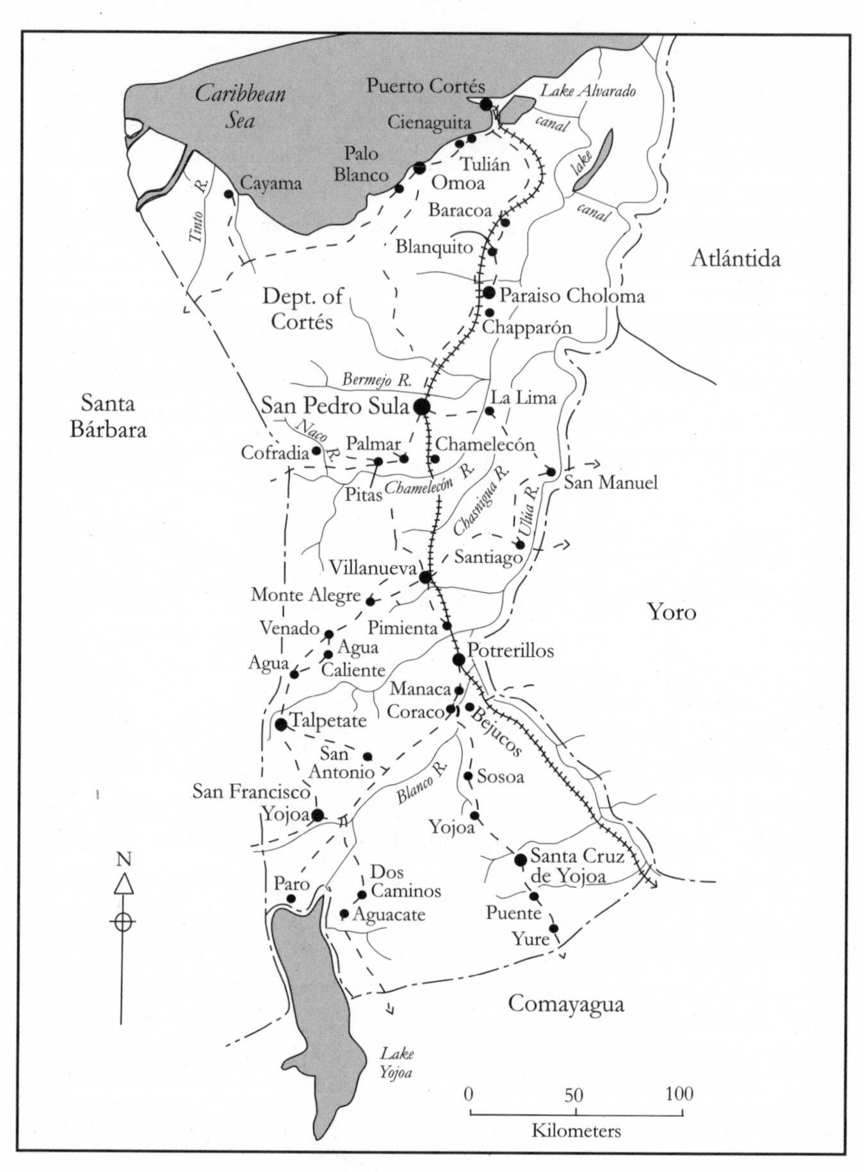


Map 3. Department of Cortés, 1930 (adapted from original by John V. Cotter; courtesy of *Mesoamérica*)

approached the Honduran North Coast but did not travel into the country's interior. He thus missed encountering an amazing variety of chiefdoms and sedentary tribes that occupied distinctive topographic, demographic, and cultural areas, including the Sula Valley. During the colonial period (1520s–1821) the Sula Valley, like other Caribbean lowlands, maintained tenuous links to the highland regions of Honduras's Western Zone (see Table 1.2). The fragile connection between San Pedro Sula and its interior survived primarily because of export and import harbors established on the Caribbean coast itself, ports for which San Pedro Sula served as a trading post of official and contraband commerce, a situation that changed little until the nineteenth century.

## San Pedro Sula before the 1870s

For most of the colonial period San Pedro Sula barely existed, its dwellers often repelling French and English pirates. Like the territory as a whole, the peoples of the Sula Valley suffered a massive demographic collapse during the conquest by the Spaniards. On the eve of independence, Honduras's pre-colonial population of 800,000 had dropped to about 62,000 inhabitants, most of whom lived in the southern departments of the Western Zone.[4] The Sula Valley's indigenous population never recovered. In 1860 San Pedro Sula authorities reported that only thirty-eight Indians lived there.[5]

In the mid-eighteenth century, the Spanish Crown responded to British imperialism by erecting various forts throughout the Caribbean. In Honduras, it built the Fort of Omoa, in the northwestern corner of the Department of Cortés, some twenty miles west of old Puerto Cortés. Finished in 1775, the fort became a key port for commerce between the Honduran Western Zone and European markets.[6] Spanish defensive efforts also translated, in 1780, into another reconstruction of Trujillo, not only to protect Spanish interests in Colón and Gracias a Dios, but also to help Omoa, which the British occupied in 1777.[7]

Omoa again made San Pedro Sula an intraprovincial entrepôt for exports originating in Santa Bárbara and Comayagua and for imports transported from England via Jamaica, Belize, and the Bay Islands. Nonetheless, after independence San Pedro Sula remained a small and impoverished village functioning mainly as a conduit for trade in the interior of the country. One commercial network extended from Omoa, through San Pedro Sula and other villages, directly south into the Sula Valley, and then southwestwardly into the more prosperous north-central regions of the Western Zone.

A second trade network that included San Pedro Sula in its path emerged in Comayagua and the northern rims of the Departments of Lempira and Intibucá and the southern region of the Department of Santa Bárbara. Taken together, these trade networks represented the commercial lifeblood of Honduras's Western Zone.[8] In the 1840s and 1850s Omoa's nineteenth-century population peaked at around 2,000, about four times the number of residents in San Pedro Sula.[9]

Between the 1830s and 1850s Omoa emerged as Honduras's most important port. It served not only as a transshipping point from Santa Bárbara and Comayagua, but also as the key place of entry for European imports destined for trade fairs in El Salvador.[10] In the 1840s and 1850s ships from the United States began stopping in Omoa. Regional commerce from Belize paralleled the more "global" trade, especially logging operations along the Ulúa and Chamelecón Rivers.[11] The U.S. consul for Omoa and Trujillo, Augustus Follin, and his British counterpart, Frederic Debrot, monopolized logging concessions during the 1840s and 1850s.[12] These diplomats joined a coterie of other Europeans buying and exporting cattle, indigo, hides, deerskins, and sarsaparilla cultivated and collected by Hondurans from the interior.[13]

These processes did little to transform San Pedro Sula. Despite a general demographic growth recorded throughout the country and particularly in the Western Zone, San Pedro Sula's population in 1860 still only amounted to about six hundred people, a growth rate of 0.4 percent since 1801.[14] The rural hinterland of San Pedro Sula remained virtually unoccupied. After the 1860s its communal territory remained attractive to newcomers from the interior, enough so that the banana boom recorded after the 1870s took place through cultivation of communal land. The majority of the city's oldest families migrated to the area from Copán, Comayagua, and Santa Bárbara in order to enjoy the flexible land tenure of the Sula Valley.[15]

## La Reforma, San Pedro Sula, and the Emergence of the Banana Industry

U.S. District Consul Frank E. Frye, stationed in the Bay Islands, reported in 1875 that San Pedro Sula's population stood at 1,200, twice its 1860 count, and now deeply affected by banana cultivation on the northern coasts.[16] Three years later, in 1878, municipal officials characterized the town as "pressed by the new necessities of its emerging progress."[17] The officials attributed the city's progress to the "instantaneous expansion motivated by the town's importance and central location in the construction of the railroad; its proximity to the ports, the richness of the area's soils, and the unmatched beauty of the town's surroundings."

San Pedro Sula's agricultural prosperity did not mean that subsistence crops were flourishing. The voyages by banana schooners from *el norte* now mattered in the economic life of the town. The 1878 report acknowledged the "extensive" cultivation of plantains, bananas, and cacao. It also recognized that "agricultural empresarios" were directing "grand works." A new social type now lived in San Pedro Sula, one that hired *operarios* (laborers) for *jornadas* (wages).

"The development of the plantain industry," claimed the authorities in 1878, "is the easiest and most productive, but is presently constrained because of two circumstances: first, a lack of means for export, and secondly, because of the liberty and permission allowed to the grazing of cattle." This was an important warning. Municipal elites perceived a contradiction that persisted for the next forty years. Cattle grazing on municipal land, known as *ejidos*, was an old practice in rural economies, but now local officials condemned grazing liberties associated with communal tradition.[18]

This rhetoric resulted from the ascendancy of a banana-planting class at the local level. Of the fifty-nine mayors that assumed power in San Pedro Sula between 1884 and 1945, thirty-three, or 56 percent, can be identified as banana growers who at one time or another marketed their products through the banana companies. Before the banana companies fully controlled the North Coast economy, that is, before 1920, thirty-five mayors governed San Pedro Sula, of which twenty-eight were banana growers; hence the measure of mayors as banana planters during this period climbed to 80 percent. The companies thus faced few or no enemies among the local political elites.[19]

The municipal report of 1878 also linked San Pedro Sula's growth in the 1870s to the presence of a railroad in Cortés. Built between 1869 and 1874, the so-called Interoceanic Railroad originated in old Puerto Caballos (renamed Puerto Cortés in 1869), traversed San Pedro Sula, and extended some fifteen miles south into the Sula Valley. This Tegucigalpa-inspired development project assumed that the railroad would continue into the Departments of Comayagua, Francisco Morazán, and Valle and finally connect a Pacific port with Puerto Cortés instead of with Omoa.[20] By the 1880s and 1890s banana exports from Cortés were critical to Honduras's emerging status as Central America's major exporter of bananas, then with cultivation largely in Honduran hands.[21]

It is important, crucial perhaps, to make clear that after the 1910s, when the bananas exported from Cortés were controlled by Samuel Zemurray, he did not mercilessly exploit all Hondurans of the Sula Valley. In fact, after 1918 Zemurray complemented his original Cuyamel Fruit Company with a complex network of subsidiaries designed to administer the railroads, raise cattle, cultivate banana and sugar plantations, and refine sugar to fill the local demand and to contract into the rum monopoly. What is most interesting about the Zemurray enterprises is the structure of the capital shares of each company.

Most of the Zemurray businesses in Honduras originated as joint ventures with prominent local capitalists, most of whom had been or would be municipal officials and major banana planters in the Sula Valley (see Table 2.1). Zemurray's association with Honduran capitalists and municipal officials in San Pedro Sula achieved at least two objectives. The joint ventures exempted him from U.S. corporate taxes because locally incorporated companies were identified as "Honduran" enterprises, despite the fact that Zemurray and his U.S. associates usually controlled more than 80 percent of the invested capital.

Involving important local elites in the Zemurray ventures in the 1920s also increased the Cuyamel Fruit Company's influence among different power

Table 2.1. Organizational Structure of Zemurray Enterprises after 1918

| Company | Minor Investors |
| --- | --- |
| Empresa Hondureña de Fomento<br>Incorporated on 1 May 1918. Transferred to the Empresa del Ulúa, incorporated on 12 February 1923. | Albert Greely<br>W. C. MacSouth<br>A. Bennaton<br>Jacob Weil<br>Leonardo Romero |
| Compañía Agrícola de Sula<br>Incorporated on 13 April 1919 as a subsidiary of the original Cuyamel Fruit Company, incorporated in South Dakota in 1911. | Juan R. López<br>Dr. Roman Bográn<br>Servando Muñoz<br>Salomon Bueso V.<br>Dr. Antonio Bográn |
| Sula Sugar Company<br>Incorporated on 17 April 1919. Transferred to another Cuyamel Fruit Company, incorporated in Delaware on 24 January 1923. | Juan R. López<br>W. F. Coleman<br>A. Bennaton<br>Salomon Bueso V.<br>Leonardo Romero<br>Luis Melara |
| Compañía Ganadera de Sula<br>Incorporated on 19 April 1919. Transferred to the Cortés Development Company on 19 January 1927. This firm was established on 27 August 1919 and under trust of the second Cuyamel Fruit Company since 1923. | A. Bennaton<br>Luis Melara<br>Leonardo Romero<br>Isidro Mejía |
| Compañía Bananera de Santiago<br>Incorporated on 22 April 1919. Transferred to Empresa del Ulúa on 8 December 1923. This firm was transferred to the Cortés Development Company on 2 May 1925. | Juan R. López<br>Rafael López Padilla<br>Salomon Bueso V.<br>Luis Melara<br>José Cabus |

*Sources:* Registro Mercantil de Cortés, San Pedro Sula 6, 1 May 1918, pp. 6– 22. Also see RMC 9 (12 February 1923, pp. 239–50), 6 (13 April 1919, pp. 109–14), 6 (17 April 1919, pp. 114–20), 6 (19 April 1919, pp. 124–26), 16 (18 June 1935, pp. 235–49), 13 (12 July 1930, pp. 381–86), 6 (22 April 1919, pp. 126–33), 10 (8 December 1923, pp. 35–38), 15 (October 1933), pp. 205–49; and Document No. 10, "Correspondencia y Escritos, 1943–1953," Documentos Privados del Ing. Rafael López Padilla. A good friend of Samuel Zemurray in the 1910s and 1920s, López Padilla invested in a number of Zemurray's projects in the Sula Valley.

brokers, an important step if Zemurray hoped to contain similar efforts by the United Fruit Company in Yoro and Atlántida. In this way, the Cuyamel Fruit Company integrated into its enterprises important regional elites from even the coffee-growing regions. A primary example is the Bográn clan, originally from Santa Bárbara.

Luis Bográn, observed Robert G. Williams, was "Honduras's only coffee grower president [1883–91]." Luis was born in the city of Santa Bárbara in 1849 and died in 1895. His father, Saturnino Bográn (1810–1869), a caudillo, served as Santa Bárbara's deputy in the Honduran Congress in 1848 and 1865 and briefly as minister of finance in 1867.[22] Before the presidency, Luis was appointed governor of Santa Bárbara by Marco Aurelio Soto and enjoyed a close friendship with Justo Rufino Barrios. That is how he became president in 1883. By 1889 Bográn was a shareholder in the Banco de Honduras, a concern established by the commercial and mining bourgeoisie of the interior, particularly around Tegucigalpa.

Luis was the brother of Francisco Bográn, president of Honduras briefly during 1919–20 and a confidant of General Manuel Bonilla and Samuel Zemurray. Moreover, Luis Bográn was the first cousin and godfather of Miguel Paz Barahona, also born in Santa Bárbara, then a resident of San Pedro Sula, and president of Honduras from 1925 to 1929.[23]

More importantly, by the 1910s two of Luis's sons, Antonio Bográn Morejon and Roman Bográn Morejon, owned shares in one of Samuel Zemurray's enterprises, the Compañía Agrícola de Sula, a company eventually purchased by the United Fruit Company.[24] That is not all. The Bográns became elite landowners in the Sula Valley, reaping, in short, the benefits they accrued via the creation of the Department of Cortés in 1893. Antonio and Roman were born in Santa Bárbara in the 1880s and 1890s; they died in San Pedro Sula, where they had emigrated in the wake of the banana transformation. As in their father's case, coffee cultivation was never a serious option.

## The Structure of San Pedro Sula's Economy after the 1870s

In May 1904 merchants Juan R. López, W. H. Bennaton, Silio V. Bento, George Abadie, Federico Bean, George Zuroester, W. F. Coleman, Daniel Muñoz, J. M. Mitchell, and Ricardo Collier, most of whom later owned shares in the Cuyamel complex, offered the San Pedro Sula municipality a loan of 16,000 pesos to cover expenditures for an aqueduct that might complement another built in 1883–84. Efforts to obtain a loan from the German firm P. Maier and Company in 1900 and 1903 had failed, along with Coleman's attempt to borrow the needed capital from merchant houses abroad.[25]

The merchants volunteered to loan the money in 1904 because they feared that the municipality would increase taxes on wares they imported for their commercial establishments. Merchant interest in the tax base of municipal finances was not new in San Pedro Sula. It could not be. Unlike previously, after the 1880s the administration of local income had been integrated with a municipal treasury whose expenditures depended on outside commerce. By 1889 municipal authorities recognized that the treasury's major revenues originated in local import duties.[26]

A significant consequence for San Pedro Sula's fiscal structure, and hence for the potential for modernizing the city, was that banana planters generally excluded their exports from city taxes. An evaluation of eight city budgets between 1901 and 1935 showed that only the 1905 and 1915 budgets projected revenues from taxes on the exports of domestic banana planters. This meant that officials placed the city's tax burden largely on imports and the domestic merchants. Seven budget projections between 1905 and 1935 demonstrated a range of expected revenues from these types of taxes, from a high of 59 percent of total revenues in 1915 to a low of 34 percent in 1905. The average expected revenues from this data base amounted to 46 percent of expected total revenues.[27]

San Pedro Sula's revenues from taxes on the foreign banana firm located in its jurisdiction, namely, the Cuyamel Fruit Company, depended on clauses in the concessions agreed to by the national governments. Most of these concessions obliged the company to pay the national treasury one cent per bunch of bananas exported, as well as one-half cent per bunch exported to the municipalities from which the company had extracted the bananas. San Pedro Sula's revenues increased substantially from this process, surely more than those of any other municipality on the North Coast.[28]

It is equally important to recognize that the 1904 meeting between San Pedro Sula merchants and municipal officials demonstrated a connection between the expanding banana export economy and increasing opportunities for commercial accumulation in the region. But the specific merchants attending that meeting revealed a peculiarity about who was taking advantage of, and thus profiting from, the new economic opportunities. Of the ten merchants present, only Juan R. López and Daniel Muñoz were Hondurans. The remainder were mostly West Europeans.[29] This tiny immigration had begun in the last two decades of the nineteenth century (see Table 2.2).

The transformations wrought by the banana industry in Cortés also changed San Pedro Sula. By the 1910s San Pedro Sula's economy assumed characteristics that were radically different from those it had possessed in the nineteenth century, characteristics that solidified in the 1920s, 1930s, and early 1940s. During this period (1880s–1940s), neither national nor regional governments produced statistics outlining San Pedro Sula's economic structure.

Table 2.2. Estimated Population of Non–Central Americans in Honduras, Selected Years, 1887–1945

| Nationality/ Ethnicity | Year | | | | | |
|---|---|---|---|---|---|---|
| | 1887 | 1910 | 1926 | 1930 | 1935 | 1945 |
| German | 43 | 177 | 246 | 289 | 324 | 135 |
| Italian | 50 | 94 | 322 | 166 | 180 | 131 |
| French | 72 | 122 | 242 | 112 | 100 | 50 |
| Spanish | 77 | 196 | 464 | 643 | 726 | 589 |
| Chinese | — | 44 | 192 | 269 | 315 | 307 |
| E. European | — | — | 1 | 44 | 103 | 106 |
| Arab* | — | 200 | 1,066 | 780 | 768 | 868 |
| U.S. | 185 | 668 | 1,757 | 1,313 | 1,508 | 1,014 |
| British | 1,017 | 4,710 | 3,977 | 2,921 | 3,180 | 2,093 |
| Total | 1,444 | 6,211 | 8,267 | 6,537 | 7,204 | 5,293 |

*Sources:* Dirección General de Estadística y Censo, "Censo, 1887," in Vallejo, *Primer Anuario Estadístico*, p. 153, "Censo, 1910," in Barahona, *Evolución Histórica de la Identidad Nacional*, p. 263, *Resúmen del Censo . . ., 1926* (n.p.), *1930* (p. 32), *1935* (p. 10 and generally), and *1945* (pp. 10, 46).

*"Arabs" include Turks, Lebanese, Syrians, and Palestinians.

The analysis here draws on business incorporation documents available in the Registro Mercantil de Cortés in San Pedro Sula. Restructured for this study, RMC data allow for the documentation of investment patterns across economic sectors and for the aggregation and disaggregation of these patterns among many enterprises.[30] Investment patterns in San Pedro Sula from 1905 to 1918, for example, show that most investments were directed to and reinvested in import and export businesses (see Table 2.3).

Agricultural investments went mostly into banana plantations and sugar cultivation and refineries, with lumber works accounting for smaller amounts. U.S. capitalists controlled all of these ventures. Investments in manufacturing were minimal, even less than Table 2.3 suggests. Analysis of these transactions shows that the liquor and rum "factories" were usually associated with investments in sugar plantations and refineries.

This analysis highlights the investment process. Although it confirms a general situation at a point in time, it does not verify that investment patterns correlated with the commercial and industrial structure *actually* established in that process. This problem is dealt with by analyzing data from the tax assessments of commercial and industrial establishments prepared by municipal authorities to estimate the revenue base.[31] These data show that general stores, often, but not necessarily, associated with prestigious import and export

Table 2.3. Percentage of Total Investment Value Registered in San Pedro Sula, by Economic Sector, 1905–1918

| Economic Sector | Percentage |
|---|---|
| Import/export commerce | 67 |
| Agriculture | 16 |
| Manufacturing | 8 |
| Drugstores | 2 |
| Services | 3 |
| Other | 23 |

*Source:* Registro Mercantíl de Cortés, 1905–18. The methodology is explained in Euraque, "Merchants and Industrialists," app. I, pp. 763–70.

houses, served as the most important tax base for revenues from the local economic structure (see Table 2.4).

This information confirms the process already outlined for the major sectors of the emerging elite commercial structure of San Pedro Sula. San Pedro Sula's economy in the 1920s and 1930s reinforced these patterns. Almost half of the total investments registered in the San Pedro Sula RMC between 1919 and 1936 were directed to and reinvested in import and export enterprises.[32]

Again, this analysis draws primarily from the registered investment process. Although it reinforces tendencies already present in the 1920s, it cannot confirm that investment patterns actually correlated with the commercial and industrial structure established in the 1920s. Table 2.5, which presents the structure of tax assessments made by the municipality in 1927 and 1935, shows that the situation had not changed much since the late 1910s. The municipal revenue base still depended on general stores and commercial agencies for more than 50 percent of projected expenditures derived from established commerce. Hence, well into the 1930s the sources for important accumulation were import and export businesses, since they served as wholesale distributors to retailers.

## Arab Merchants and the Organization of Capital

*Revista Económica*, a journal published in Tegucigalpa by the Austrian immigrant Barón de Franzestein, made revealing comments in 1914 on the geography, nationality, and ethnicity of Honduras's import-export commerce. It proclaimed that "in the wholesale business the white race strongly predominates,

Table 2.4. Percentage of Total Tax Assessment of Commercial and Industrial Enterprises in San Pedro Sula, 1918

| Enterprise | Percentage |
|---|---|
| General stores | 32.2 |
| Commercial agencies | 22.9 |
| Services/entertainment | 19.2 |
| Factories | 8.1 |
| Banks | 7.0 |
| Neighborhood grocery stores | 6.4 |
| Drugstores | 4.5 |

*Source:* "Clasificación de Establecimientos Comerciales e Industriales," *Libros de las Actas de las Sesiones de la Corporación Municipal de San Pedro Sula*, vol. 17, 22 March 1918, pp. 79–81. The methodology is explained in Euraque, "Merchants and Industrialists," app. III, pp. 794–99.

as in Costa Rica and Guatemala." By then, capital from the United States outdistanced earlier German investments, particularly in the southern departments, primarily because of U.S. investments in railroads and the banana industry.[33] In his discussion of wholesale commerce," Barón de Franzestein noted that "in [the] retail business the native element and the Turks (Syrians and Armenians) are the most important factors, the latter also taking a rather important part in the direct importing business and to some extent in house to house peddling as well."[34]

In the same issue, the editors of *Revista Económica* observed that "unusually annoying competition is found on the north coast, a nuisance consisting in the importation of goods free of duty under the shadow of the countless concessions granted" to the banana companies. As a consequence, "a white man with little capital finds it hard to succeed in business." Finally, "the wholesale business here swallows up the retail, leaving only Syrians and Chinese with their well known low standard of living and willingness to endure privations as an exception."[35]

This scenario is telling of another phenomenon that accompanied foreign capitalists' control of the banana industry: foreign domination of elite urban commerce. It is not surprising that over 60 percent of the thirty-five founding members of the Cortés Chamber of Commerce in 1916 were immigrants from Europe and the United States, at a time when German, Italian, French, Span-

Table 2.5. Percentage of Total Tax Assessment of Commercial and Industrial Enterprises in San Pedro Sula, 1927 and 1935

| Enterprise | Percentage | |
|---|---|---|
| | 1927 | 1935 |
| General stores | 42 | 32 |
| Commercial agencies | 18 | 20 |
| Services/entertainment | 15 | 17 |
| Factories | 7 | 14 |
| Banks | 4 | 3 |
| Neighborhood grocery stores | 10 | 8 |
| Drugstores | 4 | 6 |
| Specialty stores | 1 | .001 |

*Source:* "Clasificación de Establecimientos Comerciales e Industriales," *Libros de las Actas de las Sesiones de la Corporación Municipal de San Pedro Sula*, vol. 21, 4 December 1927, pp. 402–6, and vol. 26, 15 April 1935, pp. 285–90. The methodology is explained in Euraque, "Merchants and Industrialists," app. III, pp. 794–99.

ish, and U.S. citizens accounted for no more than 1,500 inhabitants in the entire country. The founding members of the chamber included three Hondurans, two Britons, one Nicaraguan, one North American, one German, and two Palestinian Arabs.[36]

In 1935, as in the late 1920s, the Arab Palestinian population represented less than half a percent of Honduras's approximately 960,000 residents. Of course, we cannot determine the total count of Middle Eastern Arabs living in Honduras because the census data do not distinguish between naturalized "Honduran Arabs" and other Arabs. In the 1940s most Arabs resided in Cortés, and most had not acquired citizenship. According to municipal records, from 1930 to 1940 Arab immigrants (Palestinians, Lebanese, and Syrians) never accounted for more than 0.7 percent of San Pedro Sula's total population, which ranged from about 24,500 in 1930 to about 40,500 in 1940.[37] On the other hand, during this period Palestinians represented 95 percent of the Arab population in San Pedro Sula.

The full story of Palestinian immigration to Honduras has yet to be told, but available research offers the following conclusions.[38] First, most Palestinians who settled in Honduras were Christian, and most originated in Bethlehem, Beit Jala, and Beit Sahur, usually fleeing Ottoman persecution or the post–1948 diaspora. Second, most of the Christian Palestinians who came were not poor peasants, as often believed; on the contrary, they were rather sophisticated peddlers with historic ties to European commercial networks that often reached back well into the nineteenth century and before. (The first Palestinian Arab mentioned in the documentation for this book is Salomon Handal, identified as a San Pedro Sula merchant in 1899.)[39]

Third, most of these immigrants settled on the North Coast, benefiting from the commercial entrepôts created during the upsurge of banana exports from the 1880s to the 1920s. Fourth, most of them maintained close ties with extended family in and near Bethlehem. Finally, this pattern was reinforced by general ethnic endogamous marriage patterns well into the 1940s. The historiography lacks detailed studies of how the latter aspect of Palestinian immigration contributed to economic power on the North Coast, but it surely began playing an important role as far back as the 1910s, when the number of immigrants multiplied fivefold (Table 2.2).

During the late 1910s Christian Arab merchants in San Pedro Sula obtained control of the major sectors of the city's elite economic structure, especially large-scale commerce. In the 1920s Christian Arab immigrants also emerged as important innovators in certain small-scale manufacturing enterprises that developed in response to an emergent market on the North Coast.

Patterns of registered investments in San Pedro Sula between 1919 and 1936 show that Arabs surpassed all other nationalities in staking money on manufacturing. Arabs participated in few of the joint ventures that constituted the vast majority of manufacturing investments in San Pedro Sula. Most joint ventures involved Europeans, U.S. immigrants, and Hondurans as minor investors. Arab manufacturing investments focused on a general product line: clothing.[40]

The real strength of Arab investors, however, resided in their almost complete control of the import and export commercial sector. RMC data provide the structure of investments in the San Pedro Sula import and export sector by nationality or ethnicity between 1919 and 1936. Unlike the Hondurans, in fact, unlike all other foreigners involved in San Pedro Sula's elite commerce, the Arabs by the 1930s widely distributed their investments not only in Cortés but also elsewhere on the North Coast. In the 1920s, according to RMC records, prominent Arab families opened branches in nascent towns throughout Cortés and other departments of the North Coast.[41] Among other foreigners, the British Bennaton interests, of Jewish descent, branched out in this way on the North Coast, but none of the European or U.S. investors matched the range and distribution network established by the Arabs. Municipal tax assessment data confirm this. Table 2.6 presents the structure of the tax assessments of general stores by nationality or ethnicity for 1927 and 1935.

This situation placed the Arab commercial leadership in a difficult position: that of arousing criticism of the "company stores" introduced by banana companies near banana plantations. After the 1910s, the major companies on

Table 2.6. Percentage of Total Tax Assessment of General Stores in San Pedro Sula, by Nationality or Ethnicity, 1927 and 1935

| Nationality/Ethnicity | Percentage | |
|---|---|---|
| | 1927 | 1935 |
| Arab* | 41 | 43 |
| Honduran | 24 | 19 |
| U.S. | 9 | 0 |
| German | 7 | 5 |
| British | 5 | 5 |
| European/U.S. | 4 | 2 |
| Joint ventures | 4 | 4 |
| Other | 6 | 19 |

*Source:* "Clasificación de Establecimientos Comerciales e Industriales," *Libros de las Actas de las Sesiones de la Corporación Municipal de San Pedro Sula*, vol. 21, 4 December 1927, pp. 402–6, and vol. 26, 15 April 1935, pp. 285–90. The methodology is explained in Euraque, "Merchants and Industrialists," app. III, pp. 794–99.
*"Arabs" include Turks, Lebanese, Syrians, and Palestinians.

the North Coast established general merchandise stores to supply the increasing numbers of workers on the larger plantations. Because concessions allowed the companies duty-free import privileges, company stores sold their goods at cheap prices, encouraging workers to buy the bulk of their subsistence goods in these stores. This practice naturally deprived local merchants of a larger regional market.[42]

Arab censure of the banana companies in Cortés was not evident, but Arabs did encourage the abolition of the company stores elsewhere on the North Coast. In 1924 U.S. consuls in La Ceiba and Puerto Castilla, near Trujillo, blamed a recent strike on non-Honduran "agitators," among them Syrians, Armenians, and Palestinians who objected to the banana companies' commercial monopoly through their commissaries.[43] Honduran agitation against the Arabs increased, and by 1929 and 1934 new laws severely restricted immigration by whole groups of nationalities, races, and ethnicities, including Palestinian Arabs.[44] This situation had critical implications for the nature of organized capitalists in and around San Pedro Sula and probably for all of the North Coast as well.

Between the 1910s and the 1920s most Hondurans saw that even accumulation opportunities in the niches of the banana economy fell into foreign hands. Although the Hondurans worked on the banana plantations and in the few factories, cleaned the streets, built the roads, and served in political office, the ownership and control of the local economy lay with *los Turcos*, recently arrived Arabs from a foreign land most Hondurans had never heard of. Moreover, apparently the Arabs' minority status in their homeland, reproduced numerically in Honduras, served to re-create their special social culture.[45] The archetypical encounter between Honduran and Arab in San Pedro Sula, and probably in most North Coast towns at the time, took place in urban stores. Arabs located primarily in important commercial towns and generally remained distant from the social life of the vast majority of the Honduran people, most of whom lived in rural areas.

The recently arrived Arabs cultivated their religious and cultural traditions apart from most Hondurans, and initially even apart from the Honduran social and political elite. A 1927 article in the La Ceiba Chamber of Commerce's *Revista Comercial* indicated that San Pedro Sula's first chamber of commerce, established in 1916, disappeared in the early 1920s "because Turks made up the majority of its membership and the minority did not want to be oppressed by the Turks."[46]

In the long run, this situation created a cleavage between economic power and its social-cultural expression and legitimacy; in effect, it denied the new commercial and industrial elite the opportunity to command positive social acknowledgment from most of the Honduran population, including members of the new working class.[47] Further, before the 1950s most Palestinian Arabs themselves did not view Honduras as a permanent home. A recent important ethnographic account suggests that these immigrants brought and nourished a "permanent migration ideology" and that "throughout the first half of this century most Palestinians considered Honduras a backwater in comparison with what they had left behind."[48]

The fact that Hondurans transformed the *turco* characterization from its nationalist identification to a socially pejorative expression identified with individual stinginess must be understood in the historical context outlined here. The sons and daughters of Arab immigrants who settled in Honduras grew up in this peculiar social position, despite their class status as children of a regional petite bourgeoisie that was transforming itself into a regional industrial bourgeoisie. A prominent observer touched on the historical implications of this situation: in the 1960s a Lebanese and Syrian sector of an "emerging new class of wealth" tended "to be excluded from political activity, partly by their own choice and partly as a result of the unwelcoming attitudes of the native middle class from which most political leadership is drawn."[49]

## The Travails of Organized Labor: San Pedro Sula in the National Context

The peculiar process of elite class formation on the North Coast represented only one structural aspect that differentiated this region's historic development from other areas in Honduras. The history of its working people also promoted a social and political culture that broadly contrasted with that of the interior. The elite and nonelite processes of class formation on the North Coast affected one another in ways that together produced a different civil society, especially by the 1950s. However, that history was linked as well to events and developments in the 1920s and 1930s.

In December 1943 Ambassador John D. Erwin in Tegucigalpa responded to various questions from the U.S. Department of State regarding the labor situation in Honduras. Asked about the "present attitude of the Government towards labor," Erwin answered matter-of-factly that "the Government has not had occasion to assume an attitude" because "the present regime is a dictatorship and the President is suspicious of all organizations not controlled by himself." Indeed, he acknowledged the absence of any legislation or regulations governing individual or collective labor contracts or of "any organized method, either government or private, of handling relations between employer and employees."[50]

One of the State Department's concerns in 1943 revolved around strikes, and so it asked the ambassador to "please furnish information for the period beginning [with] 1940 on the number of strikes which have occurred including any readily available data such as the number involved, the cause and duration and basis of settlement." Erwin's answer was not surprising. "According to the Ministry of Development, Agriculture and Labor," he wrote, "the only strike in recent years was one of the shop workers of TACA [*Transportes Aéreos Centroamericanos*], which was settled after three days. President Carías [1933–49] supported the Company in its dismissal of several of the leaders." The ambassador also indicated that "the United Fruit Company has not had any strikes in recent years" and that "the New York and Honduras Rosario Mining Company states that strikes on its property 'are unknown.'" Finally, Erwin submitted a statement from the Standard Fruit and Steamship Company in La Ceiba, the second largest employer in Honduras that read as follows: "In recent years we have had several short strikes on the wharf. None were occasioned by serious grievances, none caused property damage and all were settled in a few hours. The last of these was in April 1942. . . . The last serious strike was by farm labor in January–February 1932."[51]

In response to another query, Erwin reported that the Ministry of Development believed that the Federación Obrera Hondureña, established in Tegucigalpa in the early 1920s, had "disappeared," but that the New York and Honduras Rosario Mining Company maintained that the FOH "still exists but has been inactive for many years." He also wrote that an artisan association said to have existed in La Ceiba "operated as a social group rather than a labor union." Ironically, given subsequent developments in the late 1940s and 1950s, and even the immediate history of the 1920s, San Pedro Sula's labor situation in 1943 did not merit any attention in the Erwin report. Perhaps it should have.

In the late 1920s San Pedro Sula became a center of artisan activism and left-wing meetings and organizations, as well as a transit point for organizers and militants traveling from Tegucigalpa to Tela, Progreso, La Ceiba, Trujillo, and other banana towns on the North Coast. A road connecting Tegucigalpa and San Pedro Sula, with boat transport across Lake Yojoa, became fully serviceable to automobiles between 1920 and 1924, and heavy truck traffic began in 1926. Moreover, the extensive railroad system that connected the various banana towns, about 1,000 miles by 1926, facilitated a mode of regional communal life unique to that part of Honduras. San Pedro Sula, by then the North Coast's most important town, was easily accessible to all the banana towns east of the Ulúa and Chamelecón Rivers.[52]

Along with the greater concentration of workers on the banana plantations by this period (in 1925 about 13,000, five times the number of laborers a decade earlier), the transportation nexus between the interior and the North Coast facilitated the movement of people and ideologies from the interior to a region that concentrated new kinds of social relations and energies. The U.S. consuls on the North Coast, always apprehensive of developments that might affect the interests of the banana companies, took note of the situation early. In January 1920 the consul for the Puerto Cortés district, home to the Cuyamel plantations, reported seven short strikes "all among the employees of the Cuyamel Fruit Company." He attributed the organized nature of the strikes, repeated in Tela and Trujillo, to outside agitators, as "there never was such restlessness among [the laborers] before."[53]

It is therefore not surprising that in 1927 San Pedro Sula served, after an initial gathering in La Ceiba, as the place for the organization of Honduras's first Communist Party.[54] Two years later its most prominent leaders, including Manuel Calix Herrera, helped establish, in Tela, the Federación Sindical Hondureña, a left-wing counterpart to the Tegucigalpa-based FOH. The FSH's commitment, unlike that of the FOH, was to develop a strategy for dealing with the conflicts between capital and labor. Thus key militants in the organization, including Calix Herrera, participated in a walkout in La Ceiba that the Standard Fruit Company, in 1943, eleven years later, called its "last serious strike."[55]

It is easier to understand the death of the FOH and the FSH in the wake of General Carías's persecution after 1933 than it is to evaluate their activities between their establishment—the FOH in 1921 and the FSH in 1929—and their demise in the early 1930s. In fact, Carías's repression of these and other labor organizations affected more than labor militancy as such. Even the important communist militants that established another Partido Comunista de Honduras in 1954 enjoyed only ephemeral recollections of the struggles of the 1920s.[56] Little has been written about these issues, but a few points are instructive here.

The key social confrontations around which the FSH organized, despite the fact that most of its members were urban artisans, turned on the labor practices of the banana companies, including the manipulation of wage contracts, the monopoly enjoyed by the commissaries, and the problems faced by independent banana growers who remained after the banana companies acquired control of the export economy as a whole. This social structure, unique to the North Coast, required labor organizers to appeal to these sectors, for the region lacked an "oligarchic" landed elite even in the production of domestic crops. Moreover, its commercial elite, largely of Palestinian Arab extraction, demonstrated little solidarity with the repressive role and tactics of the local political elites.

Two reasons explain this. First, foreign merchants stood to benefit from the collapse of the commissary system. And available evidence shows that most of the spontaneous strikes that occurred up to 1932, mostly of short duration (usually less than a week), received the support of many merchants and even of independent banana growers.[57] Second, before the 1940s the foreign commercial elite did not enjoy familial or political links to governors, military commanders, customs officials, and other administrative and political officers usually appointed in Tegucigalpa and from that city's inner circle of power. The ethnic schism created when non-Arab merchants ostracized their Middle Eastern counterparts created more obstacles to a united commercial and industrial opposition to worker militance.

For these reasons labor agitators on the Honduran North Coast, at least until 1930, did not suffer the systematic repression from the state visited on labor elsewhere in Central America, especially in Guatemala and El Salvador.[58] Moreover, by this time the left wing of the Liberal Party campaigned directly on North Coast plantations, in effect competing with old socialist, left-wing appeals to labor. Thus a certain articulate and public liberalism existed on the North Coast not found in other parts of the country. Even the leading communists most closely associated with the FSH, Manuel Calix Herrera and Juan Pablo Wainwright, did not die directly at the hands of Honduran repressive forces. Wainwright was executed in Guatemala in 1932 after escaping from a prison in Omoa, where authorities also imprisoned Calix Herrera in 1932. Calix Herrera died of tuberculosis in Olancho in 1939.[59]

Finally, the fact that the destruction of labor militants occurred during a National Party government bestowed on them a legacy that the Liberal Party exploited soon after Ambassador Erwin wrote his report in 1943. That effort, however, originated with tragic events. In July 1944 San Pedro Sula became, in some ways in the spirit of the late 1920s, the scene of organized protests of the Liberal Party against the Carías dictatorship. Carías's local henchmen responded with a brutality that resulted in the massacre of more than fifty people.[60]

Many liberals of San Pedro Sula's elite families fled into exile and two years later consolidated into a radical wing of the Liberal Party.[61] The Partido Democrático Revolucionario de Honduras, as it was called, challenged both traditional parties. It is difficult to imagine the emergence of this party anywhere else in Honduras. Indeed, the establishment of the PDRH in San Pedro Sula and its role in Honduran politics from 1946 to 1954 represented but a moment in the differentiation between the North Coast and the interior.

# HONDURAN POLITICS AND THE RISE OF THE NORTH COAST, 1876–1945

William S. Stokes, in the most important work ever written in English on the Honduran political system, which was published in 1950, observed that on the North Coast "a new balance of power is in the making, and the old mutually hostile interior departments are being forced to combine in opposition to the growing might of the north coast. . . . [The] obvious implication [is] . . . that the north coast not only may be able to oppose the interior departments numerically, but in time may raise an urban-rural conflict."[1] Stokes was keenly aware of the emerging demographic differences between the North Coast and hostile political power in the interior. For example, he asserted, "from 1920 to 1930 Congress voted only two changes in apportionment."[2] Only in 1942 did reapportionment begin to reflect the demographic transformations discussed earlier.

Demographic redistribution is only one important change deserving attention here. The relationship in the early 1970s between military populism and North Coast personalities cannot be fully understood without exploring the emergence of the PDRH in the context of the Carías regime as the major expression of the dictatorial politics that developed in Honduras between 1876 and 1948. A radical young wing of the Liberal Party, Carías's nemesis since the 1920s, established the Partido Democrático Revolucionario de Honduras in San Pedro Sula in 1946. At that point the PDRH materialized as a political party distinct from the Frente Democrático Revolucionario Hondureño, an organization that united mainstream liberals who were exiled during the dictatorship and especially after the killings in San Pedro Sula in 1944. In 1946 the PDRH represented a leftist social democracy illustrative of the radical liberalism of Guatemala's Juan José Arévalo in 1946 and 1947.[3] By 1948 the U.S. ambassador in Tegucigalpa, as in the Guatemalan case, characterized the PDRH's ideology as dirtied with "slightly diluted Communist phraseology."[4]

Lists of PDRH members from 1946 until the party's demise in 1954 are difficult to come by. Membership lists of the Partido Comunista de Honduras also are hard to acquire and, when available, especially from U.S. intelligence services of the period, make little distinction between leftist liberals, socialists, and communists of different colors.[5] The association between the PCH and the PDRH remains unexplored, but a close relationship did exist.[6] It seems that between 1946 and 1948 the PDRH attracted a range of members and sympathizers, including radical and mainstream liberals and exiled and local left-wing supporters of the Arévalo regime in Guatemala. Two personalities exemplify the variety of people who played critical roles in the PDRH.

The first personality was Dr. Rodolfo Pastor Zelaya, who as a young man led a student contingent in anti-Carías protests during July 1944.[7] Two years later he became a founding member of the Partido Democrático Revolucionario, forerunner of the PDRH in San Pedro Sula. Sometime between 1946 and 1948 he married the daughter of Roberto Fasquelle, a wealthy friend of Samuel Zemurray. Pastor Zelaya published nationalist and anti-imperialist articles in the PDRH's *Vanguardia Revolucionaria* and also served as one of its directors in 1947. Whereas his articles in that periodical remained free from explicit Marxist language, his essays published elsewhere did not.[8] To many of his left-wing contemporaries he represented the unique persona of an "emerging anti-imperialist national bourgeoisie" capable of leading the "bourgeois-democratic" stage of the revolution.[9]

After Carías stepped down, Pastor Zelaya rejoined the Liberal Party, but he never abandoned the radical liberalism he had cultivated in the late 1940s. Indeed, in the 1960s he helped lead the San Pedro Sula bourgeoisie in a challenge to the López Arellano regime and at one point was accused of plotting with left-wing insurrectionists. In 1970 the Liberal Party nominated Pastor Zelaya its vice-presidential candidate in the elections of 1971. His economic interest in San Pedro Sula dated from at least 1946, when he purchased shares in San Pedro Sula's first private hospital.[10]

Another prominent member of the PDRH and writer for *Vanguardia Revolucionaria* was Ramón Amaya Amador. Amaya Amador was born in 1916 and grew up near the banana plantations of the Standard Fruit Company in the Department of Yoro. After graduating as a schoolteacher in La Ceiba, he worked on the banana plantations. Studies of radical literature encouraged him to denounce the exploitation in the "green prisons" in a periodical published first in 1943. Facing repression in La Ceiba, Amaya Amador fled to Guatemala in 1947, where he supported the Arévalo regime, a government that he believed represented a "democratic-bourgeois revolution." From there he endorsed Honduran communists who played prominent roles in the PDRH and helped establish a clandestine PCH in the 1950s. He also became a major novelist whose works portray the conditions and experiences of the country's working people.[11]

The cases of Amaya Amador and Pastor Zelaya suggest the amalgamation of archetypal militants who joined and endorsed the PDRH ideology at least until 1954, when the party lost the membership that officially established the PCH. Moreover, their personal histories, like the backgrounds of those who would follow, imply two propositions. First, the urban-rural conflict that Stokes projected in 1950 had a unique origin in the conditions and cultural history of the North Coast, particularly of San Pedro Sula. Second, with the PDRH's emergence in the mid-1940s the Carías dictatorship seemed doomed in the face of the very forces that he had fomented since his alliance with the fruit companies in the 1920s. Ironically, Carías was born in 1876, the same year that liberal reformists assumed power in Honduras. His demise in the late 1940s represented a closure of one chapter of Honduran political history, but a chapter that must be addressed in order to explain military populism in the early 1970s.

## Politics and Militarism in the Post–Reforma Period, 1877–1919

In the long run, the extent of the military's autonomy from direct elite control in the early 1970s traces back to the armed forces' lack of institutionalization after Marco Aurelio Soto assumed power in 1876. That circumstance, in turn, must be viewed in the context of the relationships between the country's economic system after 1876 and state formation and civil society in the aftermath of the Reforma period (1877–83). More specifically, this requires reconsidering issues explored in Chapter 1: namely, the implications of new relationships between regions of Honduras and the world economy, elite class formation, and the acquisition of state revenues that could sustain a standing army, train recruits, and purchase equipment and weapons.

Late in 1914 John Ewing, the U.S. minister in Tegucigalpa, acknowledged recent State Department instructions that he "write fully and frankly concerning all matters that enter into or tend to control the internal political situation and conditions here, and I would not be reporting unreservedly if I failed to direct the attention of the Department to a source which is an ever present factor. I speak of the United Fruit Company and its subsidiaries and its railroad connections." After outlining the company's economic system and its relationship to concessions, Ewing admitted that, "in order to obtain these concessions and privileges and to secure their undisturbed enjoyment, it [the United Fruit Company] has seen fit to enter actively into the internal politics of these countries, and it has pursued this course so systematically and regularly until it now has its ramifications in every department of the government and is a most important factor in all political movements and actions."[12]

Ewing also remarked that "government officials throughout the whole of the North Coast are subject to its influence and it is openly asserted that even in the Cabinet it has its friends and advocates." Finally, he wrote, "President [Francisco Bertrand] and some of his Cabinet are chafing under its domination but feel themselves too weak to act contrary to its demands unless assured of the support of our Government."

Few doubts should cloud an understanding of the dramatic predicament facing Francisco Bertrand in 1914, one that was partly of his own making. He himself surely recognized the power of the fruit companies and the U.S. government's acquiescence to this form of imperialism. Bertrand had assumed the presidency in 1913 after the death of President Manuel Bonilla, whose insurrection in 1911 Samuel Zemurray financed.

In June 1919, on the eve of Bertrand's own bloody ouster, but while he was encouraging the imposition of his brother-in-law Nazario Soriano in the October presidential election, Edward W. Ames, a confidential agent of the U.S. State Department, summarized the political situation: "There is, in my opinion, one and only one logical way to prevent a very serious outbreak in Honduras between now and the end of October, viz: for the U.S. government to say politely but firmly to President Bertrand that we put him where he is, that we expected certain things of him, that he is not meeting these expectations and that we, therefore, want him to step down and out for the obvious good of his country." More pathetic but instructive here is another excerpt from Ames's report: "President Bertrand told me the whole history of the 'Tacoma' Conference [which transferred power to the Bonilla insurgents in 1911] and frankly acknowledged his parentage, saying very naively that he was a nonentity politically at the time and that he could never understand why Mr. [Thomas C.] Dawson, the U.S. Government official mediating the Conference, selected *him*."[13]

Bertrand's troubles in 1914 and 1919 were not unique. His predecessors and successors had been and would be involved in the kind of dramatic circumstances that accompanied his resignation in September 1919, a reaction to the insurrection predicted by Ames earlier in the year. Presidential successions in Honduras before 1876 usually occurred in the midst of civil wars, themselves providing the contexts for resignations of presidents, unconstitutional transfers of power, or other extracivil resolutions of political conflicts. When presidential elections did occur, they involved only a tiny minority of the Honduran population. In 1877, given restrictions on electoral privileges, only 7.2 percent of the people could vote. (Because women were not enfranchised until 1955, only 18 percent of the population could cast their ballot as late as 1948.)[14]

This did not prevent militarist caudillos from practically destroying civil society. Between 1870 and 1949 many Hondurans were killed in 146 military engagements, probably involving the mobilization of no more than 5,000 troops in any one engagement. Few researchers have offered data on casualties sustained in these battles. In 1928 the U.S. embassy in Tegucigalpa offered rough estimates on fatalities in the major civil wars from the 1890s to 1924: in 1892–94, the bloodiest war of the nineteenth century, 5,000 dead; in the 1906–7 war, 1,500; in the 1910–11 battle, 500; in the 1919 conflict, 1,000; and in the 1924 civil war, the most macabre battle of this century, 5,000. The other military engagements documented during this period probably rarely caused more than 50 or 100 deaths, similar to the numbers recorded for conflicts during the period 1827–79.[15]

Between 1877 and 1948 the Honduran political system witnessed seventeen presidential elections, usually involving only the Liberal and the National Parties (see Table 3.1). When given the chance, each party used most means, including force and fraud, to achieve overwhelming victories, in large part, as Stokes astutely asserted long ago, because all Honduran constitutions since 1824 insisted "that a presidential candidate receive an absolute majority for election."[16] In the case of pluralities, Congress selected a winner among the candidates. When candidates winning pluralities did not receive a favorable vote in Congress, they almost always revolted.

During preelection periods, candidates attempted to promote conditions for total victories, such as control over Congress. Stokes demonstrated this in various analyses. He showed that from 1896 to 1941, Congress passed almost every bill proposed by the sitting executive. In fact, the percentage of executive decrees approved by Congress during this period ranged from a low of 63 percent in 1931 to 100 percent in 1896–98, 1901–2, 1906–7, 1909, 1915, 1919, and 1938–39. Stokes put it emphatically: "the legal powers of Congress have merely been a cloak behind which the executive has performed the real work of government."[17]

By the beginning of the twentieth century, the old liberal coalition empowered by the Guatemalan general Rufino Barrios in 1876 had fallen apart, especially after the civil war of 1894. According to Stokes, every important political leader in Honduras between 1894 and 1945 fought in the 1894 war.[18] From the 1890s to 1919 loyalists of warring caudillos did not establish standing political parties (see Figure 1). In 1919 Francisco Bertrand, presumably a National Party heir to Manuel Bonilla, established the Liberal Constitutionalist Party. When Bertrand tried to impose his brother-in-law Soriano, a nonentity

Table 3.1. Results of Presidential Elections in Honduras, by Party, 1877–1948

| Year | Liberal Party | % | National Party | % | Other Parties | % | Total Vote |
|---|---|---|---|---|---|---|---|
| 1877 | 16,603 | 81 | — | — | 4,032 | 19 | 20,635 |
| 1880 | 24,521 | 82 | — | — | 5,274 | 18 | 29,795 |
| 1883 | 3,500 | 8 | 40,598 | 92 | — | — | 44,098 |
| 1887 | 5,326 | 12 | 38,394 | 88 | — | — | 43,720 |
| 1891 | 12,300 | 26 | 34,362 | 74 | — | — | 46,662 |
| 1894 | 42,667 | 99+ | — | — | 499 | — | 43,166 |
| 1898 | 36,746 | 85 | — | — | 7,834 | 15 | 44,580 |
| 1902 | 27,195 | 36 | 42,234 | 55 | 7,008 | 9 | 76,437 |
| 1908 | — | — | — | — | — | — | — |
| 1911 | 12 | −1 | 72,989 | 99+ | — | — | 73,001 |
| 1915 | 100 | −1 | 75,000 | 99+ | — | — | 75,000 |
| 1919 | 76,000 | 81 | 18,000 | 19 | — | — | 94,000 |
| 1923 | 33,000 | 34 | 46,800 | 48 | 18,000 | 18 | 97,000 |
| 1924 | — | — | 52,431 | 99+ | 274 | −1 | 53,250 |
| 1928 | 62,319 | 57 | 47,745 | 43 | — | — | 110,064 |
| 1932 | 61,047 | 43 | 80,512 | 57 | — | — | 141,559 |
| 1948 | 472 | −1 | 255,496 | 99+ | — | — | 255,968 |

*Sources:* For the 1877–98 period, see Salgado, *Compendio de Historia*, pp. 156, 158, 163, 166, 170, 203, 209; for 1902, see Suazo Rubí, *Auge y Crisis Ideológica del Partido Liberal*, p. 219. In 1908 the president was elected indirectly via a Constituent Assembly. See Salgado, *Compendio de Historia*, p. 271. Returns for the 1911–32 period are from the following U.S. Embassy reports in the National Archives, Washington, D.C.: in Record Group 59: Charles D. White, 1 November 1911, 815.00/1393; John Ewing, 3 November 1915, 815.00/1639; E. M. Lawton, 30 October 1919, 815.00/2102; Franklin Morales, 30 October 1923, 815.00/2732; Stokely W. Morgan, 8 January 1925, 815.00/3536; Herschel V. Johnson, 15 December 1928, 815.00/4330; and in Record Group 84: Julius G. Lay, 13 January 1933, Confidential U.S. Diplomatic Records, Honduras: 1930–1945, microfilm, reel 7, 116–20. For 1948, see Mario R. Argueta, *Tiburcio Carías*, p. 333.

like himself who had lived most of his life in El Salvador, the opposition revolted. In the face of this new civil war, the U.S. government pressured Bertrand to resign in favor of a transitional government that might oversee elections. He resisted, but by September 1919 the State Department, tired of his resistance, threatened armed intervention. Bertrand left for Costa Rica.[19]

Despite the similarities of the civil wars leading up to the elections of 1877, 1894, 1911, and 1919, the debacle of 1919 and General Rafael López Gutierrez's ascendance in 1920 marked a turning point in the relationship between

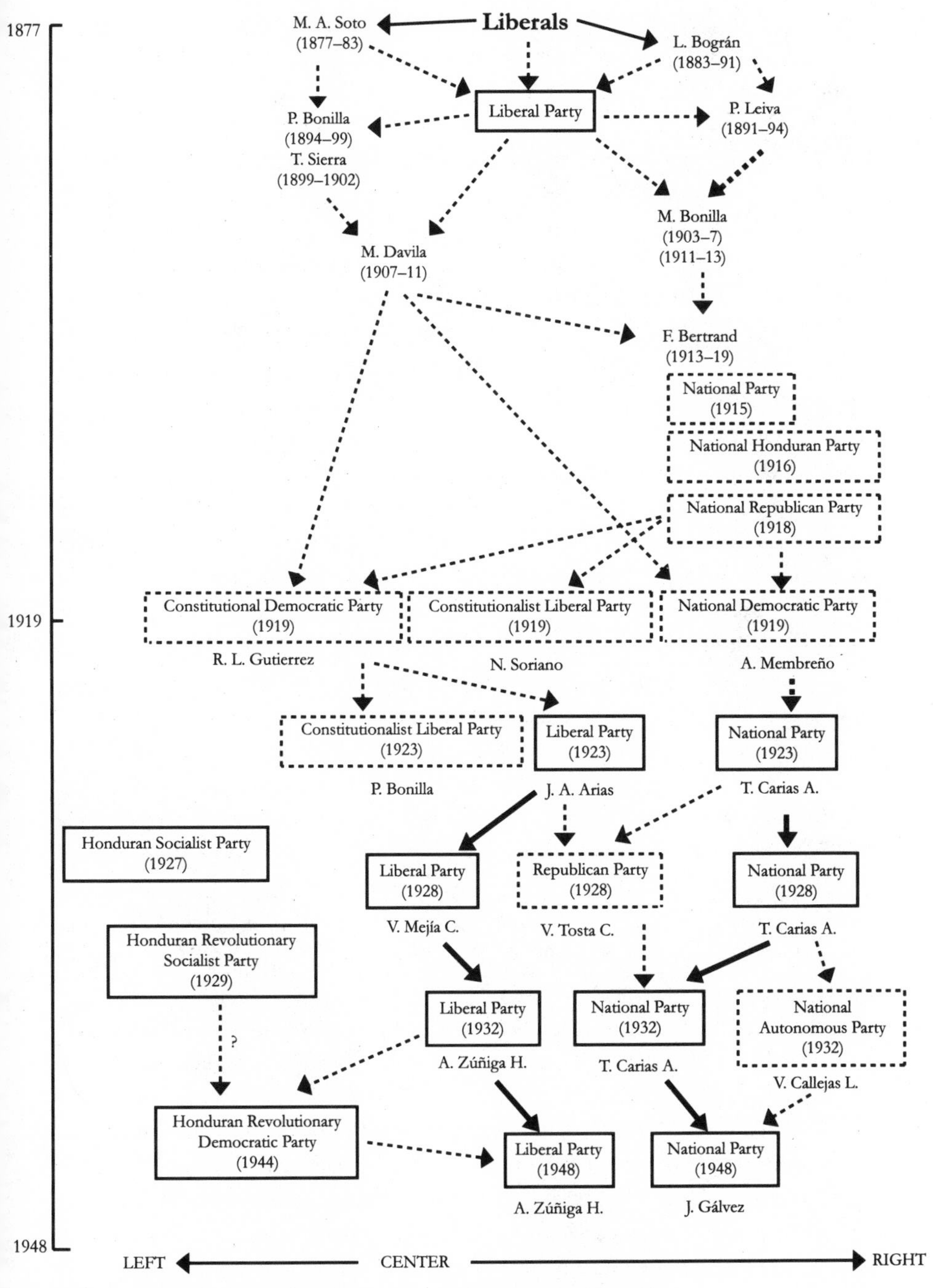


Figure 1. Evolution of Political Parties in Honduras, 1877–1948

militarist politics, Honduran society, and the state. It occurred in a very different context from previous civil wars. First, the greatest growth in U.S. investments between 1897 and 1919 occurred from 1908 to 1919, most of it on the North Coast banana plantations. Second, of fifty-seven concessions granted to the major banana companies or their predecessors between 1900 and 1930, 65 percent were granted from 1910 to 1920. Moreover, by the late 1910s the value of potential government revenues lost to specific banana company concessions doubled.[20] By the mid-1910s the exceptions represented between 40 and 50 percent of national government revenues. What is more, when Manuel Bonilla died in 1913, only about 2,480 laborers worked on banana plantations; by 1920 that figure had risen to nearly 10,000.[21] Finally, the political militarism into which the Reforma period collapsed after 1877 assumed a parasitic relationship to the little available revenues provided via the municipal and national taxes that survived the concessionary system.

In 1914 the U.S. minister in Tegucigalpa already had reported that "on account of an erroneous economic system [the country's] resources are insufficient for its needs, its treasury is often empty and it is constantly compelled to seek financial aid in the shape of temporary loans in order to tide over its pecuniary difficulties. . . . its principal reliance in such times of stress has been through foreign, principally German, commercial interests." Interestingly enough, at this point local capitalists still played a crucial role in financing government revenue deficits, a role that the major banana companies assumed in the 1920s. Data for 1892–1912 show that claims on state revenues resulting from war damages and loans to cover battle procurements were largely made by Hondurans. The sources of temporary loans changed after World War I. From that time, all three major banana companies subsidized government expenditures of outgoing administrations and new administrations assuming power, usually after bloody military engagements. This happened in 1919 and 1920 and continued into the 1930s.[22]

The entanglements between Honduran militarists and foreign capitalists are indicative of a broader phenomenon: that between the late nineteenth century and the late 1910s, the structural problem linked to the concessionary system also became enmeshed in the drain on revenues and loans demanded by the incessant insurrections promoted by virtually every leader of either political party. When General López Gutierrez assumed office in 1920, his government contracted with a U.S. State Department financial expert who in 1921 filed an extensive report on Honduran finances. The report began thus: "The history of Honduras shows clearly the grave effects of civil wars upon public finances. The expenditures of the Department of War completely dominate the financial situation during a revolution and for many succeeding months."[23]

Between fiscal years 1911–12 and 1919–20, the War Department's budget usually represented 30–35 percent of the total budget, followed closely by the budget for the Finance Ministry, mainly to cover the public domestic debt accumulated over the years.[24] Comprehensive statistics for the period 1877–1911 are lacking, but data representing the War Department's budget as a percentage of the total budget for 1894, 1900, 1901, 1902, and fiscal years 1903–4 and 1904–5 vary little from the picture amply documented for the period 1911–20. The percentages for years prior to 1911 break down this way: 1894, 31; 1900, 34; 1901, 42; 1902, 37; 1903–4, 36; and 1904–5, 38.[25] The government surely maintained these budget levels for the War Department from 1906 to 1910, when two wars, among other insurrections, during those years overthrew two presidents: Manuel Bonilla during 1906–7 and Miguel R. Dávila during 1910–11.

Ironically, War Department budgets from 1900 to 1920, if not at least from 1892 to 1920, paid only for war material and the mobilization of soldiers. These monies did not go for recruiting and sustaining a strong military. Steve C. Ropp, in an important study long ago, noted that during the nineteenth and early twentieth centuries "no military institution existed in Honduras. . . . While there was always the semblance of structure, the military did not develop to the extent that any real institutionalization occurred."[26] Besides the structure-revenue problem, Ropp discussed other factors that contributed to the nonexistence of a military identity separate from the political order. These included unpunished desertions, severe inequalities and injustice within mobilized militias, and the absence of military academies.

Ropp attributed these factors to the "chronic instability of the national government." But the broader issue was the nature of the integration into the world economy and hence the lack of a viable ruling class with a direct stake in a state with sufficient potential force to discipline civil society. As Minister John Ewing put it from Tegucigalpa in 1914, "the higher classes are composed of wealth, education, and refinement and these classes really constitute the governing element and dominate all public action. There is, however, no unity of purpose or action amongst them. They are divided into numberless factions, each faction representing some individual of dominant intellectual ability, or qualities of leadership, or possession of such personal charms as attract or draw other men unto them."[27]

At any rate, the existence in El Salvador and Guatemala by the late nineteenth century of relatively strong military academies, supported by relatively solid financial ties with their respective states, permitted, generally speaking, more organic relationships between the coffee oligarchies in those countries and "their" governments. Such relationships resulted from the repressive police force and military necessary to sustain the exploitative labor relations on coffee plantations. Cultivation in Nicaragua and Costa Rica between the late nineteenth and early twentieth centuries emerged in different contexts and hence engendered different military traditions: little militarism in Costa Rica, and, by the 1920s, a National Guard in Nicaragua under U.S. tutelage.

## Political Party Reorganization in the Aftermath of 1919

Bertrand's efforts to impose his brother-in-law's election via his Liberal Constitutionalist Party in 1919 resulted in the final polarization among men who had fought with and/or against Manuel Bonilla between 1903 and 1911 (Figure 1). Bertrand's alliance with his wife's brother had actually represented a feeble attempt to deal with the untimely deaths of Manuel Bonilla's real military successors: General Jeronimo J. Reina in December 1918 and Francisco J. Mejía in January 1919. In 1918 these generals had emerged as the anointed candidates of the National Republican Party. They had fought with Bonilla in 1903 and served as ministers of war and the interior during Bertrand's administrations (1913–18).[28] Their deaths prompted Bertrand to establish his Liberal Constitutionalist Party in March 1919.

All of this suggests that in 1919 the old Liberal Party founded by Policarpo Bonilla in the aftermath of the Reforma period had yet to recover from the disarray into which it fell after General Manuel Bonilla and Samuel Zemurray overthrew President Miguel Dávila in 1911. Various events changed this in 1919 and soon afterward: first, General López Gutierrez's military victory against Bertrand in late 1919; second, his electoral defeat of National Democratic Party candidates Alberto Membreño and Antonio Madrid in the October 1919 elections; third, and connected to the ascendancy of López Gutierrez, the imprisonment until Spring 1920 of prominent founders of the National Democratic Party, including Saturnino Medal, Antonio M. Callejas, Silverio Laínez, and Francisco López Padilla.[29]

In 1920 and 1921 these events spawned two developments: first, the redoubling of efforts by the National Democratic Party leadership to reconstitute a political party to oppose López Gutierrez, and second, the creation of space in which a new generation of self-proclaimed liberals might reconstitute something different from the Liberal Party established in 1891. These efforts facilitated preparations for the presidential election of October 1923.

Between 1920 and 1923 Paulino Valladares, General Tiburcio Carías, and old followers of Bertrand's Liberal Constitutionalist Party formed the present National Party. Moreover, albeit not yet well documented, it was probably in this context that key militarists associated with Membreño initiated ties with the United Fruit Company, especially General Carías Andino. Meanwhile, the regrouping of liberals during this period produced divisions indicative of new generations assuming influence and power within post–Reforma liberalism. In 1920 old followers and enemies of Presidents Manuel Bonilla, Miguel R. Dávila, and Francisco Bertrand convened in Tegucigalpa to reorganize the party. While important older liberals felt excluded, a prominent young man of thirty-five years served on the reorganized Liberal Party's Supreme Council and reigned as president of the National Convention in 1920: he was Angel Zúñiga Huete, who eventually became the Liberal Party's most influential ideologue and remained so until his death in 1953.[30]

Years after the 1920 convention, Zúñiga Huete recognized that between 1891, when the Liberal Party's formal constitution was drafted, and 1920, no new ideas had been added to its program.[31] In 1920, however, the party's Supreme Council produced a platform that showed not only Mexican revolutionary influences, but also a realization that Honduras, especially the North Coast, had changed dramatically since the 1890s. This document called for reforms that distanced it dramatically from its 1891 counterpart. The reforms included (1) "complete revision" of state finances, (2) abolishing mining monopolies, (3) limiting the quantities of land that the state could alienate to individuals, and (4) halting "man's exploitation of man" and "in the future, secure the socialization of land and the instruments of labor."[32]

The 1920 platform, regardless of its effectiveness at the time, served to distinguish the new Liberal Party not only from its past, but also from the program of Paulino Valladares's National Democratic Party of 1919. Whereas the National Democratic program called for the reform of state finances, it remained silent on regulating foreign investment, instead calling for facilitation of "the investment of foreign capital under the liberalism and justice allowed by the law and experience."[33] And though the latter program advocated reforming the existing agrarian law, its language de-emphasized issues of existing exploitation. The National Democratic Party also pressed for various measures to help workers, yet it lacked the Liberal Party's unequivocal call for "the organization of labor."[34]

Of course, its appeal for labor organization did not mean that the Liberal Party supported radical labor unionization, and in many ways its agenda differed little from the National Democratic conception. Nevertheless, some points deserve emphasis. First, the transition during 1919–20 not only marked the clear differentiation between the 1920 program and the ideological conceptualizations of the Liberal Party of 1891, but it also produced a subtle and simultaneous distinction among political factions during the reorganization that occurred after 1919.

Second, the influence of the Mexican Revolution on a sector of the young generation of the Liberal Party, especially its nationalist sentiments, rekindled in the 1920s some party efforts to support General Augusto Sandino of the

Liberal Party in Nicaragua, at least from 1926 to 1928. Despite the tenuousness of these relationships, in the eyes of U.S. diplomats and the banana companies they indicated that key leaders of the Liberal Party, especially Angel Zúñiga Huete, had become deadly threats.[35] This served to further distance the Liberal Party as a whole from the National Party opposition.

Finally, this differentiation occurred in the context of labor concentration and militancy on the North Coast, which political elites had to confront for the first time. This phenomenon in the 1920s and 1930s did not produce "a critical conjuncture" and a realignment of state-labor relations as it did in the larger countries of Latin America.[36] That occurred in the 1950s in Honduras. But the transition to the 1920s did serve to distinguish intra-elite party affiliations and, as such, made the North Coast the center of reformist impulses simultaneous with the socialism advanced by leftists.

## General Carías and the Liberal Party's New Demise, 1923–1932

When in late 1922 the U.S. chargé d'affaires in Tegucigalpa, Walker Smith, identified potential candidates for the 1923 presidential election, one, Jacinto A. Meza, seemed out of place. According to Smith, "Dr. Meza is an attorney practicing on the north coast and enjoys a very good reputation as a lawyer. He is very little known in the capital and has held no important political offices." Moreover, "the inhabitants of his part of the country, who are the producers and who contribute most of the revenue to maintain the Government, are disgusted with the administration of affairs by the leaders in control at the capital."[37]

Equally important, continued the diplomat, "the planters and businessmen in that section consider the office holders in Tegucigalpa as professional politicians who are willing to sacrifice the economic welfare of the Republic in order to remain in power and administer the exchequer." More ominously, "it is possible that the people of the richest section of the country may assert themselves in the approaching election campaign and center about Dr. Meza, or some other favorite, for the purpose of getting control over the affairs of state and have them administered along business like lines."[38]

Meza had emigrated from Comayagua to San Pedro Sula, where he practiced law as early as 1911.[39] He served on the municipal advisory board fourteen times between 1904 and 1931 and was the board's legal council in 1913 and 1916.[40] Meza did very well in the thriving city when its elites were allied with Samuel Zemurray. (In 1930 he would serve the Standard Fruit Company as a privileged attorney.) More important, in 1921, a year before Walker Smith submitted his report to Washington, Meza joined San Pedro Sula's elites in establishing their own social club, the Casino Sampedrano. Among its founding members were Luis Bográn, Roberto Fasquelle, Henry T. Panting, Juan R. López, future Honduran president Juan Manuel Gálvez, and Samuel Zemurray.[41]

Meza's candidacy represented the public moments of nonpolitical elite differentiation between the North Coast and the interior. Its tentativeness showed that long before Stokes's comments of 1950, North Coast elites were cognizant of the structural differences between their sources of wealth and elite power in Tegucigalpa. They also realized that they had to assume responsibilities vis-à-vis the working people of the area that seemed and were distant to Tegucigalpa elites. The absence of large labor concentrations in and near the Honduran capital kept the "social question" at bay. It is little wonder that in 1923 the U.S. minister suggested to Secretary of State Charles Evans Hughes that Meza might be considered a compromise candidate to the bitter rivalries among liberals and nationalists.[42]

In 1920 Meza had confronted issues concerning the "social question" head on. In August of that year, about 1,000 workers abandoned banana plantations near La Ceiba and crowded that city to protest low wages. In response, General López Gutierrez declared a state of siege and deployed troops. He also named a Mediating Commission drawn from Casino Sampedrano citizens from San Pedro Sula, including Jacinto A. Meza; Juan R. López, the city's mayor in 1899 and 1905 as well as an investor in Zemurray enterprises in the Sula Valley; and three prominent emigrants from the coffee-growing regions of Santa Bárbara: Dr. Miguel Paz Barahona, a cousin of two former presidents; former president Luis Bográn (1883–91); and Francisco Bográn, the provisional president after Francisco Bertrand's departure in 1919.[43] The strike was resolved without bloodshed.

Unfortunately for Meza and his friends, the North Coast's presence in the national economy, while extremely important, remained connected to the import-export sector's prominence and the overwhelming presence of foreign capital. Though commercial and manufacturing concerns already served to distinguish San Pedro Sula within the North Coast and from Tegucigalpa and the interior, the lack of structural differentiation between local industrial capital accumulation and foreign agricultural capital established the boundaries of San Pedro Sula's political power vis-à-vis Tegucigalpa. Moreover, the exclusion of Arabs and Jews from elite social clubs like the Casino Sampedrano until well into the 1930s and 1940s weakened the elite's economic solidarity and political action.[44] Jacinto A. Meza was thus not a serious contender in the elections of 1923.

On the other hand, the Liberal Party platform of 1920 failed to ignite a close relationship between Zúñiga Huete's liberalism and the working people of the North Coast. Various factors explain this. First, although the Supreme Council seemed to be under Zúñiga Huete's influence, its control between 1920 and

1923 remained with the council president, General Miguel Oquelí Bustillo.[45] Further, in the early 1920s Policarpo Bonilla, Juan Angel Arias, and others like General Oquelí remained the party elders, despite their own bitter animosities. They enjoyed both the historic prestige of having founded the party and, while nourishing patron-client relationships, using the resources of the executives they served.

Although these and other factors made the 1923 elections a rather traditional bout between old-line politicos, the fact is that party realignment and reorganization in the aftermath of 1919 did lead to new developments. First, the 1919 campaign penetrated into most areas of the country, and during 1922–23 both parties established electoral clubs throughout Honduras.[46] These clubs aligned themselves with the old-line politicians, but in the post–1919 context the process began to cultivate party affiliations that extended beyond the leaders, at least in a way that was substantially different from the pre–1919 period.

By the late 1920s the National Party had achieved a rather widespread dominance of municipal power based on party affiliation. In the 1927 elections, National Party loyalists won 68 percent of 232 municipalities. By 1928 the U.S. minister in Tegucigalpa reported that "the National Party has control of the election machinery practically throughout the country." In 1931 the nationalists won 88 percent of the municipal governments, and in 1933 their candidates secured victories in 69 percent of the country's local governments.[47]

Among the official candidates in the October 1923 elections were three old friends now turned bitter enemies: General Carías of the National Party, Juan Angel Arias of the Liberal Party, and Policarpo Bonilla, who was supported by General López Gutierrez's government. The vice-presidential choices were indicative of old loyalties and new realignments, and it seems that only Carías and Paulino Valladares astutely understood the emerging relevance of North Coast elites to party campaigning. The nationalists nominated Dr. Miguel Paz Barahona, a man not only with intimate ties to San Pedro Sula's Bográn family, but also widely popular on the North Coast.[48]

The old liberals, in contrast, neglected strategic appeals to the North Coast. Policarpo Bonilla's running mate was Mariano Vasquez, a former adherent of Manuel Bonilla and a cabinet member in Bertrand's administrations in the 1910s. Bonilla's nomination might have resulted from attempts to win over old nationalists uncomfortable with Carías, but the choice seemed irrelevant to the new demographics and economics of the period. Arias's vice-presidential candidate was General Miguel Oquelí Bustillo.[49] This selection remained tied to officialist, pre–1919 liberalism, again lacking the appeal that someone like Paz Barahona or even Jacinto A. Meza might have brought to the ticket.

In the end the Carías–Paz Barahona slate won in 1923, but with only a plurality of 48 percent. As in 1902, the Congress, mostly liberals divided between loyalty to Bonilla and Arias, accepted responsibility for choosing a president. The liberals were not about to select General Carías, but they also declined to unite and name one of their own. They feared that if they did so Carías and most nationalists would revolt, very much like General Manuel Bonilla rebelled against Juan Angel Arias in 1902.

On the other hand, General Carías knew that victory by war would prevent him from assuming power because Honduras early in 1923 had signed the General Treaty of Peace and Amnity. Signatories to the treaty agreed not to recognize governments empowered through war. The Congress failed to choose a winner, and war ensued in early 1924. The opposition forces eventually won. But the revolution produced two new generals without loyalties to either Carías or the National Party: Gregorio Ferrera and Vicente Tosta, both from departments near the Guatemalan border yet with military strength on the North Coast.[50] These generals joined the new insurrection but had their own programs.

During the 1924 war, as in 1919, the relationship between the personal agendas of the warlords of both parties became entangled with the banana companies. The United Fruit Company, wishing to avoid a repetition of the Cuyamel Fruit Company's gains with the liberal general Ernesto Alvarado in 1919–20, now fully supported General Carías's forces in war, much as it did during the political campaign.[51] United Fruit officials did so not only because of the historical lessons they had discerned in the wake of 1919, but also because they were apprehensive that General Gregorio Ferrera, ostensibly a liberal like old General Alvarado, also enjoyed ties with Zemurray. Moreover, Zúñiga Huete's presence in López Gutierrez's government or any other Liberal Party regime did not bode well for exploitative foreign capitalists as a whole.

Tegucigalpa ultimately fell to the rebels, and negotiations led to the provisional presidency of Vicente Tosta, an independent-minded general who had fought against Bertrand and for López Gutierrez in 1919, in the process nourishing some pro-Liberal Party tendencies. Though Tosta was not allied with Carías or Ferrera, his cabinet consisted mainly of founding members of the National Democratic Party and followers of Carías. Two token liberals who had not participated in the 1924 debacle were also appointed. During the Tosta administration, Ferrera, feeling betrayed over government appointments, rose up against the president and remaining liberals joined him. Tosta personally defeated the small insurrection and in the process almost destroyed post–1920 liberalism.[52] Presidential and congressional elections in 1924 led to the single candidacy of Miguel Paz Barahona (1925–28), who won the presidency with about 99 percent of the vote (Table 3.1).

Paz Barahona's administration turned out to be one of Honduras's most peaceful. This has often been attributed to Paz Barahona's democratic credentials and his lack of personal ambition.[53] There is some truth in this. In 1928, when the liberals actually returned to power, Paz Barahona presided over perhaps the cleanest election in Honduran history. Unlike the sitting presidents in the elections of 1903, 1919, and 1923, Paz Barahona remained neutral in 1928 and did not try to impose his candidate. He, in effect, allowed the contending parties to campaign relatively undisturbed. But too much has been made of Paz Barahona's democratic nature in explaining the radical differences between the 1923 and 1928 presidential elections.

First of all, after 1923 General Carías remained the jefe of the consolidated National Party, a position he held until 1963. Therefore, any effort to impose a presidential candidate in 1928 faced Carías's enormous opposition. Indeed, in 1925 Paz Barahona became president primarily because U.S. diplomats stressed the 1923 General Treaty of Peace and Amnity accords and opposed Carías's candidacy.[54] In fact, the period of Paz Barahona's term represented the first time in twentieth-century Honduran history that a sitting president did not enjoy full control over the official policy of his party. As Carías's National Party obtained municipal power after 1925, its prospects in the 1928 elections seemed very promising.

Other factors explain the stability of Paz Barahona's presidency. From 1925 to 1928 old-line Liberal Party chieftains failed to recover from the devastation suffered in 1924. Not only did the major candidates—Bonilla and Arias—and their followers almost kill one another as they oversaw the destruction of the López Gutierrez administration in 1924, but also in the process few institutional legacies remained between old liberals and new ones like Zúñiga Huete, who stayed in exile until 1928. Worse, the Liberal Party's institutional death in the 1920s paralleled the deaths of its most prominent patrons. Policarpo Bonilla and Juan Angel Arias died in 1926 and 1927 respectively.[55] This left the party in shambles at the very time that the nationalists won the presidency and that General Carías molded the National Party in his own image.

Moreover, in this situation the Liberal Party came under the influence of young nationalist liberals like Vicente Mejía Colindres. In 1913, when the United States intervened in Nicaragua, Mejía Colindres penned a critical "open letter" to the U.S. government. By 1922, apparently because of close ties to Zúñiga Huete, Chargé Walker Smith, ever watchful of Hondurans questioning the empire, characterized Mejía Colindres as "a socialist" who enjoyed the support "of certain elements of the younger generation who believe in some form of communism, just one or two shades less radical than the kind now dominating in Soviet Russia." By 1928 Mejía Colindres is said to have personally promised General Sandino, if elected president, to keep the Honduras-Nicaragua border open to assist in his struggle.[56]

More interesting is the fact that the reorganized 1927 Liberal Party Supreme Council also included prominent anti-imperialist intellectuals like Froylán Turcios and even a progressive capitalist from San Pedro Sula, indeed, none other than Jacinto A. Meza. Beginning in late 1926, Froylán Turcios published reports of Sandino's struggle against the Conservative–U.S. Marine alliance in Nicaragua. Sandino and Turcios secretly corresponded from 1927 to 1929, and Turcios publicly supported his cause.[57] It is understandable that in July 1928, on the eve of a presidential election, United Fruit officials in Washington feared that Turcios might support a rebellion and link it to "the All-America Anti-Imperialist League."[58] This did not occur.

Ironically, Carías lost in 1928. But so did the Liberal Party. In 1928 the nationalist candidate was, of course, General Carías. The liberals, on the other hand, achieved something unique in Honduran history. General José María Ochoa Velasquez, General López Gutierrez's vice-president in 1919, stepped aside for compromise candidate Vicente Mejía Colindres. Unlike some U.S. officials, General Vicente Tosta did not consider Mejía Colindres a socialist and threw his support to him. Therefore, the nationalists faced not the Liberal Party, but a coalition called the Liberal Republican Party that enjoyed popular liberal support and, crucially, the mobilized support of followers of General Tosta, a hero of the 1924 war, especially on the North Coast. In fact, Mejía Colindres's 14,000 majority vote was largely the consequence of Tosta's backing.[59]

This, of course, also meant that without Tosta, given nationalist control of municipal government and the Congress (in 1928, nationalists accounted for twenty-two of forty-seven congressional seats), the liberals might lose in 1932. General Tosta died in 1930 and General Ferrera was assassinated in 1931.[60] Tosta's death practically assured a Liberal Party defeat in 1932. It also signaled the end of a major *military* challenge to General Carías.

## The 1932 Elections and the Carías Dictatorship

The Liberal Party lost the presidential election in October 1932 by about 20,000 votes (see Table 3.1). Although the absence of Generals Ferrera and Tosta was a critical factor in the vote, a more crucial determinant was the impact of the depression. As early as December 1929, eleven months after Mejía Colindres assumed power, Tegucigalpa's *El Cronista* recognized a downturn in the economy locally. By April 1930 the newspaper linked the economic slump at home with the New York stock market collapse.[61] In Honduras, as in most of Latin America in the 1930s, the depression served as prelude to dictatorship.

The 1932 presidential election pitted old enemies. During Mejía Colindres's administration, Angel Zúñiga Huete had recovered the leadership of the Liberal Party and secured its nomination. Unlike in 1923, his present running mate, Francisco Paredes Fajardo, appealed directly to San Pedro Sula, the North Coast, and the western departments. At the time Paredes's brother, José Antonio, was governor of Cortés. In the course of the campaign, Zúñiga Huete traveled extensively on the North Coast, appealing directly to the plight of unemployed banana laborers. He was followed closely by informants associated with the U.S. embassy.[62]

During the campaign U.S. officials frequently linked Zúñiga Huete's appeals to labor throughout the North Coast with the simultaneous activism of socialists and communists. The United States and banana company spies kept an eye on both processes, searching for a possible alliance between Zúñiga Huete and communists. Actually, they had little to fear, for by 1930 Mejía Colindres declared a state of siege on the North Coast to repress strikes against wage cuts. In 1931–32 Mejía Colindres did an exceptional job of smothering socialists and communists. Whatever promises he had made to Sandino in 1928, by 1930 the Honduran president often asserted his wish to see Sandino's downfall.[63]

General Carías, of course, became the National Party's candidate and surely the United Fruit Company's choice. In April 1933, after his victory, the U.S. ambassador noted that "no Fruit Company, I believe, ever exercised a more powerful influence and control of a Honduran government (with the possible exception of the Government of Manuel Bonilla, created out of a revolution aided by the Cuyamel) than does the [United Fruit Company] now on the Government of President Carías." By this time Cuyamel belonged to the United Fruit Company, for Samuel Zemurray sold his interest to its old enemy in 1929. It is not surprising, then, that a month before the ambassador's statement, *Fortune* magazine published an extensive article on Zemurray's exploits, recognizing his chairmanship of United Fruit and observing that he "swallowed a Boston-bred empire of six republics and 50,000,000 bananas."[64]

General Carías's vice-presidential candidate in 1932, General Abraham Williams Calderón, did not disturb that empire. In fact, he may have visited United Fruit's offices in Boston in the 1910s when he studied engineering at the Massachusetts Institute of Technology. After returning from Boston, Williams Calderón served in various posts of the Paz Barahona administration. His standing in the government was based on his family's economic and political power in the southern departments, particularly in Choluteca, in landed estates whose economic importance originated in the mid-nineteenth century.[65]

Moreover, Williams Calderón represented a vengeful nemesis to the Liberal Party, which since the 1920s he had held responsible for his father's death during a civil war in 1894. The nationalist general's campaigns focused primarily on travels in the interior. Carías, the U.S. embassy officials reported with some regret in June 1932, rarely left his stronghold near Tegucigalpa; worse, he never once visited the North Coast in 1932.[66] In many ways, the four candidates and their histories represented aspects of the demographic contradiction that Williams S. Stokes discussed in 1950.

On the other hand, the conflict was not simply an urban-rural clash, even if that process was surely part of it. The main dispute turned on the emerging opposition between North Coast elite and working-class liberalism, even tinged with left-wing socialism, and the more conservative social and political culture of the interior and Tegucigalpa. The latter's social actors took power via the 1932 elections and maintained it afterward through a brutal dictatorship. However, the pre–1930s legacy of North Coast uniqueness, combined with the resurgence of the world and local economies by 1945, eventually deposed the Carías regime. That process, in turn, played a crucial role in the eventual relationship between North Coast development and military reformism in the early 1970s.

# POLITICS AND THE MODERNIZATION OF THE STATE AND MILITARY, 1945–1957

Municipal officials in San Pedro Sula sent a delegation to Tegucigalpa in 1937 to consult with the "central powers" about "issues related to the development of this Municipality's administrative program."[1] The delegates must have felt an urgency about their trip, as transportation difficulties alone might have discouraged other San Pedro Sulans from making the arduous journey into "the interior." The dusty road turned and twisted out of the flat Sula Valley and out of Cortés, a road that for some miles paralleled the old Cortés railroad once controlled by Washington S. Valentine and Samuel Zemurray.

The journey did offer some provincial if momentary luxuries, including a short meal at General Tiburcio Carías Andino's restaurant in Zambrano, where his wife Elena prepared Honduran rural cuisine.[2] However, by the mid-1930s General Carías and Doña Elenita Carías spent most of their time in Tegucigalpa, where, a loyalist claimed in 1942, the general embodied an "intelligent dictatorship" willing to "stain its hands with blood."[3]

By 1937 General Carías Andino held power in Tegucigalpa as dictator. In the previous year San Pedro Sula authorities had unanimously endorsed his continuation in office beyond the four-year term for which he was elected in 1932.[4] The 1936 "constitutional reform" extended his presidency to January 1943. The 1937 consultative meetings between San Pedro Sula's municipal officials and the "central powers" responded to the centralization of command that leaders in the new dictatorship envisioned early in 1935.[5] The unanimous endorsement of this procedure in March 1936 had been a foregone conclusion because Carías's adherents controlled the municipality. In late 1939 congressional devotees of the new dictatorship decided again to amend the constitution and prolong the Carías administration until January 1949.[6] As in 1936, the San Pedro Sula municipality unanimously approved the ruling.[7]

In early 1941 the official acts of the newly appointed council sessions had to be recorded in volumes first signed by the minister of the interior.[8] Successive municipal authorities in San Pedro Sula applauded these and other measures emanating from Tegucigalpa; they celebrated the Carías dictatorship by financing a Boulevard Carías and by erecting a bust of the general that stood in front of the Municipal Palace until liberals destroyed it in 1958.[9]

The economic structure of Honduras had changed by the late 1950s, when new personalities and class actors entered the political stage in San Pedro Sula and Tegucigalpa. These people eventually became involved in the reformist agenda of the Honduran military after 1972. The personalities included old left-wing liberals once associated with the PDRH, a reinvigorated working class on the North Coast, and progressive capitalists espousing a new political vision regarding the relationship between capital and the state. These actors were in many ways reminiscent of Dr. Jacinto A. Meza, but the new post–World War II economy produced different expectations and even promoted the political involvement of Arab merchants and industrialists.

## Economic Growth and Class Structure

The destruction of the Carías bust in San Pedro Sula early in 1958 signaled major changes in the political relations between the central state and the municipal government. These changes dated back to the military coup of 1956 and the ascendancy of the Liberal Party after the presidential election in 1954. The municipal officials who assumed power in San Pedro Sula after the 1956 coup accepted their appointments once the military had assured them that they would be allowed greater control of administrative expenditures at the local level.[10]

The San Pedro Sula officials who sought budgetary flexibility wanted to remove the constraints imposed by Carías. Besides, military leaders in 1956 had encouraged the economic liberalization recommended by the Banco Nacional de Fomento and the Banco Central de Honduras, both inaugurated in 1950.[11] In fact, Roberto Ramírez, the president of the BCH, and other prominent members of these banks, including Gabriel A. Mejía, Carías's tax revenue administrator in Cortés from 1940 to 1949, played important roles in the 1956 coup and the military government of 1956–57.[12]

Moreover, the leaders of the 1956 coup broke tradition and appointed regional officials suggested by the organized sectors of the regional business associations.[13] By March 1957 the military junta decreed that the new National Elections Council incorporate into its membership appointments offered by "the commercial, industrial, agricultural and cattlemen associations" of Honduras.[14] According to the leadership of the Cámara de Comercio e Industrias de Tegucigalpa, this showed that governments "were acquiring a new conscience, since in the past the Chambers of Commerce and Industry were inert organizations and they were not consulted on vital issues."[15] Later the 1957 Constituent Assembly obtained specific counsel on incorporating explicit ideas on the "economic regime" that should then guide economic policy.

Like Roberto Ramírez and Gabriel A. Mejía, the economic experts that advised the Constituent Assembly were prominent members of the BNF and BCH, and most had studied graduate-level economics abroad—at the National Autonomous University of Mexico, Yale, and Harvard. These and other economic advisers had been working closely with the CCIT, Cámara de Comercio e Industrias de Cortés, and Asociación de Ganaderos y Agricultores Sula since 1950, when the BNF and BCH charters officially incorporated representatives from these commercial sectors into the governing boards of these important agencies of the post–Carías state. In 1950 the CCIC leadership praised this development, proclaiming that the CCIT, CCIC, and AGAS were "organizations that represent the nation's *fuerzas vivas*," that is, the motivating economic forces, excluding, of course, workers and peasants.[16]

The changing political relations between the state and local government in the mid-1950s began with more general structural changes in the Honduran economy after World War II. The value of banana exports climbed rapidly after 1943–44, and even coffee became an important exchange earner.[17] During the period 1946–52 coffee exports represented, on the average, 9 percent of total exports.[18] After 1943 this recovery in the external economy contributed to the growth of government revenues and increased government expenditures, especially in public works (Table 4.1).

Other measures show a regenerating postwar economy. The Honduran gross domestic product enjoyed a strong recovery after 1945, and by the early 1950s it surpassed the expansion recorded during the late 1920s. Export agriculture's share of GDP growth declined steadily in the 1930s, 1940s, and 1950s, with domestic agriculture's share assuming an important position during the 1930s and 1940s. Unlike the GDP growth recorded for most of the 1920s, the sectoral structure of GDP growth of the 1940s and early 1950s showed significant changes.[19] The manufacturing share of the Honduran GDP rose steadily in the late 1940s and 1950s, particularly in San Pedro Sula.[20]

Between the 1930s and 1950 factory-based manufacturing in Honduras's major cities never employed more than 4,000 workers in a given year. Moreover, it rarely employed more than 1,500 workers in any one city, except Tegucigalpa in the late 1940s (see Table 1.5). The surge in factory employment levels occurred in the 1960s (see Table 4.2).

Table 4.1 Indicators of Economic Decline and Recovery in Honduras, 1929–1950 (in millions of lempiras)

| | | | National Government | |
|---|---|---|---|---|
| Fiscal Year | Banana Exports | General Imports | Revenues | Expenditures |
| 1929–30 | 46.0 | 31.8 | 12.0 | 8.4 |
| 1930–31 | 34.6 | 20.5 | 11.1 | 8.9 |
| 1931–32 | 27.9 | 16.7 | 9.6 | 8.9 |
| 1932–33 | 23.5 | 12.5 | 8.4 | 8.1 |
| 1933–34 | 19.5 | 16.7 | 8.6 | 8.0 |
| 1934–35 | 15.8 | 19.1 | 9.7 | 7.9 |
| 1935–36 | 11.9 | 17.4 | 9.1 | 7.8 |
| 1936–37 | 12.6 | 20.7 | 8.9 | 7.8 |
| 1937–38 | 8.5 | 18.9 | 8.8 | 8.3 |
| 1938–39 | 12.5 | 19.4 | 9.6 | 8.5 |
| 1939–40 | 12.6 | 20.1 | 9.5 | 8.1 |
| 1940–41 | 13.4 | 20.5 | 9.5 | 7.9 |
| 1941–42 | 11.7 | 22.3 | 9.5 | 8.3 |
| 1942–43 | 3.9 | 20.5 | 10.3 | 8.7 |
| 1943–44 | 9.2 | 26.6 | 12.1 | 10.5 |
| 1944–45 | 12.9 | 30.3 | 14.0 | 12.1 |
| 1945–46 | 12.3 | 39.1 | 17.9 | 13.1 |
| 1946–47 | 16.0 | 58.8 | 21.8 | 16.4 |
| 1947–48 | 14.6 | 71.2 | 23.2 | 19.0 |
| 1948–49 | 20.5 | 67.9 | 27.9 | 19.2 |
| 1949–50 | 20.3 | 68.4 | 35.3 | 20.9 |

*Sources:* Banana Export data for 1929–30 to 1947–48 are from Márquez et al., *Estudio Sobre la Economía*, p. 36. Banana export data for 1948–49 to 1949–50 represent calendar years figures for 1949 and 1950; see Ellis, *Las Transnacionales del Banano*, p. 403. Import data are from Ministerio de Hacienda, *Informe de Hacienda, Crédito Público y Comercio, 1949–1950*, p. 221. Revenues and Expenditures are from Thompson, "Economic Analysis," pp. 54, 176–77. The data on revenues and expenditures represent calendar years between 1929 and 1950.

On the other hand, the evolution of banana company employment from the early 1930s to the early 1960s, compared to factory-based manufacturing, shows significant differences, especially up to 1954. This, of course, is not surprising. What is interesting is the dramatic recovery of banana company employment in the 1940s and early 1950s, a structural change that eventually had social and political ramifications for class relations in Honduras as a whole.

Post–1930s census data show another interesting phenomenon recorded

Table 4.2. Banana Enterprises and Factory Employment, Selected Years, 1950–1970

| | Banana Enterprises | Factories |
|---|---|---|
| 1950 | 30,841 | 5,800 |
| 1960 | 15,449 | 14,800 |
| 1965 | 19,436 | 19,400 |
| 1970 | 26,511 | 25,500 |

*Sources:* Ellis, *Las Transnacionales del Banano*, p. 408; Del Cid, "Honduras," p. 89. For the 1950 figure, see Euraque, "Merchants and Industrialists," p. 310 n. 174.

during the transition from the 1940s to the 1950s and after: a rapidly increasing artisan workforce located in the departmental residencies of Tegucigalpa, San Pedro Sula, and La Ceiba.[21] Like the rural proletariat on the banana plantations, the urban artisan workforce lacked an institutional presence to represent its economic force, but the fact of its existence signified an economic "emergence" on the North Coast as important as the organized merchants, manufacturers, agriculturalists, and cattle raisers of the CCIC, CCIT, and AGAS. Nonetheless, in the early 1950s these representative organizations of capital were the first to fully engage the *caudillista* state.

## Modernizing State Institutions and Practices

The CCIC's research in December 1950 showed that the Department of Cortés provided more than 30 percent of total central state revenues, and that as such San Pedro Sula and its problems required national attention. Municipal authorities had made similar claims a few days earlier.[22] The commercial recovery of the late 1940s motivated these statements, which San Pedro Sula merchants and government officials had been making since the turn of the century. Now, however, the historical context was different, and this mattered.

Cortés cattlemen and agriculturalists founded AGAS in 1948 in the midst of the post–1945 recovery. The CCIC, influenced by the CCIT and the Tegucigalpa Rotaries, reorganized in 1946–47. In 1949 the country's chambers of commerce convened in a national assembly in Tegucigalpa for the first time in almost twenty years. During that meeting Honduras's leading capitalists made a series of recommendations that Carías's successor should consider as part of the new economic policies—everything from municipal tax reforms to liberalized local commerce to tariff reforms to protect manufacturing.[23]

In 1951 the BCH conducted a thorough study of San Pedro Sula's financial structure. Directing the project were Paul Vinelli and other economists associated with the International Monetary Fund's advisory team to the BCH since 1949. Preparations for the study began in 1950, when representatives of the BCH, the BNF, municipal government, and the CCIC and AGAS gathered to discuss the BCH-inspired fiscal reforms. By 1952 local Liberal Party notable Abraham Bueso Pineda, the CCIC president (1951–58), visited the nationalist municipal authorities to encourage closer contacts between the CCIC and the local government.[24]

After Carías left office in January 1949, a government committee considered the financial reforms necessary to establish the BCH and the BNF. By December 1949 Gabriel A. Mejía, the former administrator of tax revenues for Cortés, headed a delegation that traveled to El Salvador to learn from similar legislation implemented there.[25] By the 1960s Mejía had become the most prominent leader of a group of San Pedro Sula capitalists who used the CCIC to confront the autocratic military government established after the coup of 1963. Further, his appointment as director of the newly established General Bureau of Income Revenues (1949–56) placed him in an excellent position to closely oversee the relationship between the new direct taxes on capitalists and their contribution to the expanding tax-based revenues of the state.[26]

The economic orthodoxies offered by the IMF and the World Bank advisory missions consisted, generally, of fiscal reforms to more efficiently collect and allocate revenues for central state distribution to infrastructural projects and for the support of private investment, local and foreign. From 1950 to 1954 the BNF formulated only rudimentary statements on the question of a National Development Plan along World Bank lines.[27] Before late 1954 Honduran officials never established the "planning machinery" necessary to prioritize, mobilize, and allocate resources. But efforts in this direction produced, in February 1955, a Consejo Nacional de Economía charged with coordinating intraministerial agencies in the design of a World Bank "Economic Development Plan" for the country as a whole. But although the CNE prepared a World Bank–style plan in 1955, the CNE remained largely moribund until 1961.[28]

Despite the CNE's mainly inactive status between 1955 and 1961, its creation represented a significant innovation at the levels of macroeconomic evaluation and policy formulation in Honduras. It professionalized economic assessment, and it further legitimized technocratic influence within the state, a process bound to antagonize caudillos who were accustomed to governing on the basis of short-term spoils manipulation and even intuition. The CNE grouped the directors of the major agencies and institutions that after 1950 formulated and oversaw state macroeconomic policy: the presidents of the BCH and the BNF, the ministers of finance, development, and natural resources, and representatives of capital.[29]

The technocratic elite of the CNE remained under the influence of international professionals who appreciated capital's historical role in economic development, especially BCH consultants like Dr. Paul Vinelli, who also invested in many leading San Pedro Sula enterprises, including a Pepsi-Cola bottling plant that opened in 1957.[30] Equally important, the CNE technocrats represented a generation of professionals who had studied abroad prior to 1950 or who had gained expertise by means of BCH-sponsored scholarships. Finally, these experts considered caudillo politics as the major obstacle to economic development.[31]

A good example of a pre–1950 trained technocrat was BCH President Roberto Ramírez, who had studied in Mexico in the 1940s and worked closely with the IMF consultants since 1949. Characterizing a BCH-sponsored student was René Cruz. In 1950 Cruz worked in the Honduran embassy in Washington. Two years later the BCH sent him to Yale, where he obtained a master's degree in economics. By 1957 he held stock in San Pedro Sula's Pepsi-Cola bottling plant. In the same year he served as an economic adviser to the Constituent Assembly that elected Ramón Villeda Morales president.[32]

## MILITARY MODERNIZATION PRIOR TO THE COUP OF 1956

In October 1956 the Honduran armed forces ousted from the presidency Julio Lozano Díaz, another old-time caudillo of the National Party. The top conspirators included Colonel Héctor Caraccioli, head of the air force; Major Roberto Gálvez Barnes, minister of development; and General Roque J. Rodríguez, director of the military academy in Tegucigalpa. These officers then organized a military government with General Rodríguez as its apparent leader, primarily because of his seniority.[33] By July 1957, however, Rodríguez resigned from the government due to the pressures and machinations of the minister of defense, aviation colonel Oswaldo López Arellano.[34] In this way the leading sector of the armed forces consolidated its power within the military triumvirate.

López Arellano's control of the government and his eventual dominance of the armed forces as a whole reflected both his personal ambition and the historical trajectory of the air force within Honduras's military structure. Unique among branches of the Latin American armed forces, the Honduran air force as of 1955 accounted for 32 percent of the country's total armed forces strength.[35] Moreover, the professionalization of its officers and the institutionalization of its prominence within the military complex originated with training abroad. This occurred years before Carías, counseled by U.S. military advisers, established the first regular infantry battalion in Tegucigalpa in 1947.[36]

The relationship between the Honduran air force and U.S. military trainers began in 1942 under the auspices of programs sponsored by the United States in 1941, especially those created by the Lend-Lease Act. Carías used the situation to strengthen the training and hardware available to the Honduran military aviation school established in 1933. He sought to structure a military option capable of confronting insurgencies that he would probably face, particularly after installing his dictatorship in 1936. Thus, by 1942 the Honduran air force consisted of twenty-two planes manned by pilots and mechanics trained in the United States, including Colonel López Arellano. In fact, from 1941 to 1949 Carías used 62 percent of the Lend-Lease funds to buy airplanes and related equipment.[37]

The military coup of 21 October 1956 represented a major turning point in the post–World War II restructuring of Honduras's political system. It did so not only because it represented the armed forces's first modern intervention in national governance, a point often made by the current historiography, but also because of the civilian personalities involved in the coup and the administrative trajectory of the military government of 1956–57. (This crucial issue is rarely mentioned in the current historiography.)[38] Indeed, the 1957 Constituent Assembly that elected Villeda Morales president also granted the Honduran military "more freedom of action," according to one scholar, "than any document since Paraguay's constitution of 1844."[39]

The context for the 1956 coup emerged from several sources: the ascendancy of the Liberal Party after 1949 and its mobilization of banana working-class support; the struggles over the presidential election of 1954, which for the first time since the Carías dictatorship allowed for a rupture in the political system controlled by caudillos; and the longer-term economic processes already outlined, which made traditional caudillo politics seem more archaic and encouraged the political ambitions of new military leaders.

## San Pedro Sula, the New Liberalism, and the Demise of Carías

The first contested municipal elections in Honduras after 1933 did not take place until 1950, under the presidency of Juan Manuel Gálvez. That year the nationalists obtained over 90 percent of the votes and won every municipality except one.[40] During the 1930s and 1940s Carías represented only one of various dictatorships established in the area after 1931 and amply supported by the U.S. government in the 1940s. But unlike the other dictators of the period, Carías was the only one to hand over power in an orderly manner to his chosen successor. In the international context of democratic idealism cemented during the victory over fascism in Europe, the dictators early in 1944 confronted resistance to their quasi-fascist regimes—first in El Salvador and soon in Guatemala. Public resistance ranged from general strikes to military coups.

By May 1944 Carías confronted strikes in Tegucigalpa led largely by students, professionals, and the wives of prominent liberal dissidents. Exiled Liberal Party chieftain Angel Zúñiga Huete, who had been directing the liberal opposition in Mexico via the Comité Liberal Democrático Hondureño, early in July 1944 traveled to Washington to get State Department help in ousting Carías.[41] The State Department never accepted his proposals.

In Honduras, critical developments overtook Zúñiga Huete's efforts in Mexico and Washington. On 6 July 1944, five days after General Jorge Ubico abandoned power in Guatemala, Carías's local henchmen in San Pedro Sula challenged a demonstration with a brutality that resulted in the massacre of more than fifty people.[42] That bloodbath produced immediate and long-term effects that were critical to the presidential election of 1954, especially the ascendancy of Liberal Party strength on the North Coast in general and in San Pedro Sula in particular.

The foremost effect of the killings in the short term was the organization of the exiled community that settled in El Salvador and Guatemala late in 1944.[43] By August 1944 exiles in Guatemala had established a Frente Democrático Hondureño whose membership consisted of a new generation of Liberal Party exiles who were different from those, like Zúñiga Huete, who had fled Honduras in the 1930s. The ideological projection of the 1944 exiles was more in tune with that of Juan José Arévalo and other radical liberals of the period; the FDH exiles thus rejected Zúñiga Huete's leadership and the traditional *caudillismo* he represented.[44] These divisions doomed the organized resistance of the exiled population.

Amid these difficulties, a radical young wing of the Liberal Party in San Pedro Sula established, early in 1946, the Partido Democrático Revolucionario. Though different from the exiled membership of the Frente Democrático Revolucionario Hondureño, the FDH's successor, the PDR certainly was in consonant with the FDRH's rejection of Zúñiga Huete and generally approved of the radical liberalism of Juan José Arévalo in 1946 and 1947. Zúñiga Huete's domination of the Liberal Party continued after his return to Tegucigalpa in February 1948. The party's convention in April thus excluded liberals associated with either the FDRH or the PDR.[45]

In August 1948 a segment of the Liberal Party joined the PDRH, the successor of the PDR of San Pedro Sula. These divisions in the leadership of the Liberal Party, coupled with repression by the Carías dictatorship, signaled the collapse of Zúñiga Huete's preeminence. By September he pulled his party from the October elections. On the eve of the elections a general associated with him undertook a hopeless military expedition, and soon afterward Zúñiga Huete left Honduras for his final exile. In the uncontested elections of 10 October, the National Party secured 85 percent of the vote. Juan Manuel Gálvez assumed office in January 1949.[46]

With Zúñiga Huete out of the way, Dr. Ramón Villeda Morales took over the Liberal Party. Villeda Morales represented a new generation of liberal politicians quite different from San Pedro Sula's Abraham Bueso Pineda, a prominent member of the CCIC since its more modern establishment in 1931. Even in 1948, when the two men tried to wrest control of the Liberal Party from Zúñiga Huete, Villeda Morales acted as an aspiring junior partner of Bueso Pineda.[47]

In 1948 Villeda Morales was forty years old and Bueso Pineda was fifty-five. But more than different generations distinguished these elite Hondurans. For years Bueso Pineda had enjoyed close relations with foreign banana company interests in San Pedro Sula; Villeda Morales had not. In this respect, Bueso Pineda belonged to the generation of Carías and Gálvez, elite caudillos whose political fortunes were rooted in great part in their intimate connections to the banana companies since the 1920s. Villeda Morales entered the university in Tegucigalpa in the late 1920s and eventually earned a medical degree (1934), in the process writing a thesis on the social problems related to venereal diseases. After postgraduate work in Hamburg, Germany, in 1938–39, he opened a clinic in Tegucigalpa and soon joined the Rotarians. In the mid-1940s he became a recognized social commentator in the Honduras Rotaria as well as one of its most active members.[48]

A self-styled urban petty bourgeois reformer, Villeda Morales at times was even linked with the liberal radicalism of Víctor Raúl Haya de la Torre of Peru, Luis Muñoz Marín of Puerto Rico, José Figueres of Costa Rica, Juan José Arévalo of Guatemala, Ramón Grau San Martín of Cuba, Juan Bosch of the Dominican Republic, Rómulo Bétancourt of Venezuela, Germán Arciniegas of Colombia, Pedro Joaquín Chamorro of Nicaragua, and others. In the mid-1950s he was supported and befriended in the United States by well-connected, anticommunist liberals like Adolf A. Berle, later a policy adviser to the Kennedy administration.[49]

During the final months of the 1948 electoral campaign, groups disaffected with Zúñiga Huete's command of the Liberal Party pressed to replace him with either Abraham Bueso Pineda of San Pedro Sula or Ramón Villeda Morales.[50] From this point Villeda Morales may have remained attuned to the liberal radicalism of President Arévalo in Guatemala, but whatever ties he once had to the PDRH were now abrogated. The consolidation of Villeda Morales's control over mainstream liberalism in 1949 changed the fluctuating relations between the left-wing, liberal, and radical liberal segments of the PDRH.

After 1951 the left-wing elements of the PDRH assumed intellectual predominance within the party, leading finally, probably by 1953, to the disintegration of their loose association with even the radical liberals. The deepening radicalism of the Arbenz government in Guatemala (1951–54) no doubt also contributed to the efforts to establish a local Communist Party. Preparations for the presidential election of October 1954, beginning with the May 1953 Liberal Party convention, surely helped to wrest more liberals from the PDRH, further adding to the downfall during 1954–55 of the left-wing–liberal association in the PDRH.

## Villeda Morales's Bid for Power and Military Institutionalization

Liberal leaders in 1953 must have felt confident about Villeda Morales's chances in 1954. A feud between Gálvez and Carías, which had erupted in 1952, continued in 1953 and 1954, decisively dividing the National Party.[51] Moreover, this party's historic association with repressing labor on the banana plantations finally began to cripple its electoral prospects.

In May 1954 President Gálvez, conspiring to overthrow Jacobo Arbenz Guzmán, faced the greatest strike ever attempted against banana companies during this century; it involved 40,000 workers, who were later characterized by Ramón Amaya Amador, a Communist Party intellectual, as Honduras's "Paris Commune." The general strike, led by communists, left-wing liberals of the PDRH, and laborers radicalized in the process of the conflict, paralyzed not only banana company operations, but also all other sectors associated with the export economy. The leadership of the San Pedro Sula bourgeoisie, certainly not communists, also supported the laborers with moral and financial assistance.[52]

As a result, Villeda Morales won the October 1954 election, but only by a plurality of votes—48 percent. This placed the selection of the president in the Congress because the presidency could be won only with an absolute majority. The nationalists united briefly to prevent Villeda Morales from taking control. This constitutional crisis led to the assumption of dictatorial powers by Gálvez's vice-president, Julio Lozano Díaz, who had in turn been assigned command by Gálvez. Between late 1954 and 1956, Lozano Díaz tried to promote another nationalist presidency by fraudulent elections. This established the context for the coup of 1956.[53]

The Lozano Díaz regime collapsed for a number of reasons, some connected to the culture of Tegucigalpa politics and intrigue, others to more systemic social and economic changes experienced by Honduran society after World War II. In 1955 the Liberal Party leadership was not about to allow a longtime henchman of the National Party assume power through the calculated maneuver of another long-standing servant of the old Carías dictatorship. Moreover, the outcome of the 1954 presidential ballot demonstrated that the Liberal Party could muster the electoral votes needed to defeat the nationalists, even if the divided nationalists were to unite, something that did not happen until 1962.

Also, in the early 1950s the liberals finally began to accumulate political power at the local level, a process demonstrated in the municipal elections of November 1954. On that occasion liberals won 98 of 237 municipalities, whereas in 1950 they had prevailed in only one municipal government.[54] Finally, the emerging relationship between the North Coast working-class leadership and the liberals, unlike the experience of the 1920s, could be helpful not only in another electoral confrontation but also in mobilizing against any of Lozano Díaz's maneuvers.

In August 1956 the chief of the Honduran armed forces, Colonel Armando Velásquez Cerrato, recognized as a National Party sympathizer, began floating the idea of sponsoring a military coup against Lozano Díaz.[55] Once Velásquez Cerrato's queries had circulated in other branches of the armed forces, other military leaders, mainly from the air force, planned a "double-coup," one against Velásquez Cerrato, probably because of his relationship with the infantry and his past connection with Lozano Díaz, and the other against Lozano Díaz because of his incompetence. The motivations and actions supporting the air force coup emerged from various sources: (1) power struggles within the armed forces, (2) the traditional opportunism of Cariístas and liberals, and (3) the influence of a technocratic elite disgusted with Lozano Díaz's bad management.[56]

The armed forces appointed three civilians to tell Lozano Díaz of his dismissal: Gabriel A. Mejía, director of the Bureau of Income Tax Revenues; Roberto Ramírez, president of the BCH; and Jorge Bueso Arias, head of the CNE since its inception in 1955. Thus, not only were Mejía, Ramírez, and Bueso Arias intimates in the social world of Tegucigalpa elites, they represented some of the top leaders that took over the evaluation and making of macroeconomic policy in Honduras after 1949. The military coup of 1956 therefore represented more than the ascendancy of the air force; it signified as well the consolidation of a technocratic elite's influence over economic policy formulation within the Honduran state. Villeda Morales's image and the Liberal Party benefited from both processes. The military leadership immediately appointed Villeda Morales as ambassador to the United States, undoubtedly to reconcile his image with Washington's suspicions over his "leftism" of the mid-1940s.[57]

## THE REGIONAL EMPOWERMENT OF THE SAN PEDRO SULA BOURGEOISIE

The military leadership that assumed power in 1956 immediately committed itself to a quick return to a popularly elected civilian government. But the trajectory of that return to civilian government in 1957 was conditioned by the power struggles within the armed forces. The military's cabinet appointments in 1956 included Villeda Morales's liberals and Carías's nationalists, undoubtedly a sign of reconciliation among Tegucigalpa political elites.[58]

Conciliation within the armed forces, however, meant the rise to power of Colonel Oswaldo López Arellano, whom the military leadership appointed minister of defense. In 1957 he used his position to marginalize General Rodríguez and Major Gálvez Barnes within the junta. By late 1957 only Colonel Caraccioli remained of the original junta, and in November Colonel López Arellano himself became part of the junta with Caraccioli.[59] Meanwhile, in July the military leadership scheduled Constituent Assembly elections for September 1957.

By this time Villeda Morales's chances for finally winning the presidency seemed outstanding. Soon after his return to Honduras in August 1957 from his intermittent ambassadorship in Washington, he and López Arellano struck a deal.[60] If Villeda Morales would allow the military a constitutionally based autonomy from civilian control, the military leadership, in this case López Arellano, would support Villeda Morales's presidential election via the Constituent Assembly. This arrangement, of course, would give the liberals access to government spoils from which Carías and Gálvez had excluded them for decades.

Besides allowing Villeda Morales to appoint his own cabinet, the military would authorize his minister of the interior to restructure the country's municipal governments. In this Villeda Morales would be limited by new constitutional exigencies, more democratic than those of the Carías dictatorship, but the situation would enable Villeda Morales to appoint municipal leaders throughout the country, including those in powerful cities like San Pedro Sula. Villeda Morales's appeal to the working class of the North Coast could be used to support the mobilization of labor.

The Liberal Party won over 60 percent of the vote in 1957.[61] This gave the liberals control of the Constituent Assembly and allowed them to explore the possibility of persuing the scenario described above. The liberals soon deployed their forces and elected Villeda Morales president (1957–63), even before the assembly had an opportunity to discuss the articles of the new constitution.[62] Thereafter Villeda Morales appointed his own liberal cabinet, except that López Arellano, now chief of the armed forces, was allowed to "suggest" that a colonel friend be named minister of defense.[63]

Villeda Morales's deal with the armed forces, probably underwritten by the United Fruit Company and the U.S. embassy,[64] was not the only threat to the future of the National Party. In December 1957 Villeda Morales's minister of the interior appointed municipal authorities throughout Honduras.[65] This allowed the liberals to control the municipalities, and, more important for the story here, it enabled the local bourgeoisie to influence directly decision making in San Pedro Sula. This was a major juncture in the social and political empowerment of local merchants and manufacturers. Whatever its consequences, the San Pedro Sula bourgeoisie's first direct access to local power during the postwar period resulted from Villeda Morales's election by the Constituent Assembly of 1957.

From 1957 to 1965, San Pedro Sula officials drew the membership of the Municipal Advisory Council from among the CCIC's most prominent young capitalists and Rotarian friends of Villeda Morales, including Dr. Rodolfo Pastor Zelaya of the old PDRH, Henry Holst Leiva, Eduardo Kawas, Guillermo Paredes, Jaime Rosenthal, and Donaldo Panting.[66] These and other local capitalists identified not only with President Villeda Morales but also with the minister of economics, Fernando Villar (1958), and especially the minister of finance, Jorge Bueso Arias (1959–63), noted capitalists themselves, both of whom were part of the technocratic elite that had controlled macroeconomic policy since the early 1950s.[67]

The CCIC's identification with Jorge Bueso Arias deserves emphasis. Bueso Arias was the nephew of Abraham Bueso Pineda, a San Pedro Sula intimate of Samuel Zemurray, president of the CCIC (1951–58), and nationally recognized leader of the Liberal Party dating back to the 1930s and 1940s. Bueso Arias joined the Tegucigalpa Rotary Club in 1944 and soon became part of that same generation of urbanite petty bourgeoisie from which Villeda Morales emerged. (Recall that Bueso Arias became a critical player in the military coup of 1956.) In fact, much of the state modernization often attributed to "the Villeda Morales regime" was designed by the technocrats first fully empowered during the military government and allowed free reign during the Villeda Morales administration.[68]

Unlike Villeda Morales, however, Bueso Arias came from a prominent merchant and landowning family with banking interests and investments in major San Pedro Sula firms, including a Pepsi-Cola bottling plant, sugar refineries, and the country's only cement plant; the cement plant was financed primarily by San Pedro Sula investors in 1956. Moreover, after 1959 Bueso

Arias became one of the key figures in Villeda Morales's cabinet who supported the technocratic push to involve the Honduran economy in the movement for Central American economic integration—under way since the early 1950s.[69]

Bueso Arias's role as executive secretary of the CNE from 1955 to 1958, a time when he fully supported economic integration, added to his prestige among CCIC leaders after 1959.[70] The military's ouster of Villeda Morales late in 1963, as well as the trajectory of the military government thereafter, represented, for the leadership of the San Pedro Sula bourgeoisie, not only the reentrenchment of traditional Tegucigalpa-based caudillo politics, but also a slap to the regional identification of San Pedro Sula elites with the Villeda Morales presidency. This process seemed more cruel because the traditionalist CCIT supported Villeda Morales's ouster, despite the fact that its longstanding leader, Roque J. Rivera, was a prominent member of the Liberal Party himself and a close friend of Villeda Morales.[71]

The reaction of Honduran civil society to the 1963 coup was radically different from its response to the military coup of 1956. This was true not only because the military conspirators of 1963 assumed different postures from the military leaders of 1956. By the early 1960s the segments of civil society themselves had changed, especially social forces localized on the North Coast in general and in San Pedro Sula in particular. These changes and their regional distribution were caused not only by the structural economic changes that took place after World War II, but also by the institutional innovations introduced into the state after 1949. This process meant not just the demise of Carías; it embodied the empowerment of the North Coast, with an industrializing San Pedro Sula as its capital.

# NEW INDUSTRIALIZATION AND THE ORGANIZATION OF HONDURAN CAPITALISTS

The streets of San Pedro Sula in late September 1968 remained under the watchful stare of Honduran soldiers charged with enforcing a violently imposed state of siege. This action represented President Oswaldo López Arellano's (1965–71) answer to a so-called subversive movement promoted by leaders of the Cámara de Comercio e Industrias de Cortés. The CCIC had been planning a "capital strike" to pressure López Arellano to redress grievances that had been accumulating since the coup of 1963. The organization paid a heavy price for its "subversive" politics. Some of its leaders fled into exile, others went into hiding locally, and still others sought face-saving arrangements directly with López Arellano. Loyalists of the president threatened key Arab members of the CCIC with deportation.[1]

The motivations of the leaders of the San Pedro Sula bourgeoisie emanated from the changing class structure of Honduras after World War II, the resulting nature of regional class formation, and the relationship between the economic agencies of the modernizing central state and the economic and urban growth experienced by San Pedro Sula in the 1950s and 1960s. The events of 1968 expressed the contradictions inherent in the preceding decades of economic and social development, but they also foreshadowed the reformism of the post–1972 era.

The origins of the 1968 events dated from processes that consolidated prior to the coup of 1963. In fact, by the time Ramón Villeda Morales returned to Tegucigalpa from his Washington ambassadorship in 1957, economic policy formulation lay firmly with the visionary and expectant technocrats who in

1958 simply encouraged him to support their policies—from fiscal reforms to Honduras's incorporation into the economic integration schemes of the United Nation's Economic Commission for Latin America.

## Honduras and the Central American Common Market

Economic advisory missions of the World Bank did not take concrete, systematic steps to install planning institutions in Central America between 1950 and 1954. The Truman administration (1945–53) largely avoided committing major resources to a "planned" development program for Latin America, and the Eisenhower administration (1953–61) only changed its policy on this issue in 1958.[2] By that time, ECLA's technocrats had become very influential among many of the technical experts who were formulating macroeconomic policy in Central America. The latter technocrats and their local allies, especially the ministers of finance, induced the industrial sector of the region to embark on an economic process that encouraged new social and political expectations of the capitalists who had risen to economic prominence during the post–World War II recovery.

Central American officials signed the first ECLA-inspired "economic integration" treaties in June 1958.[3] State makers in Central America had dreamed of a politically integrated region since the postcolonial period, but such efforts always failed. After 1950, ECLA economists suggested that a customs union be formed to support the specific process of manufacturing industrialization as a complement and alternative to the established pattern of export-oriented growth. The first significant ECLA mission to Honduras arrived in 1952, headed by the Argentine economist Raúl Prebish, ECLA's secretary-general and key theoretician.[4]

By February 1957 a special Honduran delegation attended the fourth meeting of the Committee for Economic Cooperation to discuss the Multilateral Treaty on Free Trade and Central American Economic Integration.[5] The members of this important contingent made up a Who's Who of technocrats and economists trained abroad after World War II. They were associated with the Banco Central de Honduras, the Banco Nacional de Fomento, and the Consejo Nacional de Economía—all of which were motivating the CCIC and the Cámara de Comercio e Industrias de Tegucigalpa to institutionalize their social and political expectations in the 1950s. Gabriel A. Mejía, as minister of finance, headed the Honduran delegation.[6]

Before the 1950s Honduras did not formulate an industrialization policy geared specifically to accelerate the manufacturing sector. Government administrators supported industrialization mainly by trying to lessen the cost of imports required for domestic production, a policy difficult to sustain because import duties continued to be crucial to central state revenues. Manufacturers depended largely on the concessionary system, on special importing privileges provided by tariffs, or simply on executive-ordered exemptions. The state did not provide or facilitate direct manufacturing credits originating in its own reserves or through international loans, even during the 1950s and early 1960s. Before the late 1950s commercial banks rarely offered credit to manufacturing ventures.[7]

In January 1957 Gabriel A. Mejía and other key advisers to the military government established in 1956 formed various economic advisory commissions.[8] These commissions studied not only the economic integration projects of ECLA but also tariff and fiscal reform and a law of industrial development. The industrial development law differed from tariff provisions because it eliminated import duties on manufacturing inputs and allowed qualifying firms to enjoy tax exemptions on profits and sales, making the incentives greater than the old concessionary system, especially considering the changes introduced into the tax structure earlier in the decade. The program recommended by Mejía and company became law in April 1958, a few months after Ramón Villeda Morales assumed the presidency.

The Industrial Development Law of 1958 was the most important institutional catalyst supporting manufacturing investments in the 1960s. Businesses began taking advantage of the law gradually, but its importance increased dramatically after the full establishment of the Central American Common Market in 1960. During the period 1958–60 only about 15 companies qualified for the law's profitable exemptions. By 1962 55 manufacturing firms enjoyed its tax exemptions. The number rose to 92 early in 1964 and to 155 by the end of 1965. Fiscal revenues exempted under the law rose from $115,211 in 1960 to over $2 million in 1964.[9]

After 1965 the number of registered firms applying for qualification under this law climbed rapidly, with companies from San Pedro Sula outdistancing those from all other regions, including Tegucigalpa. Thus, in the 1960s San Pedro Sulans witnessed a new urban sprawl that accompanied a massive increase in the "industrial area" occupied by and designated for the location of new factories. From 1964 to 1975 the city's "industrial area" increased 417 percent, while its "commercial area" climbed 319 percent. By 1968 San Pedro Sula's factories accounted for 45 percent of total factory-based manufacturing in Honduras, more than doubling similar measures for Tegucigalpa.[10] Consequently, in the 1960s a new generation of San Pedro Sula's business class, then deeply enmeshed in the institutional catalysts behind the decade's manufacturing investments, assumed the task of organizing a bourgeoisie supported through national interlocking institutions but led by what Rafael Leiva Vivas, a keen admirer of the San Pedro Sula capitalists, called "The Free Republic of San Pedro Sula."[11]

## Peripheral Industrialization, Investment Groups, and Class Formation

Rafael Leiva Vivas wrote the cited article amid a frenzy of political activism instigated by the San Pedro Sula bourgeoisie after the fraudulent municipal election of March 1968. Soon afterward the CCIC secretly plotted to challenge the López Arellano regime. Leiva Vivas's public comments complemented these covert maneuvers, which most San Pedro Sula capitalists of an older generation would have thought absolutely out of place. Besides condemning the electoral fraud, Leiva Vivas noted the "civility" with which San Pedro Sulans participated in the election, when the Liberal Party won this important municipality. But, he suggested, "It appears that the rest of the Republic is indifferent to the . . . serious threats to our institutions." He placed special blame on "Tegucigalpa . . . where the bureaucracy, government, and politics are concentrated, and where, it seems, fear and cynicism impede consideration of the national interest."[12]

Leiva Vivas identified San Pedro Sulan "civility" and "consideration of the national interest" with what he later characterized as the "emergence of a dynamic capitalist bourgeoisie capable of forging institutional changes without vacillation and halting compromises." Indeed, Leiva Vivas was one of the few intellectuals of the period who articulated the historical role of the San Pedro Sula bourgeoisie.[13]

After World War II the Honduran gross domestic product rose from $26.4 million in 1945 to $37.0 million in 1955 and to $60.2 million in 1965. By 1970 the figure stood at $73.8 million. The manufacturing share of the GDP also climbed steadily, accounting for about 4.5 percent in 1949, 7.5 percent in 1959, and 10.0 percent by 1969, significant increases from the 1920s and 1930s, when manufacturing accounted for slightly over 3 percent of the GDP. During the same period agriculture's share of the GDP remained the major component of the economy, but the export sector's share experienced a secular decline, with domestic use agriculture assuming a much more important role. In 1939 export agriculture's percentage share of the GDP stood at 22.9, whereas in 1949 it dropped to 19.6 percent and in 1959 to 12.7 percent.[14]

Honduras's incorporation into the CACM added new and dynamic elements to these macroeconomic measures. One of the most critical elements discussed in the CACM literature involves the issue of investment capital employed in the intensification of manufacturing industrialization in Central America in the 1960s. The broad finding for all of Central America is that direct foreign investment in manufacturing in the 1960s resulted in the general control of that economic sector primarily by U.S. capitalists. In Honduras the numbers were equally clear by the late 1960s, with various studies specifying the degree of foreign control over the largest manufacturing enterprises, measured usually by value of productive output, labor employed, and profit margins.[15]

On the other hand, the national macroeconomic statistics mask the economic power of the North Coast generally and San Pedro Sula in particular. By 1970 the Department of Cortés accounted for about 55 percent of the country's factory-based manufacturing output, whereas Francisco Morazán, the department seat of Tegucigalpa, registered a parallel measure of only about 25 percent. San Pedro Sula manufacturing establishments also exhibited a greater value of capital invested in fixed assets than similar measures for Tegucigalpa. Moreover, 1969 data show that San Pedro Sula's factories employed about 8,050 workers, whereas factories in Tegucigalpa had about 6,800. Finally, the San Pedro Sula plants on the average employed more workers per factory than their counterparts in Tegucigalpa and paid higher wages than factories elsewhere in the country. In short, during the 1960s San Pedro Sula emerged as the "industrial capital" of Honduras.[16]

Many factors account for these findings, including San Pedro Sula's short and cost-saving access to Puerto Cortés, the country's most important port, especially when it received a costly overhaul after 1966.[17] Direct access to the banana plantation markets certainly encouraged increased capacity, especially in the production of consumer goods. The rapidly growing population in and near San Pedro Sula also added to the new marketing possibilities for advancing the manufacturing process.

The most critical factor for actually establishing new plants and refurbishing others, however, was the mobilization of capital for manufacturing production on a scale unseen before the 1960s. As this study has shown, domestic wealth in Honduras had rarely been systematically deployed into manufacturing production. The Industrial Development Law of 1958 changed the conditions for risking accumulated capital in manufacturing, and in San Pedro Sula a coterie of merchants and industrialists, particularly Arab families, took advantage of this new incentive as well as drew on historical investment patterns established long before the 1960s.[18]

In addition, after World War II La Ceiba's Standard Fruit Company continued a diversification process that dated to the first decades of the century in that region, but whose beginnings in San Pedro Sula originated in the 1930s. By the time of the CACM, the Standard Fruit enterprises, supported by Banco Atlántida resources, consolidated into a critical financial structure around which the San Pedro Sula bourgeoisie organized locally. This historical pattern of peripheral industrialization in San Pedro Sula allowed for new and more dynamic forms of manufacturing accumulation in the 1950s and 1960s. Nevertheless, the process also revealed a Faustian bargain, one that ultimately set new limits to bourgeois social and political potential, vision, and expectations despite the fact that some individuals at one time had thought otherwise.

Outside the apparel and sugar industries, the manufacturing industry employing most workers in San Pedro Sula during the 1940s and 1950s was the brewery complex organized by the Standard Fruit Company in the late 1930s, a set of enterprises that, by the early 1950s, employed from 270 to more than 380 people. The trajectory of Standard Fruit's investments in Cervecería Hondureña, S.A., from the 1930s to the early 1960s shows the complex and intimate details of an investment group that, before the CACM, directly controlled almost every major manufacturing concern other than textile plants, including the region's sugar plantations and refineries, flour mills, and cement factory—that is, the city's leading factory-based employers outside the apparel industry.[19]

The Standard Fruit Company's efforts to establish a brewery complex in San Pedro Sula dated back to the 1930s, long after the firm had opened a brewery in La Ceiba known as Compañía Industrial Ceibeña. In 1935 Standard Fruit representatives Antonio Mata and Reginald Hammer organized the CEHSA probably as a holding company to later absorb San Pedro Sula's Cervecería Unión, S.A., a small brewery established by Samuel Zemurray associates in the late 1920s. In February 1939 associates of the Standard Fruit Company founded the Compañía Embotelladora Hondureña, S.A., which a few months later did absorb San Pedro Sula's CEUSA. Investors in COEHMSA included most of the older investors in CEUSA.[20]

By 1944 CEHSA, the firm organized in 1935, became the holding company of both the CIC and COEHMSA, probably in an attempt to fight competition from a German-owned brewery in Tegucigalpa. In 1949 CEHSA obtained another major concession through President Juan Manuel Gálvez, who had held a small number of shares in the brewery complex since the late 1930s. By the end of 1951 CEHSA finally absorbed COEMSA and the CIC, and by 1952 it controlled the brewery and bottling industries in San Pedro Sula, Puerto Cortés, and La Ceiba.[21]

After 1951 CEHSA's major shareholder continued to be the Standard Fruit Company. During the critical years 1953–56, however, CEHSA also incorporated into its capital structure most of San Pedro Sula's major immigrant merchants and manufacturers, including José Brandel, Antonio Mata, Boris Goldstein, Elias J. Kattan, Yankel Rosenthal, Jacobo Weizenblut, and associates of the Canahuatis, Siwadys, and Yujas.[22] But the link between these investors and CEHSA did not originate only by means of this channel. The expanding relations can be viewed through other processes as well, especially via the organization of the region's sugar plantations and refineries from the late 1930s to the late 1940s. These became the first large publicly held companies of the period, all intimately connected with San Pedro Sula's most important Arab families.

In 1931 Samuel Zemurray encouraged his old friend Roberto Fasquelle to plant sugar on banana lands that had been decimated by disease a few years earlier. Helped by a significant concession, Fasquelle in 1938 reorganized his family business into a major share-holding enterprise that drew members of the local Arab commercial elite, including Larachs and Siwadys, but Arab investors from Tegucigalpa as well, among them the Facusses and Barjums. Fasquelle also tapped into the local and national political leadership, from General Abelardo Bobadilla and Colonel Eduardo Galeano in Cortés to Minister of the Interior Juan Manuel Gálvez in Tegucigalpa.[23] In the 1940s and 1950s Fasquelle's Compañía Azucarera Hondureña, S.A., was one of the few firms that received major loans from the Standard Fruit Company's Banco Atlántida.[24]

Perhaps the single most important industry that the Standard Fruit Company came to control during the 1950s turned out to be the Honduran cement industry, which also was organized by merchants and manufacturers from San Pedro Sula. The historical trajectory of this enterprise in the 1950s is interesting because it offers a special example of the various forces at work at the time that Gabriel A. Mejía emerged as a prominent figure, not only in San Pedro Sula but in Tegucigalpa as well. Mejía, by then an experienced former minister of finance, became in late 1959 the cement firm's general manager, a position offered to him by Yude Canahuati, perhaps the most dynamic investor within the coterie of San Pedro Sula's Arab families.[25]

Efforts to establish Cementos de Honduras, S.A., began in 1948 with San Pedro Sula Rotarian and banana company executive Antonio Mata. (A close friend of the Canahuatis, Rosenthals, Kattans, and Mejía, Mata was an official consultant to the leadership of the CCIC from 1966 to 1972.) Mata's project did not materialize, but in 1952 the BNF engaged a United Nations expert to study its feasibility again. The expert chose San Pedro Sula as the headquarters of a factory to be located a few miles from where the raw materials were readily available. San Pedro Sula's merchants and manufacturers bought most of the initial shares in 1956; CCIC vice-president Yude Canahuati was the principal shareholder. The other investors included Yankel Rosenthal, former IMF official Paul Vinelli, CNE director Jorge Bueso Arias, José Brandel, and many immigrant businessmen in San Pedro Sula and La Ceiba.[26]

The regional range of investors in CEMSA represented an innovation associated with the accentuated levels of commercial accumulation on the North Coast during the postwar economic recovery. However, other elements of the CEMSA investment structure also demonstrated the growing complexity of investment patterns. That structure not only involved a wide range of individual investors buying into a "publicly held company," but also represented a concentration of "institutional investments" from significant local enterprises, a process of capital mobilization specific to this period and unique in San Pedro Sula. Among the corporate investors were Luis Kafie y Cía., Jorge J. Larach y Cía., Jacobo D. Kattan Industrial, S.A., Elias J. Kattan y Cía., Antonio D. Kattan y Cía., and the BNF. By 1959 CEMSA increased its working capital by accepting major investments from Cervecería Tegucigalpa, S.A., and Cervecería Hondureña, S.A., both controlled by the Standard Fruit Company.[27]

As is well known, local capitalist industrialization also benefited from major loans from the CACM-inspired institutions like the Bank for Central American Economic Integration and even from the U.S. Agency for International Development. In Honduras, these external capital sources were best used by the San Pedro Sula bourgeoisie. The BCIE immediately became the major creditor of factory-based manufacturing investments in Honduras.[28] In the process, moreover, the BCIE fully supported major enterprises of the San Pedro Sula–Standard Fruit Company investment group, formed in the 1950s.[29]

In 1961–62 the newly established Center for Technological and Industrial Cooperation, supervised by consultants from AID, contacted Honduras's leading manufacturers to encourage the creation of an industrial investment bank capable of mobilizing local capital for manufacturing ventures. This effort resulted in the founding in January 1964 of the Financiera Hondureña, S.A., in San Pedro Sula. A few months later FICENSA received a loan of $5 million from AID. In 1966 AID provided another $3 million, and in 1971 the BCIE granted the organization major loans. At any rate, by late 1965 San Pedro Sula's FICENSA became the main source of long-term manufacturing credit in Honduras and the institutional channel for foreign capital investments, most certainly destined for firms classified under the Industrial Development Law of 1958.[30]

Whereas loans from the United States represented FICENSA's main capital resources in 1964, San Pedro Sula's major merchants and manufacturers emerged as its most important individual investors, including Gabriel A. Mejía, Yude Canahuati, José Brandel, Yankel Rosenthal, Antonio Mata, Berti R. Hogge, Boris Goldstein, Nicolas J. Larach, Jorge J. Larach, Jaime Rosenthal, Jacobo D. Kattan, and others. These individual investors, in turn, were intimately connected with the corporate investors who purchased shares of FICENSA stock in 1964.[31]

## San Pedro Sula Capitalists in the National Organization of the Honduran Bourgeoisie

Late in November 1969 Gabriel A. Mejía and the CCIC sponsored the "Third Reunion of Honduras's *Fuerzas Vivas*," a meeting that Mejía hoped would address a favorite subject of San Pedro Sula's leading merchants and manufacturers: "The Unification of Honduras's *Fuerzas Vivas*—A Critical Necessity in Confronting the Decade of the 1970s." Mejía must have been proud of this event, because ever since assuming the CCIC's presidency in 1964 he had struggled against many obstacles to unify the policy and political claims of the Honduran bourgeoisie, especially the powerful faction in San Pedro Sula.[32]

Mejía was now fifty-eight years old, and San Pedro Sula had changed dramatically since his first visit to the area in the early 1930s. By 1969 he had fought many battles against the disintegrating tendencies in the collective action of representative capitalist institutions in Honduras. The CCIC won some battles and lost others.[33] However, the struggle itself showed that the transition to peripheral industrialization in Honduras did activate a new generation of business leaders in San Pedro Sula who envisioned a distinct political position for their merchants and manufacturers and even for labor. This young generation joined Mejía in rejuvenating the CCIC along these lines and in the process instigated the reforms enacted after 1972.

Gabriel A. Mejía officially assumed the presidency of the CCIC in early 1964. It was a difficult time, primarily because of widespread business apprehension over the ultimate impact of the CACM on local manufacturing and Honduras's balance of trade within Central America. In late 1962 and 1963 the country's trade with Central America had increased dramatically, but Honduran exports were losing the positive balance of trade recorded during the previous decade.[34]

There were also problems within the CCIC. For most of the 1950s the organization had been administered by Abraham Bueso Pineda, the old Zemurray associate, as president and Yude Canahuati as vice-president. When Bueso Pineda stepped down in 1958, Canahuati's economic prominence made him a logical candidate for the presidency. Nevertheless, his Arab immigrant status precluded this option, not only because of the high public visibility of the job, but also because CCIC's leaders would be required to engage in the politics of government economic policy in Tegucigalpa, a responsibility for which Canahuati had neither the initiative nor the experience.[35]

In 1964 Gabriel A. Mejía appeared to be the best candidate for the CCIC presidency. The 1963 coup and its aftermath had excluded him from consideration as the next president of Honduras, a post to which he aspired as late as the spring of 1963. After October the National Party, in which Mejía had been an influential player since the late 1940s, was no longer under the direct control of General Tiburcio Carías Andino, his close friend for many years.[36] Mejía's political experience, however, would be invaluable to the CCIC. His friends within the leadership of the San Pedro Sula bourgeoisie certainly knew this, because their personal collaboration with Mejía dated back to the 1940s when he was Cortés's administrator of tax revenues, a position of vast influence given the importance of Cortés to the central state's revenue base.

Mejía's friendship with Yude Canahuati, Antonio Mata, José Brandel, Boris Goldstein, Jacobo Weizenblut, Yankel Rosenthal, Abraham Bueso Pineda, Roberto Fasquelle, and other prominent merchants, manufacturers, and agriculturalists in San Pedro Sula and Cortés did not begin simply because of their contacts while Mejía was a tax administrator. Since the mid-1940s he had been a minor shareholder in San Pedro Sula's small—yet important and innovative—investments, from modest factories manufacturing hats and paper bags to a highly regarded private hospital founded in early 1946. When Mejía left for Tegucigalpa in 1949 to preside over the newly established National Bureau of Income Tax Revenues, he enjoyed the profits from a small stock portfolio including some of San Pedro Sula's most prestigious enterprises. By the time he took over the CCIC, his investments and management connections had undergone considerable expansion.[37]

In an urgent letter of December 1964 to other institutions representing commercial, manufacturing, and banking concerns in the country, Mejía noted that recently the minister of economics and finance had asked the CCIC and similar organizations to study and offer an "Exposition" on Honduras's role in the CACM. Mejía had announced an interest in the project a month earlier, but apparently he hoped that the CCIC and other institutions might collectively employ outside consultants to provide a systematic evaluation. Despite continuing trade problems within the CACM, few regional interest groups responded to Mejía's initiative. Throughout 1965 top economic policymakers emphasized the difficulties, and in December Mejía again appealed for the unification of the private sector and admonished "regionalism."[38]

It is unclear why other commercial and manufacturing organizations would not support Mejía's proposals to assess the troubles of the CACM. Part of the problem may have stemmed from the general inertia that characterized the efficient operations of these institutions even in the early 1960s.[39] On the other hand, at the time San Pedro Sula merchants and manufacturers probably had a greater economic stake in the CACM than any other capitalist sector in Honduras. So why not leave the matter up to them? Other evidence suggests that the CCIC did not get support on this issue because institutions like the Tegucigalpa-centered CCIT feared that they would lose their traditional hold on policy formulation regarding Honduran business operations in their dealings with the state. Jealousies of this nature arose in 1965, when the CCIC tried to reorganize the national directorate of all business organizations under new terms.

In 1965 the CCIC underwent a critical change in its top leadership, one that motivated the chamber during the years 1965–69 to transform the San Pedro

Sula bourgeoisie into a national political force. When Mejía became president in 1964, the CCIC leadership consisted of a Junta Directiva, a governing board traditionally composed of San Pedro Sula's top merchants and manufacturers, usually the older, more experienced men among them.[40] The governing board, including the CCIC president, would meet to formulate "Expositions" on government economic legislation directly affecting their interests. Before the 1950s the CCIC leadership generally discussed changing bills on tariffs and foreign exchange supplies. After 1950 the issues of direct concern to the chamber changed dramatically, now covering new national income and corporate tax regulations, central banking reforms, industrialization policy, the introduction of sales taxes, and labor legislation as well.

As we know, in 1965 CCIC policy formulation became the task of Gabriel A. Mejía and a coterie of young capitalists and business managers—mostly in their late twenties and early thirties—who held a new vision of capitalism's historic role in the country's economic, social, and political life. Officially, this new generation organized the CCIC's newly created advisory committee, an innovation introduced by Mejía (he later characterized it as the intellectual powerhouse behind CCIC activism after 1965).[41] The CCIC advisory committee included principal members of the San Pedro Sula bourgeoisie and a sector closely associated with a progressive wing of the local Liberal Party that had controlled the San Pedro Sula municipality since 1957. Among these people were Jaime Rosenthal Oliva, Mauricio Weizenblut Oliva, Henry Holst Leiva, Reginaldo Panting, Antonio José Coello Bobadilla, and, most important, Edmond L. Bográn, perhaps the group's major intellectual force.[42]

Bográn studied law, specializing in banking legislation, at Mexico's National Autonomous University in the early 1950s, apparently while exiled for his "subversive" political activities with the Liberal Party, largely because of ties with its left wing.[43] He presented his thesis on the legal aspects of Honduras's central banking system in 1956, at the age of twenty-six.[44] Bográn soon settled in Tegucigalpa, where from 1957 to 1959 he served as general secretary of the Honduras National Autonomous University. He also assumed management positions with various organizations, was treasurer of the Asociación Nacional de Industriales, and staunchly defended the agrarian reform project introduced into Congress by President Villeda Morales in 1962. By late 1964 Bográn bought significant shares in FICENSA. Finally, he became FICENSA's manager in San Pedro Sula, a post he held until December 1968.[45]

From the point of view of class politics, Bográn's most important project of the period was the founding, in late 1964, of *La Prensa*, a newspaper intended to project the vision and expectations of San Pedro Sula under the leadership of its manufacturing and commercial bourgeoisie.[46] Its first editorial on 26 October 1964 put it this way: "*La Prensa* is born as an act of Love and Hope . . . , without attachments to transient powers." Yet, as in the case of most social phenomena, that editorial also expressed an apparent contradiction in motivations, for besides its birth as an "act of love and hope," *La Prensa* attached its birthright to "an imperative social necessity." Honduras's North Coast, it argued, "needs a verb of its own."[47]

In other words, Tegucigalpa's *El Cronista* and *El Día* could not express the concerns of the "nation's interests" on the North Coast.[48] By May 1966 Tegucigalpa's elites were reading *La Prensa*, which was distributed in their city; in this way San Pedro Sula's social and political commentary was extended beyond the North Coast.[49] The Tegucigalpa bourgeoisie did not produce a similar newspaper until the 1970s.

Bográn's scattered writings demonstrate a specific understanding of manufacturing capitalism's central position in "modern" societies, from its economic role to its political role, as well as the bourgeoisie's historic role in Europe's capitalist transition.[50] By the early 1960s Bográn was also cognizant of the difficulties of the capitalist transition in Central America, especially because of his experiences in El Salvador and its coffee oligarchy's marginalization of what in 1970 he called "the small urban petty bourgeoisie." Moreover, his early association with the Liberal Party, particularly after the coup against Villeda Morales, prompted him to make *La Prensa* the expression of a new political vision, one that might extricate the Liberal Party from the political morass into which it had plunged after October 1963.[51]

In 1965 Bográn, who once plotted against Gabriel A. Mejía's close friend, General Carías, now joined Mejía on an interesting trip. They visited Mexico's Confederation of Industrial Chambers to draw on its experiences and perhaps apply them to the overall effort to create a federation of Honduras's chambers.[52] According to Mejía, they learned two impressive facts about Mexico's chambers: first, that the chambers had an efficient organization and a "high cooperative spirit of their membership," and second, Mexico's "private and public sectors" enjoyed a close working relationship. In short, "collaboration between private enterprise and government is such that any situation or problem impacting the economy, industry or national commerce is not decided upon by the government until securing the opinion of the organizations of the *fuerzas vivas*."[53] This situation did not exist in Honduras in 1965.

By November 1965 Mejía and Bográn's work resulted in the establishment of a Central Chamber of Commerce and Industry under the provisional presidency of the CCIT's Juan Elías Flefil and the CCIC's Mejía. However, this Central Chamber never functioned because the CCIT wanted to maintain the presidency in Tegucigalpa, with the other chambers serving it as "satellites." The CCIC opposed this, and apparently the dispute finally terminated this initial project.[54]

When addressing the CCIC General Assembly in December 1965, Mejía alluded to these problems by condemning the lack of unity in the private sector and its "isolated actions and regionalisms."[55] Actually, the Tegucigalpa Chamber of Commerce had always served as the "central" directorate for the country's other chambers. By the early 1960s, however, the CCIC represented a San Pedro Sula commercial and manufacturing elite that was unwilling to subscribe to the old ways. Its leaders would forge ahead with or without support from Tegucigalpa capitalists or the dominant political system.

# THE RADICAL LIBERALISM OF NORTH COAST LABOR, 1950S–1960S

San Pedro Sula capitalists were not the only targets of persecution directed from Tegucigalpa in 1968. From 1965 to 1968 North Coast labor traversed a similar road of confrontation with the country's political system. Indeed, the general strike promoted by San Pedro Sula's Cámara de Comercio e Industrias de Cortés in September 1968 actually lost steam and only regained strength when the unions themselves declared a general strike.[1] The union leaders made up a new and dynamic roster of labor militants—among them, Céleo González, Oscar Gale Varela, and Saúl Martínez Guzmán. In late September 1968 the Tegucigalpa authorities declared a state of siege, jailing some of these men and exiling others; in the end, however, they accommodated North Coast resistance. The 1968 confrontation represented the culmination of events involving the anti–Ramón Villeda Morales coup of October 1963, though its long-term roots stemmed from earlier processes.

North Coast labor activism, of course, dated back to the 1920s and early 1930s. After its dormancy during the Carías dictatorship, a new vibrancy emerged among labor leaders. The structural basis for greater participation in the 1950s stemmed from two broad phenomena: first, the recuperation of plantation labor in the late 1940s and the growth of an artisan and manufacturing force, especially on the North Coast; and second, the demographic shift from the interior to North Coast departments, as noted by William S. Stokes in 1950. In 1935 banana plantation employment amounted to slightly over 17,000 workers. By the late 1940s that figure had doubled, and by 1953 it peaked at slightly over 38,000. The first Honduran president to fully understand the implications of this process was an old friend of Samuel Zemurray, Juan Manuel Gálvez (1949–54).

## Labor Legislation during the Gálvez Administration

In 1949 President Gálvez signed a 1948 Organization of American States charter that guaranteed formation of unions. Although this represented a major departure from the Carías period, the mild labor measures introduced after 1949 should have been passed during the Carías dictatorship because the 1936 constitution called for such legislation. Yet until 1949, nothing was done. In the mid-1940s a climate of labor repression had persisted. From Tegucigalpa in 1946, Ambassador John D. Erwin confidently observed: "there is no unrest among the laboring classes. The well-to-do classes must have confidence in President Carías and in his ability to install an eventual successor without major disorders."[2]

Erwin's assurance was due to his own close ties with Carías, as well as to the absence of militant opposition to the regime. The liberal factions in exile remained divided among mainstream liberals like former president Vicente Mejía Colindres, himself living in self-imposed exile since 1935; caudillista liberals such as the now elderly Angel Zúñiga Huete, a nemesis to the State Department since the early 1920s; and left-wing liberals with links to Guatemala's Juan José Arévalo. Moreover, socialist organizers associated with the May 1944 protests in Tegucigalpa became the targets of a new wave of repression; many fled to Guatemala and El Salvador, where a more hospitable environment awaited them after the overthrow of dictators Jorge Ubico and Maximiliano Hernández Martínez.[3]

In Central America, the mid- to late 1940s saw innovations in state and labor relations that preceded the OAS charter provisions signed by Gálvez. Before the emergence and consolidation of the Cold War, local governments, reformist and dictatorial, accommodated the new relations between management and labor. The first labor code in Central America was legalized in 1945 under the auspices of General Anastasio Somoza García. Somoza's response to the growing urban working class in Nicaragua was an astute move that projected populism from a regime that had been widely despised.[4] In 1947 Juan José Arévalo followed with a labor code for Guatemala. The 1948 OAS charter thus represented regional legitimization of a process existent in South America but new to Central America.

In Honduras the 1948 OAS-inspired legislation provided legal grounds for new efforts to unionize labor. Various groups joined the fray, especially on the North Coast. The left wing of the Liberal Party, the Partido Democrático Revolucionario de Honduras, socialists, and communists all hoped to link their agendas with the repressed aspirations of labor. However, in 1948 the

Liberal Party continued to be dominated by a now conservative Zúñiga Huete; only when Villeda Morales took over in 1949 did the possibility for reform become concrete.[5] Meanwhile, left-wing activists, especially members of the PDRH, displayed rapid initiative in organizing the working class, at least in Tegucigalpa.

By late 1950 nine unions existed in Tegucigalpa—in factories producing matches and textiles, and in artisan shops making shoes and printing materials—largely formed under the auspices of the PDRH. But attempts to unionize in San Pedro Sula and the North Coast between 1949 and 1954 generally met with immediate government repression.[6] In fact, it would appear that Gálvez wished to confine workers' organizations to 1920s-style mutual aid associations, and that the sole responsibility for overseeing new labor legislation rested with a state whose workers had never enjoyed serious representation.

In February 1952 the Honduran Congress established the Bureau of Labor and Social Welfare within a newly organized Ministry of Development and Labor. Its purpose was to implement the limited labor legislation introduced in the same year, including laws governing overtime work, women and child labor, factory-based accidents, and compensation.[7] In some measure, the bureau represented an effort by the National Party to redress its social sins during the dictatorship. But strong unions, that is, those that could wrest economic and social benefits from management, particularly in the banana companies, seemed out of the question.

Ambassador Erwin acknowledged in April 1952 that the fruit companies were not pleased with attempts to establish labor unions as such. Likewise, U.S. efforts to involve the American Federation of Labor in Honduran labor-management relations did not receive the approval of the local elite. According to Erwin, "the visit of Serafino Romualdi of the American Federation of Labor in 1950 caused trepidation in government circles. The activities of Argentine labor attachés are resented by the Government." Erwin's anxieties were prompted by labor policy initiatives arising from President Harry S. Truman's Point Four Program, which encouraged "countries to establish fair labor standards and to develop free labor union movements as collective bargaining agencies."[8]

Erwin's uneasiness regarding Serafino Romualdi's visit must be placed in the broader context of Point Four Programs in Honduras, hence the new legitimacy of promoting labor union movements. Truman's Point Four Program, announced on 20 January 1949 as part of his foreign policy agenda, offered scientific and industrial expertise to underdeveloped countries like Honduras. The project was to build on the work of the Institute for Inter-American Affairs. During World War II this U.S. government agency had responsibility for everything from distributing anti-Nazi propaganda, to building strategic roads like the Pan American Highway, to undertaking joint public ventures for financing and building better sewage treatment and public drainage systems; sometimes it sprayed mosquito-ridden areas. The IIAA programs, which "had an overriding concern for United States National Security," focused on clearing and developing areas "that might become bases for United States troops or sources of strategic materials."[9]

The IIAA's relations with the modernizing Honduran state during the Gálvez administration legitimized the tours of the area made by Serafino Romualdi and others.[10] In the 1940s Romualdi worked for Nelson A. Rockefeller's Office of the Coordinator of Inter-American Affairs, an agency established by President Franklin D. Roosevelt to coordinate programs promoting hemispheric unity during World War II. The OIAA created the IIAA. Romualdi joined the OIAA as a labor researcher early in the 1940s after submitting reports on fascist influence in South America. After the war he became the Latin American representative of the AFL, which had determined to organize a regional inter-American labor confederation to challenge socialist and communist influence and organizations in the region. In the late 1940s this project took Romualdi to Latin America again. On his first visit to Honduras, in 1947, he noted that "there were no labor leaders in Honduras that we could approach for our purpose."[11]

These developments did not seem to have much effect on the ideological and programmatic statements of the National Party regarding labor. As late as March 1954 Carlos Izaguirre, the party's major ideologue at the time, confined the "state's protection" to workers' organizations interested in establishing "vocational and cultural centers in which to strengthen the individual's moral and civic values." Izaguirre's retrograde paternalism had been evident in his quasi-fascist reflections of the 1920s; apparently these had not changed in thirty years.[12]

By the 1940s Izaguirre viewed the activism of liberals and communists with hostile disdain. In late in 1946 Ambassador Erwin reported to Washington a conversation with Izaguirre regarding the anti-Carías activism of various liberal and left-wing groups in Honduras and abroad. As a solution to the problem, according to Erwin, Izaguirre "asserted that if Carías would arrest a half dozen men and place them in jail the agitation against the Administration in Honduras would end immediately. He believes it is all superficial, that it has its inception in the personal ambitions of certain 'outs' and has no real support among the populace."[13]

This was not the case. Through a general strike beginning in May 1954, workers on the North Coast finally assumed their own autonomous struggle and in the process broke the established limits of "national" decision making based almost entirely on the whims, expectations, and obsessions of Tegucigalpa elites. This dramatic shift in the Honduran political system no doubt surprised President Gálvez and General Carías, National Party leaders who for years had helped the banana companies repress labor discontent on the plantations. The geographic aspects of this shift had a significant effect on the different national politics of the 1960s and eventually the reformism of the early 1970s. Indeed, many young men involved in the 1954 strike, such as Céleo González and Oscar Gale Varela, became the principal reformist labor leaders of the early 1970s.

## The Strike of 1954: Origins and Implications for Unionization

The revolt in 1954 involved not only the over 35,000 banana company workers, but also most of the laborers in the small factories of San Pedro Sula, La Ceiba, and Tegucigalpa. It began in late April with a wildcat strike over overtime wages at the Tela port in the Department of Atlántida. The Tela dispute sparked protests elsewhere on the North Coast. By early May the workers called a general strike that was not settled until early July.[14] In the process, the liberals, the PDRH, and the communists attempted to define the agenda of the strike.

Insiders have asserted that the modern Partido Comunista de Honduras was founded in April 1954. The PCH existed largely because of the schism within the PDRH in the early 1950s and because left-wing liberals abandoned the PDRH for the post–Zúñiga Huete Liberal Party, including young men like Rodolfo Pastor Zelaya and Edmond L. Bográn. According to Ramón Amaya Amador, who became a leading PCH intellectual in the 1950s, once the PDRH's Vanguardia Revolucionaria became a victim of repression in 1953, most "regional committees" of the PDRH were transformed into "Marxist study circles," apparently in preparation for formally establishing the PCH.[15] Though set up by left-wing leaders in San Pedro Sula in April 1954, the PCH remained a clandestine organization and some of its members participated in the still legal PDRH, whose leaders publicly rejected accusations of being "manipulated by communists."[16]

During the strike the PDRH assigned key members as consultants to the first strike committee. In May the consultant to the strikers was José Pineda Gómez, the PDRH president and a Tegucigalpa lawyer who in 1931 had served as secretary to the Liberal Party convention. By the late 1940s Pineda was a member of the PDRH. (After 1954 he returned to the fold of mainstream liberalism; in 1957 he became president of the Honduran Supreme Court.)[17] Other PDRH members established the PCH, an organization that U.S. diplomats, as always, followed with great attention. In September 1954 a Honduran colonel employed in "intelligence activities" on behalf of the banana companies submitted information to the U.S. embassy that characterized Pineda as a "Vanguardista-Comunista."[18]

Between May and July 1954, therefore, the radicalization of North Coast labor was subject to the appeals and influence of organizers from the formal PDRH, from mainstream liberals like Villeda Morales, and from the clandestine PCH, some of whose militants still remained in the PDRH. However, the first strike committee consisted mostly of members of the PDRH and PCH militants. Late in May, during negotiations with the United Fruit Company, the government-established mediating commission, and the workers' strike committee, the latter's principal leaders were arrested.[19] By early June a new strike committee replaced the first one. This second committee was more amenable to U.S. government foreign labor policies of the Point Four Program and the attempt to overthrow President Jacobo Arbenz in Guatemala. Its leaders wrote to the AFL-CIO's leaders, including Serafino Romualdi, to offer their help in the aftermath of the strike negotiations.[20]

This drama assumed a major urgency in late June because of the U.S. intention to use Honduras to overthrow the government in Guatemala. A cable of 26 May from the U.S. embassy in Tegucigalpa to the State Department suggested that U.S. policy toward the general strike should be to arrange for a fair settlement while excluding the communists, "either by force or by effective public relations." Regional operatives of the Central Intelligence Agency in 1954 publicly admitted their close oversight of strike events.[21] Even before the government negotiators settled the strike, U.S. labor consultants, backed by the U.S. embassy in Tegucigalpa and associated with CIA operations, arrived on the North Coast to counsel the anticommunist labor leaders and Honduran president. These "interesting" relationships continued into the 1960s. The important consultants were the AFL-CIO's Serafino Romualdi and Arturo Juaregui, whom Philip Agee, a former CIA agent in Latin America, pinpointed as CIA operatives.[22]

Pressed by the presidential election scheduled for October 1954 concurrent with his country's involvement with the CIA operation on the Guatemalan border, President Gálvez employed a policy combining accommodation and repression and settled the strike in July. The banana companies promised wage increases, other benefits, and support for legal unionization. This relatively nonviolent resolution of the conflict, especially given Central American standards, set an important precedent for the future of labor-management relations. Moreover, the fact that the negotiations took place in San Pedro Sula, with the direct input of prominent representatives of its commercial and industrial sector, including Gabriel A. Mejía, linked the more general shift in state-labor relations with the new presence of the region's nonlanded elite and ethnic bourgeoisie.[23] During the strike this explicit relationship manifested itself in various ways.

The strike movement received widespread popular support in Honduras, especially on the North Coast. That was expected. Most interesting, however, was the extensive backing given to the strikers by the North Coast bourgeoisie, including the CCIC. The chamber's official stance was one of "neutrality," but in the middle of the strike its newsletter asserted that individual members were left to their own consciences regarding monetary donations to sustain the strikers. By 1957 the CCIC more openly acknowledged the ample monetary contributions made to the striking workers, including a large sum donated by none other than its vice-president, Yude Canahuati. What a position for Canahuati to assume! He was born in Bethlehem, Palestine, in 1900, settled in El Salvador in the 1910s, and then moved to San Pedro Sula in 1933. By the early 1950s Canahuati was one of the city's most prominent business leaders.[24]

San Pedro Sula also became the seat of the Committee to Help the Banana Strikers, which was composed of many commercial and manufacturing elites, including Dr. Rodolfo Pastor Zelaya, a militant in the anti-Carías march of 1944, an erstwhile member of the PDRH, and in 1954 a member of the nonsocialist left wing of the Liberal Party.[25] In the 1960s Pastor Zelaya was a key promoter of Liberal Party–based reformism with deep roots in San Pedro Sula's long-standing struggle against dictatorship. His latter role, however, must be understood in the context of the 1954 strike and of San Pedro Sula's reformist legacy beginning in the 1920s and early 1930s.

Along with labor legislation passed after 1949, the settlements in 1954 finally opened the way for full unionization in Honduras the following year. In February 1955 the state legalized fifty unions, including the union of greatest importance—the one representing the thousands of workers of the United Fruit Company. Some of these organizations dissolved and some merged with other unions; nonetheless, unionization remained legal after 1955 (see Table 6.1).[26]

By the late 1960s Honduran workers had achieved the highest level of unionization in Central America. In 1961 union membership in Central America amounted to 109,000 workers, with Honduran labor representing about 16 percent of the total, or some 18,000 workers; that figure already exceeded the number of union members in Nicaragua and Guatemala and ranked second to that for Costa Rica and El Salvador.[27] In 1967 Honduran unions had 22,377 members, and by 1970 that number swelled to 30,779.[28] By this point Honduran labor was well on its way to becoming the most organized working class in Central America. Indeed, in light of the reformist military installed in 1972, union membership reached an unprecedented proportion, bypassing that in all other Central American countries (see Table 6.2).

Table 6.1. Number of Unions Registered with the Ministry of Labor, 1956–1967

| Year | Agriculture | Mining | Manufacturing | Construction | Services* |
|---|---|---|---|---|---|
| 1956 | 1 | 1 | 3 | — | 11 |
| 1957 | — | 1 | 9 | 1 | 4 |
| 1958 | 2 | — | 7 | 1 | 8 |
| 1959 | 1 | — | 4 | — | 2 |
| 1960 | 2 | — | 5 | — | 7 |
| 1961 | — | 1 | 2 | — | 3 |
| 1962 | 1 | — | 3 | 1 | 7 |
| 1963 | 1 | — | 1 | — | 5 |
| 1964 | 2 | — | 4 | — | 3 |
| 1965 | — | 1 | 5 | — | 4 |
| 1966 | — | — | 5 | — | 5 |
| 1967 | — | — | 5 | — | 5 |
| Total | 10 | 4 | 53 | 3 | 64 |

*Source:* Secretaría de Trabajo y Previsión Social, *Estadísticas Del Trabajo*, p. 7.
*Services include transportation, commerce, and electricity.

Of course, the majority of unions represented workers on banana plantations and in urban centers of the North Coast departments of Atlántida and Cortés, namely, La Ceiba and San Pedro Sula. In 1970 union membership in Atlántida and Cortés constituted about 66 percent of total organized labor in Honduras. In Francisco Morazán, the department home to Tegucigalpa, only 24 percent of the workforce belonged to unions, whereas Cortés alone contained about 47 percent of all union members in Honduras.[29]

## North Coast Labor during the Regimes of Lozano Díaz and the Armed Forces

Given the National Party's role in repressing labor prior to 1954, relations between the government and the emerging union movement did not start on a good footing during the regime of Julio Lozano Díaz (1954–56). Besides the fact that Lozano Díaz had supported the Carías dictatorship throughout the 1930s and 1940s, his first comments on North Coast's labor leaders did not bode well for an amicable relationship. In January 1955 he indicated his hope that a labor code would free "the workers from the exploitation they suffered under some of their leaders."[30]

Despite a visit to the North Coast in late 1955, Lozano Díaz's relations with the union leadership deteriorated sharply. In February 1956 he imprisoned

Table 6.2. Number of Union Members in Central America, 1973

| Country | Total | Agriculture | Mining and Manufacturing | Services and Other |
|---|---|---|---|---|
| Honduras | 67,956 | 39,251 | 7,573 | 21,132 |
| Costa Rica | 58,263 | 11,353 | 3,976 | 42,934 |
| El Salvador | 54,387 | 1,432 | 24,464 | 28,491 |
| Guatemala | 29,186 | 15,283 | 4,220 | 9,683 |
| Nicaragua | 10,419 | 602 | 1,796 | 8,021 |
| Total | 220,211 | 67,921 | 42,029 | 110,261 |

*Source:* Cline and Delgado, *Economic Integration*, p. 188.

certain leaders of the 1954 strike, including Céleo González and Oscar Gale Varela. As of June 1954, González was a key member of the strike committee purged of its original left-wing leadership, namely, communists and other radicals of the PDRH. In August 1954 he and Gale Varela cofounded the country's largest union—the Sindicato de Trabajadores de la Tela Railroad Co., which represented the United Fruit Company subsidiary. Gale Varela became president of SITRATERCO and held that position well into the 1970s; González, on the other hand, became president of the Federación Sindical de Trabajadores Norteños de Honduras. The labor leadership, supported by U.S. consultants, established the FESITRANH in April 1957, with the SITRATERCO as its major union.[31]

Imprisoning González and Gale Varela in 1956 turned out to be a serious mistake, for two reasons. First, it obviously was just another example of traditional nationalist repression of working-class leaders, anticommunist or not. Second, the move was a slap in the face for U.S. labor policy in Honduras since the 1954 strike, particularly in view of the reformist winds blowing since the announcement of the Point Four Program. According to testimony before the U.S. Congress on 15 October 1954 by John R. Leddy, a State Department operative in the region, U.S. policy in the aftermath of the May strike included encouraging "American private organizations, particularly labor organizations, to enter into Honduras and assist in the organization of labor and to furnish from their own ranks competent, capable labor organizers who cannot merely compete with but take the play away from the Communists."[32]

Leddy noted that U.S. policy also included bringing "to the United States as large a number of Honduran leaders in labor and education as we can within the limitation of the funds available to the Department." This covered everything from CIA support of the SITRATERCO since late 1954 to U.S. embassy–coordinated training of the SITRATERCO leadership in Puerto Rico beginning in January 1955. Many of these activities were carried out through the Inter-American Regional Labor Organization, headed by Serafino Romualdi and established in 1951 to promote anticommunist labor programs and cooperation between management and labor. Unlike during his trip to Honduras in 1947, Romualdi did find labor leaders amenable in 1954. The SITRATERCO had enjoyed membership in ORIT since its founding. By September 1954 ORIT's Honduran representatives in Tegucigalpa and San Pedro Sula discussed the repression of communists and debated the PDRH's leftist tendencies with U.S. embassy officials.[33]

At any rate, when the military overthrew Lozano Díaz in October 1956, Céleo González and Oscar Gale Varela were still part of SITRATERCO's leadership as well as its president and general-secretary, respectively, posts they had assumed the previous August. (They had served on the Junta Directiva since 1954.) The changed political atmosphere after October facilitated the SITRATERCO's centralization of "national" working-class leadership on the North Coast, while also allowing union leaders to make its social and political claims more forcefully.

During the military government of 1956–57 González and Gale Varela served as liaisons with the United States in U.S. efforts to establish a regional federation of the North Coast's significant unions. That goal was achieved in April 1957, when González, Gale Varela, the other SITRATERCO leaders, and U.S. foreign labor policy operatives formally constituted the FESITRANH. By late 1957 the FESITRANH leadership, still in the hands of González and Gale Varela, publicly reminded Villeda Morales of his earlier promise to provide a labor code. On the other hand, by this time some kind of a labor code seemed inevitable, as representatives from the International Office of Labor had been consultants on the issue even during the Lozano Díaz regime.[34]

In short, elite labor's participation in the political system now became institutionalized under the electoral reform policies encouraged during the military government of 1956–57. By June 1957 military leaders selected Salvador Ramos Alvarado as labor's representative in that year's Electoral Commission. The military leadership chose Ramos Alvarado for this position because he worked for one of the country's oldest corporations, the United Fruit Company. In 1963 Ramos Alvarado became secretary-general of Honduras's first national confederation of union membership, the Confederación de Trabajadores de Honduras; he remained in the position until 1966.[35]

## VILLEDISMO AND NORTH COAST LABOR

Ramos Alvarado broadened his role after 1958 by becoming labor's representative in the Liberal Party–dominated Honduran Congress; in 1958 he had joined Villeda Morales's personal entourage during a whirlwind trip to South America. Meanwhile, foreign experts from the IOL continued to elaborate a labor code, which the Honduran minister of labor, Oscar A. Flores, presented to the press in August 1958.[36]

Between August 1958 and June 1959, when Congress approved the labor code, a debate raged among contending groups with a stake in its provisions. What is most interesting, however, is the fact that although North Coast labor did not obtain the code it sought, most of the major organizations representing domestic and foreign capital chided the liberal majority in Congress for its neglect of suggestions for change and President Villeda Morales for his enthusiastic backing of the code.[37]

Before the overthrow of Villeda Morales in 1963, other policy initiatives strengthened the social and political ties between the elite leadership of the organized Honduran working class and the Villeda Morales government.[38] Scarcely a few months after President Kennedy's announcement of the Alliance for Progress, Villeda Morales complemented his earlier support of the labor code with efforts to promote SITRATERCO's welfare with Alliance for Progress funds. This stands out as a unique policy initiative for various reasons.

In August 1961 SITRATERCO received executive authorization to contract a $300,000 loan with the U.S. International Cooperation Administration, the predecessor of the Agency for International Development, for the purpose of financing low-cost housing for members of SITRATERCO. By 1963 union leaders offered their membership a housing project that they surely never expected when they first organized in the 1950s. In November 1964 FESITRANH finalized the transaction to obtain an even more massive loan from the Inter-American Development Bank. This loan, for $2 million, allowed González and Gale Varela to offer many North Coast unions credit lines for housing on a scale undoubtedly unforeseen before 1961. The FESITRANH housing project was also unique because it had the full support of the CCIC leadership in San Pedro Sula.[39]

The collaboration between North Coast capitalists and labor during the strike of 1954 translated into a very uncommon relationship. In 1965 and 1966 the CCIC, headed by Gabriel A. Mejía, even gave this project financial support. By 1971 the chamber reported a debt of over $300,000 resulting from this initiative.[40] Therefore, after 1958 the Honduran organized working-class movement, led by the self-appointed leadership of SITRATERCO and

FESITRANH, assumed a status unique in its history, and it further distinguished the North Coast region from the interior of Honduras.

### North Coast Labor and the Origins of the Honduran Peasant Movement

The administrator of San Pedro Sula's municipal market, expressing the abundance of the post–World War II economic recovery, in early April 1955 reported record fiscal revenues. But at the same time he acknowledged a new necessity: the construction of another municipal market because more and more people wished to rent the old market's stalls. This upsurge, he explained, resulted in part from the "massive displacement brought about by the [banana] companies that operate on the north coast, as well as a result of the recent floods that pushed many families to seek refuge in this city." Thus, in early 1955 a social process, banana company employment policies, and a natural disaster—a hurricane that had damaged North Coast agriculture the previous fall—converged to create a potentially explosive social and political situation. Eventually, these events combined with historical legacies of the North Coast to mark the region with another singular phenomenon: the beginnings of a powerful Honduran peasant movement, one of the strongest in Central America.[41]

In September 1954, scarcely two months after the dramatic strike on the North Coast was resolved and only a month before the presidential election that eventually empowered Ramón Villeda Morales and the liberals, a powerful hurricane struck the North Coast. It damaged over 70 percent of the United Fruit Company plantations and knocked about 30 percent of them out of production. Losses in the Sula Valley climbed rapidly in late 1954, as the CCIC pointed out. Beginning in 1955, the banana companies, hard hit by the strike and the hurricane, used the occasion to justify massive layoffs.[42] For example, in 1953 banana company employment amounted to about 36,321 workers; by the end of 1955 that figure dropped to 24,878, and by 1959 the Standard Fruit Company and the United Fruit Company together employed only 16,045 laborers.[43]

Some of the thousands of newly unemployed emigrated to North Coast urban centers like San Pedro Sula; others, however, pressed authorities for plots of land in or near old banana plantations. This process represented a massive effort by former peasants to return to the land.[44] It meant that between 15,000 and 20,000 landless workers now floated within the rapidly unionizing and radicalizing urban centers like San Pedro Sula, La Ceiba, El Progreso, and elsewhere on the North Coast. As in the case of the dramatic circumstances surrounding the strike from April to July 1954, after 1955 governments faced a new phenomenon: militant cries for land. Many issues surfaced requiring the various parties to deal with a second "social question" beyond the plantation workers.[45]

Left-wing activists from the PCH tried to organize pockets of these thousands of "new peasants." Ramón Amaya Amador's historical novel records the existence of a Peasant Committee in Defense of the Land in Cortés in 1954, but one that nonetheless fell prey to the repression meted out to PCH militants in that period. On the other hand, Lorenzo Zelaya, a PCH activist during the 1954 strike, achieved some success when, between 1959 and 1961, he and others organized the Comite Central de Unificación Campesina. Zelaya's group became involved with colonization programs on lands abandoned by the old Cortés Development Company, established by Samuel Zemurray in 1919. By 1962 Zelaya and others transformed the CCUC into the Federación Nacional de Campesinos de Honduras.[46]

These developments did not escape the scrutiny of the North Coast labor movement generally or of the U.S. government. Years later Andrew McLellan, ORIT's permanent delegate to Central America and instrumental in establishing the FESITRANH in 1957,[47] recalled the operations carried out to block left-wing organizations like the CCUC and the FENACH:

> In early 1962, communist activists became active in La Lima and Progreso. The activists were collecting money from peasants . . . presumably to pay the expenses of land surveyors who would begin surveying land to which those campesinos would ultimately receive title. Concerned with this campaign, Oscar Gale and Céleo González suggested that perhaps some effort should be made to create a democratically-oriented campesino organization which, if necessary, could become the revolutionary political arm of the North Coast labor movement and as such, pressure the Villeda Morales administration into enactment of the Agrarian Reform Law.[48]

Inspired by the Guatemalan and Bolivian laws of 1952 and 1953 respectively, Liberal Party platforms, dating back to at least May 1953, committed its leadership to agrarian reform supported by the "principle of expropriation for reasons of public utility and necessity" and a willingness to "limit land concentration in the hands of latifundistas." The Honduran Ministry of Natural Resources had been preparing some kind of agrarian reform legislation since 1958, legislation whose principles the Liberal Party introduced into the constitution of 1957. Therefore, the SITRATERCO idea coincided with a region-wide movement. In the end, the efforts led to the establishment, rightfully enough, in the offices of the SITRATERCO, in La Lima, Cortés, of Honduras's first and most important anticommunist peasant organization: the

Asociación Nacional de Campesinos de Honduras. Moreover, the occasion allowed President Villeda Morales to personally present an agrarian reform law to the first ANACH leaders in an impressive ceremony.[49]

The ANACH's first secretary-general was Ezequiel Cruz Guevara, whom the SITRATERCO's newspaper in 1966 proclaimed as one of its founders in 1954. The ANACH's second president (1964–66) was Efraín Díaz Galeas, a former Liberal Party mayor of Santa Rita in the Department of Yoro. Despite the repression suffered after the 1963 coup, the ANACH grew rapidly under the leadership of Cruz Guevara and Díaz Galeas. In 1967 the Ministry of Labor recorded the association's membership at 11,660 peasants, all residing on the North Coast; in the same year the FESITRANH had slightly over 16,000 members.[50] That the ANACH was established on the North Coast with impressive ties to the militant if anticommunist leaders empowered via the strike of 1954 signaled another source of North Coast reformism critical to understanding the military reformism of 1972.

## Organized Workers Contest López Arellano's Regime

Villeda Morales's relations with organized elite labor and the emergent peasant movement were two of the rather formidable obstacles confronting the National Party in the presidential election in late 1963. What is more, the violence with which López Arellano eventually deposed Villeda Morales further alienated the North Coast labor leaders from Tegucigalpa. Paralleling Julio Lozano Díaz's actions in February 1956, security forces jailed Céleo González in the aftermath of the coup.[51]

Besides the liberals' increasing domination of electoral politics since 1954, the National Party's fortunes in mid-1963 seemed gloomy for other reasons. During the campaign, the organized working class consistently encouraged both parties to engage in a "civil" electoral process. However, the nationalists surely regarded its leadership as duplicitous, because even in 1963 it was still evident that the Liberal Party's ascension to power in the late 1950s was closely related to working-class support on the North Coast. The fact that the SITRATERCO, the most important union of the San Pedro Sula–based FESITRANH, roundly condemned the 1963 coup, confirmed not only the unions' claims to endorse democracy, but also their older relationship with the Liberal Party.[52]

This did not bode well for a smooth political transition between Colonel López Arellano's coup in 1963 and his efforts to obtain a National Party endorsement for his presidential bid in 1965. In addition to condemning his action in late 1963, the FESITRANH again roundly denounced the violence of the coup in April 1964. Early in 1965 the Liberal Party nominated three prominent labor leaders, including Céleo González, as candidates for election to the Constituent Assembly in February 1965.[53]

By May 1965 San Pedro Sula's *La Prensa*, led by Edmond L. Bográn, quoted Karl Marx in characterizing the Honduran working class as having been transformed from "a class in itself to a class for itself." The editorialists also argued that "political sectarianism" had confounded Marx's views on the necessity of "a dictatorship of the proletariat." Instead, they maintained, Marx "wanted the proletariat united as a factor of production and as a partner in the production process."[54]

Earlier, in September 1964, Céleo González had warned of the possibility of working-class leaders establishing their own "political institution," because, declared González, "we are a class that thinks, and why are we to be denied this right."[55] González made these remarks on the eve of helping to form the CTH, which for most of the 1960s remained largely an appendage of the SITRATERCO and FESITRANH. González directed his threats primarily against the nationalists, but the Liberal Party's response to the nationalist-military machinations in 1964 and 1965 also gave elite labor many reasons for not wholeheartedly embracing mainstream liberalism either.

On the other hand, the liberals' inclusion of recognized labor leaders like Céleo González in their electoral slate of 1965 again demonstrated the close ties between the liberals and the organized sectors of the Honduran working class on the North Coast. By 1968 this translated into persecution by the López Arellano regime that paralleled the repression meted out to Edmond L. Bográn, Jaime Rosenthal Oliva, and others. Yet the 1968 confrontation represented the culmination of the 1963 coup against Villeda Morales, both in its local dimensions and in its involvement with regional and international events beyond Honduras.

# 7

## THE MILITARY COUP OF 1963: ORIGINS AND OUTCOMES

On 2 October 1963 General Theodore F. Bogart, commander of U.S. military forces stationed in Panama, was a guest in Tegucigalpa on the eve of yet another military coup and, worse, just before a presidential election scheduled for 13 October. Bogart had been sent to the Honduran capital to try to persuade Colonel Oswaldo López Arellano not to overthrow President Ramón Villeda Morales, with whom López Arellano had contrived, in 1957, to grant the Honduran military virtual autonomy from civilian control. General Bogart's mission failed.[1] On 3 October 1963 Villeda Morales and Modesto Rodas Alvarado, the president of the Congress and an old foe of General Carías since the 1940s, found themselves on a plane to Costa Rica.

Rodas Alvarado's unexpected trip also must have seemed ironic given who had "asked" him to depart. Although his association with the post–World War II Honduran armed forces had never been warm, after the 1956 coup Rodas Alvarado had outdone many Liberal Party chieftains in praising the "glorious" military. And in the 1957 Constituent Assembly he had argued passionately in favor of erecting an architectural monument to commemorate the military's "revolutionary" support of the liberals' indirect rise to executive power late that year.[2]

By late 1963, however, the almost amorous relations that developed between López Arellano and the liberals in 1957–58 fell prey to contradictions connected with various events and processes. President Villeda Morales assumed office early in 1958, a critical year not only for local history but also for the country's relations with other nations in the region and with the United

States. In 1958 Villeda Morales signed some of the major documents that established the Central American Common Market in 1960. But this program unleashed forces that would have a greater impact on the regime installed after 1963 than that of Villeda Morales.

Other events that took place in 1958 and soon afterward did affect Villeda Morales's regime as well as the one that followed. Early in 1962 the president received a visit from his old friend Adolf A. Berle, the New Deal liberal and Harvard alumnus whom the CIA in 1956 had asked to determine Villeda Morales's possible ties to communists or fellow travelers.[3] Later, Berle recalled the meeting with some satisfaction, noting that "when Ramón Villeda Morales came in we thought him a good, honest well-intentioned man but questioned whether he was strong enough to swing it. Well, he was." Berle's confidence in Villeda Morales's regime actually belied, at least by 1962, a suspicion that liberals like Villeda Morales and others in the region were often still too soft on communists and "crypto-Communists."[4]

In the summer of 1958 General Fulgencio Batista of Cuba ordered a final military offensive from which his regime never recovered. Late in the year Fidel Castro, Ché Guevara, and others leading the insurrection against Batista felt victory close at hand. On 31 December Batista abandoned Cuba for the Dominican Republic, where General Rafael Leónidas Trujillo, the ferocious dictator of that country since 1930, must have wondered about his own future. Soon afterward Trujillo saw Cuban-inspired and supported incursions in Panama, against Somoza in Nicaragua, and, by June 1959, against his own regime. Some evidence suggests that Villeda Morales stood behind the anti-Somocista rebels in their first forays from Honduras in early 1958.[5]

Trujillo's concerns stemmed not only from Batista's collapse, but also from the January 1958 overthrow of General Marcos Pérez Jiménez in Venezuela. The leadership that toppled that government, personified best by Villeda Morales's good friend, Rómulo Bétancourt, had frequently pronounced itself bitterly hostile to the region's dictators. By late 1958 even President Dwight D. Eisenhower appeared hesitant about the political viability of the dictators that his and previous administrations had amply supported in the past. Villeda Morales, on the other hand, smelled the shifting winds early. In 1958 he and an enormous entourage traveled to South America to visit most of his ideological counterparts in the region.[6]

In August 1958 Eisenhower for the first time made a strong public statement recommending representative government for Latin America as a whole. Late in the year he finally approved the establishment of the Inter-American Development Bank, and by early 1959 he also extended his backing for the CACM, albeit under U.S. tutelage. By 1960 his administration intervened in the CACM process by openly using its financial leverage with the Bank for Central American Economic Integration to press for policies compatible with U.S. economic concerns in the region.[7]

Eisenhower's turnabout in his Latin American policy during the period 1958–60 ushered in a very different hemispheric context for realizing Villeda Morales's liberalism in Honduras. The emergence of the Cold War in the early 1950s had already crushed any possible alliance between Villeda Morales's liberalism and local left-wing sectors. The radicalization of the Cuban Revolution in 1959, especially as a result of the agrarian reform begun in Cuba in the middle of the year, offered reactionary sectors locally and in the United States abundant "evidence" for the kind of misgivings that Adolf A. Berle voiced in his diary in 1962. In fact, Berle himself saw the American Molasses Company, on whose board of directors he had served since the 1940s, adversely affected by the Cuban agrarian reform in 1959.[8]

## Villeda Morales and the Aspirations of the San Pedro Sula Capitalists

Adolf Berle was not a blind reactionary. His foreign policy expertise generally as well as his close ties to Latin American liberals like Villeda Morales were widely recognized by the Washington foreign policy establishment. This made Berle an excellent consultant in the kind of foreign policy shift under way under Eisenhower after 1958 and further elaborated under President John F. Kennedy. In late 1960 Berle became the head of a task force charged with drawing up a broad new policy for Latin America, finally announced in March 1961 as the "Alliance for Progress."[9]

In Honduras Villeda Morales disclosed, in late 1961, a policy counterpart to the alliance called "The March Towards Progress." This program was viable primarily because of the broad loan potential pledged by Kennedy through the IDB, and it was to be administered by the Agency for International Development. The fact that The March Towards Progress was closely associated with technocrats who controlled macroeconomic policy within the old Consejo Nacional de Economía had enormous significance for the San Pedro Sula bourgeoisie's eventual confrontation with the López Arellano regime in the 1960s.[10]

From the time of its establishment in 1955 until its transformation into the Consejo Superior de Planificación Economía in 1965, the CNE was controlled by three men: Jorge Bueso Arias, Carlos H. Matute, and Miguel Angel Rivera. Bueso Arias also served as Villeda Morales's minister of finance from 1959 to 1963, and Rivera was Matute's second at the CNE. Matute resigned in 1964 in protest over National Party obstructions to the National Economic

Development Plan for 1965–69. Rivera, a San Pedro Sula–based engineer closely associated with the town's construction industry, was the director of CONSUPLANE until he, too, resigned in disgust in 1967.[11]

Of the three CNE leaders, Bueso Arias was the most influential. His liberalism and his economic ties to San Pedro Sula's industrial capitalism expressed the city's identification with Villeda Morales's rise to power, his administration, and its downfall in 1963. San Pedro Sula's status as a Liberal Party stronghold since the late 1940s was further strengthened by the generational and ideological bond between Villeda Morales's liberalism and youthful charisma and the leadership of the class interests that came to control the city's economic and political fortunes in the late 1950s.

Like other young technocrats of the period, Bueso Arias studied in the United States; he returned to Tegucigalpa with a degree in business administration from Louisiana State University, Baton Rouge (1941). In 1942 his family connections landed him a job with La Compañía Aseguradora Hondureña, a large insurance company founded by Tegucigalpa elites whose wealth had come from late colonial money as well as the new silver exports after the 1880s. By 1948 Bueso Arias sat on the board of La Capitalizadora Hondureña, an investment bank established in that year by the elites associated with La Compañía Aseguradora Hondureña.[12]

By the 1950s Bueso Arias's interests extended beyond his family's commercial and tobacco investments in western Honduras. Among his additional investments were shares in his family's Banco de Occidente, San Pedro Sula's Embotelladora Sula, S.A., the local Pepsi-Cola bottling plant, a significant amount of stock in the country's only cement factory, and money in Cortés's Compañía Azucarera Hondureña, S.A., owner of the country's most powerful sugar plantations and mills.[13] In the early 1960s these enterprises remained intimately connected with the Standard Fruit Company's "economic group."

Bueso Arias's social and political world from the 1940s onward revolved around San Pedro Sula and Tegucigalpa, far beyond his origins in the Departments of Copán and Santa Bárbara. His ties to Villeda Morales went back to at least the forties, when both men were up-and-coming members of the Tegucigalpa Rotary Club. Besides his economic and social interests in San Pedro Sula, Bueso Arias enjoyed impeccable Liberal Party credentials. His great-grandfather was Céleo Arias, the party's founding ideologue in the 1880s; his grandfather, Juan Angel Arias, was a liberal cabinet member in the 1890s, the country's president for a few months in 1903, and one of three liberal candidates opposing General Carías in the 1923 presidential election. Finally, he was married to a granddaughter of Policarpo Bonilla, the liberal president of Honduras from 1894 to 1899.[14]

By the time Villeda Morales took charge of the Liberal Party in 1949, Jorge

Bueso Arias was a major player in the new generation that had wrested control of the party from Angel Zúñiga Huete. But his role in the coup of 1956 represented more than his high Liberal Party connections. His position as executive secretary of the CNE from 1955 to 1958, as well as his economic portfolio, made him a crucial figure to advance the kind of macroeconomic policy encouraged by the Economic Commission for Latin America at the time and supported during the Alliance for Progress. Moreover, the fact that his uncle, Abraham Bueso Pineda, was president of the Cámara de Comercio e Industrias de Cortés (1951–58) further allied San Pedro Sula's elites with the vision and promise of the Villeda Morales regime. On 3 October 1963, the day of the coup, Minister of Finance Bueso Arias was in Washington negotiating with the International Monetary Fund.[15]

## Kennedy, the Democratic Left, and the Cuban Revolution

In Washington, Bueso Arias's reaction to news of the 1963 coup must have been tinged more with bitterness than surprise. Rumors of the takeover had been rampant for months, and Bueso Arias knew perfectly well, from his part in the 1956 coup, that the military could be turned against Villeda Morales as well. He surely also realized that the National Party remained bitter about the deal cut between the liberals and López Arellano in late 1957, when the military high command sanctioned the election of Villeda Morales as president. From 1958 to 1963 relations between the liberals and the Honduran military were subject to many forces, contradictions, and ambitious personalities unique to that period.

The Alliance for Progress's economic program offered ammunition to Villeda Morales's potential enemies, especially in its support of structural agrarian reform and the possible impact on the banana companies.[16] But, as previously in Honduras, the politics of those and other kinds of conflicts became intertwined with the machinations of key individuals who rose to prominence within the military and the National Party in the aftermath of the 1956 coup, namely, Colonel Oswaldo López Arellano and Ricardo Zúñiga Augustinus.

After the 1963 coup Zúñiga Augustinus, legal counsel of the Ministry of Defense since 1956, became the political liaison between the National Party and the regime of López Arellano. Their personal ambitions, in turn, became entangled with the efforts of the National Party's old leadership to make the party viable under its control. In the early 1960s a U.S. Department of State confidential report suggested that Carías remained "head of the opposition National party" and, though "very old," "in charge of the party."[17] López Arellano, Zúñiga Augustinus, and other factions within the National Party fought against Carías and against a Liberal Party abundantly supported by the

Kennedy mystique and largess. Only the coup in 1963 removed Carías's stranglehold on the National Party.

The 1963 coup represented the culmination of various attempts to overthrow President Villeda Morales, including some that involved Anastasio Somoza, Rafael L. Trujillo, and a Honduran former chief of staff named Colonel Armando Velásquez Cerrato. In early 1959 Juan Ramón Ardón, a reporter who accompanied Villeda Morales on his South American trip in 1958, published a short tract denouncing the Somoza–Trujillo–Velásquez Cerrato alliance.[18] Interestingly enough, Ardón praised the victory of Fidel Castro's guerrillas. Batista had abandoned Cuba on 31 December 1958, and the Cuban Revolution had yet to implement radical measures. This and more changed in 1959, including the implications of Villeda Morales's covert support of the anti-Somoza insurgency, the counterattacks by Velásquez Cerrato, and López Arellano's evaluation of this and other aspects of the Villeda Morales government.

In 1959 the Cuban revolutionaries assumed themselves to be part of the regional vanguard against Latin America dictators. A Ché Guevara–sponsored invasion of Panama failed in April 1959, as well as another traditional anti-Somocista incursion from Honduras into Nicaragua in May and June. By this time, however, the Nicaraguans in the eastern Honduran mountains were divided into Castro radicals and leftists and the traditional caudillista factions initially supported by Villeda Morales and generally tolerated by the Honduran armed forces.[19]

Villeda Morales's political viability depended on this changed hemispheric context, as well as on whether his local enemies could manipulate the situation for their own purposes. His enemies were not only the nationalists, but also powerful economic interests opposed to his brand of liberalism and its possible sympathy with the Cuban Revolution. The fact that the Alliance for Progress also pledged itself to reformism allowed Villeda Morales some breathing space after 1961, but that space finally closed in 1963.

By April 1960 the Cuban agrarian reform had taken a heavy toll on U.S. investments, from extensive confiscations in the sugar industry as a whole to large-scale appropriation of property belonging to the United Fruit Company. The Cuban government offered the company about $6 million in bonds as "appropriate compensation," but the company demanded $56 million. In the end, the Cubans confiscated all U.S. investments and the investors rejected the compensation offered. Early in the year Cuban exiles had been training for the 1961 invasion of their homeland on estates bordering United Fruit banana plantations in Guatemala.[20]

In Honduras Villeda Morales denied accusations made by liberals in Congress that he sympathized with the Cuban Revolution. At the same time, he encouraged proposals for OAS assistance in elaborating a Honduran law of agrarian reform. Pressured by North Coast unemployment after the 1954 strike and hurricane, Villeda Morales continued his plans for agrarian reform in 1961, now also encouraged by the support offered to this kind of reformism by Kennedy's Alliance for Progress and even by the National Party.[21]

In August 1962 the University of Honduras in Tegucigalpa hosted a radio-broadcasted forum on the agrarian reform law to be taken up by the Congress. The broadcast afforded Hondurans the first public discussion of this law. The guardians of the empire, however, had been considering it for some time. Charles F. Burrows, the U.S. ambassador, had long been reviewing the projected law with Villeda Morales so that, according to State Department official Edwin M. Martin, Villeda Morales and other Honduran officials "would be aware of our interest in ensuring that the law was both constructive in its effects on agricultural productivity and incomes and would not adversely affect the legitimate interests of the present property owners, including United States corporations."[22]

Despite Burrows's early discussions with Villeda Morales, the liberal leader apparently still felt that he could demonstrate some independence from Washington and the banana companies. For example, he "failed" to show United Fruit Company officials copies of agrarian legislation prior to debate in the Honduran Congress. The company then contacted U.S. senators to pressure the State Department to again impress upon Villeda Morales the company's disgruntlement with parts of the law.[23]

Villeda Morales first assured Washington that his signing of the law would be accompanied by public declarations reflecting Washington's recommendations. He then mustered some autonomy and did not make the declarations. But yet another visit by Burrows forced Villeda Morales to announce the empire's recommendations. As Assistant Secretary of State Martin recalled, "our Ambassador spoke to him on October 1 [1962] and on October 3 [Villeda Morales] publicly and personally made an oral statement to the press confirming the commitment he made to us." This satisfied Washington and Burrows, despite the fact that the United Fruit Company continued to claim that the Honduran Agrarian Law of 1962 put Honduras, as Martin remembered it, "on the path of Cuba and Communist China."[24]

These setbacks led Ambassador Burrows in late 1963 to actively discourage López Arellano's coup by warning that President Kennedy would suspend economic aid if the revolt took place. When López Arellano did remove Villeda Morales from power, his conservative opponents answered Burrows's threats by arguing that any aid cutoff by Washington would be momentary and that Burrows and company "would be back in six months."[25] Indeed, Kennedy's reaction to coups elsewhere in the region in 1962 and 1963 had given

Villeda Morales's most virulent enemies ample hope of enticing López Arellano back into the political arena. All the Latin American presidents overthrown in the latter two years were friends of Villeda Morales. Some he had visited on his tour of South America in 1958, including Arturo Frondizi (1958–62) of Argentina and Manuel Prado (1956–62) of Peru.

Starting in 1961 the president's enemies had viciously red-baited his regime, despite Ambassador Burrows's reassurances to Villeda Morales and despite Villeda Morales's public denunciations of communism in general and its Cuban variety in particular. Villeda Morales suspended diplomatic relations with Cuba in April 1961—before he signed the alliance charter in August. Even right-wing opponents recognized his constant recriminations against "Castro-Communism." Nonetheless, by the time López Arellano ousted Villeda Morales, it was a foregone conclusion that the new regime would justify the coup at least partly because of "the communist menace" to local civilization, property, and so forth.[26]

### López Arellano, Carías, and the Nationalists

The cabinet assembled by Colonel López Arellano after the coup reflected his abandonment of earlier ties to the liberals and new associations with the National Party.[27] Indeed, after October 1963 the nationalists provided civilian caudillo support to his ambitions. But the nationalists' actions represented more than that. First, the nationalist-military connection in 1963, unlike the liberal-military connection of 1957, expressed the National Party's desperate attempts to survive the factional infighting that dated back to the early 1950s. Second, the nationalists' participation in the 1963 coup reflected their efforts to arrest the liberals' increasing influence over modern Honduran politics and the state, especially given the economic prominence of the industrializing North Coast.

The present crisis of the National Party had its origins in the early 1950s, when party loyalists divided into factions supporting one of three dominant caudillos: General Tiburcio Carías Andino, General Abraham Williams Calderón, and Juan Manuel Gálvez, the latter two long associated with the Carías dictatorship (1933–49). The National Party convention of February 1960 still passed a resolution confirming Carías as the party's *jefe supremo*, thereby postponing unification with the other caudillos. Discussions on unification continued in 1961, and formal consolidation resulted in early 1962. On the other hand, Carías's feud with Juan Manuel Gálvez persisted into the next year.[28]

Although this rivalry posed major obstacles to the nationalists in the presidential election scheduled for October 1963, other events further complicated the political scenario. In 1962 the liberals, nationalists, and all other interested elite powers realized that the results of the municipal elections scheduled for

November 1962 would be used to evaluate the prospects for each party's presidential candidates in 1963. At this point, nationalists found themselves in a tragic situation. First, the liberal-military connection of 1957 had allowed its leadership to further consolidate the party's grip on municipal government in ways only imagined in the post-Carías period. And second, the nationalists boycotted the municipal elections of 1960, charging that the liberals and "their" Civil Guard would maneuver to keep them from the polls.[29] In 1962 the nationalists could ill afford to boycott yet another round of municipal elections, especially in the context of Kennedy's ample support of Villeda Morales liberalism and the persistent feuding between Carías and Gálvez.

The results of the 1962 municipal elections seem to have doomed the National Party. The liberals won over 70 percent of 278 municipalities. More important, they consolidated their power throughout the North Coast, winning virtually every municipality in the Departments of Cortés, Atlántida, Yoro, and Colón. The liberals also won in fourteen of the eighteen departmental capitals, including San Pedro Sula. This victory solidified the local power of the business class interests that had taken control of San Pedro Sula in the late 1950s; it also represented workers' power in the region. Early in 1963 the nationalists thus found themselves on the verge of political extinction, reduced to charging electoral fraud. In February they gathered in a national convention to nominate a presidential candidate to confront Modesto Rodas Alvarado, the liberals' sure winner that year. Preconvention candidates included Juan Manuel Gálvez, General Carías's son, Gonzalo Carías Castillo, and, less publicly, Colonel López Arellano. Carías controlled most of the delegates but not enough to name his son. He then apparently offered López Arellano the nomination.[30]

General Carías, perhaps senile by now, may have thought this a good move because it secured his hold on the party, it rebuffed Gálvez, now his arch enemy, and it offered the nationalists a way of intensifying the deteriorating relations between the military and the liberals. López Arellano, however, turned down the nomination because, according to his biographer, "of reasons beyond my control."[31] What forces beyond López Arellano's control could possibly have kept one of the country's most powerful men from a presidential candidacy?

In early March 1963 Ambassador Burrows found himself denying National Party accusations that the U.S. government had persuaded López Arellano to reject the Carías nomination. Not only did the entire Tegucigalpa press make the charge, but a delegate to the nationalist convention, Joaquín Bonilla, later publicly denounced Burrow's intervention as well. Moreover, Bonilla condemned Washington for dismissing López Arellano's candidacy when elsewhere in the region President Kennedy did recognize military governments.[32]

When the nationalists reconvened in May, Gálvez and Carías put aside their differences and allowed the nomination of Dr. Ramón Ernesto Cruz to go forward. Cruz, an elderly lawyer, had served both the Carías dictatorship and the Gálvez administration; he had also helped in Julio Lozano Díaz's efforts to remain in power in 1956.[33] His nomination reflected more a compromise candidate of the party's old caudillos than a man of broad appeal to the rural masses or the organized working people of the banana plantations. Certainly he held little attraction for the new generation of capitalists in San Pedro Sula.

In light of Rodas Alavarado's wide appeal in rural Honduras, recognized even by National Party militants, the nationalist candidate in 1963 seemed to be a sure loser. But it was not just because of Cruz's ignominious political history. Immediately after the May convention, Carías resigned as the party's jefe supremo and with his son formed the Popular Progressive Party. Despite the almost surreal claim by some conservative journalists that Carías's new party could be linked with communists, this division of the nationalists further weakened their party.[34] General Carías would not campaign for his old friend. It was probably at this point that disaffected nationalists teamed up with López Arellano, Zúñiga Augustinus, and others to depose Villeda Morales.

## The Constituent Assembly of 1965 and the San Pedro Sula Municipality

On 5 October 1963, the date of yet another hot and humid day in San Pedro Sula, municipal authorities met for an unexpected and extraordinary session—to debate their official reaction to the 3 October coup, the state of siege, and the prospects for political autonomy from Tegucigalpa.[35] At the time, these officials made up a who's who of the region's old, powerful economic interests, mostly members of the Liberal Party, and of young capitalists who were receiving their first taste of authoritarian government directed from Tegucigalpa.

Presiding over the somber session was Mayor Felipe Zelaya Zelaya, co-founder in 1948 of the Asociación de Ganaderos y Agricultores Sula and former president of the local Rotarians. Among Zelaya's councilmen were Dr. Abraham Bueso Arias, a cousin of Jorge Bueso Arias, the recently deposed minister of finance; Henry Holst Leiva, a prominent investor in Empacadora Alus, S.A., a beef exporting venture established in 1960; and Camilo Rivera Girón, the governor of Cortés. Rivera Girón's prominence in the early 1960s as a wealthy, independent banana plantation owner (with membership in AGAS and the CCIC) actually belied his humble beginning in the 1940s as a schoolteacher in a United Fruit Company–financed school.[36]

Mayor Zelaya's Board of Advisers included men like Elías J. Kattan, who, a decade after arriving from Palestine in 1933, had founded a shirt factory producing Camisas Bolívar. In 1962 Kattan refurbished his plant in a new building, and by 1964 he obtained the fiscal privileges offered in the Industrial Development Law of 1958. Kattan also owned stock in Compañía Azucarera Hondureña, S.A., owned primarily by Roberto Fasquelle, an old friend of Samuel Zemurray. Fasquelle's son-in-law, Dr. Rodolfo Pastor Zelaya, was another prominent member of the Board of Advisers. Pastor Zelaya had been a young leader of the Partido Democrático Revolucionario de Honduras, the Liberal Party's left wing during the anti-Carías struggles of the mid-1940s. After 1965 he became a key liaison between the leaders of the CCIC and the Liberal Party's most progressive wing in San Pedro Sula. Pastor Zelaya was joined by other young liberal-minded capitalists such as Mauricio Weizenblut Oliva and his cousin, Jaime Rosenthal Oliva.[37]

Jaime's father, Yankel Rosenthal, must have been proud of his son's political participation, for despite enjoying enormous economic influence throughout the region, he himself had been prevented from entering politics. Educated at the Massachusetts Institute of Technology, Jaime Rosenthal, like Edmond L. Bográn, was a representative young leader of the San Pedro Sula bourgeoisie. As did many of his colleagues in the municipal government of 1962–65, Rosenthal in 1965 would own shares in the enterprise that began publishing *La Prensa* that year.[38]

At the meeting on 5 October 1963, Mayor Zelaya and his colleagues, though decrying the violent form by which López Arellano had removed the chief executive, nonetheless voted to remain in office if the military government "respected" municipal autonomy. López Arellano did so until January 1965, when he finally removed Mayor Zelaya and company and appointed officials loyal to himself and the National Party.[39]

The colonel's actions represented not just the displacement of yet another municipal government in order to consolidate his power. Such tactics had been part and parcel of caudillo politics in Honduras for decades. Now, however, López Arellano's maneuvers were an affront to the class aspirations of the new economic power holders of San Pedro Sula and its working class, and that seemed to matter in the mid-1960s. Unlike their counterparts in Tegucigalpa, the CCIC leaders in San Pedro Sula did not send members to the Electoral Commission established in December 1963 to prepare for the assembly elections of 1965.[40] Needless to say, the important Sindicato de Trabajadores de la Tela Railroad Co. and the Federación Sindical de Trabajadores Norteños de Honduras also failed to join the Electoral Commission of 1963–64.[41]

At any rate, López Arellano's takeover of the San Pedro Sula municipality in early 1965 signaled the final step in the nationalist project to dress the existing military regime in constitutional garb. In November 1963 President Kennedy and López Arellano made a deal: diplomatic recognition of the López Arellano regime in exchange for the dictator's public promise of a return to the constitutional order at an unspecified date. But the nationalists acted quickly in late 1963 and 1964. In November 1963 López Arellano ordered preparations for elections to a Constituent Assembly in February 1965.[42]

Throughout 1964 López Arellano publicly denied his political ambitions. Ricardo Zúñiga Augustinus, whom Burrows called the "number two man," continued his liaison with the nationalists, especially via the Ministry of the Interior. This ministry historically remained the key venue for maneuvering local governments into the orbit of centralization and political realignment from Tegucigalpa. Early in the year Darío Montes, the Liberal Orthodox leader first appointed minister of the interior in 1963, resigned his post. Montes charged that his undersecretary, Mario Rivera López, had subverted his authority and "converted his office into a political club."[43]

Rivera López's presence in the Ministry of the Interior surely had shown liberals the kinds of experienced politicos that López Arellano now employed in his project. Rivera López was the son of Antonio C. Rivera, minister of education during the presidency of Miguel Paz Barahona (1925–29). More important, from 1933 to 1939 Antonio was president of the Congress, and in 1936 he played a critical role in establishing the Carías dictatorship through the ploy of amending the constitution. In the early 1950s Mario Rivera López loyally served in the nationalist governments of the period. In short, his skills in negotiating Tegucigalpa's political currents were crucial to López Arellano's success.[44]

The nationalist influence in the military regime continued unabated in 1964, despite the fact that sectors from the armed forces begrudged the relationship encouraged by Zúñiga Augustinus and accepted by López Arellano. According to a U.S. CIA memorandum of 1 April, Zúñiga was "resented by the military for isolating López from them." In December even López Arellano's minister of defense, Colonel Armando Escalón, resigned and denounced the nationalists' political clout. (In April 1965 López Arellano would remove Escalón from his post as chief of the armed forces.)[45]

Escalón's resignation created a major scandal because he had helped plan both the 1956 and 1963 coups. Apparently López Arellano and Zúñiga Augustinus never told him in 1963 of their intention to advance the ambitions of López Arellano as well as to rescue the National Party from extinction. The CIA reported that military disaffection with the Zúñiga Augustinus–López Arellano alliance continued in 1965, but there is no evidence that López Arellano faced a serious challenge to his authority.[46]

López Arellano's removal of San Pedro Sula's authorities in January 1965, as part of a national strategy, strengthened his party there and countrywide on the eve of Constituent Assembly elections scheduled for February. The results of those elections, now supervised by the nationalists and local military commanders, paved the way for López Arellano's assumption of "legitimate" constitutional power. The National Party deputies to the Constituent Assembly of March 1965 represented a majority that, like the liberals in 1957, "elected" López Arellano president. In 1965, of course, the nationalist leadership reminded Hondurans and liberals alike that, in the words of Julio Galdámez Zepeda, "we are pledged to do what the National Constitutional Assembly of 1957 did."[47]

The liberal deputies protested, but most eventually joined the body that soon transformed itself into a Congress, again following the liberal practice of 1957. Liberal deputies came under great pressure from many quarters to accept the situation, including from Ambassador Burrows. Villeda Morales himself joined the chorus demanding subservience, arguing that the deputies should "assume a virile and energetic attitude and defend the interests of democracy and the country." The aged Adolf Berle visited Villeda Morales in those days and, "with a great deal of soul-searching," advised him "not to go into revolution."[48]

Villeda Morales was no revolutionary, even of the liberal kind. But some liberal deputies denounced López Arellano, the nationalists, and even the mainstream liberals who listened to Burrows, Villeda Morales, and others. Seven out of thirty liberal deputies refused to take their seats in the assembly of March 1965. Three of the "Rebel Seven" represented the Department of Cortés and resided in San Pedro Sula. The major figure of the three was none other than Dr. Rodolfo Pastor Zelaya, a college pal of Villeda Morales in the early 1930s, a prominent member of the CCIC, a friend of Edmond L. Bográn, and a substantial investor in San Pedro Sula's *La Prensa.*

## San Pedro Sula and the Origins of Reformism in the 1960s

In the spring of 1965 Rodolfo Pastor Zelaya must have harbored bitter feelings about the aftermath of the 1963 coup. (He publicly distributed leaflets denouncing the coup.) He had joined the Liberal Party in the early 1940s, at a time when the Carías dictatorship repressed most opposition that it encountered, including the early reformism of Villeda Morales and others of his generation. Pastor Zelaya himself had witnessed the massacre of liberals in San Pedro Sula in the summer of 1944. Now, twenty years later, he watched the imposition of yet another dictatorial regime, with the ironic difference that the nationalists now legitimated a government that came to power despite Carías's efforts to retain control of political power even at the age of eighty-seven.

On the other hand, whatever bitterness Pastor Zelaya may have felt, he surely understood that Carías's demise resulted from not only his declining age but also the country's changing social structure after World War II. Undoubtedly he also recognized that the late 1950s and early 1960s represented sharper periods of social and political change than most Hondurans had experienced until then. Indeed, up to October 1963 it seemed that perhaps Villeda Morales's presidency finally could assert that it was a maximum expression of the progressive changing times.

After 1963 López Arellano and the nationalists put an end to the liberals' monopoly to claims of that kind. After 1965, however, he and his party confronted the social and political implications of processes under way even before the earlier liberal–López Arellano machinations in 1957. A crucial element of those processes that came to fruition in the mid-1960s involved the empowerment envisioned by Pastor Zelaya, Edmond L. Bográn, and other leaders of the San Pedro Sula bourgeoisie, as well as the high expectations of North Coast rural and urban constituents. López Arellano and Zúñiga Augustinus surely never expected that their authority would be challenged from as far away as San Pedro Sula. But if López Arellano did not expect the challenge, Pastor Zelaya, Edmond L. Bográn, Céleo González, Oscar Gale Varela, and others eventually made sure that he had to dealt with it. That confrontation produced the conjuncture that generated the reformist agenda of 1972–75.

# 8

# SAN PEDRO SULA CAPITAL AND LABOR CONFRONT CAUDILLISMO AND DICTATORSHIP, 1965–1968

On 19 September 1968 *El Día*, the conservative daily of Tegucigalpa, published dramatic headlines: "*La Prensa* Suspended Last Night, State of Siege Declared throughout the National Territory," then "Late Breaking News: The Government Sends Troops to San Pedro Sula." Two days later the paper informed its readers that the Financiera Hondureña, S.A's "Edmond L. Bográn [Was] Forced to Leave for Nicaragua" and displayed a communiqué earlier released by General López Arellano. The bulletin condemned a "capital" strike encouraged by San Pedro Sula merchants and manufacturers and demanded that commercial activities resume within twenty-four hours. Merchants and manufacturers faced fines ranging from $25 to $1,000, "depending on the seriousness of the infraction and the number of workers affected." These penalties could be complemented by "other responsibilities that the competent authorities might declare."[1]

Finally, the central government chastised the foreign elements of San Pedro Sula's bourgeoisie for "having made their life in this country and even accumulated riches under the auspices of a protective and fraternal environment that noble Honduran people have afforded them without expecting material recompensation." More ominously, General López Arellano threatened to bring foreign merchants and manufacturers participating in the strike before "competent authorities so that, according to the established procedures, their residency permits might be canceled and that they be invited to leave the country in the time prescribed by the law." According to the newspaper, these threats were "directed especially to the Arab merchants of San Pedro Sula."

For San Pedro Sula's elites, *El Día*'s pages after 19 September, particularly its characterization of the wrecking of *La Prensa*'s offices by police as of "little importance," only confirmed the paper's defense of López Arellano since 1963. Equally telling was *El Día*'s editorial of 24 January 1967 portraying *La Prensa* "as the property of an economic consortium carrying much weight in national activities."[2] In this way, *La Prensa*'s politics were linked with San Pedro Sula's capitalism.

*El Día*'s hostility toward *La Prensa* was shared by *El Nacional*, also published in Tegucigalpa, which virulently denounced President Villeda Morales and *La Prensa*. More interesting, *El Nacional* argued that *La Prensa*'s editorial policy seemed "manifestly inclined toward the democratic left while also harboring a phobia towards the present government that is only faintly concealed." Moreover, in July 1967 *El Pueblo*, then produced by the Liberal Party's left wing, the Izquierda Democratica, declared that "*La Prensa* of San Pedro Sula is throughout Honduras considered the authorized voice of the country's most powerful business sector."[3]

General López Arellano's repression of *La Prensa* in 1968 was the climax of a confrontation that had been brewing since the military chieftain removed San Pedro Sula's liberal municipal government in 1965. Nonetheless, the origins and course of this conflict between López Arellano and the Liberal Party elites in that city were the consequences of various mid- and long-term processes, including (1) the character of bourgeois class and North Coast working-class formation in San Pedro Sula in this century and (2) Honduras's role in the Central American Common Market and San Pedro Sula's subregional relation to it. Finally, elite business support of the left-wing Izquierda Democratica must be seen in light of how mainstream, caudillo liberalism responded to the nationalist-military mafia that wielded power from 3 October 1963 until López Arellano's ascent to the executive in June 1965.

## San Pedro Sula and the Erosion of Mainstream Liberalism

General López Arellano singled out the North Coast for repression in 1968. He saw the region as a hotbed of subversion possibly coordinated with the activities of Izquierda Democratica. But the course of San Pedro Sula's relationship with the Liberal Party's democratic left in 1965–66 had been anything but smooth. The enemies of that relationship included elements in addition to the National Party, the right-wing sectors of the military, and the local business elites with a historic apprehension of "involvement in politics." In trying to establish their influence over the Liberal Party, business leaders in San Pedro Sula had to deal with resistance within the party, especially from mainstream liberalism and its right wing, the small but vociferous Partido Republicano Ortodoxo, headed by the president of the Cámara de Comercio e Industrias de Tegucigalpa, Roque J. Rivera.[4]

The 1963 coup had left mainstream liberalism in disarray. President Kennedy's message to General López Arellano that his regime would receive U.S. diplomatic recognition if he promised a return to constitutional rule did not bode well for liberalism. The fact that López Arellano called for organizing an Electoral Commission soon after he reached an understanding with Kennedy placed mainstream liberalism in a difficult position. Finally, President Lyndon B. Johnson's commitment to López Arellano on a scale that paralleled Kennedy's support of Villeda Morales was another point for the liberals to consider.[5]

Apparently mainstream liberalism saw only a few options when confronted with the coup of 1963. Its leadership could either send the required members to the Electoral Commission, and thus legitimate nationalist-military ambitions for power, or it could boycott the process entirely and risk political extinction. Faced with pressures from the U.S. embassy and blinded by their own political myopia, mainstream liberals like Villeda Morales encouraged supporters to fight for "democracy" through participation in "the constitutional process." Villeda Morales and others chose this road while they tried to obtain promises from López Arellano that he would not persecute the liberals and that he would declare a general amnesty.[6]

Thus between late 1963 and mid-1965 mainstream liberalism failed to mobilize its appeal in the popular sector and directly confront the nationalists and the military. This could have been done in various ways, ranging from mass mobilizations to short-term strikes or perhaps even a general strike.[7] Mainstream liberals apparently did not even think along these lines, for it would have meant abandoning old caudillismo politics. Instead, Villeda Morales, pressured also by the U.S. ambassador and Adolf A. Berle, committed the party to the upcoming Constituent Assembly elections.[8]

Widespread violence and fraud marred those elections in February 1965. U.S. correspondents generally condemned them as just another fraud in a long line of "Honduran style elections." Berle, whom López Arellano allowed into the country as an observer, later recalled that the process "was a beautiful exercise on how to steal an election." According to Berle, Ambassador Burrows also acknowledged that General López Arellano and the nationalists had stolen the election.[9]

Only a handful of liberal deputies boycotted the fraudulent assembly elections that would designate General López Arellano president of Honduras. Five liberals pledged not to enter the assembly regardless of their party's

Consejo Central Ejecutivo decree to return. This first group of dissidents included Dr. Rodolfo Pastor Zelaya, Carlos Roberto Reina, Felipe Elvir Rojas, Enrique Rodríguez Zúñiga, and Leonardo Godoy Castillo.[10]

By 23 March the liberals who initially had heeded the CCE's call now abandoned their seats in the assembly to protest the nationalist plan to elect General López Arellano. The next day the CCE approved their action in a formal decree that was accompanied by a blistering manifesto again denouncing the 1963 coup and the nationalist project of 1965. Further, the Liberal Party's "labor" candidates, including Céleo González, president of the Federación Sindical de Trabajadores Norteños de Honduras, denounced López Arellano's victory and also left the assembly.[11]

Simona Paredes and Armando Elvir Cerrato, who were elected deputies from the Department of Cortés, joined the original five dissidents. (This group of Liberal Party rebels came to be known as the "Dissident Seven.") However, liberal resistance stopped here, a fact roundly condemned by *La Prensa*. The Dissident Seven were the only ones, along with Céleo González, who remained true to the original protests of mid-March. The other liberals slowly trickled back to the assembly. This process, in turn, spurred a major crisis of CCE authority over high Liberal Party officials.[12]

During the assembly deliberations, the newly formed Association of Professional Liberals, led by Carlos R. Reina, one of the Dissident Seven opposing the fraud of February 1965, called for and obtained the resignation of various officials of the 1964 CCE. Among those departing were Roberto Suazo Cordova, Juan Murillo Duron, and Jorge Bueso Arias. The APL then took control of the vacant CCE positions.[13] Under this new leadership, the Liberal Party's official program projected a different political vision.

The APL dated back to 1962. According to one of its founding members, the association contained the party's most prominent professionals.[14] In July 1964 the APL's founders sought to make it a kind of corporate organization that would serve as "an auxiliary organism" to the CCE—that is, the CCE's moral and intellectual mini think tank. By June 1965 APL leaders took over the CCE. Carlos R. Reina, Honduras's current president, remained in that post until the 1966 convention, associating his party with San Pedro Sula liberals of the Cámara de Comercio e Industrias de Cortés.

After June 1965 the CCE called on liberals throughout the country to join the local councils that would elect delegates to a national convention scheduled for 1966. In October some prominent liberals in San Pedro Sula, including the capitalists Rodolfo Pastor Zelaya and Jaime Rosenthal Oliva, met at the home of Simona Paredes, of Dissident Seven fame, to consider possible candidates for the council in their city.[15] This meeting of minds of liberal politicians and businessmen represented more than just a response to the democratic leftist appeal of the new CCE based in Tegucigalpa. It also indicated a certain convergence of the economic class elements responsible for San Pedro Sula's emerging role as the "industrial capital" of Honduras and the failure of mainstream liberalism to move beyond traditional Tegucigalpa-style politics. In this way, Gabriel A. Mejía's decisions at the CCIC showed the enormous historical distance between that organization and Jacinto A. Meza's fledgling representation of San Pedro Sula capital in the 1920s.

At any rate, in 1965 the clouds surrounding Honduras's role in the CACM got darker. On 14 December Gabriel Mejía's friend Roberto Ramírez, president of the Banco Central de Honduras, again emphasized the country's "unbalanced development" within the CACM. Thereafter, the CCIC challenged López Arellano's handling of CACM policy. Late in December Mejía publicly encouraged the general to govern the state in more "dynamic ways."[16] From the viewpoint of the CCIC, the López Arellano regime, besides having to contend with its fraudulent origins, also had yet to prove its administrative capacity. Beginning in 1966, CCIC leaders evaluated the government in Tegucigalpa based on to how it dealt with the CACM.

## Militant Capitalists and the Democratic Left's Early Demise

The liberal CCE elected in 1966 consisted of Rodolfo Pastor Zelaya as president, Edgardo Paz Barnica, past APL president; Gilberto Osorio Contreras, old militant of the extinct Partido Democratico Revolucionario de Honduras; José Medina González; Leonardo Godoy Castillo, one of the Dissident Seven; and Carlos F. Hidalgo, past APL official and Villeda Morales's director of the Honduran Alliance for Progress.[17] During the final months of 1966, this CCE elaborated a new political vision that culminated, on 31 December, in formal adherence to what it called the democratic left in Latin America.

The 1966 CCE publicized its new position in a historic document entitled, "The Liberal Party of Honduras Defines Its Political Platform."[18] It condemned the 1963 coup, noting that the coup followed the pattern of other military regimes that took power in Latin America in that decade. In many ways the 1966 document represented a major restructuring of party laws that paralleled Angel Zúñiga Huete's redefinition in 1920 in the context of the emerging "social question" posed by the contours of the then "new" North Coast's agro-export economy. In 1966, however, the redefinition took place in the context of San Pedro Sula's key industrializing role detailed in Chapter 5.

Next, the document recounted the Honduran Liberal Party's history. Up to the 1960s, the party had traversed two stages. In the first stage, which started in the decades prior to independence and ended in the middle nineteenth century, the Liberal Party assumed a laissez-faire approach to society and the economy; it also incorporated the ideas of the French Revolution. A second stage began in the late nineteenth century, when party leaders presumably realized that the state should play a role in social and economic development and complement "particular interests." According to the CCE, this second stage soon faded into history. The Liberal Party needed a new ideological orientation. The document offered in December 1966 was a step in that direction.

This periodization seems to have had its origins in an earlier study by Angel Zúñiga Huete, the Liberal Party's main ideologue from the 1920s until his death in 1953. But the 1966 document's main intellectual roots lay in the analyses offered by the old PDRH in the late 1940s, especially statements on Honduran liberalism available in the party's *Vanguardia Revolucionaria*.[19] (Rodolfo Pastor Zelaya served on its editorial board in 1947.) On the other hand, the democratic leftist discourse offered in the mid-1960s was the San Pedro Sula bourgeoisie leadership's alternative to mainstream liberalism and the oligarchic political and caudillista system in Tegucigalpa.

According to Honduran democratic leftists in December 1966, modern social concerns demanded that liberalism modify its focus on five issues: (1) the organization of society, (2) liberty and individual rights, (3) the role of the state, (4) foreign relations, and (5) social equality. Democratic leftism considered modifying its ideology because of pressing world problems and especially because Honduran society in the last decades had undergone momentous changes. These included the rise of the working-class movement, the formation of organizations representing private enterprise, the movement toward economic integration, and the projected new political parties. As a consequence, the democratic leftists pledged to force the Liberal Party to develop positions on agrarian reform, the working-class movement, tax reform, credit legislation, foreign investment, and economic integration. In doing so, the new CCE promised to remain between the extremes of right and left.[20] Nonetheless, in January 1967 Pastor Zelaya and his colleagues faced attacks from mainstream liberals, the party's right wing, and, of course, opponents in the Arellano regime and beyond.

On 27 January 1967 *La Prensa* published Pastor Zelaya's answer to accusations made in Tegucigalpa by a former Liberal Party official in the dramatic headline, "Medrano Lies! I Am Not a Communist!" Gerardo A. Medrano, expelled by the CCE for plotting an internal party coup, had charged Pastor Zelaya not only with having "communist sympathies," but also with encouraging a guerrilla insurrection in 1965. Pastor Zelaya claimed that Medrano made the allegations because he was working for the police.[21]

Pastor Zelaya weathered the crisis over the Liberal Party's democratic leftism and its so-called sympathies with communism. However, his task remained isolated from the party's major players and from its representatives in

Congress and elsewhere.[22] In August 1967 the mainstream liberals Villeda Morales and Roberto Martínez met with the dissident Carlos R. Reina to discuss party statutes and ideology. Faced with a crisis of authority, as well as the issue of liberal participation in the municipal elections scheduled for March 1968, Pastor Zelaya and other CCE leaders agreed to form commissions to take up the the party's controversial bylaws and ideology.[23]

Pastor Zelaya's agreement to name consultative commissions after the discussions among Reina, Villeda Morales, and Martínez closed the first chapter in the efforts of San Pedro Sula capitalists to secure predominance in Liberal Party politics. This did not mean that Bográn and others in the business establishment had abandoned their commitment to obtain an electoral victory over National Party caudillismo. In fact, in October 1967 Pastor Zelaya, Edmond L. Bográn, and their associates published a manifesto calling on liberals to register to vote in the municipal elections of March 1968.[24]

Bográn and other business leaders in San Pedro Sula likewise did not abandon their more general task of questioning caudillista policy outside of party and electoral politics. The San Pedro Sula agenda for reformism only paralleled the APL's objectives after 1965; it did not supplant them. The reaction of Bográn and other elite San Pedro Sulans to the nationalist–López Arellano political nexus after 1965 stemmed from their stake in Cortés's broader economic transformation in the course of their city's role in the CACM. In short, Pastor Zelaya and Bográn's politics represented more than progressive Honduran liberalism. It revealed a social and political vision that they encouraged within the CCIC and that paralleled the vision of militant labor, even if in 1966 and early 1967 labor remained marginal to the movement.

## The Cortés Chamber of Commerce and Industry and the San Pedro Sula Critique of Caudillismo and Dictatorship

*La Prensa* on 21 December 1967 carried a revealing editorial headline: "Clear Words." The paper warned that "public opinion and power could not remain divorced." That is, Tegucigalpa's political system could not continue to disregard "the public" on important policy questions. *La Prensa*'s main concern was Honduras's role in the CACM. Its conclusions were based on a variety of issues and events—ranging from economic planning to General López Arellano's apparent hostility to international traffic at San Pedro Sula's new airport.[25]

The newspaper recognized that in May 1967 "a high level functionary" had offered valuable criticism of development policy made by the Consejo Superior de Planificación Economía, the successor of the Consejo Nacional de Economía. The published version of this criticism, the so-called Rivera Report, then sparked spontaneous public solidarity for this "not so frequent event." *La Prensa* then acknowledged that San Pedro Sula "recently witnessed a meeting of varied individuals trying to plan the study of national problems by establishing a center to channel public opinion into public power." According to Rafael Leiva Vivas, the center sought to organize "a group to pressure public power and the political parties to obtain concrete responses to the crisis in Honduras."[26]

Leiva Vivas had reported in April 1967 that San Pedro Sula's FICENSA, Honduras's most prestigious industrial investment bank, then headed by Edmond L. Bográn, recently "offered Honduran investors fifty thousand shares" during its last capitalization. But Leiva Vivas did not limit his discussion of FICENSA to recent stock distributions or more technical financial matters; he also raised important social and political issues. According to him, FICENSA represented a "typical case" of Honduran effort and talent, based on "Honduran capital," representative "of that petty national bourgeoisie that is taking the reins of the country."[27]

Actually, Leiva Vivas's celebration of the San Pedro Sula bourgeoisie's successful embarkment on the road to taking state power proved premature. By 1967 the regional and local economic terrain in which FICENSA flourished after its establishment in 1964 showed signs of suffering more severe cracks than those recorded during 1965 and 1966. In May 1967, a month after Leiva Vivas published his laudatory reflections, Miguel Angel Rivera, CONSUPLANE's executive secretary, offered General López Arellano the Rivera Report on the economy, the CACM, and their relation to public policy, particularly the obstructions by Ricardo Zúñiga Augustinus, the presidential minister. López Arellano reacted by protecting Zúñiga Augustinus, whereas he linked Rivera to liberal machinations and fired him.[28]

The nationalists missed their mark when they focused entirely on Rivera's relationship with liberalism at large. First, explaining the Rivera Report requires locating Rivera's motivations within the travails of Honduras's role in the economic integration movement at large and within San Pedro Sula's subregional relationship to that broader process. And second, the report must be viewed in the context of the CCIC's role and Gabriel A. Mejía's leadership in trying to redefine their old relationship with Tegucigalpa-based merchants and industrialists.

The 1965 reorganization of the CCIC by its Advisory Board (comprised of Mejía, Bográn, and others)—as a first step to establishing a national federation of the country's chambers of commerce and industry—challenged Tegucigalpa's lackluster control of policy criticism emerging from traditional sectors of organized capitalists. As such, the Cámara de Comercio e Industrias de Tegucigalpa rejected the CCIC's efforts to establish its political hegemony in the context of CACM-supported industrialization, especially when important sectors of the CCIT opposed economic integration because of its implications for accumulation in Tegucigalpa and the interior.[29]

The CCIC nevertheless continued to press the issue in 1966. Mejía and his advisers hired a New York–based consultant from the Latin American Council on Commerce and Production, and meetings were held for most of the year. By December Honduran capitalists finally integrated their sectors into the Consejo Hondureño de la Empresa Privada under the presidency of Gabriel A. Mejía. The specific reasons behind this turn of events are unknown, but they probably originated with frustration over the increasingly contradictory process of economic integration and the deterioration of Honduras's trade in 1965 and 1966.[30]

Despite the increasing absolute volume and value of intraregional trade, the Honduran economy still endured disproportionate levels of imports from the region, particularly El Salvador, which constituted Honduras's chief regional trading partner. By 1966 Honduran manufacturers and merchants were encouraging an unofficial boycott of Salvadoran goods. Publicly, the manufacturers continued to insist on obtaining a special "Protocol" to CACM agreements that would allow industrial development laws to provide Honduras greater fiscal incentives as a way of catching up with manufacturing development elsewhere in Central America.[31]

Honduran manufacturers obtained a commitment to such a protocol in January 1966, a situation that further motivated the country's chambers to work more closely in preparing a strategy to take advantage of this change, especially via the establishment in April of a National Commission for Industrial Development.[32] Despite these positive moves, relations between San Pedro Sula's business establishment and Tegucigalpa's political regime remained strained, hence the "Clear Words" editorial in *La Prensa* in December 1967.

In the aftermath of the Rivera Report, Bográn, Rosenthal, and other young CCIC leaders invited members of the Honduran *fuerzas vivas* to an organizational meeting of the projected San Pedro Sula–based think tank in November 1967. A month later labor representatives were invited to join the project.[33] A select group attended the first organizational meeting on 15 December. The participants included all previous executive secretaries of CNE-CONSUPLANE (Jorge Bueso Arias, Carlos H. Matute, and Miguel Angel Rivera). They were joined by economists employed by the Central American Bank for Economic Integration and the Permanent Secretariat for Central American Economic Integration, the authority empowered by the region's governments to oversee CACM treaty implementation.[34]

Other notable personalities joined the young CCIC leaders and the technocrat contingent at that December 1967 meeting: the liberal-oriented, anti-communist leadership of North Coast organized labor, pillars of the Confederación de Trabajadores de Honduras based in Tegucigalpa. They included Céleo González, FESITRANH's leader since 1957, who was temporarily imprisoned after the 1963 coup; and Oscar Gale Varela, president of the United Fruit Company's union, the Sindicato de Trabajadores de la Tela Rail Road Co., since its founding in 1954.[35] (Recall that SITRATERCO's membership accounted for a majority of FESITRANH's overall affiliation.)

Bográn's projected think tank never got beyond the planning stage, and it is difficult to explain why. Rafael Leiva Vivas, then closely connected with the 1967 meetings, remembers only that the project "failed."[36] Probably more pressing matters arising in early 1968 overtook San Pedro Sula's elites and their sympathizers elsewhere. The more immediate problem revolved around the municipal elections in March. The Liberal Party, from its democratic leftist faction to its right wing, feared that General López Arellano and his National Party supporters might organize an electoral fraud on the scale of that in 1965.

On 31 March 1968 López Arellano and the nationalists did just that; the magnitude of the deception was equal to that in 1965. The result was that nationalists secured 235 of 260 mayorships. As in 1965, the democratic leftist CCE enjoined liberal administrators to stay away from their offices. Generally the North Coast municipalities complied, with the critical exception of the San Pedro Sula mayor, who changed loyalties to the mainstream liberalism of Villeda Morales and others.[37]

Despite the collapse of the San Pedro Sula think tank project and amid the continuing Liberal Party crisis, Bográn and other young leaders of the CCIC found another way to challenge the Tegucigalpa political system specifically and caudillismo rule generally. By early 1968 Honduras's deteriorating position within the CACM became clearer, adding substance to the 1967 Rivera Report's charge that López Arellano's economic development plan for 1965–69 had failed. In March the post-Rivera CONSUPLANE continued studying a "Plan of Action" to complement the 1965–69 plan, but even then the CCIC questioned its feasibility given the current personnel in the López Arellano administration. Gabriel A. Mejía voiced his skepticism over the 1968 Plan of Action in a historic meeting with López Arellano held in Tegucigalpa on 29 April 1968. Besides its significance in terms of the issues discussed, this meeting, also attended by Céleo González and Oscar Gale Varela, represented a critical shift in San Pedro Sula's continuing challenge to López Arellano generally. In fact, from this perspective the origins of the 29 April meeting deserve comment as well.[38]

As in February 1965, the FESITRANH in April 1968 publicly blasted the López Arellano–nationalist axis on yet another electoral imposition. Unlike in

1963 or 1965, however, in 1968 CCIC leaders joined Céleo González, Oscar Gale Varela, and others in criticizing López Arellano's regime. In fact, the 29 April meeting resulted from earlier private letters signed by Mejía, González, and Gale Varela. The letters ranged from denouncing the electoral imposition to asking General López Arellano for a meeting attended by him, his military advisers, and the organizations that Mejía, González, and Gale Varela considered to be "the country's main business, sindicalist, peasant and agricultural organizations."[39] The public and private exchanges between López Arellano and North Coast business and labor leaders before 29 April again demonstrated the geographic and economic axis of conflict between modernizing Honduran capitalism and Tegucigalpa and interior caudillismo.

The meeting on 29 April did not offer positive results. Only the continuing crisis of the CACM brought a new round of correspondence and meetings. From late 1967 to early 1968 CACM officials and government representatives, in talks held in San José, Costa Rica, discussed the CACM's most immediate problems. These included (1) deteriorating balance of payments, in part a function of deteriorating foreign exchange earnings from traditional exports, and (2) fiscal pressures caused by falling revenues as a consequence of tax incentives for industrial development itself and intraregional tariff suspensions accorded in CACM treaties.[40] Worse, although these macroeconomic problems affected Central America as a whole, by 1968 Hondurans from across the ideological spectrum and from all sectors of organized capital and labor realized that Honduran industrialization did not keep pace with that of its neighbors, especially El Salvador.

CACM's official response to these problems, revealed in San José in early June 1968 and known eventually as the "San José Protocol," consisted of two major policies: (1) in defense of balance of payments, a 30 percent surcharge on imports from outside the CACM, except capital goods, raw materials, and some intermediate goods, and (2) to deal with the fiscal pressures, excise taxes, from 20 to 10 percent, on various luxury consumer goods. Economists offered these measures as alternatives to austerity or income tax reform, which they assumed might be more politically explosive than the San José Protocol.[41]

Official reactions by organized capital and labor ranged from toleration to the taxes by the Asociación Nacional de Industriales de Honduras, then headed by National Party member Cesar A. Batres, to moderate intolerance by the CCIT and the CCIC. Both the CCIT and the CCIC asked for other measures as well as further study. North Coast labor leaders rejected the protocol, and SITRATERCO's Oscar Gale Varela resigned as labor's representative in CONSUPLANE. *La Prensa* condemned the protocol early on, arguing that it failed to address the root of the country's economic problems, especially as outlined in the Rivera Report of 1967.[42]

On 21 June 1968 *La Prensa* published an interesting letter dated 30 April. Addressed to General López Arellano and signed by Gabriel A. Mejía, Céleo González, and Oscar Gale Varela, it—for the first time—publicized details of their 29 April meeting, one that turned out to be a major disappointment to the CCIC. López Arellano had simply ignored the CCIC-FESITRANH agenda.

In June the relevance of this letter revolved around two issues. First, that the CCIC and the FESITRANH now took it upon themselves to "lead the country" in a struggle against the San José Protocol. From that time until mid-August 1968, *La Prensa*, the CCIC, and the FESITRANH constantly condemned the protocol on the grounds that it did not address structural problems and that the excise taxes would hike the cost of living for the "Honduran majorities." The first of these charges was true, but López Arellano did not sign the protocol to deal with "structural economic development." It represented only an emergency policy to save the CACM, a fact that CCIT and ANDI directors eventually accepted, if grudgingly. The second charge was untrue because the excise tax only affected luxury items, not the basic consumer goods of even the better-off members of the organized working class.[43]

A second issue associated with *La Prensa*'s publication of the CCIC-FESITRANH letter turns on the continuity of the critical discourse developed between the April initiatives and the June expositions. This discourse assumed a common element between the April initiative, related first to the farce of the municipal elections in March, and the administrative myopia the CCIC and FESITRANH ascribed to the San José Protocol: that the López Arellano–nationalist axis of the 1960s merely represented another in a long line of authoritarian regimes, unresponsive to the fuerzas vivas and imposed on the Honduran people by the traditional political parties. Unlike leaders of the CCIT and ANDI, however, CCIC directors now confronted the more general problem by challenging the protocol.

National Party legislators passed the 30 percent surcharge in a final debate on 7 August 1968. This occurred despite secret meetings, in mid-July, between López Arellano and the elders of the San Pedro Sula bourgeoisie—men like Antonio Mata, José Brandel, Yankel Rosenthal, Yude Canahuati, Reginaldo Panting, and Gabriel A. Mejía.[44] On 20 August the CCIC and FESITRANH sent the general another private memorandum that reiterated charges dating back to the 29 April meeting and the subsequent secret meetings in July, and that demanded a definitive answer to those charges in order to "alleviate the pressures which we confront."[45] López Arellano did not respond.

## The General Strike of 1968

Soon after the 20 August memorandum, National Party loyalists in Congress passed the excise taxes associated with the San José Protocol.[46] These taxes were to take effect on 12 September. Meanwhile, the advisory board of the CCIC, composed of the San Pedro Sula core of the democratic leftist CCE, which governed the Liberal Party from 1966 to May 1968, planned a commercial and industrial strike to retaliate against the López Arellano regime. This undertaking grew out of discussions between young CCIC leaders and FESITRANH veterans like Céleo González and SITRATERCO president Oscar Gale Varela. The overall project involved the CCIC and the FESITRANH in the mobilization of their constituencies for a general strike that would paralyze the North Coast economy.[47]

The specific project, however, placed the CCIC at the vanguard of the movement. On 24 August Gale Varela closed a SITRATERCO assembly by attacking the San José Protocol and announcing that various resolutions taken there would be discussed at the next FESITRANH meeting.[48] The FESITRANH then scheduled an "extraordinary" assembly for 17 September. Interestingly enough, the CCIC also called an "extraordinary" assembly for the same day to discuss its position on the protocol.

At some point between 24 August and 17 September 1968, the CCIC made a deal with the FESITRANH. First, the CCIC pledged to declare a commercial and industrial strike late on 17 September. (Everyone interviewed on this question agreed that until that day, the majority of San Pedro Sula's elite merchants and industrialists promised to participate in the "capital strike.") Second, the FESITRANH pledged to complement the CCIC action by declaring a general labor strike *after* the CCIC initiative was endorsed in a general assembly of the chamber. But official CCIC support never materialized.

General López Arellano discovered the plot before 17 September and retaliated quickly. He struck at the heart of the San Pedro Sula bourgeoisie: the foreign contingent of the North Coast business establishment, especially its Arab sector.[49] López Arellano's henchmen, including his infamous minister of the presidency, Ricardo Zúñiga Augustinus, initiated a campaign to privately intimidate key representatives of the San Pedro Sula elite. Among their tactics were telephone calls and personal visits to Arab businessmen by members of the San Pedro Sula elite.

A major figure making these visits was Julio Galdámez Zepeda. In 1968 Galdámez Zepeda was the nemesis of the CCIC because of his politics and his previous relationships with the San Pedro Sula elites. First, he enjoyed impeccable National Party credentials; in 1962 he had been the party's candidate for mayor of San Pedro Sula. In 1965, after strongly supporting the 1963 coup, he got himself elected to the Constituent Assembly that made López Arellano president. In fact, he played a key role in the congressional maneuver itself. Galdámez Zepeda was a crucial player in passing the San José Protocol in Congress in July and August 1968. In the process, he took a swipe at *La Prensa* during a television program, calling the paper "an enemy of the government."[50]

Galdámez Zepeda's social and business ties in San Pedro Sula were just as important as his political credentials. A past president of the San Pedro Sula Rotaries, he had invested extensively in agricultural enterprises, including the region's only modern milk processing plant. His stake in the land allowed him a prominent position in the Asociación de Ganaderos y Agricultores de Sula since its founding in 1948. Finally, his investments in industry and finance complemented those in agriculture, allowing him a place on the CCIC Board of Directors starting in 1963.[51] Galdámez Zepeda also bought stock in Cementos de Honduras, S.A., owned primarily by Yude Canahuati and Kattan family interests. And, like most of the San Pedro Sula elite, he held shares in FICENSA, the San Pedro Sula investment bank headed by Edmond L. Bográn between 1964 and the fateful year of 1968.[52]

Galdámez Zepeda's admonitions, accompanied by pressure and intimidation from Tegucigalpa, took their toll. Late on 17 September 1968, the CCIC General Assembly voted against a strike. Instead, it decided to present General López Arellano with another set of petitions. CCIC militancy now turned to more talks and policy positions. This left the FESITRANH isolated, yet pressed by collective frustration with the regime and by the militant pronouncements of FESITRANH officials in 1967–68, as well those dating back to the aftermath of the 1963 coup. On the morning of 18 September 1968 Céleo González and other FESITRANH leaders declared a general strike on their own. López Arellano responded with a state of siege and dispatched troops to San Pedro Sula. By 23 September security forces had captured González and the entire strike committee. Further repression thereafter broke the workers' resistance.

Persecution of the more militant businessmen in San Pedro Sula continued. Late on 18 September security forces closed *La Prensa*, owned at that time primarily by Jorge J. Larach. The repression also extended to radio stations blamed for "inciting" the population. Jorge J. Sikaffy's "La Voz de Centroamerica," one of the city's oldest broadcasters, was shut down. Even so, San Pedro Sula merchants closed their establishments despite the CCIC's official position. This defiance after the declaration of the state of siege forced López Arellano to publicize his communiqué that threatened the foreign elements of the business class with deportation and expropriation. The Arab merchants and industrialists were terrorized. Within a short time security forces imprisoned Jaime Rosenthal Oliva, who was snatched directly from the offices of *La Prensa*. Edmond L. Bográn escaped into exile, and San Pedro Sula's business community fell silent.[53]

Soon after these events, Jorge J. Larach decided to make a trip that signified the changed times and the contradictions of Honduran history. Representing *La Prensa* as a whole, Larach traveled to Tegucigalpa to negotiate the reopening of his young newspaper. General López Arellano imposed two conditions: first, restructure the newspaper's militant editorial board, and second, take a less critical editorial line. The repression worked. *La Prensa*'s first subsequent editorial, on 15 October, reflected the changed discourse.[54]

On 14 October 1968 *El Día* reported that security forces still seemed bent on apprehending Edmond Bográn when he returned from exile. A month after the fateful events of September, Bográn saw his house surrounded by troops. In fact, the government persisted in legally prosecuting Bográn for his involvement in the September events. Eventually he resigned from his post at FICENSA and later, along with Jaime Rosenthal Oliva, founded his own newspaper—*Diario Tiempo*.[55] Nonetheless, the collective business militancy that Bográn and his democratic leftist colleagues encouraged from 1965 to 1968 left its mark. In 1969 the CCIC continued to challenge Tegucigalpa's political system, even if it now harbored few of the dreams offered by Bográn and others. On the other hand, the inclusion of militant North Coast labor in the movement against the López Arellano regime strengthened the region as a whole.

# THE NORTH COAST AND THE ROAD TO MILITARY REFORMISM, 1969–1972

"The bombing operation," recalled a Honduran writer years later, "lasted only four hours, and so the powerful Honduran air force could not immediately respond." On 14 July 1969, Eduardo Bahr wrote, Hondurans living near Toncontín airport in Tegucigalpa watched, surely with great astonishment, as the crews of low-flying planes maneuvered bombs from external racks that they then flung overboard. A few bombs destroyed homes, others failed to explode, and some just lodged themselves into the dirt and pavement. The Honduran foreign minister, Tiburcio Carías Castillo, registered the Salvadoran strike at 6:25 P.M. The attack "marked the first war between Latin American nations since 1941."[1]

The Salvadoran air force's raid on Tegucigalpa failed utterly—unlike the army's blitzkrieg over land. The Honduran air force, composed of twenty-three combat aircraft, did not suffer any direct hits. Despite careful planning, the Salvadoran air raid confronted problems even prior to arriving near Tegucigalpa. Before taking off from Ilopango air base near San Salvador, two Salvadoran aircraft collided on the runway. Worse, the commander responsible for leading the attack on Toncontín failed to find the air base. He became separated from his squadron and eventually flew to Guatemala City.[2]

On 15 July 1969 Gabriel A. Mejía sent an urgent telegram to General Oswaldo López Arellano: "In this trying time for the country, we reaffirm our unconditional support. We are providing decisive support to the departmental civic committee. Attentive and affectionate greetings." Soon afterward Mejía headed the Cámara de Comercio e Industrias de Cortés's Regional Committee of Pro-Defense Bond Sales. Key CCIC members coordinated the subregional bond sales committees. Antonio Bográn, the grandson of former Honduran president Luis Bográn (1883–91), assumed responsibility for the Departments of Cortés, Yoro, Atlántida, and the Bay Islands; Camilo Rivera Girón, who was deposed by López Arellano from the Cortés governorship in 1965, took charge of the Departments of Santa Bárbara, Copán, Intibucá, and Lempira.[3]

Other important organized social sectors from the North Coast assumed critical roles in the defense against the Salvadoran invasion. Like Mejía, Oscar Gale Varela, president of the Sindicato de Trabajadores de la Tela Railroad Co., took up a post with the diplomatic team charged with advising Foreign Minister Carías Castillo on possible tactics and strategies. Gale Varela, then also serving on the executive committee of the Confederación de Trabajadores de Honduras, likewise helped mobilize the country's organized working class. The CTH's secretary-general, Andrés Víctor Artiles, characterized the Honduran workers in those moments as "civilian troops" responding to a direct request from General López Arellano.[4]

Even during this national emergency, Gale Varela must have thought it ironic that López Arellano requested the help of the country's organized working class. Surely neither men, nor their respective constituencies, had forgotten that only a year before, Gale Varela, as well as Céleo González, president of the Federación Sindical de Trabajadores Norteños de Honduras, suffered the repression of a "national" state of siege designed to crush their "subversive" movement. González, perhaps more than any other top leader of the CTH, may have felt somewhat smug even in this dire situation; in September 1968 López Arellano's security forces attacked him near San Pedro Sula, confined him in a Tegucigalpa jail, and then forced him into exile. In fact, in the same month López Arellano had sent Gale Varela to relay the news of exile to González.[5]

By July 1969 Gale Varela, González, and other CTH leaders seemed on the road to some kind of rapprochement with at least the Honduran armed forces, if not with López Arellano himself. This situation arose during an important CTH national convention held in Puerto Cortés in March 1969. The convention, initially scheduled for November 1968 but postponed because of the strike declared by the FESITRANH during the previous September, produced a critical document entitled "*Llamamiento* a la Conciencia Nacional" (A Call to the National Consciousness). In this paper, the CTH recognized that "in the present conjuncture, the Armed Forces [are] a factor of real power in the country."[6]

The CTH's *Llamamiento* indicated a new appreciation of the Honduran armed forces beyond the simple recognition of their political power. It also linked the armed forces' political intervention to "the power vacuum resulting from the absence of real political parties that represent the permanent and authentic interests of the country's popular sectors."[7] This analysis is significant in and of itself and in light of other points made in the *Llamamiento*. Its inherent importance is that it dismissed a broadside that might have characterized the armed forces' political intervention as a function of ambition or militarism per se. In the posited scenario, the real miscreants in Honduras's political history turned out to be the leaders of the Liberal and National Parties, characterized in the document as "oligarchs."

The *Llamamiento* also offered the following tidbit: "the organized working class considers that the military, when acting within its own juridical regime and helping with development plans, constitutes a positive factor of the nationality."[8] This and other comments in the *Llamamiento* suggest that between September 1968 and March 1969, Gale Varela, González, and others in the CTH gradually came to recognize the benefits of encouraging not only a disassociation of the armed forces from the National Party, but also perhaps even the institutionalization of the military's role in the country's development. The drama of and the national mobilization against the Salvadoran invasion offered a unique conjuncture for reorienting a San Pedro Sula discourse and vision that dated back to at least 1967.

Also, as of March 1969, the Honduran armed forces, if not General López Arellano himself, might have found the CTH's characterization of their potential role in national development more appealing than in a different decade or even in the early 1960s. Two broad issues were involved. First, by the late 1960s most of the officer corps of the Honduran armed forces had been exposed to a special worldview provided through training in U.S. military academies. According to one scholar, after World War II and with the beginning of the Cold War, the U.S. military taught its foreign students a "new global strategy based on the need for a permanent alliance in the face of a presumably permanent war." In this scenario, "the enemy was not merely a nation, or even a group of nations, but rather an ideology"—communism.[9]

Second, after the Cuban Revolution, U.S. military analysts deployed a global strategy within all Latin American countries. In February 1959 President Eisenhower announced a new comprehensive military policy for the region, one by which the United States might "strive to be the sole supplier of military hardware to Latin America" as "a means of maintaining U.S. influence over Latin American military forces and through such forces on the political orientation of Latin American governments."[10]

Beginning in 1960, U.S. military strategy in Latin America emphasized nontraditional forms of training: counterinsurgency and "civic action." Counterinsurgency would deal with leftist guerrillas, whereas civic action involved the military in projects ranging from building bridges to "community development." Civic action programs encouraged the Latin American officer corps to view themselves as "nation builders."[11] The *Llamamiento* assumed that its appeals to the armed forces' potential for national development might tap into this new training.

## The Salvadoran Invasion and Its Implications for San Pedro Sula–Based Political Reformism

The Salvadoran invasion destroyed many myths, especially the one of a homogeneously "friendly" El Salvador. Notwithstanding propaganda from both sides, it seems that the war destroyed more myths than lives. Death squads at home killed more Salvadorans (ca. 2,641) between May and July 1980 than the combined number of Salvadoran and Honduran combatants and civilians who died in July 1969. An OAS-ordered cease-fire stopped most of the fighting on 18 July 1969. OAS observers reached the border area on the nineteenth and twentieth. However, at that moment the Salvadoran army still occupied 1,600 square kilometers of Honduran territory. The invading army returned to El Salvador in early August only because of severe diplomatic threats from the OAS.[12]

Before, during, and immediately after the war, elite Hondurans finally "discovered" that El Salvador was ruled by an oligarchy. In June 1969 Tegucigalpa's conservative *El Día* characterized it as "Latin America's most closed oligarchy." Jorge Fidel Durón, contributor to *El Día*, Rotarian, corporate lawyer, former foreign minister, National Party intellectual, and member of the Banco Atlántida Board of Directors, blamed El Salvador's "oligarchy" and "Salvadoran capitalism" for the war.[13] Juan Ramón Ardón, an ardent supporter of former president Villeda Morales, attacked El Salvador's "feudal lords" and their monopoly of the country's land. In 1970 Edmond L. Bográn condemned the Salvadoran "coffee barons" and their "oligarchic regime."[14]

Hondurans from across the political spectrum clearly understood that the Salvadoran invasion was a "final solution" to that country's systemic social and economic problems, especially its demographic explosion and its exploitative and unequal structure for land tenure. By 1969 Honduran territory had become home to 250,000–300,000 Salvadorans in search of land.[15]

Between early 1967 and the invasion of 1969, a number of contradictions associated with both countries' transitions to peripheral capitalism adversely affected sectors of each country's elites and their historic reluctance to deal with land problems. The elites, in turn, made different demands on their political systems originating in the changed economic structure of the 1960s. In Honduras, by November 1967 organized landowners called for the expulsion of Salvadoran squatters as one way to deal with the record levels of peasant mobilization. The removals began in May 1969, and by mid-July 1969

Honduran authorities had deported 15,000–20,000 Salvadorans. In El Salvador, one sector of the oligarchy called for an invasion of Honduras as a way to deal with internal economic and social problems that would be greatly exacerbated by the return of thousands of Salvadorans.[16]

The Salvadoran oligarchy's recent penetration of the peasant economy, particularly through cotton cultivation, had reached a new stage. This process not only fortified an already powerful relationship between the old Salvadoran ruling class and the state, it also radically differentiated the nature of capital mobilization for manufacturing in El Salvador and Honduras. In El Salvador, old and new factions of "the oligarchy" invested heavily in CACM-sponsored industrialization. Indeed, by 1971 thirty-six of the country's largest landowners controlled 38 percent of the country's top 1,429 firms.[17]

In Honduras, something quite different happened. Local capital mobilized for CACM-sponsored manufacturing came primarily from earlier commercial accumulation and from an area, San Pedro Sula, whose access to the state did not even approximate the historic and organic association between the Salvadoran oligarchy and "its" state. In the late 1950s CCIC officials were well aware of this situation, and they often praised the extent and quality of collaboration between the Salvadoran government and capitalists. Finally, San Pedro Sula capitalists believed that El Salvador's industrial development law offered more protection and incentives for industrialization than did similar inducements in Honduras.[18]

Leaders of the manufacturing bourgeoisie in San Pedro Sula recognized their comparative backwardness in the Central American context and tried to deal with it, thus sparking the crisis of September 1968. Until 1967 the manufacturing bourgeoisie had enjoyed substantial support from agricultural interests associated with the CCIC, mainly the Asociación de Ganaderos y Agricultores Sula. For example, in early 1967, when Rodolfo Pastor Zelaya declared the Liberal Party to be on the "democratic leftist" road, some of the area's most influential agricultural investors supported his position.[19] This changed between late 1967 and 1969.

Later in 1967 the cordial relations between AGAS and liberal democratic leftism fell prey to contradictions inherent in Honduran agrarian capitalism. In August a *La Prensa* editorial condemned the new official attitude toward agrarian reform as "leftist." By November José Eduardo Gauggel, in an interview published in the "democratic leftist" *La Prensa*, characterized López Arellano's government as "socialist" because of its efforts to revive the moribund Agrarian Reform Law of 1962.[20] Peasant resistance to the new agricultural capitalism presented a challenge to the CCIC-AGAS cooperation forged in the post–World War II economic recovery.

In 1966 peasant organizations that had been tamed into submission after the 1963 coup returned to the struggle. One of them, the Asociación Nacional de Campesinos de Honduras, threatened to conduct a "hunger march" to Tegucigalpa to protest problems with the agrarian reform.[21] More important, ANACH emerged from the dispute over land in the Sula Valley once owned or rented by Samuel Zemurray. What is more, the land involved was also claimed by two scions of one of San Pedro Sula's most prestigious families—Antonio Bográn Paredes and Luis Bográn Fortin, the sons of former Zemurray associates in the valley. By August 1967, in an assembly held at the CCIC offices, the Bográns characterized tentative government support of peasant positions in the Sula Valley as "communist."[22]

By mid-1968 the Federación Nacional de Agricultores y Ganaderos de Honduras, of which AGAS was a prominent member, also faced peasant militancy in southern Honduras, especially in the Departments of Choluteca and Valle. There, peasant groups organized formally in 1964 as the Asociación Campesina Social Cristiana de Honduras. During the period 1965–68 ACASH's leadership received training in Peru, México, and Guatemala, as well as from progressive sectors of the Catholic Church. By that time, ANACH activists had transferred their land recuperation strategies from the Sula Valley to Choluteca and Valle. At last, in December 1968, General López Arellano authorized bond sales of $15 million to support projects of the Instituto Nacional Agrario. A Honduran-Salvadoran immigration treaty of 1965 was allowed to expire in January 1969.[23]

López Arellano's new domestic and foreign policies reflected, broadly speaking, reactions to the changing structure of Honduran agrarian capitalism. By the mid-1960s rural society finally began to suffer the social polarization evident long before in Guatemala, El Salvador, and Nicaragua. In those three countries, even the original coffee export–based economies produced a general assault on peasant land tenure and subsistence crops not induced by Honduras's banana export system. The North Coast banana plantations occupied a largely underpopulated area at a time of low demographic growth rates. This contrast meant that Honduran peasants enjoyed access to community-owned lands on a scale impossible in Guatemala and especially El Salvador.[24]

Increasing rural landlessness in the 1960s was a by-product of a new cycle in Honduras's involvement in the world economy. As in El Salvador, beginning in the 1950s Honduran state agencies supported, through technical expertise, credits, and sometimes even capital, a series of export products that diversified the old banana export economy and provided sources of foreign exchange. Cotton production in Honduras had jumped from 1,000 bales in 1941 to 21,000 bales by 1963. And whereas in the late 1950s there were only 57 cotton farms, by the mid-1960s cotton farms numbered about 417, creating a cotton bourgeoisie that was represented in FENAGH.[25]

The capitalization of a rural cotton bourgeoisie in southern Honduras connected to exports to the world economy also paralleled equally new investments in sugar cultivation and exports and cattle grazing for beef exports to the United States. Investors in the southern departments of Honduras, particularly in Choluteca and Valle, now established concrete financial relationships with sugar and beef exporters from the North Coast departments of Cortés, Atlántida, and Colón. Moreover, as in manufacturing, foreign investors, including the Standard Fruit Company investment group, played a dominant role in this new rural capitalization.[26]

In short, by the late 1960s there had emerged a Honduran agrarian bourgeoisie dominated by an old imperial connection that undoubtedly arrested anti-imperialist, pronationalist bourgeois concepts of visionaries like Bográn and Rosenthal at *La Prensa*. So, just as one cannot comprehend General López Arellano's failure to renew the 1965 immigration treaty early in 1969 without understanding the course of Honduran agrarian capitalism, one cannot appreciate the origins and nature of López Arellano's 1972 coup outside that same economic and social process.

### The 1969 Agendas for Reformism: The CTH *Llamamiento* in the Postwar Context

Rafael Leiva Vivas in 1967 offered an interesting characterization of business-led reformism in San Pedro Sula. Choosing the dynamic Financiera Hondureña, S.A., as his point of departure, Leiva Vivas described this investment bank as "a Honduran enterprise, organized by Honduran effort and talent and with Honduran capital, which, in a few years has structured itself as the representative of the national petty bourgeoisie that is taking control of the country."[27]

Nineteen sixty-seven was a heady year for the San Pedro Sula bourgeoisie, which saw the Rivera Report, access to the Liberal Party via democratic leftism, and Bográn's projected think tank. Most of this died in September 1968. Nonetheless, in the post–14 July 1969 context Leiva Vivas offered telling remarks about the potential emergence in Honduras of "a dynamic capitalist bourgeoisie capable of forging institutional changes without vacillation and halting compromises [that] reflected the changing times."[28] Dr. Jacinto A. Meza would have been proud.

The Salvadoran invasion changed many political agendas, including the post–1963 alliance between a Zúñiga-led National Party and a López Arellano–led military. After September 1968, National Party conventions consistently and proudly reiterated the party's support for General López Arellano. This did not bode well for Hondurans generally, for San Pedro Sula reformism, or for a practically moribund Liberal Party. Worse, in early 1969 rumors suggested that the Zúñiga Augustinus–López Arellano axis might be preparing another electoral fraud or constitutional maneuver to stay in power beyond the presidential election scheduled for March 1971. This remained a possibility after July 1969, and as late as July 1970 prominent liberals vowed to "violently" confront *continuismo*.[29]

The mobilization for the national defense, however, effectively reduced the space for undertaking a fraudulent project, especially given unresolved problems following the destruction of the CACM and sporadic military confrontations with Salvadoran forces as late as January and February 1970. Finally, the successful Salvadoran attack on land demonstrated the Honduran army's corruption and lack of military preparedness for the conflict. An institutional reorganization was due, and surely such a process might not survive another political nexus with the National Party.[30]

The last Salvadoran troops left Honduras in early August 1969. By 18 August leaders from the North Coast working class, the Liberal Party, Liberal and National Party splinter groups, and university organizations signed a public manifesto, directed to General López Arellano, that represented a first effort to create a national reformist agenda in the post–July 1969 context. The manifesto demanded administrative reforms similar to those found in the CTH *Llamamiento* published in March. Moreover, it called for "institutionalizing a civic organism of National Unity" to be integrated by the country's organized social forces and political parties. Although this "civic organism's" responsibilities would be specified by the participating organizations, its general task remained ensuring the "national unity" achieved during the defense mobilization as well as the commitment to a reformist agenda. This project did not survive past September 1969.[31]

At this juncture, in October 1969, Gabriel A. Mejía, as president of the Consejo Hondureño de la Empresa Privada, responded to the CTH *Llamamiento* initiative of March 1969 by convening what was officially called the "Third Reunion of Honduras's *Fuerzas Vivas*." These events prompted Leiva Vivas to identify the San Pedro Sula bourgeoisie as Honduras's "emerging national bourgeoisie." In effect, this third reunion of the fuerzas vivas, scheduled for November in San Pedro Sula, represented the revival of San Pedro Sula–led reformism dating back to 1966–67 and repressed in September 1968. Oscar Gale Varela, a keynote speaker at the November reunion, explicitly linked the COHEP-sponsored event with the confrontation of 1968 and the March 1969 *Llamamiento*. This gathering and its resolutions was dominated by progressive individuals from the North Coast bourgeoisie and combative North Coast union leaders like Gale Varela and Céleo González. Business sectors unsympathetic with the CCIC's control of COHEP, located mostly in the interior, resented the CCIC's command of the event.[32]

A major resolution adopted at the Third Reunion dealt with how the fuerzas vivas might "participate in politics." This resolution and the meetings associated with the 1969 CTH-COHEP movement in San Pedro Sula bore fruit quickly. On 13 February 1970 leaders of COHEP and CTH met with General López Arellano and delivered a *planteamiento* outlining a potential CTH–COHEP–armed forces accord that could be offered to the political parties as the basis for competing in the 1971 elections.[33]

This document called for free elections, a cabinet of capable professionals, a single slate of congressional deputies, a civil service law, and a minimal government plan to be elaborated by all subscribers to the accord. The CTH-COHEP plan named López Arellano and the armed forces as possible guarantors of a San Pedro Sula–based reformism emanating from outside the traditional political parties. López Arellano did not act on the planteamiento until December 1970, and for most of that year liberals and nationalists debated different formulas for jointly administering the state after March 1971. Both feared being outflanked by the CTH-COHEP document.[34]

In December 1970, days before liberals and nationalists were to convene and choose candidates for the 1971 elections, General López Arellano finally approved a CTH-COHEP planteamiento similar to the one proposed in February. Subscribers to the December accord then offered the document to the liberals and nationalists for their consideration. In the process, López Arellano broke with Zúñiga Augustinus and the National Party and essentially cut a deal with most of the enemies he had accumulated from 1963 to 1968. Signatories to the 8 December planteamiento from the labor and peasant sectors included Céleo González and Oscar Gale Varela, presidents of the FESITRANH and SITRATERCO respectively; Andrés Víctor Artiles, temporarily detained in 1968 as secretary-general of the CTH; and Juan Reyes Rodríguez, head of ANACH since 1968 and a cofounder of the association in 1962.[35]

Reyes Rodríguez's signature was critical because it demonstrated López Arellano's new sympathy with ANACH's struggles over land. On the other hand, from the viewpoint of the new rural bourgeoisie represented in FENAGH, Reyes Rodríguez's formal inclusion in the CTH-COHEP planteamiento was more than a mere "coincidence" involving Mejía and his radical friends, Edmond L. Bográn and Jaime Rosenthal. (FENAGH president Héctor Callejas Valentine charged that Mejía had not consulted him on the substance of the talks on the planteamiento.) Reyes Rodríguez, a nearly illiterate peasant from one of Honduras's poorest departments, "never went to school even one day of his life, but he [had] learned to read and write during six months that he [had] spent in jail for his part in agrarian conflicts of the ANACH in the Department of Santa Bárbara." Moreover, recalled a close friend, he "was a great campesino leader when he started, with extraordinary courage for standing up against the rich landowners and their gunmen."[36]

Signatories to the planteamiento from the capitalist sector were Gabriel A. Mejía, president of COHEP and the CCIC; Captain Armando San Martín, COHEP vice-president and godfather of one of Mejía's children; Rafael Pastor Zelaya, CCIC board member since 1963 and brother of the democratic leftist Rodolfo Pastor Zelaya; and Cesar A. Batres, National Party corporate lawyer, former president of the Asociación Nacional de Industriales, and legal adviser to COHEP. These men were not "radical capitalists" on a par with Edmond Bográn, Jaime Rosenthal, and others who had plotted the capital strike of 1968. Instead, they represented more reformist capitalists who had gradually shed their old ties to National Party politics, especially when they fell under the influence of Zúñiga Augustinus.[37]

Mejía and Pastor Zelaya, however, were obviously intimately connected with 1968 reformism generally, as both joined Céleo González and Gale Varela in establishing a first dialogue with López Arellano in the aftermath of the fraudulent municipal elections that year. Batres, as president of ANDI in 1968, had also supported the 1968 reformist dialogue that originated in San Pedro Sula. Captain San Martín's reformist credentials were established as early as 1956, when, like Mejía and the young López Arellano, he participated in the military coup that ousted National Party dictator Julio Lozano Díaz.[38]

The association of these personalities with the redemption of General López Arellano did not bode well for the National and Liberal Parties, both of which initially rejected the planteamiento. On the one hand, the general's break with Zúñiga Augustinus and his acceptance of the planteamiento meant that he had finally accommodated his San Pedro Sula critics at least as far back as the 1964–65 period. On the other hand, these actions also meant that he implicitly accepted San Pedro Sula's critique of mainstream liberalism as well. But why should he not do so? López Arellano recognized the political bankruptcy of both parties, for his own climb to power had been tied to the political ambitions of each party in 1957 and 1965.

How did other organized social sectors view the convergence between 1968 reformism and talks on the 1970 planteamiento? FENAGH resented its exclusion from the discussions but for the time being resigned itself to the outcome. Newly formed and as yet unregistered parties like the Partido de Inovación y Unidad and the Christian Democrats also were offended because they had been omitted. Of course, the latter organizations questioned the planteamiento on different grounds than FENAGH, especially the Christian Democrats. Their roots lay precisely in helping peasant organizations in Choluteca recover lands claimed by FENAGH. These parties' questions regarding the planteamiento paralleled other groups' concerns over their own exclusion from the reformist agenda, including students as well as Liberal and National party splinter groups.[39]

The Federación Central de Sindicatos de Trabajadores Libres de Honduras, FESITRANH's weaker counterpart in the interior and a member of the CTH, formally protested the "private" actions of Céleo González, Gale Varela, and Artiles. The CTH leaders later explained that they had not consulted the head of FECESITLIH, Gustavo Zelaya, because they needed to act quickly before liberals and nationalists assembled for their December conventions.[40] But González, Gale Varela, and Artiles probably knew that Zelaya was a Zúñiga Augustinus loyalist and that his formal inclusion in the talks might have helped Zúñiga Augustinus to obstruct the CTH-COHEP agenda. Moreover, González and Gale Varela recalled that the FECESITLIH had failed to mobilize in support of the FESITRANH's abortive strike of 1968 and that Zelaya's leadership at FECESITLIH had begun with a political maneuver dating back to the repressive year of 1965.[41]

FECESITLIH's resentment over the course of the CTH-COHEP planteamiento was less important than FENAGH's increasing perception that the leaders from the North Coast, organized manufacturing capitalists and workers alike, were bent on development at the expense of the land. To FENAGH, López Arellano's support of the 1970 planteamiento seemed to confirm that his personal redemption might be achieved at their expense, despite the fact that Honduran agrarian capitalism was actually registering its most important victories in decades. How could this be? Whatever answers FENAGH might have given to this question in 1970, in 1971 and 1972 it tried to break the alliance between the San Pedro Sula bourgeoisie, reformist labor, and López Arellano. FENAGH and its allies failed—if only temporarily.

## The Final Road to the Coup of 1972

On 7 January 1971, a few months before the March presidential election, General López Arellano finally announced the results of the planteamiento talks initiated in late December 1970. The Liberal and National Parties accepted the terms of the agreement, except that they wished to name more than one candidate for the presidency. The *Convenio Político*, as the formal accord was called, instead allowed both parties to offer candidates in the upcoming election. Despite this initial setback, the *Convenio* still required a future president to choose a cabinet from among social forces not formally associated with the two major political parties. It compelled the parties to choose Supreme Court justices from a list assembled by the Honduran Bar Association. And it obliged each party to compile a list of thirty-two candidates for deputies, and to establish a congressional leadership consisting of a seven-member board, with four of these deputies belonging to one party and the remaining three belonging to the other.[42]

More important, the *Convenio* stipulated a "minimum government program" that contained most reforms called for in the CTH *Llamamiento* and resolutions from the "Third Reunion of Honduras's *Fuerzas Vivas*." The major aspects of the projected government program included (1) a search for a solution to border disputes with El Salvador, (2) coordination among all social sectors in preparing and implementing a development plan, (3) following through on the Agrarian Reform Law, (4) respect for the Civil Service Law, (5) tax reform, and (6) restructuring the CACM. The elected president, the *Convenio* stated, assumed the responsibility of carrying out this "minimum program" as prepared by the Consejo Superior de Planificación Económica. Finally, CONSUPLANE would outline the "program" as a result of "close contact with the forces proposing the December 8 planteamiento and the political parties."[43]

The January-to-March campaign pitted old enemies from both parties against each other. The Liberal Party's candidate was Jorge Bueso Arias, a moderate. Bueso Arias was nonetheless not supported by the followers of Modesto Rodas Alvarado because they identified him, as well as one of his vice-presidential candidates, Dr. Rodolfo Pastor Zelaya, with the old democratic left.[44] Consequently, Rodas Alvarado encouraged liberals to abstain from voting for Bueso Arias, a situation that bitterly divided the party and did not help his candidacy. According to one of Bueso Arias's vice-presidential candidates, the party's "internal problems drained much of that year's political campaign."[45]

The National Party candidate, on the other hand, turned out to be Ramón Ernesto Cruz, a lawyer who was linked with the most conservative sectors of the party dating back to the repressive 1930s and 1940s. In 1963 he had emerged as a compromise presidential candidate, mainly to diffuse a bitter dispute between two nationalists Cruz had served well: former presidents General Tiburcio Carías Andino and Juan Manuel Gálvez. In 1971, recalled one of Cruz's vice-presidential candidates, Cruz was given the candidacy, by a Zúñiga Augustinus–controlled convention, mainly because, in case of a victory, Zúñiga Augustinus felt that he could then remain the power behind the throne, even without support from General López Arellano.[46]

Whatever the merits of either Bueso Arias or Cruz, leaders of both parties still seemed bent on maintaining their dominion over the political system irrespective of the *Convenio*. On 27 March 1971, the day before the election, liberals and nationalists violated the *Convenio* by formally agreeing to proportionally divide, among themselves only, appointments to the state's most important institutions. The parties even agreed to apportion diplomatic and consular posts. The victor gained the right to appoint ambassadors to Washington, the OAS, Guatemala, Spain, Colombia, Venezuela, Costa Rica, Peru, Germany, Nicaragua, Mexico and Argentina; the loser could name ambassadors to the United Nations, Chile, England, France, Panama, the Holy See, the Dominican Republic, Japan, Ecuador, and Italy.[47]

On 28 March Ramón Ernesto Cruz was elected president of Honduras. His victory originated with two different, but related processes from the 1960s. First, the Liberal Party's continued bitter divisions surely demoralized party loyalists.[48] Of course, much of this party anarchy had resulted from nationalist-inspired maneuvers to "constitutionalize" General López Arellano's coup in the aftermath of the 1963 revolt. What is more, one cannot separate the National Party's electoral strength in 1971 from its control of the state from late 1963 to 1971. Whatever López Arellano's change of mind after 1969, Cruz's assumption of power on 6 June 1971 in large part proceeded from the general's alliance with the nationalists after the coup of 1963.

Cruz's inauguration speech was memorable, for in a way he seemed to prophesy his own political death. He declared that he would prefer "to die a thousand times" rather than fail to comply with his oath before the people. Cruz was not the man for the office at the time, nor perhaps for any other time. Gabriel A. Mejía, who had known him for decades, recalled that Cruz was an indecisive man who had no "executive talent." General Carías himself admitted that Cruz was a talented jurist, but that "for President of the Republic he was no good."[49]

On the other hand, if Cruz's lack of political talent prevented him from serving the country, his personal deficiencies could be manipulated to serve the talents of others, especially the omnipotent power behind the National Party throne and the upcoming administration—Ricardo Zúñiga Augustinus. Worse, Zúñiga Augustinus secured an excellent cabinet post from which to encourage his political ambitions—the Ministry of the Interior. This ministry's responsibilities included providing (and, of course, withholding) funds to local governments, which used the money to ensure loyalty to the regime. National Party loyalists made much of this structure after the coup of 1963. After March 1971 Zúñiga Augustinus could surely do the same again, especially because the nationalists now dominated 188 municipalities and the liberals only 94.[50]

The events leading up to Cruz's overthrow in 1972 can be grouped around various axes of conflict, all of which made the president's indecisiveness a target for López Arellano's new allies and even their opponents. They included (1) the usual liberal-nationalist clashes, with Zúñiga Augustinus outmaneuvering President Cruz as a backdrop, (2) disputes over the representation of various factions in different business organizations, and (3) continuing strife pitting traditional landlords and the new rural bourgeoisie against peasants and workers in rural Honduras. These arenas of conflict became the battlegrounds in which urgent government policies were contested. The "urgent" government policies, in turn, remained those first clearly stated in the CTH *Llamamiento* of 1969 and incorporated in the *Convenio* of 1971. They ranged from "agrarian reform" and civil service reorganization to ways to deal with CACM imbalances. Cruz's failure to address these problems established the basis for his ouster.

These issues might not have brought Cruz down in another era. However, as this study has suggested, by the late 1960s and early 1970s Honduras's new capitalism had produced an array of social forces that, given their respective organized visions and demands, would not patiently allow oligarchs from either party to manipulate the political system at will. Cruz, to say nothing of Zúñiga Augustinus, did not seem to understand this. In fact, by 1972 Cruz openly declared that the "government is not responsible to the so-called 'pressure groups,'" especially the newly militant peasantry. Cruz largely abandoned agrarian reform and by default supported FENAGH.[51]

Cruz's other major problem involved the immediate consequences of the CACM's destruction and the failure to restructure it. More specifically, policies developed to deal with CACM contradictions represented another terrain for struggles between Tegucigalpa interests and those from San Pedro Sula, with the difference, of course, that in 1971 and 1972 General López Arellano sided with the North Coast. Moreover, as a result of his political ambitions, Zúñiga Augustinus became involved in manipulating the intracapital struggle for his own purposes. Only the 1972 coup put an end to these and other controversies. Throughout all this Cruz remained largely an observer, incapable, according to one of his vice-presidents, of controlling the machinations of Zúñiga Augustinus.[52]

Regional consultations on CACM problems after the Salvadoran war began in October 1969 and continued throughout the next year. These failed, and Honduras formally broke with the CACM in December 1970. A new economic policy established a "uniform external tariff for all imports of the country." With the Salvadoran border already closed, this policy further consolidated Honduras's withdrawal from the CACM. Though concerned with fiscal and balance of payment problems, the new policy was a blow to Honduran interests that profited most from the CACM—San Pedro Sula capitalists generally. On the other hand, industrialists and merchants who benefited less from economic integration *and* who remained suspicious of the North Coast's hegemonic aspirations praised the new economic approach, including members of ANDI, the CCIT, and the banker's association.[53]

Divisions between North Coast capitalists and their counterparts in the interior arose over tax reform and Cruz's handling of CACM policy, conflicts further inflamed by the intervention of Zúñiga Augustinus. In mid-November 1971 Fernando Lardizabal, a National Party chieftain and high FENAGH official, joined the president of ANDI, Adolfo Facussé, in publicly accusing Gabriel A. Mejía of misrepresenting COHEP's opposition to the tax reform. Although various Mejía allies supported the CCIC president, it was clear that the November incident represented the first salvo against Mejía's dominance of COHEP and hence of the North Coast.[54] This conflict deepened in 1972.

Dramatic events occurred in Tegucigalpa between 19 and 23 May 1972. On the twentieth *La Prensa* printed this headline: "Change of COHEP's Board of Directors." The same day *Diario Tiempo*, published by Edmond L. Bográn and Jaime Rosenthal, proclaimed: "COHEP's Administration Is Assaulted." What did this mean? It turned out that on 19 May ANDI and FENAGH officials convened an unauthorized COHEP General Assembly, nullified the board's bylaws, and appointed a new commission to represent COHEP at a 23 May *Convenio* meeting called to evaluate its administration.[55] These maneuvers represented *zuniguismo*'s efforts to retaliate against López Arellano and to obstruct the general's alliance with North Coast capital and labor.

The newly appointed COHEP commission included Fernando Lardizabal; Juan Kattan, president of ANDI; and Zacarías E. Bendeck, former president of ANDI and now a member of its Consultative Council. By 22 May Zúñiga Augustinus, as minister of the interior, approved the "new" COHEP bylaws. These actions in effect ousted Mejía from the COHEP presidency, as well as the commission he had appointed for the *Convenio* talks. Mejía challenged the minister's ploy in the liberal-controlled Supreme Court, where his decision to legalize the "second" COHEP was overturned. Meanwhile, General López Arellano asked the party commissions at the *Convenio*'s talks their opinion regarding which COHEP delegation to admit to the 23 May gathering. The liberals accepted both COHEP delegations, whereas the nationalists, not surprisingly, rejected the one led by Gabriel A. Mejía. López Arellano, as supreme arbitrator, admitted both delegations.[56]

The *Convenio* evaluation talks were a total failure. The discussions did not resolve the problems that had plunged the Cruz government into a crisis that was evident in late 1971. After the May discussions, liberals and nationalists continued to struggle over the apportionment of administrative posts agreed to in March 1971. As late as November 1972 CONSUPLANE had yet to present a National Development Plan for the 1972–77 period.[57] Indeed, by mid-1972 many Hondurans publicly debated the possibility of a coup, but one very different from the militarization imposed in 1963.[58]

In late November Juan Reyes Rodríguez of ANACH threatened to lead a "Hunger March" of thousands of Honduran peasants to Tegucigalpa if President Cruz did not immediately yield to ANACH's demands on the application of the 1962 Agrarian Reform Law. Cruz's response did not satisfy Reyes Rodríguez, and in early December thousands of peasants began mobilizing for the march to the capital. By this point, Oscar Gale Varela claimed later, he and General López Arellano had already discussed the "shape a future government should take."[59] On 4 December López Arellano ousted Cruz from the presidency and redeemed himself with the sponsors of reformism from the North Coast.

# CONCLUSION

Unlike the 1963 coup, the 1972 military intervention produced no bloodshed, no state of siege, no curfews, no exiles, and no imprisonments. On the contrary, it received widespread support from organized sectors of the working and peasant classes, groups targeted for repression in 1963. In fact, rather than an institutional alliance between the military and a political party, the new regime immediately mounted a direct attack on the traditional parties. Decree No. 3 of 6 December destroyed the parties' main source of revenues and loyalties because it declared that "voluntary contributions" from state employees to political parties were illegal.[1] The party oligarchs had institutionalized these so-called contributions as a means of recruiting and retaining supporters.

General Oswaldo López Arellano's new cabinet included interesting personalities, especially in key areas associated with economic and social policy. The Economics Ministry went to Abraham Bennaton Ramos. In addition to his paternal lineage from the British Bennaton émigrés to Cortés at the turn of the century, Bennaton Ramos offered impeccable technocratic credentials. He held a bachelor's degree in economics from Tegucigalpa's Universidad Nacional Autonoma de Honduras and a master's degree from the London School of Economics.[2]

The Ministry of Labor was entrusted to Gautama Fonseca, who was born and raised (1930s–1940s) in San Pedro Sula. In the 1950s he earned a law degree and became a militant member of the Liberal Party's left wing. Indeed, in 1956 a U.S. intelligence report identified Fonseca as a "vociferous university leader" who was arrested in July 1956 by the Lozano Díaz dictatorship. In the 1960s he served as legal counsel to the Secretariat for Central American Economic Integration. His public sympathy with the modernizing forces in San Pedro Sula, as well as his democratic leftist leanings, dated from at least 1967, when Edmond L. Bográn, Oscar Gale Varela, Céleo González, and others met to establish the ill-fated "center for the study of national problems."[3]

Perhaps the most conspicuous members of the cabinet announced in 1972 were Dr. Enrique Aguilar Paz as Minister of Health and Miguel Angel Rivera as Minister of Communications and Public Works.[4] To liberals and particularly nationalists, the presence of Aguilar Paz and Rivera in the cabinet must have been a bitter pill to swallow. First of all, since early 1970 Aguilar Paz and Rivera had been founding members of the newly established Partido de Inovación y Unidad, a reformist, social democratic group headed by Dr. Miguel Andonie Fernández. As late as November 1972, Andonie Fernández, an important investor in television and radio broadcasting stations, recalled how National Party lawyers had tried to block PINU's legal registration in the National Electoral Commission.[5]

Miguel Angel Rivera's inclusion in the López Arellano cabinet of 1972 surely meant that the military chieftain was now poised to break completely with the morass into which his alliance with the National Party had plunged the country after 1965. Rivera's special place in San Pedro Sula–based reformism in the mid-1960s originated with his authorship in May 1967 of the Rivera Report, the memorandum for which López Arellano fired him from his position as executive secretary of the Consejo Superior de Planificación Económica. It is important to note that in late 1967 Rivera had assumed a post in the Provisional Organizing Committee of Bográn's projected San Pedro Sula think tank. In short, his presence in the cabinet fulfilled the hopes of many Hondurans, who, like Ramón Oquelí, an astute political commentator of the period, wished that the Rivera Report might signal the start of a "national campaign" to address the "disaster" in which the country then found itself.[6]

Three weeks after López Arellano ousted President Cruz from office, his military government decreed special and urgent agrarian legislation. Decree No. 8 of 26 December 1972 forced landowners to rent peasants uncultivated land. By 1 January 1973, López Arellano announced a major reformist agenda that proposed a new Plan of Agrarian Reform but that also incorporated many of the reformist provisions stated in the CTH *Llamamiento* of 1969 and others suggested by CCIC leaders beginning in 1966. Nonetheless, the main project of the new government centered around agrarian reform, ostensibly to deal with the problems of the impoverished, "marginalized" peasant masses. From the outset, the Federación Nacional de Agricultores y Ganaderos de Honduras mounted a fierce opposition to Decree No. 8.[7] Moreover, by this time the

Consejo Hondureño de la Empresa Privada had fallen under the direction of FENAGH sympathizers generally as well as Tegucigalpa-based merchants and industrialists. By 1975 these sectors would recover their strength, forge a counterreformist alliance with military elements opposed to López Arellano, and overthrow the now reformist general in a coup.

What are we to make of the presence of Rivera and the other conspicuous figures in the December 1972 cabinet and General López Arellano's support of agrarian reform? Is there a historical relationship between 1967 San Pedro Sula reformism, the confrontation over the San José Protocol in 1968, the Honduras–El Salvador War in 1969, and the reformist potential of the 1972 coup? Did the empowerment of Rivera and other progressive capitalists and technocrats via the coup of 1972 reflect the empowerment of an "emerging industrial national bourgeoisie" based in San Pedro Sula? What role did North Coast labor play in this scenario?

Had López Arellano now, perhaps imitating Generals Omar Torrijos in Panama and Juan Velasco Alvarado in Peru, hatched a deal with his North Coast critics of 1967 and 1968? In the case of Peru, recall that on 3 October 1968 the Peruvian military ousted President Fernando Belaunde Terry. By 1972 General Velasco had consolidated power and projected a radical transformation of Peruvian society. In the same year his regime undertook a major agrarian reform and in the process expropriated significant U.S. investments. Velasco also attacked the relevance of Peru's traditional politics and "the oligarchy."[8]

Perhaps of greater relevance here is the fact that on 11 October 1968 the Panamanian military deposed President Arnulfo Arias. By late 1969 General Omar Torrijos with the Panamanian Defense Forces embarked on a course of nationalist reformism that displaced traditional politicians—oligarchs, CTH leaders might have called them—and entrenched elites. These events had a great influence had on López Arellano's reformist thinking, although this was little known at the time. Indeed, an associate of Torrijos wrote in his memoirs that in 1972 López Arellano personally told him about the "landlords that wanted to block the agrarian reform."[9]

In this context, to what extent can the origins of the 1972 López Arellano–North Coast axis be explained by the history of regional class formation outlined in this study? In May 1973, about six months after López Arellano returned to power and well after the new regime had committed the state to a reformist mission that in many ways paralleled the Panamanian and Peruvian experiences, the general secretary of the Honduran Communist Party claimed that "the industrial bourgeoisie of San Pedro Sula was actively involved in the preparations to overthrow the Cruz government [in 1972]."[10] Was the San Pedro Sula industrial bourgeoisie been "actively involved" in preparing the coup? If so, did post–December 1972 reformism imply that Honduran capitalism had finally produced a "national bourgeoisie" a la the old Comintern's projections? Had the reformism of 1967 and 1968 been transformed into a business class-based revolutionary and anti-imperialist agenda?[11] And how can this view be reconciled with the leading role of North Coast labor in the CTH's formulation of the 1969 *Llamamiento*?

The coup of 1972 did not empower a San Pedro Sula–based national industrial bourgeoisie. Rather, López Arellano's coup empowered the agenda, or the vision, espoused by a national industrial bourgeoisie and labor as these sectors developed on the North Coast. Although the reformism of 1972–75 was central to Honduran political stability in the 1980s, that reformism must be understood in terms of the history of the Honduran North Coast in the first half of the twentieth century. Too often the historiography and general commentary dismiss the region as merely a big *plantation* of the imperialist banana companies. This view fails to scrutinize the economic, social, and political history of the North Coast. Thus, in the process of examining these factors, the present study has reinterpreted modern Honduran history.

Donald E. Schulz and Deborah Sundloff Schulz's recent monograph on the "exceptionality" of Honduran political stability in the 1980s is a major and welcomed contribution to the scholarly literature on contemporary Honduras. Unfortunately, it draws too heavily on the traditional historiography and therefore repeats most of its problems. For example, whereas the present study disputes that an oligarchy dominated modern Honduran history, the Schulzes' monograph is replete with references to "traditional" and "backward" oligarchs, even while recognizing the absence of a " 'banana oligarchy' comparable to the coffee elites in El Salvador and Guatemala."[12]

The Schulzes explain Honduran stability in the 1980s by linking the comparative restraint on the use of violence by Honduran civilian and military elites to the country's "dominant political culture."[13] By the 1970s and 1980s that culture had produced a political system that allowed for cyclical processes of reform and reaction, including the land reform decrees of the López Arellano regime after 1972 and their demise after 1975. Also, the Schulzes emphasize that the "early legalization of unions" in the 1950s and "the introduction of agrarian reform" in 1962 indicate that this political system existed.

What is more, the military elites were "not under the thumb of the rural oligarchy." Instead, until the 1956 coup the "military had served as an appendage of whatever political party or faction happened to be in power."[14] Presumably, then, the political culture did not suffer from the widespread state-sponsored military terrorism more often deployed against reformist movements elsewhere in Central America. This is not to say that the Schulzes disregard the key instances of military-sponsored repression; rather, they suggest that its comparative absence and lack of intensity confirm the existence of substantive periods of reform allowed by the political system.

Many elements in their analysis parallel issues addressed in the present monograph. The crucial difference, however, is that in this study the genesis of the "dominant political culture" is situated in a particular period in Honduran history, the 1870s to the 1930s, and in a precise region, the North Coast, especially its nexus to the history of San Pedro Sula capital and labor. Although the Schulzes raise major issues relating to North Coast modernization, their dismissal of the Sula Valley as primarily a "Cuyamel fiefdom" disregards the particular conditions that, simultaneous to banana-led modernization, produced a regional reformist political culture long before the post–World War II period.[15]

The first three chapters of this book detailed key processes and events that are relevant to this study's alternative interpretation. Chapter 1 showed how historical processes linked to North Coast development, railroad construction, and banana cultivation in the 1860s and 1870s, prior to the liberal reformers' efforts to establish a coffee-exporting state, doomed the project, which succeeded elsewhere in the region. Moreover, this postindependence development combined with the colonial history of Tegucigalpa, particularly its silver interests, in ways that made state evolution very different from the "coffee township" scenario posited by Robert G. Williams for other countries in Central America.[16] In short, the fate of coffee in Honduras was to be caught between silver and banana exports.

Various authors have addressed the mining-merchant interests associated with the establishment and early evolution of the Honduran state after 1876. Juan Arancibia Cordova tentatively suggested that the "reformers [of the 1870s and early 1880s] seemed to have represented a *comprador* mining-merchant bourgeoisie, that took over the state and tried to make it national and use it to promote its own wealth." Guillermo Molina Chocano, one of the main commentators on the period, long ago argued that "the new mining cycle [in the 1880s], inscribed in the country's mining tradition, was presided over by a small sector of domestic owners associated with foreign investors."[17]

What is more—and this is the key issue—this mining-merchant bourgeoisie, unlike the coffee patriarchs in Santa Bárbara and Choluteca, many of whom migrated to San Pedro Sula, did not have to establish cross-regional municipal alliances before controlling the Reforma state. The mining-merchant circuit turned on the bullion wealth of Tegucigalpa and its environs, which, in turn, enjoyed a rich colonial history that seems to have been reproduced in the nineteenth century prior to the institutionalization of the Liberal Reforma. President Marco Aurelio Soto transferred the "state" there in 1880 not only because he and his cabinet enjoyed shares in new mining ventures with the

Valentine family. Tegucigalpa's struggle against Comayagua went back to the eighteenth century.[18] The establishment of the state in Tegucigalpa allowed its elites, many of them descendants from the colonial period, to link municipal power and resources with the "national" state.[19]

Therefore, the Reforma leaders' concern with export agriculture remained marginal to their principal interest in mining, particularly given the difficulties inherited with the massive foreign debt incurred by the Interoceanic Railroad project. Further, the intimate relationships between some Honduran elites embroiled in the railroad debacle and the resurgent investment in mining in the 1880s suggest that the new power holders' preoccupation with enrichment left little room for promoting a national state based on agricultural exports that they controlled. A case in point was General Enrique Gutiérrez, owner of the mine later exploited by the New York and Honduras Rosario Mining Company.[20]

General Gutiérrez was the brother of Carlos Gutiérrez (1818–1892), who was authorized in the 1860s and early 1870s to contract the loans to build the frustrated Interoceanic Railroad. Briefly in 1883, when Soto was forced to resign the presidency, General Gutiérrez presided over a Council of Ministers that included General Luis Bográn, Honduras's "only coffee growing president" and whom Soto had made governor of Santa Bárbara in 1877. General Gutiérrez died while in charge of the council, and Bográn became president (1883–91). By 1889 Bográn's commitment to the mining circuit led him to investments in the Banco de Honduras, the mining bourgeoisie's financial success.[21]

After the 1890s, as indicated in Chapter 2, members of the Bográn clan became coinvestors with Samuel Zemurray in the Sula Valley. In short, Honduran elite-based coffee production in the nineteenth century succumbed to the interests of regional elites caught between the legacy and potential of silver exports and the promise of banana cultivation and exports.[22] Moreover, the victory of banana production seems to have enjoyed kinship ties that connected the old mining elite with the commercial and industrial bourgeoisie that became prominent on the North Coast. For example, General Gutiérrez's daughter Emma married Policarpo Bonilla, president of Honduras from 1894 to 1899. One of their granddaughters married none other than Jorge Bueso Arias, a scion of a clan connected with San Pedro Sula economic growth since the 1880s, the finance minister (1959–63) of President Ramón Villeda Morales, and the Liberal Party's presidential candidate in 1971.

Nonetheless, despite the continuity of kinship ties between Tegucigalpa mining elites and North Coast industrialists that Jorge Bueso Arias's life might suggest, the argument here is that the regional histories of the interior and the North Coast superseded elite family alliances in their respective impact on state evolution and national political history. Future research into kinship ties and dominant elites might change this scenario, but the data now suggest otherwise.[23] Thus, for most of the twentieth century the North Coast bourgeoisie was a very different animal than its counterpart in Tegucigalpa and in the interior overall, a differentiation that in large part was associated with the nature of banana cultivation and export in the Sula Valley.

Chapters 2 and 3 demonstrated that the Sula Valley was more than just a fiefdom of Samuel Zemurray and the Cuyamel Fruit Company. The same was true of the North Coast as a whole. Chapter 2 established that a strong, if immigrant-controlled, commercial and industrial sector emerged in San Pedro Sula that differentiated its urbanization from anywhere else in Honduras. Chapter 3 showed that although their success depended on a healthy banana-exporting economy, the region's commercial and industrial elites cultivated a political independence that separated them from the political intrigue in Tegucigalpa. By the 1960s, according to the later chapters of this book, the descendants of this regional bourgeoisie challenged the dominant political culture of Tegucigalpa and the interior.

On the other hand, the North Coast bourgeoisie did not emerge and act alone. We saw in Chapters 2 and 3 that in the 1920s San Pedro Sula became a hotbed of reformists and radical militants committed to organizing banana plantation workers throughout the North Coast. Indeed, the difference between the sentiments of the National and Liberal Parties after 1919 was based in large part on "the social question" posed by the working people of the North Coast. By the 1930s the Liberal Party's earlier programmatic appeal to labor, via the Convention of 1920, led to direct campaigning among the region's workers. The 1954 strike, which the Schulzes recognize as central to their analysis, originated not only with the deplorable labor conditions, but also with the legacy of resistance established in the 1920s and early 1930s.

The agrarian reform of 1962, again, considered central to the Schulzes' argument, cannot be understood outside the specific history of the North Coast before the 1960s. The fact is that militant efforts to push agrarian reform began in and near the Sula Valley, indeed on lands once owned by associates of Samuel Zemurray. The Asociación Nacional de Campesinos de Honduras was organized there not only to realize the aspirations of landless peasants but also to simultaneously obstruct organizing efforts by communist workers once employed by the banana companies and fired after 1954. The militant peasant movement that materialized in the southern departments of Choluteca and Valle benefited from the experiences and economic resources of the organization that formally represented labor in San Pedro Sula and elsewhere on the North Coast—namely, the Federación Sindical de Trabajores Norteños de Honduras.

Whereas Chapter 6 described the origins and aftermath of the 1954 strike, Chapters 8 and 9 showed that the North Coast labor leaders often worked in tandem with the most progressive capitalists that led the Cámara de Comercio e Industrias de Cortés in the 1960s and early 1970s. Although the progressive generation active in the 1960s drew on the reformist culture peculiar to the North Coast, Chapters 4 and 5 demonstrated that the militancy of the San Pedro Sula bourgeoisie also intensified in the context of the vibrant post–World War II economic recovery and in the industrial diversification and intensification in the Sula Valley. Macroeconomic statistics usually marginalize this regional aspect of Honduras's capitalist transition after the war.

The Schulzes' account of the development of a national bourgeoisie in Honduras unfortunately assumes a homogeneous capitalism. Their account of the 1956 military coup is indicative of this problem. In their perspective, the 1956 coup was primarily the result of accelerated institutional development promoted under President Manuel Gálvez's administration, including new military assistance treaties with the United States.[24] However, Chapter 4 in this study revealed that important personalities intimately associated with San Pedro Sula commercial and industrial capitalism, Gabriel A. Mejía and Jorge Bueso Arias in particular, played central roles in the 1956 coup, as well as in the social and economic policies decreed during the military government of 1956–57.

Similarly, the Schulzes' discussion of the 1960s period, including the crucial coup of 1963, remains mired in the traditional historiography. In Chapter 7 of this book, that period receives a different interpretation, again originating with past events in San Pedro Sula and on the North Coast. As most other historians, the Schulzes explain the 1963 coup by López Arellano as a reaction against peasant militancy, an effort to arrest Rodas Alvarado's presidential ambitions in the election of October 1963, and a bid to consolidate military autonomy against an assertive Liberal Party.

Although the present interpretation does not discount these factors, it sees the 1963 coup as the first confrontation between the Tegucigalpa political system and the political culture and ambitions of the North Coast bourgeoisie and labor. The individuals associated with the most militant resistance to the 1965 constitutionalization of the López Arellano regime were from the North Coast, especially San Pedro Sula.[25] The organizational expressions of this resistance were the CCIC, the FESITRANH, and the newspaper *La Prensa*. Among the influential figures associated with these organizations were Gabriel A. Mejía, Dr. Rodolfo Pastor Zelaya, Edmond L. Bográn, Oscar Gale Varela, and Céleo González. The road to military reformism between 1968 and 1972 was paved by these personalities, their constituencies, and the political culture of the Honduran North Coast, as outlined in Chapters 8 and 9.

Yet the triumph of North Coast social, economic, and political ambitions in 1972 did not herald the complete destruction of the old system. The difficulties that López Arellano and his loyalists confronted after 1973 showed that Honduras's continuing capitalist transition, especially in the agrarian sphere, also reconstituted older economic power blocs that CACM industrialization did not break down. FENAGH militancy in the 1960s and 1970s expressed the emergence in Honduras of a formidable agro-export bourgeoisie in the once coffee-rich areas of Choluteca.[26] The dramas and peculiar politics of the 1980s that the Schulzes analyze so well have their origins in these other processes.

The major assumption underlying the projected agrarian legislation of 1973 was that peasant poverty, and hence mobilizations in the 1960s, resulted from "rural backwardness" and "non-integration" into "the modern economy." Instead, the opposite was the case. Peasant discontent and militancy in the 1960s surfaced precisely in the areas where agrarian capitalism had been registering its greatest success, in the southern departments of Choluteca and Valle.[27] On the other hand, the difference in the historical origins of Honduras's new agrarian bourgeoisie in the Central American context itself sheds light on the peculiar militancy of the San Pedro Sula bourgeoisie and labor in the 1960s.

The prominent Central American sociologist Edelberto Torres-Rivas has argued that after the 1950s the region's "old oligarchy gave way to a modern agro-exporting bourgeoisie." But Torres-Rivas also makes the critical point that the old oligarchies, especially the coffee-based ruling classes of El Salvador and Guatemala, did not "disappear." Rather, "the dominant class modified itself slightly. What occurred was an internal restructuring—both slow and painful—that transformed the old landlord-capitalist into a capitalist-landlord."[28] This analysis is generally correct for Guatemala, El Salvador, and Costa Rica, although in Costa Rica with different political implications. The Honduran case does not "fit" the Torres-Rivas vision.

As this study has shown, particularly in Chapter 8, the Honduran agrarian bourgeoisie of the late 1950s and 1960s did not result from "an internal restructuring" of an old "oligarchy." Indeed, FENAGH's hostility to redistributive agrarian reform expressed the worries not of a reconstituted, "classical" Central American oligarchy, but of a new rural bourgeoisie closely allied with foreign capital. What is more, this relationship, mainly in the cases of cotton, sugar, and beef, remained intertwined with a commercial-industrial group associated with the Standard Fruit Company since the 1950s. Whatever tolerance imperial capitalists, as well as the U.S. embassy, showed visionaries like Rodolfo Pastor Zelaya, Edmond L. Bográn, Jaime Rosenthal Oliva, and others in the 1960s did not continue after 1972.

The upsurge of CACM industrialization encouraged a commercial-industrial bourgeois and labor militancy in the 1960s based in San Pedro Sula. However, the simultaneous restructuring of this commercial-industrial bourgeoisie into an agrarian bourgeoisie also associated with foreign capitalists left the visionaries of the strongest manufacturing sector of the class—men like Edmond Bográn—isolated and open to attack. Thus the coup of 1972 empowered aspects of Bográn and the bourgeoisie's vision and program, but not their historical actors as "a class." That potentiality died in September 1968 because of the peculiarities of twentieth-century Honduran history in the context of peripheral capitalism: from Honduras's integration into the world economy via banana exports to the consequent character of bourgeois class and labor formation on the North Coast generally and in San Pedro Sula in particular. On the other hand, the victories of North Coast reformism, in many ways a broad "social movement," bestowed on modern Honduran history social and political legacies that scholars and activists too often marginalize.[29]

# NOTES

## Abbreviations Used in the Notes

| | |
|---|---|
| AGAS | Asociación de Ganaderos y Agricultores Sula |
| BCIE | Bank for Central American Economic Integration (Tegucigalpa) |
| *BSFOA* | *Boletín de la Secretaría de Fomento, Agricultura y Obras Públicas* |
| CCA | Cámara de Comercio de Atlántida (La Ceiba) |
| CCH | Cámara de Comercio de Honduras (Tegucigalpa) |
| CCIC | Cámara de Comercio e Industrias de Cortés (San Pedro Sula) |
| CCIT | Cámara de Comercio e Industrias de Tegucigalpa |
| CDSPS | Consejo del Distrito Departamental de San Pedro Sula |
| CIA | U.S. Central Intelligence Agency |
| DGEC | Dirección General de Estadística y Censos |
| DPAGR | Documentos Privados del Ingeniero Don Amílcar Gómez Robelo (1944–48) |
| DPRLP | Documentos Privados del Ingeniero Don Rafael López Padilla (1923–62) |
| EDUCA | Editorial de la Universidad de Costa Rica |
| *IFAT* | *Informe del Ministerio de Fomento, Agricultura y Trabajo* |
| *IFATC* | *Informe del Ministerio de Fomento, Agricultura, Trabajo y Comercio* |
| *IHCPC* | *Informe del Ministerio de Hacienda, Crédito Público y Comercio* |
| *IMA* | *Informe del Ministerio de Agricultura* |
| *LAC* | *Libros de Actas de las Sesiones del Consejo del Distrito Departamental de San Pedro Sula* |
| *LAM* | *Libros de las Actas de las Sesiones de la Corporación Municipal de San Pedro Sula* |
| MCCIC | Memorias de la Labor Desarrollada por la Cámara de Comercio e Industrias de Cortés durante los Años 1964 a 1972 |
| *MBCH* | *Memoria del Banco Central de Honduras* |
| *MEH* | *Memoria del Ministerio de Economía y Hacienda* |
| *MFA* | *Memoria del Ministerio de Fomento y Agricultura* |
| *MFO* | *Memoria del Ministerio de Fomento y Obras Públicas* |
| *MFOA* | *Memoria del Ministerio de Fomento, Obras Públicas y Agricultura* |
| *MFOAT* | *Memoria del Ministerio de Fomento, Obras Públicas, Agricultura y Trabajo* |
| *MHCP* | *Memoria del Ministerio de Hacienda y Crédito Público* |
| *MHCPC* | *Memoria del Ministerio de Hacienda, Crédito Público y Comercio* |
| NA | National Archives, Washington, D.C. |
| RG | Record Group |

| | |
|---|---|
| RMC | Registro Mercantil de Cortés, San Pedro Sula |
| TIPN | Tipografía Nacional |
| UNAH | Universidad Nacional Autónoma de Honduras |

## INTRODUCTION

1. Medea Benjamin, introduction to Elvia Alvarado, *Don't Be Afraid Gringo*, p. xvi (quotation). The literature is discussed in Euraque, "La 'Reforma Liberal,'" pp. 7–11.

2. Guevara-Escudero, "Nineteenth-Century Honduras," p. 117 (quotation). The most sustained discussion of a Honduran "culture of poverty" originating in the colonial period is available in Marvin A. Barahona's excellent book, *Evolución Histórica de la Identidad Nacional*, pp. 193–222.

3. Stokes, *Honduras*, p. 24.

4. Cardoso, "The Liberal Era"; Acuña, "Las Repúblicas Agroexportadoras."

5. Torres-Rivas, *Interpretación del Desarrollo Social Centroamericano*, pp. 70–73, 90–95. His classic text is now available in English; see Torres-Rivas, *History and Society in Central America* (Austin: University of Texas Press, 1993).

6. Pérez Brignoli, "Economía y Sociedad en Honduras." A contemporary analysis similar to Pérez Brignoli's account, but originating in a different theoretical tradition, is Brand's "Background of Capitalist Underdevelopment," pp. 2–4, 114, 188–89.

7. The most recent and most systematic account that assumes most of this perspective is Schulz and Schulz, *The United States, Honduras*.

8. The notion of an absent oligarchy in Honduras is mentioned in a rich comparative essay by Gudmundson, "Lord and Peasant in the Making of Modern Central America," pp. 166–68. Some of Torres-Rivas's incisive essays of the 1970s and 1980s are available in English in his *Repression and Resistance*.

9. Woodward, "Historiography of Modern Central America," p. 469. Some of Pérez Brignoli's findings appear in his *Brief History of Central America*, pp. 88, 146.

10. Mörner, *Region and State in Latin America's Past*, pp. 9–18; Roseberry, "Beyond the Agrarian Question," p. 346.

11. The study is in many ways a response to Robert G. Williams's call for a reexamination of the history of banana cultivation in Central America within his broader concern for theorizing social evolution and state formation in the region. See Williams, *States and Social Evolution*, p. 326 n. 1.

12. The existing historiography frequently recognizes the "weak" state associated with the banana enclave in Honduras, but it fails to take the region's history seriously. See, for example, Weaver, *Inside the Volcano*, pp. 100–102.

13. The historical analysis offered here complements the work of Sieder, "Honduras."

14. Consult Eduardo Baumeister's contribution in Samper and Peréz Brignoli, *Tierra, Café y Sociedad*.

15. Ropp, "Teorías sobre el Comportamiento de los Militares Centroamericanos," p. 420. I thank Professor Ropp for pointing me to this article.

16. This followed the pattern elsewhere in Latin America. Roxborough, "Labor Control."

17. One scholar has seriously explored the implications of the 1954 strike for national political development. See Echeverri-Gent, "Labor, Class, and Political Representation."

18. Bergquist, *Labor in Latin America*; Collier and Collier, *Shaping the Political Arena*.

19. On caudillo politics in Latin America, see Hamill's introduction to his *Caudillos*, pp. 3–24. After Stokes's classic work and before the Schulz and Schulz volume, Morris's *Honduras* was the most comprehensive scholarly approach to twentieth-century Honduran history appearing in English. That volume, Morris suggested, then represented "the first comprehensive study of Honduras to be published (in English) since that of Stokes" (preface). Unfortunately, his interesting monograph remained too closely associated with the traditional views of the North Coast as "an 'enclave' society" (p. 7).

20. Schulz and Schulz, *The United States, Honduras*, p. 315.

## Chapter 1

1. Hobsbawm, *Nations and Nationalism*, p. 9.

2. Guevara-Escudero, "Nineteenth-Century Honduras," p. 84; Newson, *Cost of Conquest*, p. 330; Newson, *Cost of Conquest*, p. 330. Racial and ethnic classifications are tentatively explored in Euraque, "Labor Recruitment and Class Formation.

3. Towsend Ezcurra, *Las Provincias Unidas*, p. 21.

4. Benedict Anderson, *Imagined Communities*, pp. 50–65.

5. Calculated from "Presidents, 1824–1949, and Date of Assumption of Power" in Stokes, *Honduras*, pp. 329–30.

6. Fernández Molina, "Coloring the World in Blue," pp. 404–59.

7. Robert S. Smith, "Financing the Central American Federation," p. 486; Marichal, *A Century of Debt Crises*, pp. 43–67.

8. Guevara-Escudero, "Nineteenth-Century Honduras," pp. 236–96.

9. Frye, 20 July 1877, dispatch 67, Omoa, Dispatches from U.S. Consuls in Omoa, Trujillo, and Roatán, 1818–93, microfilm T-477, reel 4, RG 59, NA; "La Nueva Era," in Carías, *Ramón Rosa*, pp. 171–74. On Rosa's connection to the process of national imaginings in Guatemala, see Palmer, "A Liberal Discipline," p. 105.

10. The remainder of this chapter draws substantially from Euraque, "La 'Reforma Liberal.' "

11. Molina Chocano, *Estado Liberal y Desarrollo Capitalista*, pp. 39–43; K. Lendas, 27 September 1879, dispatch 21, Omoa, microfilm T-477, reel 4, RG 59, NA; *LAM* 8, 23 July 1898, pp. 252–53.

12. Marta R. Argueta, *Biografía Intelectual de Ramón Rosa*, pp. 105–9; Ministerio de Hacienda, "Tesorería de Caminos," *MHCP, 1908–1909*, pp. 14–15; Ministerio de Fomento, "Tesorería General de Caminos," *MFA, 1917–1918*, pp. 9–13; República de Honduras, "Informe del Director General de Caminos," *MFOAT, 1928–1929*, pp. 49–85. The state's financial crisis is discussed later in this chapter.

13. Delmer G. Ross, "Construction of the Railroads of Central America," pp. 27–42, 113–69; Marichal, *A Century of Debt Crises*, p. 117.

14. Yeager, "The Honduran Foreign Debt," pp. 229 (quotation), 309.

15. Reina Valenzuela and Argueta, *Marco Aurelio Soto*, pp. 155–58; Finney, "Our Man In Honduras," p. 13.

16. The fate of these products is detailed in Euraque, "La 'Reforma Liberal,'" pp. 17–27.

17. "Situación de la Agricultura del País" (p. 190) and "Francisco Morazán" (pp. 358–98), in Carías, *Ramón Rosa*; Molina Chocano, "La Formación del Estado," p. 63.

18. Schoonover and Schoonover, "Statistics for an Understanding of Foreign Intrusions into Central America," p. 101.

19. Hill, "Economic Factors in Central America," p. 241; Laínez and Meza, "El Enclave Bananero," p. 145.

20. Meza and López, "Las Inversiones Extranjeras," p. 56; Finney, "Precious Metals Mining," pp. 345–47. Officials established a tax on mining profits only in 1937. Meza and López, "Las Inversiones Extranjeras," pp. 56–57.

21. Vélez O. and Herrera, "Historia," pp. 85–114.

22. "Participation of the Chief Products," *Revista Económica*, no. 5 (March 1922): 357; Villanueva, "Institutional Innovation and Economic Development," p. 32; Ministerio de Hacienda, "De los Productos del País que Más Se Exportan. . . . [1925–26, 1935–36]," in *MHCPC, 1932–1933*, pp. 25–28, and *MHCPC, 1935–1936*, pp. 80–83. Also see Márquez et al., *Estudio sobre la Economía*, p. 36. Honduras's mining industry gets a serious comparative look in Araya Pochet, "El Enclave Minero en Centroamérica."

23. Laínez and Meza, "El Enclave Bananero," p. 144.

24. Finney, "Washington S. Valentine: The Yankee Who 'Bought' Honduras," p. 3. I thank Professor Finney for making his unpublished papers available to me.

25. "W. S. Valentine Dies in Atlantic City," *New York Times*, 18 March 1920.

26. "El Muelle de Puerto Cortés," *BSFOA*, no. 2 (February 1913): 63–66; Cruz Caceres, *En las Selvas Hondureñas*, pp. 91–92; Karnes, *Tropical Enterprise*, pp. 93–94; Ministerio de Hacienda, *MHCP, 1946–1947*, pp. 121–22.

27. Kepner and Soothill, *Banana Empire*, pp. 100–101; Pan American Union, "Honduras," p. 315; Ministerio de Fomento, "Ferrocarril de la Cuyamel Fruit Co.," *MFOA, 1913–1914*, pp. 11–15.

28. McCann, *On the Inside*, p. 19 (quotation); Whitfield, "Strange Fruit," p. 309.

29. Brand, "Background of Capitalistic Underdevelopment," p. 259 n. 610. Also see Millorn, "Loan War," pp. 44–76.

30. The most complete account of Zemurray and Manuel Bonilla's relations appears in Langley and Schoonover, *Banana Men*.

31. República de Honduras, *Indice General de Concesiones*, pp. 7–12.

32. Euraque, "Los Recursos Económicos."

33. Rovelo Landa, "Nuestra Situación Económica: Concesiones I" and "Nuestra Situación Económica: Concesiones II."

34. Noé Pino, "Structural Roots of Crisis," p. 41; Guevara-Escudero, "Nineteenth-Century Honduras," pp. 54–60.

35. Williams, *States and Social Evolution*.

36. Ibid., p. 226.

37. Ibid., p. 232.

38. Ibid., pp. 210, 324 n. 22.

39. Ibid., p. 97.

40. Young Honduran scholars have offered some evidence on the question. José S. Barahona G. et al., "La Evolución."

41. Williams, *States and Social Evolution*, pp. 211, 219.

42. Ibid., p. 324 n. 22. Also see Weaver, *Inside the Volcano*, pp. 100–102.

43. Ibid., p. 92.

44. Ibid., p. 185.

45. Molina Chocano, "La Formación del Estado"; Vélez O. and Herrera, "Historia," pp. 115–79.

46. Brand, "Background of Capitalistic Underdevelopment," pp. 80, 237 n. 364; Davis, "Agrarian Structure and Ethnic Resistance."

47. Brand, "Background of Capitalistic Underdevelopment," p. 242 n. 414.

48. Williams, *States and Social Evolution*, p. 211.

49. "La Pujanza Económica de Nuestro Departamento," *Boletín*, CDSPS, no. 71, 9 December 1950; *LAC* 41, 1 December 1950, p. 228.

50. This section draws substantially from Euraque, "Zonas Regionales en la Formación del Estado Hondureño."

51. Guevara-Escudero, "Nineteenth-Century Honduras," p. 91.

52. Wilkie, *Latin American Population*, pp. 4–5.

53. For suggestive data from the nineteenth century that use a *Registro de Abogados* and complement the information provided in this study, see Brand, "Background of Capitalistic Underdevelopment," pp. 46–48.

54. Ministerio de Fomento, "Industrias," *IFATC, 1936–1937* (pp. 65–76), *1937–1938* (pp. 40–45); *IFAT, 1938–1939* (pp. 37–48), *1940–1941* (pp. 43–55), *1941–1942* (pp. 45–60), *1943–1944* (pp. 75–97), *1944–1945* (pp. 90–108), *1945–1946* (pp. 81–89), *1948–1949* (pp. 120–30), *1949–1950* (pp. 106–15), *1950–1951* (pp. clxx–clxxxiv), *1951–1952* (pp. 176–87); *IMA, 1952–1953*, pp. 113–32.

55. Rietti, "Diagnóstico de la Industria Manufacturera Hondureña," p. 14. Bulmer-Thomas (*Political Economy of Central America*, p. 119), in summarizing the Industrial Census for 1950, shows 19,556 employees in the "industrial sector." This figure undoubtedly combines artisan- and factory-based manufacturing, as data for the 1960s, the period of greatest manufacturing growth, indicate factory-based manufacturing employment of 14,000–15,000 workers, figures that usually accounted for probably 30 percent of industrial employment. Therefore, the 1950 factory workforce probably amounted to about 5,800, which is closer to my estimate for that period. Industrial censuses distinguish factory and artisan production by the number of workers employed by a manufacturing concern. "Factories" included five or more workers, whereas "artisan workshops" employed less than five workers. The 1950 census indicated that 98 percent of industrial establishments in Honduras employed less than five workers. Mondragón Carrasco, "Naturaleza y Desarrollo de la Industria en Honduras," p. 19.

## CHAPTER 2

1. This chapter draws substantially from Euraque, "San Pedro Sula" and "Modernity, Economic Power."

2. Pineda Portillo, *Geografía*, pp. 59–70.

3. Ibid.

4. Newson, *Cost of Conquest*, p. 330.

5. Pastor Fasquelle, *Biografía*, p. 177.

6. Ibid., pp. 137–39; Newson, *Cost of Conquest*, pp. 186–87, 320.

7. Nancie L. González, *Sojourners of the Caribbean*, p. 51; Newson, *Cost of Conquest*, pp. 186–87.

8. Guevara-Escudero, "Nineteenth-Century Honduras," pp. 59–61.

9. Ibid., p. 317.

10. Ibid., pp. 302–3.

11. Naylor, "British Commercial Relations," p. 153.

12. Naylor, *Penny Ante Imperialism*, pp. 177, 191, 280 n. 37; Guevara-Escudero, "Nineteenth-Century Honduras," p. 364 n. 96.

13. Guevara-Escudero, "Nineteenth-Century Honduras," pp. 236–77.

14. Pastor Fasquelle, *Biografía*, p. 13.

15. Luque, *Memorias de un Sampedrano*, p. 6.

16. Frye, 30 September 1875, dispatch 24, Omoa, Dispatches from U.S. Consuls in Omoa, Trujillo, and Roatán, 1818–93, microfilm T-477, reel 4, RG 59, NA.

17. "San Pedro Sula en 1878," *Boletín*, CDSPS, no. 64, 31 August 1954, pp. 8–9.

18. The allocation of *ejido* land between cattle grazing and commercial agriculture remained a problem in the 1880s and 1890s. By 1900 municipal authorities discussed the "convenience of maintaining, transforming or suppressing the cattle grazing zone." *LAM* 9, 3 January 1900, p. 154.

19. The names of the mayors identified as banana growers came from *LAM* and were cross-checked with lists of growers in San Pedro Sula. For examples, see Luque, *Memorias de un Sampedrano*, pp. 111–12; *LAM* 11, 15 January 1904, pp. 220–29; and "Asociación Frutera de Sula," RMC 3, 18 January 1914, pp. 426–52.

20. Delmer G. Ross, "Construction of the Railroads of Central America," pp. 27–42.

21. Ellis, *Las Transnacionales del Banano*, pp. 53–55.

22. Williams, *States and Social Evolution*, p. 216; Antúnez Castillo, *Biografía*, pp. 21–30, and *Memorias*, pp. 125–28; Oquelí, *1862*, pp. 35, 60–61.

23. Antúnez Castillo, *Biografía*, pp. 21–30, and *Memorias*, pp. 125–28.

24. RMC 19, 17 October 1940, pp. 25–28; RMC 20, 28 July 1943, pp. 138–42.

25. *LAM* 3, 12 May 1883, pp. 57–58, 31 July 1883, p. 67, and 29 July 1884, p. 83; *LAM* 9, 9 May 1900, pp. 225–26, and 23 May 1900, p. 245; *LAM* 11, 15 April 1903, p. 143, 15 May 1903, p. 148, 19 June 1903, pp. 167–68, 1 October 1903, p. 185, 15 October 1903, pp. 187–88, and 6 May 1904, pp. 304–7.

26. *LAM* 5, 5 January 1889, pp. 98–99.

27. *LAM* 10, 24 January 1901, pp. 213–15; 11, 23 January 1905, pp. 356–58; 12, 21 January 1911, pp. 144–48; 15, 15 January 1915, pp. 127–30; 18, 13 January 1921, pp. 394–99; 20, 12 January 1925, pp. 261–63; 23, 19 January 1931, pp. 357–61; 26, 21 January 1935, pp. 151–71.

28. Reyes, *Honduras y Las Compañías Ferroviarias*, pp. 4–12; Arthur N. Young, "Financial Reform in Honduras," a report to President Rafael López Gutierrez, pp. 41–42, 815.51/442, RG 59, NA.

29. Full biographical sketches and data are available in Euraque, "Merchants and Industrialists," app. II.

30. The methodology is explained in ibid., app. I, pp. 763–70.

31. The methodology is explained in ibid., app. III, pp. 794–99.

32. Euraque, "Estructura Económica," p. 38.

33. "Commercial Activity of the White Race in Honduras," *Revista Económica*, no. 6 (October 1914): 331–33. A recent account shows that Germany's commercial prominence in Honduras, especially in Choluteca, threatened U.S. interests to such an extent that U.S. diplomats consistently sought to curtail its expansion. See Mario R. Argueta, *Los Alemanes en Honduras*, pp. 22–34.

34. Much of this section draws on Euraque, "Estructura Económica."

35. Ibid.

36. RMC 4, 15 March 1916, pp. 256–60; RMC 14, 31 May 1931, pp. 83–86.

37. Mondragón Carrasco and Tosco, *Aspectos Demográficos*, p. 8; "Movimiento de Inmigración . . . [en] San Pedro Sula . . . durante 1932 a 1942 . . . ," *Boletín*, CDSPS, no. 8, 15 March 1943, p. 15.

38. The following paragraphs are based on Nancie L. González, *Dollar, Dove, and Eagle*.

39. Perry, *National Directory of Honduras*, p. 164.

40. Euraque, "Estructura Económica," p. 42.

41. Ibid.

42. May and Plaza, *United Fruit Company*, pp. 194–95; Posas, *Luchas del Movimiento*, pp. 48–50; Marvin A. Barahona, *La Hegemonía*, pp. 135–37.

43. Karnes, *Tropical Enterprise*, p. 96; Posas, *El Sub-Desarrollo*, p. 37.

44. This issue is explored in Euraque, "Nation Formation."

45. Nancie L. González, *Dollar, Dove, and Eagle*, p. 112.

46. "La Cámara de Comercio de la Ceiba," *Revista Comercial*, Boletín, CCA, no. 4 (15 November 1927): 11.

47. It seems that before the 1950s Arabs rarely married Hondurans or other immigrants, and thus "kinship networks" among dominant class sectors probably did not socialize and reproduce the Arab membership in the social and political ruling class. Nancie L. González, *Dollar, Dove, and Eagle*, chap. 6.

48. Ibid., p. 170.

49. Charles W. Anderson, "Honduras," p. 78.

50. John D. Erwin, replying to questionnaire regarding labor matters in Honduras, 30 December 1943, dispatch 677, Confidential U.S. Diplomatic Post Records, reel 33, 190–211, RG 84, NA.

51. Ibid.

52. Ministerio de Fomento, "Informe. . . . Caminos," *MFOAT, 1928–1929*, p. 59, and *1926–1927*, pp. 54–55. For a detailed analysis of transportation systems in Honduras in the 1920s, see Bengston, "Studies in the Geography of Honduras," pp. 521–37.

53. "Labor Troubles along the North Coast of Honduras," 16 January 1920, dispatch 25, 815.5045, RG 59, NA.

54. The culture of labor organizing in La Ceiba during this period is characterized briefly in Posas, *Breve Historia*, pp. 36–40.

55. Villars, *Porque Quiero Seguir*, pp. 137–40, 324–28; Posas, *Luchas del Movimiento*, pp. 77–82, 91 n. 27.

56. Villars, *Porque Quiero Seguir*, pp. 338–40.

57. Posas, *Luchas del Movimiento*, p. 83.

58. Villars, *Porque Quiero Seguir*, pp. 120–23, 163.

59. Ibid., pp. 332–37.

60. Ferrera et al., "Gobierno del Doctor," pp. 104–6.

61. Even today the trajectory of those events has never been clarified. Liberals declare or insinuate that either the massacre was ordered from Tegucigalpa or Juan Manuel Gálvez, Carías's minister of the interior, who was visiting San Pedro Sula at the time, took it upon himself to direct the dictatorship's local thugs. Comité Liberal Democrático, *Manifiestos*. One of Carías's biographers offered a different version. See Romualdo E. Mejía, *El 4 de Julio de 1944*. A once anti-Carías nationalist who witnessed the horror basically agreed with the liberals' perspective. Peraza, *Confinamiento*.

## CHAPTER 3

1. Stokes, *Honduras*, pp. 9, 21.

2. Ibid., p. 269.

3. For an analysis of PDRH ideology, see Posas, *Luchas del Movimiento*, pp. 188–92.

4. Leonard, *United States*, p. 122.

5. U.S. Embassy, Tegucigalpa, to Secretary of State, 12 March 1950 (dispatch 121, 715.00/3-1250) and 2 April 1954 (dispatch 405, 715.00/4-254), Confidential U.S. State Department Central Files: Honduras, 1950–1954), reels 2–3, RG 59, NA.

6. Amaya Amador and Padilla Rush, *Memorias*, pp. 18–20, 74–76.

7. I thank Mrs. Gladys Fasquelle de Pastor for forwarding personal details of her life with Don Rodolfo. She kindly responded to a questionnaire in late 1989.

8. "Materialismo e Idealismo," *El Economista Hondureño* no. 4 (April 1947): 147–48.

9. Amaya Amador and Padilla Rush, *Memorias*, p. 104.

10. RMC 20, 23 April 1946, pp. 342–49.

11. Sorto Batres, *Ramón Amaya Amador*.

12. Ewing, Tegucigalpa, to the Secretary of State, 17 September 1914, dispatch 84, 815.00/1547, RG 59, NA.

13. Ames, "Memorandum of Political Outlook in Honduras," 2 June 1919, 815.00/817, RG 59 NA.

14. Enrique C. Ochoa, "Rapid Expansion of Voter Participation," p. 886.

15. Díaz Chávez, *Sociología*, p. 457; Minister George T. Summerlin, Tegucigalpa, to Secretary of State, 6 March 1928, dispatch 219, 815.00/4188, RG 59, NA; Vallejo, *Compendio*, pp. 413–20.

16. Stokes, *Honduras*, p. 104.

17. Ibid., pp. 332, p. 280.

18. Ibid., p. 215.

19. Cáceres Lara, *Efemérides Nacionales*, pp. 86, 178–79, 187–88, 195; Daniel J. Ross, "The Honduras Revolution," pp. 34–48; Luque, *Memorias de un Soldado Hondureño*,

1: 23–34; Theodore P. Wright, "Honduras," p. 216; Minister Sambola T. Jones, Tegucigalpa, to Secretary of State, 10 September 1919, dispatch 312, 815.00/2075, RG 59, NA.

20. Medardo Mejía, *Historia*, 6:194.

21. Ministerio de Fomento, *MFOA, 1913–1914*, pp. 11–12, and *1922–1923*, p. 5.

22. Minister John Ewing, Tegucigalpa, to Secretary of State, 17 September 1914, dispatch 84, 815.00/1547, RG 59, NA; Ministerio de Hacienda, "Conocimiento de las constancias de crédito extendidas por la Dirección General de Rentas. . . . por perdidas reconocidas y causadas por las guerras civiles de 1892 a 1912 . . . ," *MHCP, 1911–1912*, pp. 101–7; Ministerio de Hacienda, "Crédito Público," *MHCP, 1921–1922*, pp. 8–9; Arthur N. Young, "Reforma Financiera," p. 42.

23. Chargé d'Affaires W. Spencer to Secretary of State, 31 August 1921, dispatch 199, with enclosure, *Financial Reform in Honduras*, a report to President López Gutierrez by Arthur N. Young, Financial Adviser, 1920–21, 815.51/442, RG 59, NA.

24. Ibid., app. III.

25. Posas and Del Cid, *La Construcción*, p. 21; Bardales Bueso, *Imagen*, p. 174. War Department expenditures in 1892 amounted to 26 percent of the total. Bureau of the American Republics, *Hand-Book of Honduras*, bulletin 57 (Washington, D.C., 1894), p. 62.

26. Ropp, "The Honduran Army," pp. 505–6.

27. Ewing, Tegucigalpa, to Secretary of State, 17 September 1914, dispatch 84, 815.00/1547, RG 59, NA.

28. Stokes, *Honduras*, pp. 222–23; Bardales Bueso, *Imagen*, pp. 100–101, 107, 135; Cáceres Lara, *Efemérides*, p. 180.

29. "Memorandum of Opposition Party in Honduras," Division of Latin American Affairs, Department of State, 20 May 1921, 815.00/2258, RG 59, NA.

30. Euraque, "San Pedro Sula," pp. 238–39; Chargé d'Affaires Perry Belden, Tegucigalpa, to Secretary of State, 17 June 1920, dispatch 665, 815.00/2199, RG 59, NA; Suazo Rubí, *Auge y Crisis*, pp. 45–46; Mejía Deras, *Policarpo Bonilla*, pp. 448–52; Paredes, *Drama Político*, pp. 142–47; Instituto de Educación, *Pensamiento Liberal De Zúñiga Huete*, p. 64; Paz Barnica, *La Renovada*, p. 65.

31. Zúñiga Huete, *Idolo Desnudo*, p. 24.

32. Paz Barnica, *La Renovada*, pp. 291–301.

33. Bardales Bueso, *Historia*, p. 6.

34. Paz Barnica, *La Renovada*, p. 298.

35. Chargé d'Affaires Walker Smith, Tegucigalpa, to Secretary of State, 16 October 1922, dispatch 195, 815.00/2521, RG 59, NA.

36. Collier and Collier, *Shaping the Political Arena*.

37. Smith, Tegucigalpa, to Secretary of State, 16 October 1922, dispatch 195, 815.00/2521, RG 59, NA.

38. Ibid.

39. Fletes, *Commercial Directory of Honduras*, p. 8.

40. This information is drawn from membership lists in the *Libros de las Actas de las Sesiones de la Alcaldía Municipal de San Pedro Sula*, beginning in 1882.

41. Bascom, *Propaganda*, p. 245; RMC 9, 4 December 1921, pp. 49–53.

42 Daniel J. Ross, "The Honduras Revolution," p. 95.

43. Posas, *Luchas del Movimiento*, pp. 72–74, 90 n. 11; Antúnez Castillo, *Biografía*, pp. 21–30.

44. Pastor Fasquelle, *Biografía*, p. 379.

45. Daniel J. Ross, "The Honduras Revolution," p. 102.

46. Stokes, *Honduras*, pp. 244–45.

47. Minister George T. Summerlin, Tegucigalpa, to Secretary of State, 8 December 1927, dispatch 492, 815.00/4178, RG 59, NA; Minister Julius G. Lay to Secretary of State, 31 October 1932, dispatch, Confidential U.S. Diplomatic Post Records, reel 5, 275–80, RG 84, NA; Mario R. Argueta, *Tiburcio Carías*, pp. 66, 75, 90, 95–96.

48. Luque, *Memorias de un Sampedrano*, pp. 125–26.

49. Cáceres Lara, *Efemérides*, pp. 69–70; Mario R. Argueta, *Diccionario*, p. 140.

50. Mario R. Argueta, *Tiburcio Carías*, pp. 159–60; Cáceres Lara, *Gobernantes*, pp. 326–27.

51. Navarrete, "Latin American Policy of Charles E. Hughes," pp. 91, 97–102.

52. Luque, *Memorias de un Soldado Hondureño*, 2:179–80; Paredes, *Drama Político*, p. 405; Daniel J. Ross, "The Honduras Revolution," pp. 207–8; Minister Lawrence Dennis, Tegucigalpa, to Secretary of State, "Political Parties and Groups: Strengths, Leaders, Programs, Policies," 25 March 1925, dispatch 11, 815.00/3670, RG 59, NA.

53. Stokes, *Honduras*, pp. 53–54.

54. Mario R. Argueta, *Tiburcio Carías*, pp. 86–89.

55. Mejía Deras, *Policarpo Bonilla*, pp. 472–76; Mario R. Argueta, *Diccionario*, p. 22.

56. "Carta Abierta" to President Woodrow Wilson, 10 August 1913, in Oquelí, *Boletín de la Defensa Nacional*, pp. 119–23; Smith, Tegucigalpa, to Secretary of State, 16 October 1922, dispatch 195, 815.00/2521, RG 59, NA; Medardo Mejía, *Froylán Turcios*, p. 166.

57. Consul Herschel V. Johnson, Tegucigalpa, to Secretary of State, 18 July 1927, dispatch 400, 815.00/4116, RG 59, NA; Minister George T. Summerlin, Tegucigalpa, to Secretary of State, 16 March 1928 (dispatch 565, 815.00/4190) and 27 August 1927 (dispatch 430, 815.00/4120), RG 59, NA; Sandino to Froylán Turcios, 8 August 1927, in Ramírez, *Augusto C. Sandino* 1:146–47. Also see pp. 150–54, 206–7, 210–11, 231–32, 249–55, and 270–72.

58. Memo of a conversation between the United Fruit Co. and the U.S. Department of State, Latin American Affairs Division, officials, 14 July 1928, 815.00/4203, RG 59, NA.

59. Minister Julius G. Lay to Secretary of State, 31 October 1932, dispatch, Confidential U.S. Diplomatic Post Records, reel 5, 275–80, RG 84, NA.

60. Minister Julius G. Lay, Tegucigalpa, to Secretary of State, 11 August 1930, dispatch 54, ibid., reel 1, 579–81; Luque, *Memorias de un Soldado Hondureño*, 2:14–15, 60–67, 70, 200, and 1:134–37.

61. Finney, "The Central Americans' Reaction," pp. 92, 106.

62. Bascom, *Propaganda*, p. 341; Minister Julius G. Lay, Tegucigalpa, to Secretary of State, 4 April 1932, dispatch 443, microfilm, reel 4, 797–802, RG 84, NA; Minister Julius G. Lay, Tegucigalpa, to Secretary of State, 4 April 1932 (dispatch 416, 762–88), and "Report on Political Conditions," Vice-Consul Warren C. Stewart, La Ceiba, to Lay, 3 March 1932 (678–81), both on microfilm, reel 4, RG 84, NA.

63. Chargé d'Affaires Lawrence G. Higgins, Tegucigalpa, to Secretary of State, 10 May 1932, dispatch 475, microfilm, reel 4, 948–65, RG 84, NA; Posas, *Luchas del Movimiento*, pp. 76–77; Finney, "The Central Americans' Reaction," pp. 21–22.

64. Minister Julius G. Lay, Tegucigalpa, to Secretary of State, 28 April 1933, dispatch 775, microfilm, reel 7, 218–20, RG 84, NA; Ernest H. Baker, "Map of the Foreign Empire."

65. José F. Martínez, *Honduras Histórica*, pp. 315–17; "General e Ingeniero Abraham Williams Calderón," *Boletín de la Biblioteca y Archivo Nacionales*, nos. 9–10 (1 October 1945): 45; José S. Barahona G. et al., "La Evolución," pp. 42–48.

66. Mejía Deras, *Policarpo Bonilla*, pp. 245–49; Paredes, *Drama Político*, pp. 111–13; Minister Julius G. Lay, Tegucigalpa, to Secretary of State, 3 March 1933, dispatch 731, microfilm, reel 7, 874–84, RG 84, NA.

## CHAPTER 4

1. *LAM* 28, 7 January 1937, p. 425.

2. Graciela García, *Páginas de Lucha*, pp. 45–46.

3. Julián López Pineda, *Democracia y Redentorismo*, p. 7.

4. *LAM* 28, 25 March 1936, pp. 18–22.

5. Izaguirre, *Readaptaciones y Cambios*, p. iv; *LAM* 27, 4 January 1936, pp. 225–26.

6. Paredes, *Drama Político*, pp. 554–60.

7. *LAM* 31, 2 September 1939, p. 173; *LAM* 33, 2 December 1940, p. 146.

8. *LAC* 34, 1 January 1941, p. 3.

9. *LAM* 18, 1 February 1940, p. 31, 16 February 1940, p. 391; *LAM* 32, 15 August 1940, pp. 336–37; Baide Galindo, "Iconoclastas Ebrios."

10. *LAC* 48, 1 December 1956, pp. 97–98.

11. República de Honduras, *Boletín Legislativo*, pp. 481–515.

12. Ramírez became president of the BCH in 1950 and remained so well into the 1970s. As of 1950 Mejía headed the newly created Bureau of Income Tax Revenues. The military junta appointed Mejía minister of finance for 1956–57. Interview, Gabriel A. Mejía.

13. "Dos Miembros de la 'AGAS' en la Rectoría de Importantes Oficinas," *Boletín*, AGAS, no. 33, November 1956, p. 19.

14. "Las Fuerzas Vivas de la Nación y la Política Nacional," *Boletín*, CCIT, no. 130, September 1957, p. 3.

15. "Funciones de las Cámaras de Comercio e Industrias de Nuestro País," *Boletín*, CCIT, no. 63, February 1952, pp. 17–18.

16. "El BNF y los Representantes de las Fuerzas Vivas," *Carta Semanal*, no. 44, 20 May 1950.

17. *Boletín*, Comité Nacional de Café (Tegucigalpa), no. 11, June 1948, p. 419.

18. Noé Pino, "Structural Roots of Crisis," p. 41.

19. Bulmer-Thomas, *Political Economy of Central America*, p. 271.

20. Euraque, "Estructura Económica," p. 39.

21. David F. Ross, "Economic Development of Honduras," p. 195; Morris, "Interest Groups," p. 34.

22. "La Pujanza Económica de Nuestro Departamento," *Carta Semanal*, no. 71, 9 December 1950; *LAC* 41, 1 December 1950, p. 228.

23. "Acción Rotaria," *Boletín*, CCIT, no. 9, August 1947, p. 35; CCIT, Segunda Convención Nacional de Cámaras de Comercio e Industrias.

24. *LAC* 42, 16 June 1952, p. 220; Vinelli, "Currency and Exchange System," pp. 420–22; *Boletín*, CDSPS, no. 15, October 1950, p. 15; "Coordialidad y Mutua Cooperación," *Carta Semanal*, no. 128, 8 March 1952.

25. "Oficina del Impuesto sobre la Renta," *IHCPC, 1949–1950* (Tegucigalpa, 1951), p. 47.

26. Interview, Gabriel A. Mejía.

27. "Divulgaciones de la Cámara de Comercio e Industrias de Cortés," *Carta Semanal*, no. 54, 12 August 1950.

28. David F. Ross, "Economic Development," p. 136; Oficina de Cooperación Intelectual, *Acontecimientos*, pp. 49–50; "Programas Gubernamentales de Desarrollo Económico," *MBCH, 1954*, pp. 29–32; "El Plan de Desarrollo Económico," *MBCH, 1954*, pp. 42–43; Wynia, *Politics and Planners*, pp. 38–41, 54–57, 75.

29. Oficina de Cooperación Intelectual, *Acontecimientos*, p. 48.

30. RMC 25, 21 January 1957, pp. 459–69.

31. Carlos H. Matute, a close friend of Gabriel A. Mejía and Roberto Ramírez and associated with the CNE from the 1950s to the early 1960s, acknowledged the problems of caudillismo in "Breves Reflexiones en Materia de Política Nacional," *El Día*, 29 January 1957.

32. Marta R. Argueta, "Reseña Histórica," p. 38; René Cruz, "Dinero y Banca en Honduras." On Cruz, also see *Boletín*, CCIT, no. 41 (April 1950) and no. 98 (January 1955), and *Carta Semanal*, no. 405, 28 September 1957.

33. Unlike the elderly Rodriguez, Caraccioli and Gálvez Barnes were both in their thirties and had been professionally trained in the 1940s. Gálvez Barnes graduated from MIT with a degree in aeronautical engineering. Schleit, *Shelton's Barefoot Airlines*, p. 74. Caraccioli, born in San Pedro Sula, descended from a prominent Italian-Honduran family whose origins in that city dated back to the 1860s. Oquelí, "Gobiernos Hondureños," *Economía Política*, no. 10 (1976): 6.

34. As chief of air force internal security, López Arellano had been instrumental in the coup. Domínguez, *Ascenso al Poder*, pp. 18, 23; Natalini de Castro et al., *Significado Histórico*, p. 49.

35. Only the air forces of Chile, Uruguay, and Venezuela approached this percentage. Lieuwen, *Arms and Politics*, p. 210.

36. Ropp, "The Honduran Army," pp. 504–11.

37. Lommel, "U.S. Efforts to Foster Peace, p. 271; Mario R. Argueta, *Tiburcio Carías*, pp. 125–36; Schleit, *Shelton's Barefoot Airlines*, pp. 14–15, 46, 58–59; Ropp, "The Honduran Army," p. 509; Domínguez, *Ascenso al Poder*, p. 16; Ropp, "In Search of the New Soldier," pp. 70, 88 n. 28.

38. A recent example is Funes H., *Los Deliberantes*, pp. 181–92.

39. John J. Johnson, *The Military and Society*, p. 162.

40. Kantor, *Patterns of Politics*, p. 139.

41. Ferrera et al., "Gobierno del Doctor," pp. 104–6; Natalini de Castro et al., *Significado Histórico*, p. 37; Comité Liberal Democrata, *Manifiestos*, pp. 1–2.

42. Ferrera et al., "Gobierno del Doctor," pp. 106–8.

43. Honduran exile in San Salvador to Amílcar Gómez Robelo in Guatemala, 7 October 1944. This letter and others cited below are from Gómez Robelo's private correspondence and papers. Gómez Robelo, a liberal resident of San Pedro Sula, fled to Guatemala after the massacre in July 1944. Thereafter he served in various positions in different exile organizations, including as secretary of the Frente Democrático Revolucionario Hondureño. Henceforth letters from this private collection are indicated by reference to DPAGR.

44. Leonard, *United States*, pp. 112–13; Gómez Robelo, Guatemala, to Zúñiga Huete, Mexico, 9 October 1944, and Zúñiga Huete to Gómez Robelo, 18 October 1944, DPAGR.

45. Rafael Heliodoro Valle, Mexico, to Amílcar Gómez Robelo, Guatemala, 30 June 1945, DPAGR; "La Convención Liberal," *Vanguardia*, no. 91, 29 May 1948.

46. Mario R. Argueta, *Tiburcio Carías*, pp. 332–33.

47. Leonard, *United States*, p. 122.

48. RMC 13, 19 December 1930, pp. 427–46; Partido Liberal de Honduras, *Datos Biográficos del Dr. Ramón Villeda Morales*; Baciu, *Ramón Villeda Morales*; *Honduras Rotaria*, no. 1, April 1943; Guilbert and Callejas, *Cincuentenario (1929–1979)*, pp. 283–311.

49. Schwarz, *Liberal: Adolf A. Berle*, pp. 313, 319–20, 340–41.

50. Mario R. Argueta, *Tiburcio Carías*, p. 323.

51. Paredes, *Liberalismo y Nacionalismo*, pp. 371–73, and *El Hombre del Puro*, pp. 70–71, 77, 125–26.

52. Amaya Amador and Padilla Rush, *Memorias*, p. 23 (quotation); "Aclaraciones Necesarias," *Carta Semanal*, no. 240, 15 May 1954; "Gravísimo Precedente," *Carta Semanal*, no. 382, 20 April 1957.

53. Morris, "Interest Groups," p. 51; Paredes, *Los Culpables*, pp. 38–39; Ramón E. Cruz, *La Lucha Política de 1954*, p. 31; Secret Cables, Ambassador Whitting Willauer to the State Department, 27 November and 6 December 1954, U.S. Department of State, *Foreign Relations of the United States, 1952–1954*, 4:1320–23; Paredes, *Liberalismo*, pp. 63–65, 371–73, and *El Hombre del Puro*, pp. 125–26.

54. Oquelí, "Gobiernos Hondureños," *Economía Política*, no. 4 (January–April 1973): 7.

55. U.S. Embassy, Tegucigalpa, to Secretary of State, 18 August 1956, secret cable 71, Confidential U.S. State Department Central Files: Honduras, 1955–1959, reel 1, 715.00/8-1856, RG 59, NA.

56. The details of the technocratic origins of the coup, in conversations dating back to at least February 1956, were publicized only a few years ago by a central figure in those events. See Jorge Bueso Arias, "Lo Que Viví, durante e inmediatamente después del Golpe del 21 de Octubre de 1956," *Diario Tiempo*, 21 October 1991. Bueso Arias suggests that the U.S. government wished the coup plotters "good luck" even while it claimed not to want involvement. Adolf A. Berle, a close friend of CIA chief Allen Dulles, a consultant to the preparations of the coup against Arbenz in 1954 and a consultant on Honduran political events in August 1956, thought that the CIA "gener-

ally spread the good word and thus probably assisted." Schwarz, *Liberal: Adolf A. Berle*, pp. 319–20.

57. Natalini de Castro et al., *Significado Histórico*, p. 49.

58. Salomón, *Militarismo y Reformismo*, pp. 171–73; Natalini de Castro et al., *Significado Histórico*, p. 55 n. 32. Gabriel A. Mejía, an old friend of Carías and Lozano Díaz, was appointed minister of economics and finance. Mejía's National Party politics at this juncture began to wane in the context of the technocratic responsibilities he assumed in the 1950s.

59. Domínguez, *Ascenso al Poder*, pp. 18, 23; Salomón, *Militarismo y Reformismo*, p. 36; Natalini de Castro et al., *Significado Histórico*, p. 49.

60. Baciu, *Ramón Villeda Morales*, p. 15; Natalini de Castro et al., *Significado Histórico*, p. 55 n. 33.

61. Natalini de Castro et al., *Significado Histórico*, p. 56 n. 38.

62. The legislative debates are available in Asamblea Nacional Constituyente, *Boletín Legislativo*, vols. 1–2.

63. Fonseca, *Cuatro Ensayos Sobre*, pp. 119–20.

64. Various commentators have noted a meeting on 9 November 1957 attended by Ambassador Whitting Willauer, local executives of the United Fruit Co., State Department representatives, and Villeda Morales. MacCameron, *Bananas, Labor, and Politics*, pp. 97–98; Natalini de Castro et al., *Significado Histórico*, pp. 144–54. Only access to State Department archives or testimony by the alleged participants will clarify this issue. However, State Department records later recognized that "although the military supported the advent to power of the Villeda Morales regime, they did so with reluctance and only after being accorded special constitutional status making them semi-independent of the President." U.S. State Department, Bureau of Intelligence and Research, Intelligence Report 7954.

65. Oquelí, "Gobiernos Hondureños," *Economía Política*, no. 9 (1975): 58–59.

66. LAM 53, 5 October 1963, pp. 225–26.

67. Villar was a major stockholder in La Capitalizadora Hondureña, an investment bank established in June 1948 and later intimately associated with El Banco de El Ahorro Hondureño, founded in 1960. The major shareholders of these banks were closely allied with important leaders of the Liberal Party, including Jorge Bueso Arias, who served on the board of directors of La Capitalizadora in 1948. Anonymous, "La Compañía Aseguradora"; Marta R. Argueta, "Reseña Histórica," pp. 17–18.

68. Guilbert and Callejas, *Cincuentenario (1929–1979)*, p 314; Luque, *Memorias de un Soldado Hondureño*, 2:43; "Murió Abraham Bueso," *La Prensa*, 26 April 1965; RMC 25, 21 January 1957, pp. 472–74; RMC 25, 25 June 1956, pp. 332–62; RMC 26, 7 April 1958, pp. 124–31; LAM 53, 5 October 1963, pp. 225–26.

69. Wynia, *Politics and Planners*, pp. 46–50; "Un Cambio de Impresiones sobre el Plan Quinquenal," *Carta Semanal*, no. 289, 14 May 1955.

70. In October 1956 the military leadership accorded the Secretariat of the CNE ministerial status "because of the relations that the CNE maintains with the different branches of the State." Oquelí, "Gobiernos Hondureños," *Economía Política*, no. 6 (1973): 9.

71. *MCCIT, 1961*, pp. 8–20; Domínguez, *Ascenso al Poder*, p. 57.

## Chapter 5

1. These issues are discussed in detail in Chapters 7 and 8.

2. Rabe, *Eisenhower and Latin America*, p. 112.

3. "Ley de Fomento," *Boletín*, CCIT, no. 139, June 1958, pp. 6–10.

4. *Boletín*, BNF, no. 3, March 1952, p. 2.

5. "La Cuarta Reunión del Comité de Cooperación Económica del Istmo Centroamericano," *Boletín*, CCIT, no. 123, February 1957, pp. 3–6.

6. Mejía's critical knowledge of the post–1950 relationship between a development state and budget revenues and allocations is detailed in a budget report he submitted to the Constituent Assembly of 1957. See "Presupuesto General para 1958," Asamblea Nacional Constituyente, *Boletín . . . 1957*, 2:537–38.

7. Shepherd, "Honduras," p. 24.

8. "Informes: Mensaje de la Junta Militar de Gobierno Dirigido a la Asamblea Nacional Constituyente," *Boletín Legislativo*, 1:9.

9. Consejo Nacional de Economía, *Plan Nacional*, vol. 4, *Programa de Desarrollo Industrial*, p. 51; Ministerio de Economía, *MEH, 1959–1960*, pp. 29–30; Mario V. Rietti, "Los Incentivos Fiscales al Desarrollo Industrial en Honduras," *Revista Extra*, no. 13 (August 1966): 13; Consejo Superior de Planificación Economía, *Diagnóstico del Sector Industrial*, p. 143.

10. Ministerio de Economía, "Empresas Clasificadas y Protegidas"; Crowley, "San Pedro Sula," pp. 57–152; Hidroservice Engenharia de Proyectos Ltda., *Plan de Desarrollo Urbano*, p. 34; García Valderramo, "Municipio de San Pedro Sula," p. 104.

11. Leiva Vivas, "La República Libre de San Pedro Sula," *La Prensa*, 24 April 1968.

12. Leiva Vivas, "La República Libre de San Pedro Sula"; "Las Dos Capitales de Honduras," editorial, *La Prensa*, 12 December 1967.

13. Leiva Vivas, "La Empresa Privada Hondureña Busca Una Revolución" (quotation), and "Nuestra Pequeña Burguesía Naciente."

14. Bulmer-Thomas, *Political Economy of Central America*, pp. 308–9, 273, 271.

15. Murga Frassinetti, "Concentración Industrial," p. 85; Del Cid, "Honduras," p. 68.

16. Consejo Superior de Planificación Economía, *Diagnóstico Industrial*, pp. 21–22; Shirey, "Analysis of the Location of Manufacturing," p. 37, 25–26, 32. In 1968 factory employment in San Pedro Sula accounted for about 40 percent of factory employment nationwide. García Valderramo, "Municipio de San Pedro," pp. 104, 108.

17. "Ports of Central America," *Latin American Report* 6, no. 3 (September–October 1966): 17–21.

18. Familiar surnames deserve mention: Larach, Kattan, Yuja, and Canahuati. See Euraque, "Estructura Económica," p. 45.

19. Euraque, "Merchants and Industrialists," p. 449 n. 79.

20. República de Honduras, *MFOAT, 1927–1928*, pp. 267, 281; Karnes, *Tropical Enterprise*, p. 49; *LAM* 24, 17 October 1932, p. 378; RMC 18, 24 February 1939, pp. 279–86, and 10 May 1939, pp. 408–27.

21. RMC 20, 20 June 1944, pp. 169–79, and 27 October 1945, pp. 268–79; RMC 23, 29 November 1950, pp. 71–75, and 19 December 1951, pp. 293–98; "Concesión

Otorgada por el Consejo del Distrito Departamental a la Cervecería Hondureña," *Boletín*, CDSPS, no. 37, 31 May 1952, pp. 9–10; Ministerio de Agricultura, *Informe . . . 1952–1953*, p. 123.

22. RMC 24, 13 March 1953, pp. 60–83, and 11 October 1954, pp. 426–45; RMC 25, 12 July 1956, pp. 364–66.

23. Solorzano de Quesada, "Análisis de la Producción de Azucar," pp. 11–12; RMC 15, 12 November 1932, pp. 40–52; RMC 18, 21 October 1938, pp. 189–97, and 12 December 1938, pp. 245–52; *LAM* 31, 22 September 1939, p. 198, and 15 December 1939, pp. 280–82. Also see Pastor Fasquelle, *Memoria de Una Empresa*, pp. 51–52.

24. RMC 21, 31 August 1948, pp. 273–74; RMC 23, 7 June 1952, pp. 400–416; Pastor Fasquelle, *Memoria de Una Empresa*, pp. 131, 169–70, 185, 191, 239.

25. Interview, Gabriel A. Mejía.

26. "La Primera Piedra de Una Gran Industria," *Carta Semanal*, no. 327, 3 March 1956; Sabillón García and Avila, "Enfoque Social y Económico," pp. 1–3; RMC 25, 25 June, 1956, pp. 332–62.

27. RMC 25, 25 June, 1956, pp. 332–62; RMC 26, 1 March 1959, pp. 220–24; Instituto de Investigación Económica, "Industrialización Y Dependencia," pp. 616–17.

28. McCamant, *Development Assistance*, p. 261.

29. A good example is a $1.5 million loan the BCIE provided to the San Pedro Sula cement factory in 1963. "Préstamo de Tres Millones a 'Cementos de Honduras,'" *El Día*, 14 February 1963. By 1966 Honduras had received twenty-seven loans from the BCIE amounting to about 15 million lempiras. "Banco Centroamericano Otorga a Honduras Total de 27 Préstamos," *El Día*, Tegucigalpa, 18 February 1966.

30. "Inversionistas del País Se Reunen para Formar Financiera Industrial," *El Día*, 18 September 1962; "Fondos de la Financiera para Desarrollo Económico," *El Cronista*, 3 September 1964; "Diez Millons para la Nacional Financiera de San Pedro Sula," *La Prensa*, 12 June 1964; "Tres Millones de Dolares Presta AID a Financiera Hondureña," *La Prensa*, 14 July 1966; "Préstamo a la Financiera Hondureña," *Revista Extra*, no. 72 (July 1971): 3; "Primer Año de Operaciones," *Revista Extra*, no. 2 (September 1965): 45. According to FICENSA executives interviewed in 1964, for "foreign investors who are interested in joint ventures, *Financiera Hondureña* is well qualified to provide the local partners. . . . It can also perform as dealer and stockbroker in order to sell securities." "Fastest Growing City Sparks Coastal Development," *Latin American Report* 5, no. 8 (December 1964): 14.

31. RMC 28, 22 July 1964, pp. 461–83.

32. Gabriel A. Mejía, "La Función de las Fuerzas Vivas."

33. Interview, Gabriel A. Mejía.

34. Ibid.; McCamant, *Development Assistance*, p. 256; Castañeda, "Algunos Aspectos Debiles de Nuestra Economía" and "El Comercio Centroamericano."

35. Interview, Coello Bobadilla. After graduating with a degree in economics from the Technological Institute of Monterrey, Coello Bobadilla joined Mejía's inner circle in the CCIC as part of the "Advisory Committee." In the latter 1960s the Advisory Committee was the driving intellectual force behind CCIC activism.

36. Interview, Gabriel A. Mejía.

37. RMC 20, 23 April 1946, pp. 349–63, and 13 May 1946, pp. 368–76; RMC 21, 19 July 1949, pp. 486–89; RMC 28, 4 February 1964, pp. 271–85.

38. MCCIC, 1964, pp. 14–15; MCCIC, 1965, pp. 13–14, 29–30.

39. Andrés Felipe López, CCIC treasurer and general manager from 1964 to 1972, recalled the small office operation of the CCIC when he took over. Interview.

40. Members of the 1964 and 1965 CCIC governing boards are good examples. They included Elías J. Kattan, Jacobo I. Weizenblut, Francisco Abufele, Emilio L. Mejía, Bertie R. Hogge, Julio Galdámez Z., Nicolas Larach, and Abraham Bueso Pineda.

41. Interview, Gabriel A. Mejía.

42. Unless otherwise stated, the account of Bográn's life draws on biographical sketches and recollections by his friends published in San Pedro Sula's *Diario Tiempo* during 17–20 January 1989. Bográn died on 16 January 1989.

43. Information on Bográn's career prior to the 1960s is sketchy. He was probably exiled to El Salvador during the presidential campaign of 1948, when he was likely associated with the Liberal Party's non-Marxist left wing that formed the PDRH in 1948. For his involvement in student politics in El Salvador in 1950, see the PDRH's *Vanguardia Revolucionaria*, nos. 299 (19 August 1950), 300 (22 August 1950), and 311 (19 September 1950); also see Amaya Amador and Padilla Rush, *Memorias*, p. 8. He apparently then moved to Guatemala and afterward to Mexico, where the U.S. embassy reported that the Honduran consulate informed its "reporting officer" that Bográn belonged to the PDRH. Second Secretary William P. Hudson, Mexico City, 7 June 1954, dispatch 1942, Confidential U.S. State Department Central Files: Honduras, 1950–1954, reel 2, 715.00/6-754, RG 59, NA.

44. Bográn, "El Banco Central de Honduras." It is interesting that here Bográn thanked Paul Vinelli and Jorge Bueso Arias for the advice they had provided.

45. RMC 28, 22 July 1964, pp. 461–83; MCCIC, 1964, p. 4. Also see "Lic. Bográn y Lic. Ramiro Cabañas a Primera Reunión de Instituciones Bancarias de Desarrollo en Washington, 11/30–12/2," *La Prensa*, 23 December 1964, and "Despedida al Lic. Edmond L. Bográn . . . ," *La Prensa*, 9 December 1968. According to Gabriel A. Mejía (interview), Bográn had been a major promoter of this investment bank.

46. Bográn registered small investments in *La Prensa*, along with Henry Holst Leiva, Jaime Rosenthal Oliva, Reginaldo Panting, Andrés Felipe López, Yude Canahuati, Camilo Rivera Girón, and others. RMC 29, no. 192, 1964, pp. 340–49.

47. Cited in Euraque, "Social Structure," p. 145.

48. Alvarado Lozano, "Memorandum de Diario *La Prensa*." Alvarado Lozano was *La Prensa*'s most prominent editorial writer from 1964 to 1971. He prepared this "Memorandum" in response to a list of questions provided to him in San Pedro Sula.

49. By the late 1960s Tegucigalpa's *El Día*, established in 1948 by interests closely associated with the National Party, characterized *La Prensa* as the "property of an economic consortium that carries much weight on national activities." "El Tema de Moda," *El Día*, 24 January 1967.

50. The bibliography to his 1956 master's thesis is replete with works that deal with these issues, including Maurice Dobb's *Studies in the Development of Capitalism*. A San Pedro Sula colleague of Bográn with a similar vision was Rodolfo Pastor Zelaya of the old PDRH. Like Pastor Zelaya, Bográn married a daughter of Roberto Fasquelle, Samuel Zemurray's friend and business associate since the 1920s. I thank Mrs. Gladys

Fasquelle de Pastor for forwarding personal details of her life with Don Rodolfo and information on other matters. She kindly responded to a questionnaire in late 1989.

51. Bográn, "El Cuadro Político Salvadoreño," p. 34. Bográn described the chaos of the Liberal Party in the 1960s in "Entre el Marasmo."

52. MCCIC, 1965, pp. 16–21. Mejía began the undertaking in August 1964 during a national meeting of the country's chambers in San Pedro Sula. However, in early 1965 he reported that the project did not materialize. "Programa de la II Reunión de Cámaras de Comercio e Industrias de Honduras en San Pedro Sula . . . ," *El Cronista*, 21 August 1964 and scattered articles, 27 and 31 August 1964. Also see MCCIC, 1964, pp. 25–28.

53. MCCIC, 1965, p. 18.

54. Ibid., pp. 22–23; "Organizarón Cámara Central de Comercio e Industrias," *La Prensa*, 4 November 1965; interview, Gabriel A. Mejía.

55. MCCIC, 1965, p. 29.

## CHAPTER 6

1. Details of these issues are narrated in Chapter 8.

2. Partido Nacional de Honduras, *El Partido Nacional*, pp. 54–64; Mariñas Otero, *Las Constituciones*, pp. 369–70; Department of State, "The Question of Military Cooperation," p. 955.

3. Villars, *Porque Quiero Seguir*, pp. 185–91, 197; Liss, *Radical Thought in Central America*, pp. 107–12.

4. Gould, " 'For an Organized Nicaragua.' "

5. Suazo Rubí, *Auge y Crisis*, pp. 279–83.

6. Posas, *Luchas del Movimiento*, p. 124; Andrés Pineda, *Soy Andreo Neda*, p. 45; Posas, *Luchas del Movimiento*, pp. 124–25.

7. Partido Nacional de Honduras, *El Partido Nacional*, pp. 65–67, 85–119, 120–31, 132–46.

8. Department of State, *Foreign Relations of the United States, 1952–1954*, 4:1293–95.

9. LaFeber, *America, Russia, and the Cold War*, p. 73; Erb, "Prelude to Point Four," p. 256.

10. For U.S. financial relations and public works projects in this period, see Gálvez, *La Obra del Doctor Juan Manuel Gálvez*; David F. Ross, "Economic Development of Honduras," p. 135; and Lommel, "U.S. Efforts to Foster Peace," pp. 293–94.

11. Romualdi, *Presidents and Peons*, p. 65.

12. Izaguirre, "Ideario Político-Administrativo," pp. 72–73, and "El Obrerismo como Elemento Indispensable para el Progreso Nacional," in *Honduras y sus Problemas de Educación*, pp. 19–21. Izaguirre wrote the latter essay in the 1920s.

13. Erwin, Tegucigalpa, to Secretary of State, 4 September 1946, dispatch 2459, Confidential U.S. State Department Central Files: Honduras, 1945–1949, reel 1, 815.00/9-446, RG 59, NA.

14. Unless otherwise noted, this account draws on Echeverri-Gent, "Labor, Class, and Political Representation"; MacCameron, *Bananas, Labor, and Politics*; Posas, *Luchas del Movimiento*; and Meza, *Historia*.

15. Amaya Amador, *Destacamento Rojo*, pp. 36–37, 63–64. This is Amaya Amador's historical novel about North Coast labor from 1954 to 1957. Recently, the complex and contradictory relationship between the PDRH and the PCH has been documented in a compilation of interviews with former PDRH and PCH militants. See Marvin Barahona, *El Silencio Quedó Atrás*.

16. Amaya Amador and Padilla Rush, *Memorias*, pp. 57, 80–82; Posas, *Luchas del Movimiento*, pp. 121, 174 n. 32; MacCameron, *Bananas, Labor, and Politics*, pp. 59–60, 76.

17. Bascom, *Propaganda*, p. 154; Andrés Pineda, *Soy Andre Neda*, p. 38; MacCameron, *Bananas, Labor, and Politics*, pp. 39–40; "José Pineda Gómez Relata Visicitudes de la Lucha Liberal," *El Cronista*, 20 April 1964.

18. U.S. Embassy in Tegucigalpa to Secretary of State, 2 April 1954, dispatch 405, Confidential U.S. State Department Central Files: Honduras, 1950–1954, reel 2, 715.00/4-254, RG 59, NA. Ironically, from 1986 to 1990 Pineda served as one of Honduras's three vice-presidents. República de Honduras, *Datos Biográficos del Presidente Constitucional*, p. 36.

19. Posas, *Luchas del Movimiento*, pp. 132, 158, 155, 182 n. 117, 246–48; MacCameron, *Bananas, Labor, and Politics*, pp. 35, 39–40; Martz, *Central America*, pp. 139–41.

20. MacCameron, *Bananas, Labor, and Politics*, p. 50; Posas, *Luchas del Movimiento*, p. 159; Martz, *Central America*, pp. 139–40.

21. Immerman, *The CIA in Guatemala*; Echeverri-Gent, "Labor, Class, and Political Representation," 1:133 (quotation); U.S. House of Representatives, Select Committee on Communist Aggression, "Testimony of John R. Leddy," pp. 209–10.

22. Martz, *Central America*, pp. 139–40; MacCameron, *Bananas, Labor, and Politics*, pp. 66, 84–87; Agee, *Inside the Company*, pp. 69, 214, 237, 307. The CIA's own journal, *Studies in Intelligence*, confirms Agee's accuracy in revealing the CIA operations. The CIA's assessment of Agee's work is discussed in Agee, *On the Run*, p. 123.

23. Mejía was then living in Tegucigalpa because President Gálvez had appointed him director of the Office of Revenues and Taxes. Interview, Gabriel A. Mejía.

24. Posas, *Luchas del Movimiento*, pp. 161, 183 n. 125; "Aclaraciones Necesarias," *Carta Semanal*, no. 240, 15 May 1954; "Gravísimo Precedente," *Carta Semanal*, no. 382, 20 April 1957; "Biografía del Sr. Yude Canahuati," *La Prensa*, 22 September 1989.

25. Pastor Fasquelle, *Biografía*, pp. 425–26.

26. Secretaría de Trabajo, *Estadísticas*, p. 7; MacCameron, *Bananas, Labor, and Politics*, pp. 79–82; Meza, *Historia*, pp. 103–4.

27. Swedberg, "Honduran Trade Union Movement." Swedberg cites data from the U.S. Department of Labor's *Directory of Labor Organizations: Western Hemisphere* (Washington, D.C., 1960).

28. Secretaría de Trabajo, *Estadísticas*, p. 9, cited in Morris, "Interest Groups," p. 97.

29. Ibid.

30. Oficina de Cooperación Intelectual, *Acontecimientos*, p. 51.

31. Interview, González González; Posas, *Luchas del Movimiento*, pp. 158, 199–202; MacCameron, *Bananas, Labor, and Politics*, pp. 199–202; Meza, *Historia*, p. 156; interview, Martínez Guzmán (secretary of the FESITRANH, 1963–75); Posas, *Lucha Ideológica*, p. 40.

32. U.S. House of Representatives, Select Committee on Communist Aggression, Testimony of John R. Leddy, pp. 208–11.

33. Romualdi, "A Report on Central America Today" and *Presidents and Peons*, pp. 254–60; First Secretary Wymberley Coerr, U.S. Embassy, for the Ambassador in Tegucigalpa, 13 September 1954, dispatch 106, Confidential State Department Central Files: Honduras, 1950–1954, reel 2, 715.00/9-1354, RG 59, NA.

34. Posas, *Lucha Ideológica*, pp. 39–40; Oficina de Cooperación Intelectual, *Acontecimientos*, p. 51. According to Martínez Guzmán, in late 1954 Villeda Morales and SITRATERCO made an explicit deal that the union would support the Liberal Party's campaign in exchange for passing a labor code thereafter. Interview, Martínez Guzmán.

35. Oquelí, "Gobiernos Hondureños," *Economía Política*, no. 8 (May–October 1974): 14; Posas, *Las Centrales*, pp. 50–51.

36. Ardón, *La Ruta de los Condores*, p. 10; Oquelí, "Gobiernos Hondureños," no. 12 (May–October 1976): 7; "Honduras," *Hispanic American Report* 11, no. 2 (February 1958): 78.

37. MacCameron, *Bananas, Labor, and Politics*, pp. 102–11; "Algunos Comentarios sobre el Proyecto del Codigo de Trabajo," *Carta Semanal*, no. 452, 23 August 1958; "Los Representantes de la Libre Empresa Privada Podían Haber Contribuido con Su Experiencia a la Emisión de Un Codigo de Trabajo Eminentemente Imparcial," *Carta Semanal*, no. 476, 7 February 1959; "Primera Asamblea General Extraordinaria," *MCCIT, 1959*, pp. 10–14.

38. Posas, *Lucha Ideológica*, p. 14.

39. "Honduras: Housing for Banana Workers," *Hispanic American Report* 14, no. 6 (August 1961): 492; "Se Ultiman Detalles para el Prestamo de Cuatro Millones," *La Prensa*, 13 November 1964; "Plan de Vivienda Social de la FESITRANH," MCCIC, 1967, pp. 11–12.

40. "Relaciones con el Sector Obrero," MCCIC, 1965, pp. 21–22; "Plan de Vivienda Social de la FESITRANH," MCCIC, 1967, pp. 11–12; MCCIC, 1971, pp. 18–19.

41. *LAC* 46, 1 April 1955, p. 168. A broad outline of the Honduran peasant movement is available in Posas, "El Movimiento Campesino," pp. 28–76.

42. Posas, *Luchas del Movimiento*, p. 109; MacCameron, *Bananas, Labor, and Politics*, pp. 72–73; "La Tragedia del Valle de Sula," *Carta Semanal*, no. 65, 30 September 1954; "La Inundación," *Carta Semanal*, no. 66, 31 October 1954. According to one close analysis, "12 or 14 per cent of Honduras's wage earners (the monetized labor market) were employed by the Tela Railroad prior to 1954, while some 8 per cent remained in the [banana] Company work force immediately following the 1954–1955 layoffs." LaBarge, "La Huelga de la Costa Norte," p. 18.

43. Ellis, *Las Transnacionales del Banano*, p. 408.

44. Posas, "Política Estatal," pp. 42–44.

45. The PDRH called for agrarian reform in its platform of 1950. Posas, "Reforma Agraria," p. 106 nn. 5–6.

46. Amaya Amador, *Destacamento Rojo*, p. 187; Posas, *Breve Historia*, pp. 11–12; "Honduras," *Hispanic American Report* 15, no. 3 (May 1962): 216; "Cooperativa Guanchias," *Revista Ariel*, no. 284 (December 1975): 8; Carney, *To Be a Revolutionary*, pp. 188–89.

47. Oquelí, "Gobiernos Hondureños," *Economía Política*, no. 8 (May–October 1974): 38; Romualdi, *Presidents and Peons*, pp. 135–36, 351, 379. Philip Agee says that

McLellan was either a CIA operative or used by the CIA. Agee, *Inside the Company*, pp. 305–7.

48. Pearson, "Peasant Pressure Groups," pp. 303–4.

49. Paz Barnica, *La Renovada*, pp. 384–85 (quotation), 396; Oquelí, "Gobiernos Hondureños," *Economía Política*, no. 10 (1976): 20–21; Paz Barnica, *Las Garantías*, pp. 393–426; MacCameron, *Bananas, Labor, and Politics*, p. 114; Posas, "Política Estatal," p. 48; Posas, *Breve Historia*, p. 14.

50. Posas, *Breve Historia*, p. 14; Carney, *To be a Revolutionary*, p. 192; Secretaría de Trabajo, *Estadísticas*, p. 10.

51. Interviews, González González and Martínez Guzmán.

52. "Constitucionalidad Piden Obreros en Costa Norte," *El Cronista*, 5 November 1963.

53. "Un Precipitado Pronunciamiento de la FESITRANH," editorial, *El Día*, 27 April 1964; "Lideres Sindicalistas Explican Su No Comparecencia a la Asamblea," *La Prensa*, 26 March 1965.

54. "Primero de Mayo, Día del Trabajo," editorial, *La Prensa*, 1 May 1965.

55. "Constituida la Confederación de Trabajadores Hondureños," *El Cronista*, 28 September 1964; Posas, *Las Centrales*, pp. 5–6.

## CHAPTER 7

1. "U.S. Suspends Honduras Ties after Coup," *Chicago Tribune*, 4 October 1963.

2. Partido Liberal de Honduras, *Biografías de Personajes Liberales*, p. 22; Fonseca, *Cuatro Ensayos Sobre*, pp. 87–90.

3. Schwarz, *Liberal: Adolf A. Berle*, pp. 319–20. According to the U.S. ambassador stationed in Honduras between 1960 and 1964, Villeda Morales and Berle continued "as close friends" when Berle visited him in the early 1960s. Burrows, Transcript of Oral History Interview, pp. 6–7.

4. Bishop Berle and Beal Jacobs, *Navigating the Rapids*, p. 768 (first quotation); Schwarz, *Liberal: Adolf A. Berle*, pp. 339–41.

5. Ameringer, *The Democratic Left*, pp. 269–83; Borge, *La Paciente Impaciencia*, p. 149. This in many ways resembled President Vicente Mejía Colindres's initial support of Sandino in 1927–28. See Chapter 3.

6. Ardón, *La Ruta de los Condores*.

7. Rabe, *Eisenhower and Latin America*, p. 105; Jonas Bodenheimer, "Poder a Control Remoto," pp. 109, 115–18.

8. Schwarz, *Liberal: Adolf A. Berle*, pp. 312, 324.

9. Levinson and Onís, *The Alliance*, pp. 52–53.

10. Consejo Nacional de Economía, *Informe de las Labores*, p. 6; Thompson, "Economic Analysis," pp. 85–125; Wynia, *Politics and Planners*, p. 75.

11. Foster, *Latin American Government Leaders*, pp. 85–86; *LAC* 43, 16 March 1953, pp. 265–66; *LAC* 46, 15 June 1955, pp. 256–58; *LAC* 47, 15 October 1955, p. 93; RMC 24, 12 February 1954, pp. 251–56.

12. Robles, "Los Empresarios Deben Influir"; Marta R. Argueta, "Reseña Histórica," p. 17.

13. Yu Shan Salinas, "Historia y Desarrollo," p. 21; RMC 25, 25 June 1956, pp. 332–62, 21 January 1957, pp. 472–73; RMC 26, 7 April 1958, pp. 124–31.

14. This biographical sketch is drawn from Luque, *Memorias de un Soldado Hondureño*, 2:43; "Murió Ilustre Copaneco Don Abraham Bueso Pineda," *La Prensa*, 22 April 1965; Stokes, *Honduras*, pp. 46, 79, 216; Mario R. Argueta, *Tiburcio Carías*, p. 15; and Bueso Arias, "Lo Que Viví."

15. "U.S. Ready to Cut Ties to Honduras," *New York Times*, 4 October 1963.

16. Levinson and Onís, *The Alliance*, p. 349.

17. Matute Canizales, *Algunas Sendas*, pp. 179–84; "Ricardo Zúniga Augustinus," in José F. Martínez, *Honduras Histórica*, pp. 328–32; Department of State, "Key Personalities," in "Visit of President Villeda Morales, Washington, November 30, 1962."

18. Turcios Rodriguez, *Movimiento Militar*; Department of State, Bureau of Intelligence and Research, Intelligence Report 7954; Ardón, *Una Democracia en Peligro*.

19. Blandón, *Entre Sandino y Fonseca*, pp. 82–96; Ameringer, *The Democratic Left*, pp. 274–77.

20. O'Connor, "Agrarian Reform in Cuba," p. 169; Padula, "The Fall of the Bourgeoisie: Cuba," pp. 161–66.

21. "Honduras-Controversy Regarding Cuba," *Hispanic American Report* 13, no. 1 (March 1960): 19–20; "OAS Agricultural Mission to Honduras," ibid., no. 11 (January 1961): 779–80. Former ambassador Charles F. Burrows recalled that Villeda Morales understood his agrarian law to be "part of the Alliance for Progress." Burrows, Transcript of Oral History Interview, p. 14.

22. "Habrá Foro sobre Reforma Agraria el Lunes Próximo en H.R.N.," *El Día*, 24 August 1962; "Memorandum for the President," enclosure to "Memorandum, Edwin M. Martin, Assistant Secretary of State, to President John F. Kennedy, December 1962," in U.S. Department of State, Declassified Documents: Retrospective Collection, 1976, Fiche Collection 500E to 503E; Burrows, Transcript of Oral History Interview, p. 14.

23. Bernstein, *Foreign Investment in Latin America*, pp. 186–211. According to Burrows, the company "was battering the doors . . . in Washington to get instructions sent to me: 'Tell Villeda Morales he has to veto that thing.'" Burrows, Transcript of Oral History Interview, p. 15.

24. "Memorandum for the President," enclosure to "Memorandum, Edwin M. Martin, Assistant Secretary of State, to President John F. Kennedy, December 1962," in U.S. Department of State, Declassified Documents: Retrospective Collection, 1976, Fiche Collection 500E to 503E. For details on the broader Honduran context and the 1962 agrarian reform law, see Posas, "Reforma Agraria," pp. 75–119.

25. Burrows, Transcript of Oral History Interview, p. 35.

26. Ibid., p. 32; Vicente Machado Valle, H., "Sucesos de Honduras, 1961," *El Día*, 3 January 1962, and "Honduras Rompió con Cuba y Dio Reconocimiento a Tres Gobiernos," *El Día*, 12 October 1963; "Honduras Justifica Un Golpe," *El Día*, editorial, 13 April 1963; Paredes, *Liberalismo*, pp. 151–53; Paz Barnica, *La Renovada*, pp. 405–17; "Un Golpe a la Democracia," editorial, *El Día*, 26 September 1963.

27. Oficina de Información, *Gobierno Militar*, pp. 46–47. The 1963 cabinet included Darío Montes, a member of a dissident wing of the Liberal Party—the Partido Ortodoxo Liberal. According to a CIA document, however, Montes's "animosity to then

President Ramón Villeda Morales was stronger than his loyalty to the Orthodox leader, Roque Rivera." See CIA, "Biographical Sketch of Darío Montes." Rivera, then president of the Tegucigalpa Chamber of Commerce, had denounced Villeda Morales's unwillingness or incapacity to counter the communist threat. Filadélfo Suazo, *Rivera*, pp. 72–79.

28. "Selection of New Political Leaders," *Hispanic American Report* 13, no. 2 (April 1960): 92; "Se Ratifica Unidad de Nacionalismo," *El Día*, 23 February 1962; "Nacionalismo de la Costa Postula Como Candidato al Dr. Juan Manuel Gálvez," *El Día*, 16 October 1962.

29. "Rumors of Revolt: Solidarity with Cuban Revolution," *Hispanic American Report* 13, no. 11 (January 1961): 778; Domínguez, *Ascenso al Poder*, pp. 45–46.

30. Consejo Nacional de Elecciones, "Elecciones Municipales de 1962," *El Día*, 14 November 1962; Oficina de Relaciones Publicas del Gobierno de Honduras, "Cuadro de Elecciones Municipales," *El Día*, 13 November 1962; Partido Nacional de Honduras, *Elecciones Municipales*; "La Gran Convención del Partido Nacional," *El Día*, 16 February 1963; Paredes, *El Hombre del Puro*, pp. 75, 80–86.

31. Domínguez, *Ascenso al Poder*, p. 83.

32. Virgilio Zelaya Rubí, "Burrows Niega Ingerencia en la Política Hondureña," *El Día*, 7 March 1963; "Estados Unidos Acusado por Un Hondureño Dice el Miami News," *El Día*, 9 March 1963; "Bonilla Actuó por Su Propia Cuenta en Ciudad de Miami," *El Día*, 18 March 1963. Soon after the October coup, the conservative *El Día* reported that López Arellano had conceded that in February 1963 the U.S. embassy "discreetly insinuated" that he decline the nationalist candidacy. "Reloj de la Política," *El Día*, 5 November 1963. Burrows later recalled his discussions with López Arellano. Burrows, Transcript of Oral History Interview, p. 40.

33. José F. Martínez, *Honduras Histórica*, pp. 322–27; Paredes, *Los Culpables*, pp. 157–66.

34. "En Busca de Un Candidato," editorial, *El Día*, 23 April 1963; "Anuncian Organización de Otro Partido en Honduras," *El Día*, 13 June 1963; "Tiburcio Carías Andino No Tiene Vinculación con Partido Nacional," *El Día*, 23 September 1967; "Oposición del Partido Nacional a Inscripción del PPP," *El Día*, 6 August 1963.

35. *LAM* 53, 5 October 1963, pp. 225–26.

36. RMC 21, 17 May 1948, pp. 251–54; "Historia de Un Amor," *Boletín Rotario*, no. 770, 8 June 1966; RMC 26, 18 August 1960, pp. 437–50; Ruíz, *Apuntes Biográficos Hondureños*, pp. 173–74.

37. "En SPS Rinden Homenaje a Distinguidos Ciudadanos," *Diario Tiempo*, 27 February 1987; "Fábrica de Camisas Bolívar," *La Prensa*, 29 June 1967; Ministerio de Economía, "Empresas Clasificadas y Protegidas"; RMC 21, 31 August 1948, pp. 273–74; RMC 23, 7 June 1952, pp. 400–16.

38. Interview, Gabriel A. Mejía; "Curriculum Vitae [Jaime Rosenthal Oliva]," *Diario Tiempo*, 12 June 1993; RMC 29, agreement 192 (1964), pp. 340–49.

39. Mirtha Torres de Mejía, "Revelase Violenta Actitud en Traspaso de Municipalidad," *La Prensa*, 15 January 1965.

40. The representatives from the business association who did participate are listed in "Acuerdo 324, Integrada Comisión Electoral," Oficina de Información, *Gobierno Militar*, p. 57. Only Julio Galdámez appears to be an exception to this proposition. His

interests lay primarily in cattle in Cortés. In order to identify business association membership, membership lists of these organizations were reviewed in *La Industria* (1963–64), the journal of the Asociación Nacional de Industriales, and the CCIT's *Memorias* for 1960–64.

41. FESITRANH's counterpart in Tegucigalpa, the FECESITLIH, also was not represented in the Electoral Commission. "FECESITLIH Fuera de Comisión Electoral," *El Cronista*, 28 November 1963. It is important to note that in December 1958 FESITRANH leaders, along with U.S. labor operatives, were instrumental in organizing the FECESITLIH.

42. Matute Canizales, *Algunas Sendas*, p. 190; Burrows, Transcript of Oral History Interview, p. 53; Oficina de Información, *Gobierno Militar*, pp. 51–53.

43. "Renuncia Lic. Darío Montes," *El Cronista*, 11 January 1964.

44. Mario R. Argueta, *Diccionario*, pp. 152–54; "Mario Rivera López," in José F. Martínez, *Honduras Histórica*, pp. 394–96. According to a political commentator of the period, Rivera López "inherited the executive skills of his father." Lara Cerrato, *Radiografía de Algunos Políticos*, p. 21.

45. CIA, "Honduras," in Survey of Latin America; "Renuncia Ministro de Defensa por Desacuerdo con Jefe de Gobierno," *La Prensa*, 8 December 1964; "¿Siguen Queriendo?," editorial, *La Prensa*, 31 May 1968.

46. Domínguez, *Ascenso al Poder*, pp. 248–49; "Hubo Crisis entre Militares Manifiesta Escalón en Carta," *La Prensa*, 5 July 1965; CIA, Intelligence Memorandum on "Instability in Latin America."

47. "Constituyente Eligió Presidente Provisional al Col. Oswaldo López," *La Prensa*, 19 March 1965; "Intervención Oratoria del Ilustre Parlamentario Don Julio Galdámez Zepeda . . . ," in Asamblea Nacional Constituyente, *Boletín Legislativo . . . 1965*, 2:195.

48. "Villeda Morales Visitó Ocotepeque," *La Prensa*, 13 May 1965 (first quotation); Bishop Berle and Beal Jacobs, *Navigating the Rapids*, p. 805.

## CHAPTER 8

1. "Gobierno Dió Plazo Perentorio para Que Comerciantes Abran Sus Establecimientos." *El Día*, 21 September 1968. Colonel López Arellano was made a general by his supporters in the Constituent Assembly of 1965.

2. "La Prensa Empastelada por los Agentes del DIN," *El Día*, 29 September 1968; "El Tema de Moda," editorial, *El Día*, 24 January 1967.

3. "Dualismo de La Prensa," *La Prensa*, 9 February 1967 (*El Nacional*). *El Pueblo* is cited in *La Prensa*'s refutation of *El Pueblo*'s claim. See "Aclaración," *La Prensa*, 13 July 1967.

4. "Garantías Constitucionales Suspendidas por el Regimen," *El Día*, 19 September 1968; "Ortodoxia contra los Izquierdistas," *El Día*, 23 January 1967; Pedro Rovelo Landa, "Situación y Posición del Liberalismo Ortodoxo," *El Día*, 22 September 1962.

5. Natalini de Castro et al., *Significado Histórico*, pp. 175–98; McCamant, *Development Assistance*, pp. 37, 45.

6. "Garantías Pide Partido Liberal al Gobierno," *El Cronista*, 11 June 1964; "37 Detenidos Políticos en San Pedro Sula Quieren Salir de la Prisión al Exilio," *El Cronista*, 25 July 1964.

7. Members of a radical wing of the Liberal Party, still influenced by the Cuban Revolution, chose to confront the López Arellano regime militarily. They failed. Longino Becerra, "Redacción, Prólogo y Notas," in García, *El Jute*, pp. 7–17; "CIA, 'Honduras,'" in Survey of Latin America, pp. 138–39; Domínguez, *Ascenso al Poder*, p. 139.

8. Burrows, Transcript of Oral History Interview, p. 51; Schwarz, *Liberal: Adolf A. Berle*, p. 340; Bishop Berle and Beal Jacobs, *Navigating the Rapids*, p. 805.

9. Leiva Vivas, *Un País*, pp. 59–64; Bishop Berle and Beal Jacobs, *Navigating the Rapids*, pp. 804–5.

10. "Diputados Liberales Integraron Asamblea Nacional Constituyente," *La Prensa*, 23 March 1965.

11. "Presentan a la Constituyente el Proyecto Constitucional," *La Prensa*, 24 March 1965; "Autoridad Maxima del Liberalismo Aprueba Conducta de Sus Diputados," *La Prensa*, 25 March 1965; Becerra, *Evolución Histórica*, p. 180; "Lideres Sindicales Explican Su No Comparecencia a la Asamblea," *La Prensa*, 26 March 1965.

12. "Manifiesto de los Siete Que No Asistieron a la Constituyente," *El Cronista*, 26 March 1965; "¿Capitularon los Constituyentes Liberales?," editorial, *La Prensa*, 27 March 1965; "Sube a Cinco Número de Diputados Liberales en la Constituyente," *La Prensa*, 31 March 1965.

13. "La Renuncia de Tres Ejecutivos Exigen Profesionales Liberales," *La Prensa*, 31 May 1965; "Asumen Cargos los Nuevos Dirigentes en el Consejo Central Ejecutivo," *La Prensa*, 14 June 1965. Suazo Cordova later served as president of Honduras from 1982 to 1986.

14. Zaldívar Guzmán, *Liberalismo*, pp. 90–99.

15. "Proponen Candidatos al Consejo Liberal," *La Prensa*, 6 October 1965.

16. "Tenemos Economía y Presupuesto Desequilibrados," *La Prensa*, 14 December 1965; "Acción Más Dinamica para 1966 Pide Gabriel A. Mejía," *La Prensa*, 17 December 1965.

17. "Nuevo Consejo Ejecutivo de Liberalismo es Rodista," *El Día*, 25 April 1966; "Ayer Finalizó XVII Convención Liberal," *La Prensa*, 25 April 1966; Zaldívar Guzmán, *Liberalismo*, p. 95. Osorio Contreras was editor of the PDRH's *Vanguardia*. "Indicador de Vanguardia," no. 61, 23 September 1947.

18. Paz Barnica, *La Renovada*, pp. 421–26.

19. Ibid., pp. 305–61; "Breve Análisis de la Situación Política Hondureña," *Vanguardia*, no. 87, 28 April 1948.

20. Suazo Rubí, *Auge y Crisis*, pp. 96–99.

21. "Ortodoxia contra los Izquierdistas," *El Día*, 23 January 1967; Suazo Rubí, *Auge y Crisis*, pp. 95–106; "Expulsiones en el Partido Liberal," *El Día*, 24 January 1967; "Medrano: Yo Acuso," *La Prensa*, 26 January 1967; Leiva Vivas, "Anarquía dentro del Liberalismo"; "Pastor Zelaya Apoyaba la Rebelión," *El Día*, 25 January 1967.

22. On 8 March 1967 *El Día* publicized a manifesto signed by prominent liberals who supported the CCE's position. "Respaldo al Consejo del Liberalismo." The

majority of the liberal deputies did not sign the document. Also see Paz Barnica, *La Renovada Ruta*, pp. 103–4, and Suazo Rubí, *Auge y Crisis*, pp. 106–7.

23. "Convención Extraordinaria del Partido Liberal," *La Prensa*, 25 August 1967.

24. "A la Nación," *La Prensa*, 21 October 1967.

25. "Palabras Claras," editorial, *La Prensa*, 21 December 1967.

26. Ibid.; Leiva Vivas, "Centro de Estudios."

27. Leiva Vivas, "Exito de la Financiera Hondureña."

28. "Memorandum al Consejo de Planificación," in Quiñonez and Argueta, *Historia de Honduras*, pp. 196–205; "Destituyen Ingeniero Miguel A. Rivera," *La Prensa*, 9 June 1967.

29. Levine, *El Sector Privado*, pp. 28–29.

30. Morris, "Interest Groups," p. 110 n. 2; MCCIC, 1965, pp. 15–16; MCCIC, 1966, pp. 18–22; "La Empresa Privada Se Unifica," editorial, *La Prensa*, 14 December 1966; "Tenemos Economía y Presupuesto Desequilibrados," *La Prensa*, 14 December 1965.

31. Waiselfisz, "El Comercio Exterior," pp. 173–75; Bulmer-Thomas, *Political Economy of Central America*, p. 194; Delgado, *Evolución del Mercado Común Centroamericano*, pp. 93–113.

32. "Anexo," MCCIC, 1966, n.p.

33. Interview, Martínez Guzmán. Martínez Guzmán was then a key FESITRANH official. He noted that Bográn and others issued formal invitations to him and other labor leaders on the North Coast.

34. Leiva Vivas, "Centro de Estudios."

35. "Sindicatos Exigen López Arellano Enfrente Crisis," *La Prensa*, 22 July 1967; Leiva Vivas, *Un País*, pp. 20–21.

36. Leiva Vivas, *Un País*, p. 57.

37. Thomas P. Anderson, *Politics in Central America*, p. 69; "260 Liberales Integraron Municipalidades del País," *El Día*, 3 June 1968; "Juan F. López: Nuevo Alcalde," *El Día*, 17 June 1968.

38. Rietti, "Análisis de la Situación Económica"; Gabriel A. Mejía, Céleo González, and Oscar Gale Varela to López Arellano, 30 April 1968, published in *La Prensa*, 21 June 1968.

39. "Los Sindicatos Exigen: Respuestas al Presidente," *La Prensa*, 22 April 1968; letters in the private archive of Gabriel A. Mejía. The first letter is dated 8 April 1968, a few days after the CCE ordered its adherents in the Congress to abandon their seats the first time.

40. Wynia, *Politics and Planners*, p. 109; Williams, "The Central American Common Market," pp. 307–12.

41. Williams, "The Central American Common Market," pp. 310–11; Wynia, *Politics and Planners*, p. 109.

42. "Industriales Aceptan el Protocolo de Costa Rica," *El Día*, 14 June 1968; "Opinión de la CCIT sobre Nuevos Impuestos," *El Día*, 21 June 1968; MCCIC, 1968, pp. 8–10; Leiva Vivas, *Un País*, pp. 109–12; "El Origen de la Crisis Económica," editorial, *La Prensa*, 14 June 1968.

43. "Pedirán al Congreso Que Demore Discusión del Impuesto del 30%," *La Prensa*, 28 June 1968; "Reunión en la Cumbre sobre 30%," *La Prensa*, 28 July 1968;

Dirección General de Tributación, "Boletín de Prensa No. 26," *El Día*, 23 September 1968.

44. "En Sigilo Aprueban Protocolo San José," *La Prensa*, 8 August 1968. I am grateful to Don Gabriel A. Mejía for access to the following documents: "Estrictamente Confidencial: Memorandum [sobre] Reunión en Casa Presidencial El Día 10 de Julio de 1968. . . ." and "Estrictamente Confidencial: Memorandum de la Reunión entre el Sector Público y el Sector Privado de San Pedro Sula el 18 de Julio de 1968. . . ."

45. Confidential letter to General López Arellano, 20 August 1968, from Gabriel A. Mejía, Edgardo Dumas Rodríguez, and Rafael Pastor Zelaya of the CCIC and from Céleo González, Oscar Gale Varela, and Marco Antonio Altamirano of the FESITRANH.

46. "Congreso Aprueba Impuesto Adicional," *La Prensa*, 22 August 1968.

47. In addition to the sources cited, this account is based on interviews with Gabriel A. Mejía, president of the CCIC (1964–78); Edgardo Dumas Rodríguez, legal counsel to the CCIC (1966–72); Andrés Felipe López, CCIC treasurer (1966–72); Antonio José Coello, CCIC Advisory Board (1967–72); Céleo González González, secretary general of the FESITRANH (1957–75?); Saúl Martínez Guzmán, who occupied various posts in the FESITRANH in the 1960s, including in 1968; and Andrés Víctor Artiles, secretary-general of the CTH (1966–89?).

48. "Sindicatos Harán Nuevo Análisis de Situación Nacional," *La Prensa*, 27 August 1968.

49. Even before the 17 September meetings, National Party congressional deputies tried to introduce a bill that threatened "unscrupulous merchants" with exile or the loss of Honduran citizenship if they tried to abuse the excise taxes by unduly raising prices. "Multas para los Comerciantes Inescrupulosos," *El Día*, 4 September 1968.

50. Ricardo Gavídia, "Planilla de Alcaldes Municipales," *El Día*, 3 November 1962; "Intervención Oratoria del Ilustre Parlamentario Don Julio Galdámez Zepeda, en la Sesión de la Asamblea Nacional Constituyente . . . ," in Asamblea Nacional Constituyente, *Boletín Legislativo*, 2:195–96; "Decepción," *La Prensa*, 16 September 1968.

51. "Lista de Presidentes del Club Rotario Sampedrano," in "Historia de Un Amor," *Boletín Rotario*, no. 770, 8 June 1966; RMC 22, 3 November 1950, pp. 40–61; RMC 21, 17 May 1948, pp. 251–54. Names of the members of the CCIC Board of Directors were extracted from CCIC *Boletíns* and *Memorias*.

52. RMC 25, 25 June 1956, pp. 332–621; RMC 28, 22 July 1964, pp. 461–83.

53. "Empresas de Radio Solicitan Reapertura de Dos Estaciones," *El Día*, 30 September 1968; Andrés Alvarado Lozano, "Memorandum de Diario La Prensa," 14 September 1987. Alvarado Lozano then was the chief editor of *La Prensa*; he had also served on the paper's editorial board from 1964 to 1968 and remained an employee until 1971. He prepared this memorandum in response to questions provided to him in 1987.

54. Andrés Alvarado Lozano, "Memorandum de Diario La Prensa," 14 September 1987; "De Nuevo con Nuestros Lectores," editorial, *La Prensa*, 15 October 1968.

55. "Persecusiones en San Pedro Sula," *El Día*, 14 October 1968; "Pedimos Suspensión Proceso Contra el Lic. Bográn," *La Prensa*, 16 October 1968; Euraque, "Social Structure," p. 197.

## CHAPTER 9

1. Bahr, *El Cuento de la Guerra*, p. 45; Rowles, *El Conflicto*, p. 143; Rouquie, "Honduras–El Salvador, p. 17.

2. Thomas P. Anderson, *War of the Dispossessed*, pp. 114–15.

3. MCCIC, 1969, pp. 19, 26; "Quince Millones de Lempiras y Una Clara Definición: Bográn Fortín," *Revista Extra*, no. 50 (September 1969): 13–16.

4. Durón, "La Batalla," p. 51; interview, Artiles.

5. "Nueva Dirigencia en la CTH," *La Prensa*, 26 March 1969; interviews, González González and Martínez Guzmán. Martínez Guzmán, then and now a top official with the FESITRANH, was imprisoned with González in 1968.

6. "Consultara sobre el Regreso de Céleo González," *La Prensa*, 18 November 1968; "CTH Emite Energica Resolución," *La Prensa*, 25 March 1969; "A Todo el Pueblo Hondureño," *El Cronista*, 25 March 1969.

7. CTH Emite Energica Resolución," *La Prensa*, 25 March 1969; "A Todo el Pueblo Hondureño," *El Cronista*, 25 March 1969.

8. CTH Emite Energica Resolución," *La Prensa*, 25 March 1969; "A Todo el Pueblo Hondureño," *El Cronista*, 25 March 1969.

9. Salomón, *Militarismo y Reformismo*, pp. 232–38; Black, *Sentinels of Empire*, p. 40.

10. Rabe, *Eisenhower and Latin America*, p. 108.

11. Black, *Sentinels of Empire*, p. 41; Barber and Ronning, *Internal Security*, pp. 65–80; Ropp, "The Honduran Army," p. 522.

12. Thomas P. Anderson, *War of the Dispossessed*, pp. 126, 124; White, *The Morass*, p. 44; Rouquie, "Honduras–El Salvador," pp. 21, 40; Rowles, *El Conflicto*, p. 254; Flores Ochoa, *El Retorno de Caín*, pp. 125–33.

13. "El Salvador con la Oligarquía Más Cerrada de América Latina," *El Día*, 27 June 1969, cited in Carías and Slutsky, *La Guerra Inutil*, p. 151; Durón, "La Batalla," pp. 48, 51. On Durón's early professional and civic activities, see Hilton, "Honduras," p. 57. On Durón's ties to Banco Atlántida, see "Se Inician los Festejos del Cincuentenario del BANCATLAN," *El Día*, 9 February 1963, and "Banco Atlántida Inicia la Construcción de Moderno Edificio," *La Prensa*, 15 March 1972. For Durón's legal counsel to other multinationals, see RMC 26, 29 December 1959, pp. 324–34, and 7 June 1960, pp. 405–8.

14. Ardón, *Días de Infamia*, pp. 65–70; Bográn, "El Cuadro Político Salvadoreño," pp. 33–34.

15. Durham, *Scarcity and Survival*, p. 59. After July 1969 many foreign commentators reduced the "causes" of the war to the "passions" and "nationalist fervor" associated with soccer games played between El Salvador and Honduras that June. Both countries participated in the elimination rounds for the World Cup championships in 1970. Hondurans rejected this "analysis" early on. Simon Torres Castillo, "La Guerra de Caines Contra Abeles No la Guerra del Football," *La Prensa*, 12 August 1969.

16. Carías and Slutsky, *La Guerra Inutil*, pp. 128–34; Rowles, *El Conflicto*, pp. 52–53, 59, 141–43; Rouquie, "Honduras–El Salvador," p. 19; Thomas P. Anderson, *War of the Dispossessed*, p. 108.

17. Williams, *Export Agriculture*, pp. 197–200; Dunkerley, *The Long War*, p. 53.

18. "El Salvador Es un Pueblo Ejemplar," *Carta Semanal*, no. 445, 5 July 1958; "Las Desventajas de Nuestras Pocas Industrias," *Carta Semanal*, no. 422, 22 January 1958.

19. "Sampedranos Respaldan al Dr. Pastor Zelaya," *La Prensa*, 28 January 1967.

20. "El Gobierno Gira a la Izquierda," editorial, *La Prensa*, 28 August 1967; "Gobierno de López Arellano Puede Calificarse Como Socialista," *La Prensa*, 27 November 1967.

21. "Resolverán Problemas de Asociación de Campesinos," *El Día*, 13 December 1966.

22. *La Prensa*: "INA Apoya Campesinos contra Sr. Echeverry," 4 August 1957; "Resolución Ilegal del INA," 7 August 1967; "Expropiaremos Manifiesta Director del INA," 16 August 1967; "AGAS Se Dirige al Presidente," 24 August 1967; "Anoche en la Cámara de Comercio, Alarma en Sector Inversionista, Giro Hacia la Izquierda," 29 August 1967.

23. Posas, *Breve Historia*, pp. 15–16; Pearson, "Peasant Pressure Groups," p. 310; "Treinta Millones en Bonos para el INA," *La Prensa*, 7 December 1968; Rowles, *El Conflicto*, p. 52.

24. Brockett, "The Commercialization of Agriculture," p. 84.

25. Posas, "Política Estatal"; Pan American Union, *Economic Survey*, p. 307; Williams, *Export Agriculture*, pp. 197, 200.

26. Pastor Fasquelle, *Memoria de una Empresa*, pp. 218, 238–61; RMC 32, 11 July 1966, pp. 95–124; Williams, *Export Agriculture*, p. 68; Del Cid, "Compañías Azucareras y Productores," pp. 110, 112; Slutsky, "La Agroindustria," pp. 147, 158 n. 37; Rietti, "Exposición," p. 15; RMC 26, 18 August 1960, pp. 437–50; RMC 117, 6 November 1967, pp. 205–17; Williams, *Export Agriculture*, p. 184; Instituto de Investigaciones Econónomicas y Sociales, "Empresas Industriales"; Castillo Rivas, *Acumulación de Capital*, pp. 249–50.

27. "Exito de la Financiera Hondureña," *Revista Extra*, no. 21 (April 1967): 11.

28. Leiva Vivas, "La Empresa Privada," p. 18.

29. "Nacionalismo Reitera Respaldo al Regimen del General López Arellano," *El Día*, 28 October 1968; "¿Buscarán Asegurar Reelección de OLA?" *La Prensa*, 15 January 1969; "Partido Liberal Plantea Lucha Violenta," *La Prensa*, 16 July 1970.

30. Thomas P. Anderson, *War of the Dispossessed*, p. 132; Salomón, *Militarismo y Reformismo*, pp. 45–49.

31. Manuel Gamero, "Fuerzas Nacionales Piden Reorganización Administrativa," *La Prensa*, 26 August 1969; "Comité Civico Nacional: Un Muerto Ilustre," editorial, *La Prensa*, 19 September 1969.

32. Morris, "Interest Groups," p. 231; Gabriel A. Mejía, "La Función de las Fuerzas Vivas"; "Nuestra Pequeña Burguesía Naciente," *La Prensa*, 21 November 1969; Oscar Gale Varela, "Un Desafío a la Conciencia Nacional," *La Prensa*, 22 November 1969; "Participantes en la Tercera Reunión de las Fuerzas Vivas de Honduras," *La Prensa*, 11 December 1970; MCCIC, 1970, pp. 24–27; MCCIC, 1971, pp. 14–15; Morris and Ropp, "Corporatism and Dependent Development," p. 61 n. 41.

33. Anonymous, "III Reunión de las Fuerzas Vivas," p. 28; Morris, "The Honduran Plan," pp. 14–15.

34. Morris, "The Honduran Plan," pp. 14–15.

35. "Señores Miembros del Consejo Central Ejecutivo del Partido Liberal y Comité Central del Partido Nacional," photocopy of typed manuscript of the December 1970 planteamiento (obtained from the private collection of Gabriel A. Mejía); Morris, "Interest Groups," p. 221; Salomón, *Militarismo y Reformismo*, p. 53; Matute Canizales, *Algunas Sendas*, pp. 171–74.

36. Morris, "The Honduran Plan," p. 22; Carney, *To Be a Revolutionary*, p. 235. Reyes Rodriguez remained head of ANACH until 1978. Posas, *Breve Historia*, pp. 35–36.

37. Mejía related that Zúñiga Augustinus harbored a grudge against him because he felt that Mejía, a major National Party player until 1963, had obstructed his nomination for the presidency before the October 1963 elections. Interview, Gabriel A. Mejía.

38. Manuel Gamero, "Batres: Diálogo Debe Continuar," *La Prensa*, 13 May 1968; interview, Gabriel A. Mejía.

39. Santos M., *Díez Años de Lucha*, pp. 79–91, 3; Morris, "The Honduran Plan," p. 27.

40. Morris, "The Honduran Plan," pp. 22–23. Apparently Zelaya should have been formally consulted because he signed the March 1969 *Llamamiento*.

41. Interviews, Gabriel A. Mejía and González González. The old, repressive López Arellano regime had violently imposed Zelaya's leadership in FECESITLIH after an abortive strike in 1965. Posas, *Lucha Ideológica*, pp. 62–63.

42. "Convenio Político entre el Partido Nacional y el Partido Liberal de Honduras," *Foro Hondureño*, no. 4 (February–April 1971): 90–95.

43. Ibid.

44. The fact that Carlos R. Reina was Bueso Arias's official campaign coordinator in 1971 probably angered the *Rodistas*. "Curriculum Vitae del Abogado Carlos Roberto Reina," document distributed by Reina's presidential campaign in 1993.

45. Posas, *Modalidades del Proceso,* pp. 24–25; Paz Barnica, *La Renovada*, p. 118; Velásquez Díaz, *Reorganización Liberal*, p. 29.

46. "Dr. Ramón Ernesto Cruz," in José F. Martínez, *Honduras Histórica*, pp. 322–27; Matute Canizales, *Algunas Sendas*, pp. 237–40.

47. Posas, *Modalidades del Proceso*, pp. 185–93.

48. "Resumen Total de las Elecciones," *La Prensa*, 1 April 1971; "Paco Milla Bermúdez Ofrece Su Apoyo al Dr. REC," *La Prensa*, 25 January 1971; "Soy Liberal pero Daré Mi Apoyo al Dr. Cruz," *La Prensa*, 29 January 1971.

49. Ramón E. Cruz, *Discursos del Presidente Cruz, Año de 1971*, pp. 3–8; interview, Gabriel A. Mejía; Matute Canizales, *Algunas Sendas*, p. 245.

50. Paz Aguilar, *El Municipio en Honduras*, p. 20; "Resumen Total de Las Elecciones," *La Prensa*, 1 April 1971.

51. Ramón E. Cruz, *Discursos del Presidente Cruz, Primer Semestre 1972*, p. 6; "Concentración de Invasores Amenaza con Huelga de Hambre," *La Prensa*, 17 August 1971.

52. Rietti, "Diagnóstico de la Economía"; Matute Canizales, *Algunas Sendas*, p. 243.

53. Paz Barnica, *Reestructuración Institucional*, pp. 77–82, 85–86, 89–91, 126–27, 180; Williams, *Export Agriculture*, p. 330 (quotation); Williams, "The Central American Common Market," pp. 331–32.

54. "Cámara de Comercio e Industria Respalda a Don Gabriel Mejía," *La Prensa*, 19 November 1971.

55. "Cambio de la Junta Directiva del COHEP," *La Prensa*, 20 May 1972; ¿A Quien Representa? *Diario Tiempo*, 22 May 1972.

56. "¡Insolito! Aprueban Nuevos Estatutos del COHEP en 24 Horas," *Diario Tiempo*, 23 May 1972; "El Atraco al COHEP Termina en Fracaso," *Diario Tiempo*, 27 May 1972; "Evaluación del Pacto Comenzará Esta Noche," *Diario Tiempo*, 23 May 1972.

57. Morris, "The Honduran Plan," pp. 32–37; "Partido Liberal Requiere del Partido Nacional Si Reconoce Pactos Políticos," *La Prensa*, 21 October 1972; "Para Analizar Situaciones Políticas Reunense Hoy Diputados Liberales con el CCEPL," *La Prensa*, 9 November 1972; Mario V. Rietti, "Hay Indecisión e Indiferencia ante Crisis Económica del País," *La Prensa*, 1 November 1972.

58. Ramón Oquelí, "La Crisis, los 'Militares Patriotas' y Una Política Popular," *El Cronista Dominical*, 9 July 1972, cited in Oquelí, *Gente y Situaciones*, pp. 333–35.

59. Morris, "Interest Groups," p. 313 n. 4.

## CONCLUSION

1. "Golpe de Estado Cuenta con Tolerancia de la Ciudadanía," *La Prensa*, 5 December 1972; Posas and Del Cid, *La Construcción*, p. 186.

2. Euraque, "Merchants and Industrialists," p. 775; Grieb, "Honduras," p. 82.

3. U.S. Embassy, Tegucigalpa, to Secretary of State, 16 August 1956, dispatch 38, Confidential State Department Central Files: Honduras, 1955–1959, reel 2, 715.00/8-1656, RG 59, NA; Grieb, "Honduras," p. 83.

4. National Party ministers in the 1972 cabinet represented old but more reformist faces. Finance Minister Manuel Acosta Bonilla, Minister of Education Dr. Napoleon Alcerro Oliva, and Foreign Relations Minister Cesar A. Batres all had been involved in National Party activities since the 1950s. By 1971, however, at least Batres seemed prepared to abandon his ties to the political parties, including his own. "Solo Hombres de Fe y Buena Voluntad Podrán Hacer Efectivo el Pacto de Unidad Nacional," *La Prensa*, 5 November 1971. On the careers of Batres and the other National Party ministers, see Grieb, "Honduras," pp. 80–81, and Paredes, *Los Culpables*, pp. 157–66. López Arellano appointed to the Ministry of Natural Resources an old, experienced agricultural technocrat; Raúl Edgardo Soto had served every government since 1954. Grieb, "Honduras," p. 82.

5. "Historia del PINU," *La Prensa*, 22 November 1972; "Palabras del Doctor Miguel Andonie Fernández pronunciadas en el Programa de T.V. 'De Cara al Pueblo,' 11 de Noviembre de 1972." The latter talk is reprinted in a manuscript obtained from PINU offices in San Pedro Sula, entitled "PINU y Su Historia." On Andonie Fernández's investments in radio and television in the 1960s, see Luis Aníbal Gómez et al., *Desarrollo de la Comunicación*, pp. 3, 8.

6. Ibid.; Ramón Oquelí, "Anatomía del Desastre," *La Prensa*, 19 July 1967, cited in Oquelí, *Gente y Situaciones,* pp. 39–40.

7. Salomón, *Militarismo y Reformismo*, pp. 191–95; Posas, "Política Estatal," pp. 68–69.

8. McClintock and Lowenthal, *The Peruvian Experiment Reconsidered*.

9. Del Cid, "Los Limites de la Acción Estatal Bajo Situaciones Reformistas"; Ropp, *Panama Politics*, p. 50; Escobar Bethancourt, *Torrijos*, pp. 24–25. I am grateful to Professor Ropp for bringing Escobar Bethancourt's memoirs to my attention.

10. Ramos Bejarano, "Something New in Honduras?," p. 70.

11. An article in the Communist Party's journal published in late 1971 characterized the 1968 San Pedro Sula project as an alliance between a maturing "national bourgeoisie" and North Coast labor. "Lineamientos de la Lucha en el Frente Sindical," *Trabajo*, no. 26 (November–December 1971): 31–34. The discussion and article is cited in Posas and Del Cid, *La Construcción*, pp. 151, 176 n. 60.

12. Schulz and Schulz *The United States, Honduras*, p. 8.

13. Ibid., p. 319.

14. Ibid., pp. 14, 26.

15. Ibid., p. 12.

16. Williams, *States and Social Evolution*.

17. Arancibia C. *Honduras ¿Un Estado Nacional?*, p. 34; Molina Chocano, "La Formación del Estado," p. 56.

18. Marvin A. Barahona, "La Alcaldía Mayor." The mining-merchant circuit and world financial systems is explored in Finney, "Merchants, Miners." An important Honduran scholar recently offered an insightful analysis of the Tegucigalpa elite on the eve of the *Reforma*; see Zelaya, "Tipificación del Grupo Social Dominante."

19. This issue is tentatively explored in Vélez O. and Herrera, "Historia." An extraordinary book recently published in Honduras finally examines the country's colonial elites; see Oyuela, *Un Siglo en la Hacienda*.

20. Matheson, "History of Rosario Mine," p. 35.

21. Alfredo Léon Gómez, *El Escandolo del Ferrocarril*, p. 187; Salgado, "Noticia Biográfica del Gral. don Luis Bográn"; Vélez and Herrera, "Historia," pp. 152–58.

22. This hypothesis contrasts with prominent perspectives available in the most recent literature. See Weaver, *Inside the Volcano*, pp. 70, 90–92.

23. More recent discussion of the issue is available in Euraque, "La Metamorfosis de una Oligarquía." This essay engages the interesting ideas presented in Casaus Arzú, "La Metamorfosis de las Oligarquías Centroamericanas."

24. Schulz and Schulz, *The United States, Honduras*, pp. 19, 25.

25. Mario Posas, one of the most insightful analysts of post–World War II Honduran development, long ago described the 1963 coup as the failure of "the first bourgeois reform project of the post-war period." Posas, "Honduras at the Crossroads," p. 48. Unfortunately, Posas neglected the historic origins of that project especially on the North Coast.

26. For a different interpretation, see Sieder, "Honduras."

27. A recent account of southern Honduras details critical aspects of this region's post–World War II integration into the world economy. See Stonich, *"I Am Destroying the Land!."*

28. Torres-Rivas, *Repression and Resistance*, pp. 34, 50.

29. The militance of labor and capitalists in San Pedro Sula in the 1960s exemplified issues now explored more systematically in the "new social movements" literature; see Escobar and Alvarez, *The Making of Social Movements in Latin America*.

# BIBLIOGRAPHY

This bibliography is organized as follows:

Public and Private Archives, Collections, and Libraries
Interviews
Newspapers, Bulletins, and Other Periodicals
Special Private Collections
Honduran Government Publications and Manuscripts
U.S. Government Publications and Documents
Secondary Works on Honduras
Secondary Works on Latin America
Works on U.S. Foreign Policy
Dissertations and Theses Written in the United States
Other Works Consulted

## PUBLIC AND PRIVATE ARCHIVES, COLLECTIONS, AND LIBRARIES

### *Honduras*

*San Pedro Sula*

Archivo Histórico de la Alcaldía Municipal de San Pedro Sula
Archivo Privado del Lic. Pompeyo Melara
Archivo Privado de Don Gabriel A. Mejía
Archivo Privado del Lic. Aníbal Delgado Fiallos
Biblioteca de la Cámara de Comercio e Industrias de Cortés
Biblioteca del Centro Regional del Norte, Universidad Nacional Autonoma de Honduras
Registro Mercantil de Cortés

*Tegucigalpa*

Archivo y Biblioteca Nacional de Honduras
Archivo del Ministerio de Hacienda
Biblioteca "Colección Hondureña," Universidad Nacional Autonoma de Honduras
Biblioteca del Banco Central de Honduras
Biblioteca de la Cámara de Comercio e Industrias de Tegucigalpa
Instituto de Investigaciones Económicas y Sociales, Universidad Nacional Autonoma de Honduras

*United States*
*New York*
New York City Public Library

*Washington, D.C.*
Library of Congress
National Archives
Record Group 59: Department of State, General Records
Record Group 84: Department of State, Diplomatic Post Files

## INTERVIEWS

Artiles, Andrés Víctor. Secretary-General of CTH, 1966–90; joined North Coast labor unions after the 1954 strike in La Ceiba. Taped interview, 31 August 1987, Tegucigalpa.

Coello Bobadilla, Antonio José. Studied economics in Mexico; member, CCIC Advisory Board, 1967–early 1970s. Taped interview, 17 September 1987, San Pedro Sula.

Dumas Rodríguez, Edgardo. Minister of Finance, 1964, and Chief Legal Counsel to the CCIC, 1964–72. Taped interview, 9 September 1987, San Pedro Sula.

González González, Céleo. President of FESITRANH, 1957–80?; joined San Pedro Sula labor unions in 1954 and cofounded SITRATERCO and FESITRANH in 1955 and 1957. Taped interview, 5 October 1987, Tegucigalpa.

López, Andrés Felipe. Treasurer and General Manager of the CCIC, 1964–72; studied economics in San Pedro Sula and Brazil, and joined the CCIC when asked by Gabriel A. Mejía in 1964. Taped interview, 16 September 1987, San Pedro Sula.

Martínez Guzmán, Saúl. Secretary of FESITRANH, 1963–75; joined San Pedro Sula labor unions after 1954. Taped interview, 18 September 1987, San Pedro Sula.

Mejía, Gabriel A. Minister of Finance, 1956–57; President of the CCIC, 1964–78; and President of COHEP, 1966–72. Taped interview, 22 September 1987, San Pedro Sula.

## NEWSPAPERS, BULLETINS, AND OTHER PERIODICALS

The periodicals listed below are ones cited frequently in this study and available in public archives and libraries. Years in parentheses represent periods of consistent publishing and years consulted for this book.

*Boletín*, AGAS (1954–56)
*Boletín*, BNF (1951–58)
*Boletín*, CCH-CCIT (1921–30, 1940–42, 1950–58)
*Boletín*, CDSPS (1943–56)
*Boletín*, MFOA (1918–23)
*Carta Semanal*, CCIC (1949–63)

*Diario Tiempo*, San Pedro Sula (1970–72)
*El Cronista*, Tegucigalpa (1963–64)
*El Día*, Tegucigalpa (1962–68)
*El Economista Hondureño* (1927–30, 1937–48, 1953–58)
*Honduras Rotaria*, Tegucigalpa (1944–58)
*En Marcha*, San Pedro Sula (1954–58)
*La Prensa*, San Pedro Sula (1964–72)
*Revista Comercial*, CCA (1927–30)
*Revista de Cultura Comercial*, Tegucigalpa (1958–59)
*Revista Extra*, Tegucigalpa (1965–72)

## Special Private Collections

*Documentos Privados de Don Gabriel A. Mejía*. Mejía was the federal auditor of the country's customhouses from 1936 to 1939 and managed the Administration of Tax Revenues for the Department of Cortés in the 1940s. Between 1950 and 1956 he headed the Honduran Internal Revenue Service, then served briefly as minister of finance (1956–57). He was president of the Cortés Chamber of Commerce and Industry from 1964 to 1978 and of the Consejo Hondureño de la Empresa Privada from 1966 to 1972.

*Documentos Privados del Ingeniero Don Amílcar Gómez Robelo (1944–48)*. Gómez Robelo was a prominent liberal from San Pedro Sula who fled into exile in the mid-1940s; until the late 1940s he assumed various positions in liberal exile organizations. His extensive correspondence and other papers, which cover many issues of exile politics, are held privately by Lic. Anibal Delgado Fiallos in San Pedro Sula.

*Documentos Privados del Ingeniero Don Rafael López Padilla (1923–62)*. A good friend of Samuel Zemurray in the 1910s and 1920s, López Padilla cultivated bananas in the Sula Valley and elsewhere in Cortés until the early 1930s. His extensive correspondence and other papers cover many topics related to the presence of the United Fruit Company in the area from the 1920s to the 1950s. Don Pompeyo Melara kindly donated these documents for my private collection.

## Honduran Government Publications and Manuscripts

Asamblea Nacional Constituyente. *Boletín Legislativo de la Asamblea Nacional Constituyente, 1957*. Vol. 2. Tegucigalpa: Tipografía Ariston, 1961–62.

——. *Boletín Legislativo de la Asamblea Nacional Constituyente, 1965*. Vol. 1. Tegucigalpa: TIPN, n.d.

——. *Boletín de la Asamblea Nacional Constituyente, 1957*. Vol. 1. Tegucigalpa: TIPN, 1959.

Banco Central de Honduras. *Memoria del Banco Central de Honduras, 1958–59*. Tegucigalpa: Imprenta Calderón, 1960.

——. *Memoria del Banco Central de Honduras, 1957*. Tegucigalpa: Imprenta Calderón, 1958.

——. *Memoria del Banco Central de Honduras, 1955–1956*. Tegucigalpa: Imprenta Calderón, 1957.
——. *Memoria del Banco Central de Honduras, 1954*. Tegucigalpa: Imprenta Calderón, 1955.
——. *Memoria del Banco Central de Honduras, 1952–1953*. Tegucigalpa: Imprenta Calderón, 1954.
——. *Primera Memoria del Banco Central de Honduras, 1950–1951*. Tegucigalpa: López y Cía., 1952.
Banco Centroamericano de Integración Económica. *Primera Memoria de Labores, 1961–1962*. Tegucigalpa: BCIE, 1963.
Banco Nacional de Fomento. *Memoria del Banco Nacional de Fomento, 1966*. Tegucigalpa: TIPN, [1967?].
Consejo Nacional de Economía. *Plan Nacional de Desarrollo Económico y Social de Honduras, 1965–1969*. 5 vols. Tegucigalpa: TIPN, 1965.
——. *Informe de las Labores del Consejo Nacional de Economía*. Tegucigalpa: TIPN, 1961.
Consejo Nacional de Elecciones. "Convenio Político entre el Partido Nacional y el Partido Liberal de Honduras." *Foro Hondureño*, no. 4 (February–April 1971): 90–95.
Consejo Superior de Planificación Económica. *Diagnóstico del Sector Industrial, Periodo 1960–1972: Imagen Actual*. Tegucigalpa: TIPN, 1974.
——. *Boletín Estadístico de Indicadores Económicos de Honduras*. Tegucigalpa: CONSUPLANE, 1970.
——. *Regionalización*. Tegucigalpa: TIPN, 1968.
Dirección General de Estadística y Censos. *Honduras: Histórica-Geográfica*. Tegucigalpa: DGEC, 1980.
——. *La Estadística en Honduras*. Tegucigalpa: DGEC, 1977.
——. *Investigación Comercial, 1963–1964*. Tegucigalpa: DGEC, 1967.
——. *Directorio de Establecimientos Comerciales*. Tegucigalpa: DGEC, 1965.
——. *Directorio Industrial, 1965*. Tegucigalpa: DGEC, 1965.
——. *Directorio de Establecimientos Comerciales*. Tegucigalpa: DGEC, 1963.
——. *Investigación Industrial, 1956–1957, 1958, 1959, 1960*. Tegucigalpa: DGEC, 1961.
——. *Investigación Comercial, 1954–1957*. Tegucigalpa: DGEC, 1959.
——. *Estadísticas Industriales, 1953, 1954, 1955*. Tegucigalpa: DGEC, 1957.
——. *Estadísticas Industriales, 1953*. Tegucigalpa: DGEC, 1956.
——. *Resúmen del Censo General de Población . . ., 1945*. Tegucigalpa: DGEC, 1947.
——. *Resúmen del Censo General de Población . . ., 1935*. Tegucigalpa: DGEC, 1936.
——. *Resúmen del Censo General de Población . . ., 1930*. Tegucigalpa: DGEC, 1932.
——. *Resúmen del Censo General de Población . . ., 1926*. Tegucigalpa: DGEC, 1927.
Ministerio de Agricultura. *Informe del Ministerio de Agricultura, 1952–1953*. Tegucigalpa: TIPN, 1954.
Ministerio de Economía. "Empresas Clasificadas y Protegidas por la Ley de Fomento Industrial de 1958 y Subsiguientes Reformas, 1960–1972." Ministry of Economics Archives. (An official who wished to remain anonymous allowed me to make a copy of this important document in 1987.)
Ministerio de Fomento. *Informe de Fomento, Agricultura y Trabajo, 1951–1952*. Tegucigalpa: TIPN, 1953.

——. *Informe de Fomento, Agricultura y Trabajo, 1950–1951*. Tegucigalpa: TIPN, 1952.
——. *Informe de Fomento, Agricultura y Trabajo, 1949–1950*. Tegucigalpa: TIPN, 1951.
——. *Informe de Fomento, Agricultura y Trabajo, 1948–1949*. Tegucigalpa: TIPN, 1950.
——. *Informe de Fomento, Agricultura y Trabajo, 1945–1946*. Tegucigalpa: TIPN, 1947.
——. *Informe de Fomento, Agricultura y Trabajo, 1944–1945*. Tegucigalpa: TIPN, 1946.
——. *Informe de Fomento, Agricultura y Trabajo, 1941–1942*. Tegucigalpa: TIPN, 1943.
——. *Informe de Fomento, Agricultura y Trabajo, 1940–1941*. Tegucigalpa: TIPN, 1942.
——. *Informe de Fomento, Agricultura y Trabajo, 1938–1939*. Tegucigalpa: TIPN, 1940.
——. *Informe de Fomento, Agricultura, Trabajo y Comercio, 1937–1938*. Tegucigalpa: TIPN, 1939.
——. *Informe de Fomento, Agricultura, Trabajo y Comercio, 1936–1937*. Tegucigalpa: TIPN, 1938.
——. *Informe de Fomento, Agricultura y Trabajo, 1935–1936*. Tegucigalpa: TIPN, 1937.
——. *Informe de Fomento, Agricultura y Trabajo, 1934–1935*. Tegucigalpa: TIPN, 1936.
——. *Informe de Fomento, Agricultura y Trabajo, 1933–1934*. Tegucigalpa: TIPN, 1935.
——. *Memoria de Fomento, Agricultura, y Trabajo, 1929–1930*. Tegucigalpa: TIPN, 1931.
——. *Memoria de Fomento, Obras Públicas, Agricultura y Trabajo, 1928–1929*. Tegucigalpa: TIPN, 1930.
——. *Memoria de Fomento, Obras Públicas, Agricultura y Trabajo, 1927–1928*. Tegucigalpa: TIPN, 1929.
——. *Memoria de Fomento, Obras Públicas, Agricultura y Trabajo, 1926–1927*. Tegucigalpa: TIPN, 1928.
——. *Memoria de Fomento, Obras Públicas, Agricultura y Trabajo, 1925–1926*. Tegucigalpa: TIPN, 1927.
——. *Memoria de Fomento, Obras Públicas, Agricultura y Trabajo, 1924–1925*. Tegucigalpa: TIPN, 1926.
——. *Memoria de Fomento, Obras Públicas y Agricultura, 1923–1924*. Tegucigalpa: TIPN, 1925.
——. *Memoria de Fomento, Obras Públicas y Agricultura, 1922–1923*. Tegucigalpa: TIPN, 1924.
——. *Memoria de Fomento, Obras Públicas y Agricultura, 1917–1918*. Tegucigalpa: TIPN, 1919.
——. *Memoria de Fomento, Obras Públicas y Agricultura, 1915–1916*. TIPN, 1917.
——. *Memoria de Fomento, Obras Públicas y Agricultura, 1914–1915*. Tegucigalpa: TIPN, 1916.
——. *Memoria de Fomento, Obras Públicas y Agricultura, 1913–1914*. Tegucigalpa: TIPN, 1915.
——. *Memoria de Fomento, Obras Públicas y Agricultura, 1912–1913*. Tegucigalpa: TIPN, 1914.
——. *Memoria de Fomento, Obras Públicas y Agricultura, 1911–1912*. Tegucigalpa: TIPN, 1913.
——. *Memoria de Fomento, Obras Públicas y Agricultura, 1910–1911*. Tegucigalpa: TIPN, 1912.
——. *Memoria de Fomento y Agricultura, 1908–1909*. Tegucigalpa: TIPN, 1910.
——. *Memoria de Agricultura, 1909*. Tegucigalpa: Tipografía, 1909.
——. *Memoria de Fomento y Obras Públicas, 1907–1908*. Tegucigalpa: TIPN, 1909.

———. *Memoria de Fomento y Obras Públicas, 1903–1905*. Tegucigalpa: TIPN, 1906.
———. *Memoria de Fomento y Obras Públicas, 1902–1903*. Tegucigalpa: TIPN, 1904.
———. *Memoria de Fomento y Obras Públicas, 1901–1902*. In *Boletín Legislativo*, nos. 7–9 (January 1903): 49–72.
Ministerio de Hacienda. *Memoria de Economía y Hacienda, 1959–1960*. Tegucigalpa: MHCP, 1961.
———. *Informe de Hacienda, Crédito Público y Comercio, 1949–1950*. Tegucigalpa: Tipografía Ariston, 1951.
———. *Informe de Hacienda, Crédito Público y Comercio, 1948–1949*. Tegucigalpa: Tipografía Ariston, 1950.
———. *Informe de Hacienda, Crédito Público y Comercio, 1947–1948*. Tegucigalpa: Tipografía Ariston, 1949.
———. *Memoria de Hacienda, Crédito Público y Comercio, 1946–1947*. Tegucigalpa: Tipografía Ariston, 1948.
———. *Memoria de Hacienda, Crédito Público y Comercio, 1945–1946*. Tegucigalpa: Tipografía Ariston, 1947.
———. *Memoria de Hacienda, Crédito Público y Comercio, 1944–1945*. Tegucigalpa: Tipografía Ariston, 1946.
———. *Memoria de Hacienda, Crédito Público y Comercio, 1943–1944*. Tegucigalpa: Tipografía Ariston, 1945.
———. *Memoria de Hacienda, Crédito Público y Comercio, 1942–1943*. Tegucigalpa: Tipografía Ariston, 1944.
———. *Memoria de Hacienda, Crédito Público y Comercio, 1941–1942*. Tegucigalpa: Tipografía Ariston, 1943.
———. *Memoria de Hacienda, Crédito Público y Comercio, 1940–1941*. Tegucigalpa: TIPN, 1942.
———. *Memoria de Hacienda, Crédito Público y Comercio, 1939–1940*. Tegucigalpa: TIPN, 1941.
———. *Memoria de Hacienda, Crédito Público y Comercio, 1938–1939*. Tegucigalpa: TIPN, 1940.
———. *Memoria de Hacienda, Crédito Público y Comercio, 1937–1938*. Tegucigalpa: TIPN, 1939.
———. *Memoria de Hacienda y Crédito Público, 1936–1937*. Tegucigalpa: TIPN, 1938.
———. *Memoria de Hacienda y Crédito Público, 1935–1936*. Tegucigalpa: TIPN, 1937.
———. *Memoria de Hacienda y Crédito Público, 1932–1933*. Tegucigalpa: TIPN, 1934.
———. *Memoria de Hacienda y Crédito Público, 1930–1931*. Tegucigalpa: TIPN, 1932.
———. *Memoria de Hacienda y Crédito Público, 1929–1930*. Tegucigalpa: TIPN, 1931.
———. *Memoria de Hacienda y Crédito Público, 1928–1929*. Tegucigalpa: TIPN, 1930.
———. *Memoria de Hacienda y Crédito Público, 1927–1928*. Tegucigalpa: TIPN, 1929.
———. *Memoria de Hacienda y Crédito Público, 1925–1926*. Tegucigalpa: TIPN, 1927.
———. *Memoria de Hacienda y Crédito Público, 1924–1925*. Tegucigalpa: TIPN, 1926.
———. *Memoria de Hacienda y Crédito Público, 1921–1922*. Tegucigalpa: TIPN, 1923.
———. *Memoria de Hacienda y Crédito Público, 1920–1921*. Tegucigalpa: TIPN, 1922.
———. *Memoria de Hacienda y Crédito Público, 1919–1920*. Tegucigalpa: TIPN, 1921.
———. *Memoria de Hacienda y Crédito Público, 1914–1915*. Tegucigalpa: TIPN, 1916.
———. *Memoria de Hacienda y Crédito Público, 1913–1914*. Tegucigalpa: TIPN, 1915.

——. *Memoria de Hacienda y Crédito Público, 1912–1913*. Tegucigalpa: TIPN, 1914.
——. *Memoria de Hacienda y Crédito Público, 1911–1912*. Tegucigalpa: TIPN, 1913.
——. *Memoria de Hacienda y Crédito Público, 1908–1909*. Tegucigalpa: TIPN, 1910.
——. *Memoria de Hacienda y Crédito Público, 1903–1904 y 1904–1905*. Tegucigalpa: TIPN, 1906.
——. *Memoria de Hacienda y Crédito Público, 1901–1902*. In *Boletín Legislativo*, nos. 13–14 (February 1903): 97–112.
Oficina Hondureña de Cooperación Intelectual. *Acontecimientos en Relación al Nuevo Gobierno de Concentración Nacional*. Tegucigalpa: TIPN, 1955.
Oficina de Información de la Jefatura de Gobierno. *Gobierno Militar de la República de Honduras: Documentos*. Tegucigalpa: TIPN, 1964.
República de Honduras. *Datos Biográficos del Presidente Constitucional de la República de Honduras, Ingeniero José Azcona H. y Los Designados a la República, 1986–1990*. Tegucigalpa: 1990.
——. *Indice General de Concesiones en Honduras*. Tegucigalpa: TIPN, 1930.
——. *Boletín Legislativo de la Asamblea Nacional Constituyente, 1957*. Vol. 2, nos. 21–23. Tegucigalpa, 1961–62.
Secretaría de Trabajo y Previsión Social. *Estadísticas del Trabajo, 1967*. Tegucigalpa: TIPN, 1968.

## U.S. Government Publications and Documents

Bureau of the American Republics. "Honduras: Trade with the United States." *Monthly Bulletin*, vol. 3 (July 1895–June 1896): 503–6. Washington, D.C.: GPO, 1897.
——. "Honduras." In *Commercial Directories of Latin America*, pp. 129–33. Washington, D.C.: GPO, 1892.
Burrows, Charles F. Transcript of Oral History Interview, 1969. John F. Kennedy Library, Boston, Mass.
Central Intelligence Agency. "Honduras." In Intelligence Memorandum: Instability in Latin America, 19 May 1965, p. 3. Office of Current Intelligence No. 1758/65. The Declassified Documents Reference System, 1977, CIA, fiche 89A-91E, doc. F.
——. "Honduras." In Survey of Latin America, 1 April 1964, p. 137. Office of Current Intelligence No. 1063/64. The Declassified Documents Reference System, 1977, CIA, fiche 272c, 2 of 3 documents, pp. 137–40.
——. "Biographical Sketch of Darío Montes, Honduran Minister of Government, CIA Memo, 10/1963." The Declassified Documents Reference System, 1983, CIA, fiche 88, doc. 1547.
Department of Commerce. *Investment in Central America: Basic Information for U.S. Businessmen*. Washington, D.C.: GPO, 1956.
——. "Honduras." In *Trade Directory of Central America and the West Indies*, pp. 53–70. Washington, D.C.: GPO, 1915.
——. "Honduras." In *World Trade Directory*, pp. 164–66. Washington, D.C.: GPO, 1911.
Department of Labor. *Labor Law and Practice in Honduras*. Washington, D.C.: GPO, 1961.
Department of State. Bureau of Intelligence and Research. Intelligence Report 7954,

"Political Instability in Honduras, 19 February 1959." *O.S.S. / State Department Intelligence and Research Reports*, pt. xiv, *Latin America, 1941–1961*. Microfilm, reel 9. Washington, D.C.: University Publications of America, 1990.

——. "Visit of President Villeda Morales, Washington, November 30, 1962." The Declassified Documents Reference System, 1988, Department of State, fiche 178, doc. 2664–66.

——. Confidential U.S. State Department Central Files: Honduras, 1955–1959. Microfilm, 10 reels. Washington, D.C.: University Publications of America, 1987.

——. Confidential U.S. State Department Central Files: Honduras, 1950–1954. Microfilm, 11 reels. Washington, D.C.: University Publications of America, 1987.

——. Confidential U.S. State Department Central Files: Honduras, 1945–1949. Microfilm, 11 reels. Washington, D.C.: University Publications of America, 1987.

——. Confidential U.S. Diplomatic Post Records: Honduras, 1930–1945. Microfilm, 42 reels. Washington, D.C.: University Publications of America, 1985.

——. "Political and Economic Relations of the U.S. and Honduras." In *Foreign Relations of the United States, 1952–1954*, vol. 4, *The American Republics*, pp. 1293–1323. Washington, D.C.: GPO, 1983.

——. "The Question of Military Cooperation with the Honduran Regime as Affected by the U.S. Attitude toward Dictatorship." In *Foreign Relations of the United States, 1946*, vol. 11, *The American Republics*, pp. 955–68. Washington, D.C.: GPO, 1969.

——. "Cooperative Efforts by the U.S. to Relieve a Currency Shortage in Honduras." In *Foreign Relations of the United States, 1943*, vol. 6, *The American Republics*, pp. 372–95. Washington, D.C.: GPO, 1965.

——. *Records of the Department of State Relating to Internal Affairs of Honduras, 1910–1929*. Microfilm, 49 reels. Microcopy M647. Washington, D.C.: National Archives and Records Service, 1967.

——. *U.S. Treaties and Other International Agreements*. Vol. 12, pt. 1. Washington, D.C.: GPO, 1961.

——. *U.S. Treaties and Other International Agreements*. Vol. 6, pt. 2. Washington, D.C.: GPO, 1955.

——. *Dispatches from U.S. Consuls in Omoa, Trujillo, and Roatán, 1831–1893*. Microfilm, 6 reels. Microcopy T-477. Washington, D.C.: National Archives, 1934.

——. *Dispatches from U.S. Consuls in Puerto Cortés, 1902–1906*. Microfilm, 2 reels. Microcopy T-661. Washington, D.C.: National Archives, 1934.

House of Representatives. Select Committee on Communist Aggression. *Report of the Subcommittee to Investigate Communist Aggression In Latin America*. 83d Cong., 2d sess. Washington, D.C.: GPO, 1954.

## Secondary Works on Honduras

Acosta, Oscar. *Rafael Heliodoro Valle: Vida y Obra*. Tegucigalpa: UNAH, 1964.

Adams, Richard N. *Cultural Surveys of Panama–Nicaragua–Guatemala–El Salvador–Honduras*. Washington, D.C.: Pan American Sanitary Bureau, 1957.

Alsina Callizo, Ramón. "Aspectos Económicos de la Gganadería Vacuna en el Departamento de Cortés." Thesis, Centro Univerisatio Regional del Norte, 1965.

Alvarado, Elvia. *Don't Be Afraid Gringo: A Honduran Woman Speaks from the Heart.* Compiled by Medea Benjamin. New York: Harper and Row, 1987.
Alvarado Lozano, Andrés. "Memorandum de Diario *La Prensa*." San Pedro Sula, 14 September 1987.
Amaya Amador, Ramón. *Destacamento Rojo*. 1962. Reprint. Tegucigalpa: Editorial Universitaria, 1982.
——. *Prisión Verde*, ed. 1950. Reprint. Tegucigalpa: UNAH, 1974.
Amaya Amador, Ramón, and Rigoberto Padilla Rush. *Memorias y Enseñanzas del Alzamiento Popular de 1954*. Honduras: N.p., 1989.
Anderson, Charles W. "Honduras: Problems of an Apprentice Democracy." In *Political Systems of Latin America*, 2d ed., edited by M. Needler, pp. 75–88. New York: D. Van Nostrand, 1964.
Anderson, Thomas P. *Politics in Central America: Guatemala, El Salvador, Honduras, and Nicaragua*. Stanford, Calif.: Stanford University Press, 1982.
——. *The War of the Dispossessed: Honduras and El Salvador, 1969*. Lincoln: University of Nebraska Press, 1981.
Angulo Barahona, Raquel. "Concesiones." *Revista de Cultura Comercial*, no. 1 (May 1958): 35–41.
Anonymous. "III Reunión de las Fuerzas Vivas." *Libre Empresa*, no. 1 (May–June 1970): 22–29.
Anonymous. "La Compañía Aseguradora de el Ahorro Hondureño, S.A., Ha Cumplido Medio Siglo de Honrado y Eficáz Empeño." *Sucesos Centroamericanos* (Tegucigalpa), no. 120 (February–March 1967): 29–41.
Anonymous. "Lista de Presidentes del Club Rotario Sampedrano." In "Historia de un Amor." *Boletín Rotario*, no. 770 (8 June 1966).
Antúnez Castillo, Rubén. *Mis Memorias*. Vol. 2. San Pedro Sula: Imprenta Suyapa, 1979.
——. *Biografía del Matrimonio Bográn-Morejón* San Pedro Sula: Editora Nacional, 1967.
Arancibia C., Juan. *Honduras ¿Un Estado Nacional?*. Tegucigalpa: Editorial Guaymuras, 1984.
Ardón, Juan Ramón. *Días de Infamia*. Tegucigalpa: Departamento de Relaciones Publicas, 1970.
——. *Una Democracia en Peligro*. Tegucigalpa: Tipografía Ariston, 1959.
——. *La Ruta de los Condores*. Mexico: N.p., 1958.
Argueta, Mario R. *Los Alemanes en Honduras*. Tegucigalpa: CEDOH, 1992.
——. *Diccionario Histórico-Biográfico*. Tegucigalpa: Editorial Universitaria, 1990.
——. *Tiburcio Carías: Anatomía de Una Epoca, 1923–1948*. Tegucigalpa: Editorial Guaymuras, 1989.
——. *Bananos y Política: Samuel Zemurray y la Cuyamel Fruit Company en Honduras*. Tegucigalpa: Editorial Universitaria, 1989.
——. *Historia Laboral de Honduras: De la Conquista al Siglo xix (Aporte al Estudio de los Sin Historia)*. Tegucigalpa: Secretaría de Cultura y Turismo, 1986.
——. *Investigaciones y Tendencias Recientes de la Historiografía Hondureña: Un Ensayo Bibliográfico*. Tegucigalpa: Editorial Universitaria, 1981.
Argueta, Marta Reina. *Biografía Intelectual de Ramón Rosa*. Tegucigalpa: Editorial Guaymuras, 1986.

——. "Reseña Histórica del Sistema Bancario de Honduras." *Mundo Bantral* (July 1976): 1–55.

Artiles, Andrés Víctor. "Proyecciones Económicas de Honduras." *El Sindicalista*, 15 January 1972.

Baciu, Stefan. *Ramón Villeda Morales: Ciudadano de America*. Costa Rica: Imprenta Antonio Lehman, 1970.

Bahr, Eduardo. *El Cuento de la Guerra*. Tegucigalpa: Litografía López, 1988.

Baide Galindo, Martín. "Iconoclastas Ebrios de Triunfo." *En Marcha*, no. 91 (March 1958): 11–12.

Baker, Ernest H. "A Map of the Foreign Empire of the United Fruit Co. of Boston and New Orleans." *Fortune*, March 1933.

Baker, George W. "Ideals and Realities in the Wilson Administration's Relations with Honduras." *The Americas* 21 (1964–65): 3–19.

Barahona G., José Salvador, Luis A. Sánchez, and José Darío Izaguirre. "La Evolución de la Propiedad Privada Terrateniente en el Municipio de Choluteca, 1864–1891." Thesis, UNAH, 1989.

Barahona, Marvin A. *El Silencio Quedó Atrás: Testimonios de la Huelga Bananera de 1954*. Tegucigalpa: Editorial Guaymuras, 1994.

——. "La Alcaldía Mayor de Tegucigalpa Bajo el Regimen de Intendentes, 1788–1812." Manuscript, 1994.

——. *La Evolución Histórica de la Identidad Nacional*. Tegucigalpa: Editorial Guaymuras, 1991.

——. *La Hegemonía de los Estados Unidos en Honduras, 1907–1932*. Tegucigalpa: Centro de Documentación de Honduras, 1989.

Bardales Bueso, Rafael. *El Fundador de La Paz*. San Pedro Sula: Central Impresora, 1989.

——. *Imagen de un Líder: Manuel Bonilla*. Tegucigalpa: Editorial Universitaria, 1985.

——, comp. *Historia del Partido Nacional de Honduras*. Tegucigalpa: Servicopiax, 1980.

Bascom, John, comp. *Propaganda Pro-Honduras*. Havana: N.p., 1930.

Becerra, Longino. *Evolución Histórica de Honduras*. Tegucigalpa: Baktun, 1983.

——. "Prólogo." In *Prisión Verde*, 2d ed., edited by Longino Becerra, pp. 9–21. Tegucigalpa: UNAH, 1974.

Bobadilla, Perfecto H. *Monografía del Departamento de Cortés*. Tegucigalpa: Talleres Tipográficos Nacionales, 1944.

——, comp. *Monografía de la Ciudad de San Pedro Sula*. San Pedro Sula: Compañía Editora, 1936.

Bográn, Edmond L. "Entre el Marasmo." *Revista Extra*, no. 63 (October 1970).

——. "El Cuadro Político Salvadoreño." *Revista Extra*, no. 56 (March 1970).

——. "El Banco Central de Honduras: Ensayo de Sistematización Juridica de la Banca Central." Thesis, Universidad Nacional Autonoma de México, 1956.

Bonilla, Emma. *Continuismo y Dictadura*. Tegucigalpa: Litografía Comayaguela, 1989.

Brockett, Charles D. "The Commercialization of Agriculture and Rural Economic Insecurity: The Case of Honduras." *Studies In Comparative International Development* 22, no. 1 (Spring 1987): 82–102.

Bueso Arias, Jorge. "Lo Que Viví, durante e Inmediatamente Después del Golpe del 21 de Octubre de 1956." *Diario Tiempo*, 21 October 1991.

Cáceres Lara, Víctor. *Gobernantes de Honduras en el Siglo 20*. Tegucigalpa: Litografía López, 1992.
——. *Gobernantes de Honduras en el Siglo 19*. Tegucigalpa: Banco Central de Honduras, 1978.
——. *Efemérides Nacionales*. Tegucigalpa: Nuevo Continente, 1973.
Callejas, Jorge J. *Miseria y Despojo en Centroamerica*. Tegucigalpa: Editorial Jus, 1954.
Cámara de Comercio e Industrias de Cortés. Memorias de la Labor Desarrollada por la Cámara de Comercio e Industrias de Cortés durante los Años, 1964–1972. San Pedro Sula, n.d.
Cámara de Comercio e Industrias de Tegucigalpa. *Cuatro Años de Labores [1964–1967]*. Tegucigalpa: N.p., 1968.
——. Segunda Convención Nacional de Cámaras de Comercio e Industrias de la República de Honduras, Temario. Manuscript, CCIT Library, Tegucigalpa, 1949.
——. *Memorias de las Labores por la CCIT, 1946–1972*. Tegucigalpa: N.p., n.d.
Carías, Marcos, ed. *Ramón Rosa: Obra Escogída*. Tegucigalpa: Editorial Guaymuras, 1980.
Carías, Marcos V., and Daniel Slutsky, eds. *La Guerra Inutil: Análisis Socioeconómico del Conflicto entre Honduras y El Salvador*. San José: EDUCA, 1971.
Carney, Padre J. Guadalupe. *To Be a Revolutionary: An Autobiography*. San Francisco: Harper and Row, 1985.
Castañeda, Mauricio. "El Comercio Centroamericano de Honduras, [1956–1963]." *La Industria*, no. 124 (May 1964): 5.
——. "Algunos Aspectos Debiles de Nuestra Economía." *El Dia*, 17 October 1962.
Comité Liberal Democrata de Honduras en Mexico. *Manifiestos del Comité Liberal Demócrata de Honduras en Mexico*. Mexico: N.p., 1944.
Contreras, Carlos A. *Entre el Marasmo: Análisis de la Crisis del Partido Liberal de Honduras*. Tegucigalpa: HISA, 1970.
Cruz, Ramón E. *La Lucha Política de 1954 y La Ruptura Constitucional*. Tegucigalpa: Editorial Universitaria, 1982.
——. *Discursos del Presidente Cruz, Primer Semestre 1972*. Tegucigalpa: Oficina de Relaciones Públicas, 1972.
——. *Discursos del Presidente Cruz, Año de 1971*. Tegucigalpa: Oficina de Relaciones Públicas, 1972.
Cruz, René. "Dinero y Banca en Honduras: Reseña Histórica y Análisis de la Situación Originada por la Legislación de 1950 y la Creación del Banco Central de Honduras." Thesis, Yale University, January 1954.
Cruz Caceres, Francisco. *En las Selvas Hondureñas*. Tegucigalpa: TIPN, 1955.
Davidson, William. *Historical Geography of the Bay Islands of Honduras*. Birmingham: Southern University Press, 1979.
Del Cid, Rafael. "Economía Bananera y Desarrollo Nacional." Paper, Austin, Tex., 1986.
——. "Los Limites de la Acción Estatal Bajo Situaciones Reformistas: Los Casos de Honduras (1972–1975) y Panama (1968–1980)." *Estudios Sociales Centroamericanos*, no. 38 (1984): 13–39.
——. "Compañías Azucareras y Productores Independientes." *Estudios Sociales Centroamericanos*, no. 32 (May–August 1982): 97–129.

——. “Honduras: Industrialización, Empleo y Explotación de Trabajo.” *Economía Política*, no. 13 (November 1976–June 1977): 51–129.
Deustch, Hermann B. *The Incredible Yanqui: The Career of Lee Christmas*. London: Longman, Green, 1931.
Díaz Chávez, Filander. *Carías: El Ultimo Caudillo Frutero*. Tegucigalpa: Editorial Guaymuras, 1982.
——. *Sociología de la Desintegración Regional*. Tegucigalpa: Litografica Calderón, 1972.
Díaz Lozano, Argentina. *Aquel Año Rojo*. Guatemala: Ministerio de Educación, 1985.
Domínguez, Raúl A. *Ascenso al Poder y Descenso del General Oswaldo López Arellano*. Tegucigalpa: Imprenta Calderón, 1975.
Due, J. F. “The Retail Sales Tax in Honduras.” *Inter-American Economic Affairs*, no. 3 (Winter 1966): 55–67.
Durham, William H. *Scarcity and Survival in Central America: Ecological Origins of the Soccer War*. Stanford, Calif.: Stanford University Press, 1979.
Durón, Jorge Fidel. “La Batalla de Washington.” *Revista Extra*, no. 49 (August 1969): 47–56.
Elvir, Rafael Angel. *La Cartilla Histórica de los Teleños*. Tela: Mimeo, 1982.
Euraque, Darío A. “La Metamorfosis de una Oligarquía y las Elites de Poder en la Década de 1980: El Caso de Honduras.” In *Elites de Poder en América Central*, edited by Marta Elena Casaus Arzú. Madrid, 1996.
——. “Los Recursos Económicos del Estado Hondureño, 1830–1970.” In *Identidades Nacionales y Estado Moderno en Centroamérica*, compiled by Arturo Taracena y Jean Piel, pp. 135–50. San José, Costa Rica: EDUCA, 1995.
——. “Nation Formation: Mestizaje and Arab Palestinian Immigration to Honduras, 1880–1930s.” *Critique: Journal for Critical Studies of the Middle East*, no. 6 (Spring 1995): 25–37.
——. “The Social, Economic and Political Aspects of the Carías Dictatorship in Honduras: The Historiography.” *Latin American Research Review* (Albuquerque, N.Mex.) 29, no. 1 (1994): 238–48.
——. “Labor Recruitment and Class Formation on the Banana Plantations of the United Fruit Co. and the Standard Fruit Co. in Honduras, 1910s–1930s.” Paper presented at the Annual Conference of the American Historical Association, San Francisco, Calif., 6–9 January 1994.
——. “San Pedro Sula, Actual Capital Industrial de Honduras: Su Trayectoria entre Villorrio Colonial y Emporio Bananero, 1536–1936.” *Mesoamérica* (Vermont-Guatemala), no. 26, (December 1993): 217–52.
——. “Modernity, Economic Power, and the Foreign Banana Companies in Honduras: San Pedro Sula as a Case Study, 1880s–1945.” In *Essays in Economic and Business History*, vol. 11, edited by Edwin J. Perkins, pp. 49–65. University of Southern California, Los Angeles, June 1993.
——. “Estructura Económica, Formación de Capital Industrial, Relaciones Familiares y Poder Político en San Pedro Sula, 1870s–1958.” *Revista Polémica* (Costa Rica), no. 18 (September–December 1992): 31–50.
——. “Zonas Regionales en la Formación del Estado Hondureño, 1830s–1930s: El Caso de la Costa Norte,” *Revista Centroamericana de Economía* (Tegucigalpa) 13, no. 39 (September–December 1992): 65–102.

——. "La 'Reforma Liberal' en Honduras y la Hipótesis de la 'Oligarquía Ausente,' 1870s–1930s." *Revista de Historia* (Costa Rica), no. 23 (January–June 1991): 7–56.

Ferrera, Gloria E., Alicia Betancourth Oseguere, Maria Elizabeth Urtecho López, and Emma Yolanda Romero Gómez. "Gobierno del Doctor y General Tiburcio Carías Andino: Marco Histórico." Thesis, UNAH, 1985.

Finney, Kenneth V. "Merchants, Miners, and Monetary Structures: The Revival of the Honduran Import Trade, 1880–1900." *SECOLAS Annals* 12 (March 1981): 27–38.

——. "Our Man in Honduras: Washington S. Valentine." In *Dependency Unbends: Case Studies in Inter-American Relations*, no. 17, pp. 13–20. West Georgia College, 1978.

——. "Washington S. Valentine and the Honduras Interoceanic Railroad." Paper, Department of History, North Carolina Wesleyan College, n.d.

——. "Washington S. Valentine: The Yankee Who 'Bought' Honduras, 1890–1900." Paper, Department of History, North Carolina Wesleyan College, n.d.

Fletes, Ernesto. *Commercial Directory of Honduras*. Hamburg: Schroder and Jeve, 1911.

Flores Ochoa, Santiago. *El Retorno de Caín*. Buenos Aires: Impresiones Schmidel, 1970.

Flores Valeriano, Enrique. *La Explotación Bananera en Honduras: Capítulos del Deshonor Nacional*. Tegucigalpa: Editorial Universitaria, 1979.

Fonseca, Gautama. *Cuatro Ensayos sobre la Realidad Política de Honduras*. Tegucigalpa: Editorial Universitaria, 1982.

Funes H., Matías. *Los Deliberantes: El Poder Militar en Honduras*. Tegucigalpa: Editorial Guyamuras, 1995.

Gálvez, Juan Manuel, comp. *La Obra del Doctor Juan Manuel Gálvez en Su Administración, 1949–1954*. Tegucigalpa: TIPN, 1954.

García, Graciela. *Páginas de Lucha*. Tegucigalpa: Editorial Guaymuras, 1981.

García, Luis. *El Jute*. Tegucigalpa: Editorial Universitaria, 1991.

García de Contreras, Elvia. "Análisis de una Fábrica Textil Desde el Punto de Vista Social." Thesis, UNAH, 1967.

García Valderramo, Ulpiano. "Municipio de San Pedro Sula: Estudio Socioeconómico." Thesis, Centro Universitario Regional del Norte, 1974.

Gómez, Alfredo Léon. *El Escandolo del Ferrocarril*. Comayagua: Imprenta Soto, 1978.

Gómez, Luis Aníbal, et al. *Desarrollo de la Comunicación en Honduras: Aspectos de Investigación y Aspectos Legales*. Paris: UNESCO, 1979.

González, Nancie L. *Dollar, Dove, and Eagle: One Hundred Years of Palestinian Migration to Honduras*. Ann Arbor: University of Michigan Press, 1992.

——. *Sojourners of the Caribbean: Ethnogenesis and Ethnohistory of the Garífuna*. Urbana: University of Illinois Press, 1988.

Grieb, Kenneth J. "Honduras." In *Latin American Government Leaders*, 2d ed., edited by David W. Foster, pp. 80–85. Tempe: Arizona State University Press, 1975.

Guilbert, Henry D., and Policarpo Callejas, B. *Cincuentenario (1929-1979) del Club Rotario de Tegucigalpa*. Tegucigalpa: CETTNA, 1979.

Hidroservice Engenharia de Proyectos Ltda. *Plan de Desarrollo Urbano*. Vol. 1, *Síntesis del Plan de Desarrollo Urbano de San Pedro Sula*. Sao Paulo: Hidroservice Engenharia de Proyectos Ltda., 1976.

Instituto de Educación Política Popular del Partido Liberal. *Pensamiento Liberal de Zúñiga Huete*. Tegucigalpa: N.p., 1991.

Instituto de Investigación Económicas y Sociales. "Industrialización y Dependencia." In *Antología del Movimiento Obrero Hondureño*, edited by Víctor Meza, pp. 594–98. Tegucigalpa: Editorial Universitaria, 1981.
Instituto de Investigaciones Econónomicas y Sociales. "Empresas Industriales con el 10% O Más de Su Capital Social en Manos de Extranjeros." *Boletín del Instituto de Investigaciones Económicos y Sociales*, no. 140 (July 1984).
——. "¿Quienes Son los Representantes de la Nación?" In *Antología del Movimiento Obrero Hondureño*, edited by Víctor Meza, pp. 599–619. Tegucigalpa: Editorial Universitaria, 1981.
Izaguirre, Carlos. "Ideario Político-Administrativo del Partido Nacional." In *Historia del Partido Nacional de Honduras*, compiled by Rafael Bardales Bueso, pp. 61–87. Tegucigalpa: Servicopiax, 1980.
——. *Bajo el Chubasco: Novela de Caracter Político-Social*. Tegucigalpa: Ariston, 1945.
——. *Readaptaciones y Cambios*. Tegucigalpa: Imprenta Calderón, 1936.
——. *Honduras y Sus Problemas de Educación*. Tegucigalpa: TIPN, 1935.
Jauregui, Arturo. "The Young Free Trade Union Movement in Honduras." *Free Labor World*, no. 59 (May 1955): 26–31.
Joya, Olga, and Ricardo Urquía. "Incidencia del Estado en el Desarrollo Económico de Tegucigalpa." Thesis, UNAH, 1983.
Kattan, Héctor. "La Industria de la Ropa." *Boletín*, CCIT, no. 137 (April 1958): 19–27.
Kepner, Charles D., Jr., and Jay H. Soothill. *The Banana Empire: A Case Study of Economic Imperialism*. New York: Russell and Russell, 1967.
LaBarge, Richard A. "La Huelga de la Costa Norte: An Economic Analysis of the 1954 Strike against the UFCo. in Honduras." Paper presented to the Fourteenth Southeastern Conference of Latin American Studies, Atlanta, Georgia, 14–15 April 1967.
Laínez, Vilma, and Víctor Meza. "El Enclave Bananero en la Historia de Honduras." *Estudios Sociales Centroamericanos*, no. 5 (May–August 1973): 115–49.
Lara Cerrato, Fausto. *Radiografía de Algunos Políticos de Honduras*. San Pedro Sula: N.p., 1972.
——, comp. *Aspectos Culturales de Honduras*. Tegucigalpa: Imprenta Ariel, 1951.
Lazo, Héctor, comp. *Honduras*, U.S. Bureau of Foreign and Domestic Commerce, Bulletin No. 193. Washington, D.C.: GPO, 1924.
Leiva Vivas, Rafael. *Vacío Político, Crisis General y Alternativas al Desarrollo*. Santo Domingo: N.p., 1975.
——. *Honduras: Fuerzas Armadas, Dependencia o Desarrollo*. Chile: N.p., 1973.
——. "La Empresa Privada Hondureña Busca Una Revolución." *Revista Extra*, no. 56 (March 1970): 17–18.
——. "Nuestra Pequeña Burguesía Naciente." *La Prensa*, 21 November 1969.
——. "La República Libre de San Pedro Sula," *La Prensa*, 24 April 1968.
——. *Un País en Honduras*. Tegucigalpa: Imprenta Calderón, 1969.
——. "Centro de Estudios sobre la Problematica Nacional." *El Día*, 18 December 1967.
——. "Exito de la Financiera Hondureña." *Revista Extra*, no. 21 (April 1967): 11.
——. "Anarquía dentro del Liberalismo." *La Prensa*, 27 January 1967.

López Pineda, Julián. *Democracia y Redentorismo*. Managua: Tipografía Guardian, 1942.
——. *La Reforma Constitucional*. París: Ediciones Estrella, 1936.
Luque, Gonzálo R. *Memorias de un Soldado Hondureño*. Vol. 2. San Pedro Sula: Impresora Hondureña, 1982.
——. *Memorias de un Soldado Hondureño*. Vol. 1. San Pedro Sula: Impresora Hondureña, 1980.
——. *Memorias de un Sampedrano*. San Pedro Sula: Impresora Hondureña, 1979.
MacCameron, Robert. *Bananas, Labor, and Politics in Honduras, 1954–1963*. Syracuse: Syracuse University Press, 1983.
Mariñas Otero, Luis. *Las Constituciones de Honduras*. Madrid: Ediciones Hispánicas, 1962.
Márquez, Javier, Paul Vinelli, Alexander N. McLeod, and Julio González del Solar. *Estudio sobre la Economía de Honduras*. Tegucigalpa: BCH, 1951.
Martínez, José Francisco, comp. *Honduras Histórica*. Tegucigalpa: Imprenta Calderón, 1974.
Martínez Silva, Práxedes. "Participación de Honduras en el Programa de Integración Económica Centroamericana." *El Día*, 8 January 1965.
Matheson, Kenneth H. "History of Rosario Mine Honduras, Central America." *Mines* magazine, July 1961, pp. 22–28.
——. "History of Rosario Mine Honduras, Central America." *Mines*, June 1961, pp. 33–38.
Matute, Carlos H. "El Problema Político de Honduras." *El Cronista*, 11 February 1964.
——. "Breves Reflexiones en Materia de Política Nacional." *El Dia*, 29 January 1957.
Matute Canizales, Eugenio. *Algunas Sendas que Caminé*. San Pedro Sula: Imprenta la República, n.d.
Mejía, Gabriel A. "La Empresa Privada en Honduras en 1970." *Revista Extra*, no. 66 (January 1971): 35–37.
——. "La Función de las Fuerzas Vivas en el Desarrollo Económico y Social de Honduras." *Libre Empresa*, no. 1 (February–March 1970): 15–18.
——. "Estructuración de la Empresa Privada." *El Día*, 12 December 12, 1967.
Mejía, Medardo. *Froylán Turcios en los Campos de la Estética y el Civismo*. Tegucigalpa: Editorial Universitaria, 1980.
——. *Historia de Honduras*. 6 vols. Tegucigalpa: Editorial Universitaria, 1983–90.
Mejía, Romualdo E. *El 4 de Julio de 1944*. Tegucigalpa: Tipografía Ariston, 1945.
——. *La Vida y la Obra de un Estadista*. Tegucigalpa: La Epoca, 1942.
——. *La Obra Patriotica del Congreso Nacional* Tegucigalpa: TIPN, 1941.
Mejía Deras, Ismael. *Policarpo Bonilla: Algunos Apuntes Biográficos por Aro Sanso*. Mexico: Imprenta Mundial, 1936.
Mejía Moreno, Luis. *El Calvario de los Demagogos*. Tegucigalpa: TIPN, 1939.
——. *El Calvario de un Pueblo*. Tegucigalpa: TIPN, 1937.
Melara, Pompeyo. "El Instituto Nacional Agrario No Fomenta las Invasiones." *Revista Extra*, no. 51 (October 1969): 9–11.
Mendieta Guillen, Eduardo. "Problema Económico del Tabaco en Honduras." Thesis, UNAH, 1954.
Meza, Víctor. *Historia del Movimiento Obrero Hondureño*. Tegucigalpa: Editorial Guaymuras, 1980.

——, ed. *Antología del Movimiento Obrero Hondureño*. Tegucigalpa: Editorial Universitaria, 1981.

Meza, Víctor, and Héctor López. "Las Inversiones Extranjeras en Honduras antes del Mercado Común Centroamericano." *Economía Política*, no. 6 (September–December 1973): 47–79.

Molina Chocano, Guillermo. *Estado Liberal y Desarrollo Capitalista en Honduras*. Tegucigalpa: Editorial Universitaria, 1982.

——. "La Formación del Estado y el Origen Minero-Mercantil de la Burguesía Hondureña." *Estudios Sociales Centroamericanos*, no. 25 (January–April 1980): 56–89.

——. "Población, Estructura Productiva y Migraciones en Honduras, 1950–1960." *Estudios Sociales Centroamericanos*, no. 12 (September–December 1975): 9–39.

——. "Dependencia y Cambio en la Sociedad Hondureña." *Estudios Sociales Centroamericanos*, no. 1 (January–April 1972): 11–26.

Mondragón Carrasco, Rubén. "Naturaleza y Desarrollo de la Industria en Honduras." Thesis, Universidad Nacional Autonoma de México, 1952.

Mondragón Carrasco, Rubén, and Manuel Tosco. *Aspectos Demográficos y Económico-Sociales de la Población de Honduras*. Tegucigalpa: Banco Central de Honduras, 1952.

Morris, James A. "Honduras: The Burden of Survival in Central America." In *Central America: Crisis and Adaptation*, edited by S. Ropp and J. Morris, pp. 189–225. Albuquerque: University of New Mexico Press, 1984.

——. *Honduras: Caudillo Politics and Military Rulers*. Boulder, Colo.: Westview Press, 1984.

——. "The Honduran Plan Politico de Unidad Nacional, 1971–1972: Its Origins and Demise." Occasional Paper, Center for Inter-American Studies, University of Texas at El Paso, 1975.

Morris, James A., and Steve C. Ropp. "Corporatism and Dependent Development: A Honduran Case Study." *Latin American Research Review* 12, no. 2 (1977): 27–68.

Mossi Sorto, Perla, and Sidalia Batres Galeano, "Atecedentes Históricos Acerca del Dominio Territorial Urbano en Tegucigalpa (Siglo XIX)." Thesis, UNAH, 1982.

Murga Frassinetti, Antonio. "Industrialización y Formación de Clase: El Caso de la Fracción Industrial en Honduras." *Revista Centroamericana de Economía*, no. 17 (May–August 1985): 67–87.

——. "Industrialización Dependiente y Capital Imperialista en Honduras." *Cuadernos Políticos*, no. 31 (January–March 1982): 58–71.

——. *Enclave y Sociedad en Honduras*. Tegucigalpa: Editorial Universitaria, 1978.

——. "Estado y Burguesía Industrial En Honduras." *Estudios Sociales Centroamericanos*, no. 18 (September–December 1977): 119–55.

——. "Industrialización Dependiente y Sociedad." *Economía Política*, no. 11 (November 1975–April 1976): 39–66.

——. "Concentración Industrial en Honduras." *Economía Política*, no. 9 (April 1975): 70–78.

Murga Frassinetti, Antonio, and María Ester Caballero. "Nuevas Observaciones sobre la Concentración Industrial en Honduras." In *Honduras: Panorama y Perspectivas*, edited by Leticia Salomón, pp. 49–82. Tegucigalpa: Centro de Documentación de Honduras, 1989.

Murillo Soto, Céleo. *Un Hondureño y Una Actitud Política*. Tegucigalpa: TIPN, 1948.

Natalini de Castro, Stefanía, Maria de los Angeles Mendoza Saborro, and Joaquin Pagan Solorzano. *Significado Histórico del Gobierno del Dr. Ramón Villeda Morales*. Tegucigalpa: Editorial Universitaria, 1985.

Newson, Linda A. *The Cost of Conquest: Indian Decline in Honduras under Spanish Rule*. Boulder, Colo.: Westview Press, 1986.

——."Silver Mining in Colonial Honduras." *Revista de Historia de America*, no. 97 (January–June 1984): 45–75.

Oquelí, Ramón. *Gente y Situaciones, 1970–1974*. Tegucigalpa: Editorial Universitaria, 1995.

——. *Gente y Situaciones, 1966–1969*. Tegucigalpa: Editorial Universitaria, 1994.

——. *1862*. Tegucigalpa: Editorial Universitaria, 1990.

——. *Los Hondureños y Las Ideas*. Tegucigalpa: Editorial Universitaria, 1985.

——. "Gobiernos de Honduras durante el Presente Siglo." *Economía Política*. no. 15 (January–June 1978): 5–23.

——. "Gobiernos Hondureños durante el Presente Siglo." *Economía Política*, no. 11 (1977): 5–38.

——. "Gobiernos Hondureños durante el Presente Siglo." *Economía Política*, no. 12 (May–October 1976): 5–34.

——. "Gobiernos Hondureños durante el Presente Siglo." *Economía Política*, no. 10 (1976): 5–43.

——. "Gobiernos Hondureños durante el Presente Siglo." *Economía Política*, no. 9 (1975): 5–64.

——. "Gobiernos de Honduras durante Este Siglo." *Economía Política*, no. 8 (May–October 1974): 5–42.

——. "Gobiernos Hondureños durante el Presente Siglo." *Economía Política*, no. 7 (January–April 1974): 7–29.

——. "Gobiernos Hondureños durante el Presente Siglo." *Economía Política*, no. 4 (January–April 1973): 5–23.

——, comp. *Boletín de la Defensa Nacional*, Froylán Turcios. Tegucigalpa: Editorial Guaymuras, 1981.

——, ed. *Paulino Valladares: El Pensador y Su Mundo*. Tegucigalpa: Editorial Nuevo Continente, 1972.

Oyuela, Leticia. *Un Siglo en la Hacienda: Estancias y Haciendas en la Antigua Alcaldía Mayor de Tegucigalpa, 1670–1850*. Tegucigalpa: Banco Central de Honduras, 1994.

Pan American Union. "Honduras." *Monthly Bulletin*, vol. 33 (1911), pp. 298–315. Washington, D.C.: GPO, 1911.

Paredes, Lucas. *El Hombre del Puro: ¿Porque Carías Escogió a Gálvez?*. Tegucigalpa: Imprenta de Honduras, 1973.

——. *Los Culpables*. Tegucigalpa: Imprenta Honduras, 1970.

——. *Liberalismo y Nacionalismo (Transfuguismo Político)*. Tegucigalpa: Imprenta Honduras, 1963.

——. *Drama Político de Honduras*. Mexico: Editora Latinoamericana, 1958.

Partido de Innovación y Unidad. "Historia del PINU." *La Prensa*, 22 November 1972.

——. "PINU y Historia." Manuscript, PINU, n.d.

Partido Liberal de Honduras. *Biografías de Personajes Liberales*. Tegucigalpa: Consejo Central Ejecutivo del Partido Liberal, 1987.

——. *Datos Biográficos del Dr. Ramón Villeda Morales*. Tegucigalpa: Consejo Central Ejecutivo del Partido Liberal, 1955.

Partido Nacional de Honduras. *El Partido Nacional y la Legislación Laboral en Honduras*. San José: Talleres Antonio Lehman, 1970.

——. *Elecciones Municipales Estilo "Partido Liberal."* Tegucigalpa: Comité Central del Partido Nacional, 1968.

Pastor Fasquelle, Rodolfo. *Biografía de San Pedro Sula, 1536–1954*. San Pedro Sula: Centro Editorial, 1990.

——. *Memoria de Una Empresa Hondureña: Compañía Azucarera Hondureña, S.A.* San Pedro Sula: Centro Editorial, 1988.

——. "El Ocaso de los Cacicázgos: Historia de la Crisis del Sistema Político Hondureño." *Foro Internacional* (July–September 1985): 16–29.

Pastor Zelaya, Rodolfo. "Materialismo e Idealismo." *El Economista Hondureño*, no. 4 (April 1947): 147–48.

Paz Aguilar, Ernesto. *El Municipio en Honduras: De la Autonomia a la Servidumbre*. Tegucigalpa: Editorial Universitaria, 1984.

Paz Barnica, Edgardo. *Reestructuración Institucional de la Integración Centroamericana*. Tegucigalpa: Editorial Nuevo Continente, 1972.

——. *Villeda Morales: El Imperativo Categórico*. Tegucigalpa: Comité Central Ejecutivo del Partido Liberal, 1972.

——. *Las Garantías y los Principios Sociales en la Constitución de Honduras de 1957*. Tegucigalpa: Imprenta Calderón, 1963.

——, comp. *La Renovada Ruta del Liberalismo* Tegucigalpa: CETTNA, 1989.

Pearson, Neal J. "Peasant Pressure Groups and Agrarian Reform in Honduras, 1962–1977." In *Rural Change and Public Policy: Eastern Europe, Latin America, and Australia*, edited by William P. Avery, pp. 297–320. New York: Pergamon Press, 1980.

Peraza, José Antonio. *Confinamiento, Prisión y Destierro*. San Pedro Sula: Imprenta Antúnez, 1973.

Pérez Brignoli, Héctor. "Economía y Sociedad en Honduras durante el Siglo XIX." *Estudios Sociales Centroamericanos*, no. 6 (1973): 51–82.

Perry, G. R., comp. *National Directory of Honduras, Central America*. New York: Spanish American Directories Co., 1899.

Pincus, Joseph. *Breve Historia del Arancel de Aduanas de Honduras*. Tegucigalpa: MHCP, 1959.

Pineda, Andrés. *Soy Andreo Neda: Un Hombre Que No Quiso Ser Cucaracha*. Tegucigalpa: Editorial Guaymuras, 1981.

Pineda Portillo, Noé. *Geografía de Honduras*. 2d ed. Tegucigalpa: Editorial E.S.P., 1984.

Posas, Mario. *Modalidades del Proceso de Democratización en Honduras*. Tegucigalpa: Editorial Universitaria, 1989.

——. *Breve Historia de las Organizaciones Campesinas Hondureñas*. Tegucigalpa: Estudio de Artes Graficas, 1989.

——. *Las Centrales de Trabajadores en Honduras*. Tegucigalpa: Editorial Guaymuras, 1987.

——. "El Movimiento Campesino Hondureño: Un Panorama General (Siglo XX)." In *Historia Política de los Campesinos Latinoamericanos*, compiled by Pablo González Casanova, pp. 28–76. Mexico: Siglo XXI, 1985.

——. "Ingreso y Consolidación del Capital Imperialista." In *El Sub-Desarrollo en Honduras*, edited by UNAH as part of "Lecturas Seleccionadas De Sociología," pp. 1–45. Tegucigalpa: PROAVEH, 1984.
——. *Luchas del Movimiento Obrero Hondureño*. San José: EDUCA, 1981.
——. *Lucha Ideológica y Organización Sindical en Honduras, 1954–65*. Tegucigalpa: Editorial Universitaria, 1980.
——. "Honduras at the Crossroads." *Latin American Perspectives*, nos. 2–3 (Summer 1980): 45–54.
——. "Reforma Agraria, Lucha de Clases y Dominación Internacional: La Primera Ley de Reforma Agraria Hondureña." *Tareas* (Panama), no. 46 (1979–80): 75–119.
——. "Política Estatal y Estructura Agraria en Honduras, 1950–1978." *Economía Política*, no. 17 (November–April 1979): 29–124.
Posas, Mario, and Rafael Del Cid. *La Construcción del Sector Público y del Estado Nacional en Honduras, 1876–1979*. San José: EDUCA, 1981.
Posas, Mario, and Rafael Del Cid, "Honduras: Los Límites del Reformísmo Castrense, 1972–1979." *Revista Mexicana de Sociología*, no. 42 (April–June 1980): 607–48.
Quiñonez, Edgardo, and Mario Argueta. *Historia de Honduras*. Tegucigalpa: Escuela Superior del Profesorado "Francisco Morazán," 1978.
Ramírez, Asdrúbal. *Los Militares Patriotas y la Revolución Hondureña*. Tegucigalpa: Ediciones Compo., 1972.
Ramos Bejarano, Dionisio. "Something New in Honduras?" *World Marxist Review* 16, no. 5 (May 1973): 67–71.
Reina Valenzuela, José. "San Pedro Sula: Su Pasado, Su Presente, Su Porvernir." *La Pajarita de Papel* (October–December 1951): 89–104.
Reina Valenzuela, José, and Mario Argueta. *Marco Aurelio Soto: Reforma Liberal de 1876*. Tegucigalpa: BCH, 1978.
Rendón Madrid, Arturo. *Santa Rosa de Copán: La Sultana de Occidente*. Tegucigalpa: Secretaría de Cultura y Turismo, 1985.
Reyes, Felipe. *Honduras y las Compañías Ferroviarias* Tegucigalpa: TIPN, 1930.
Rietti, Mario V. *La Planficación del Desarrollo: Un Enfoque Internacional y Ley de Planificación de Honduras*. Tegucigalpa: COFINSA, 1987.
——. *Programas y Políticas de Desarrollo*. Tegucigalpa: López and Cía., 1980.
——. "Diagnóstico y Perspectivas de la Economía de Honduras." *Revista Extra*, no. 83 (June 1972): 49–78
——. "Análisis y Perspectivas de la Economía de Honduras." *Revista Extra*, no. 76 (Nov. 1971): 30–31.
——. "Diagnóstico de la Economía de Honduras." *Revista Extra*, no. 72 (July 1971): 43–48.
——. "Panorama Económico de Honduras en 1970." *Revista Extra*, no. 67 (February 1971): 41–45.
——. "Exposición del Lic. Mario Rietti, Gerente de la Financiera Hondureña, S.A." *La Industria*, no. 187 (May–June 1970): 12–16.
——. "Análisis de la Situación Económica de Honduras." *El Día*, 18 May 1968.
——. "Los Incentivos Fiscales al Desarrollo Industrial en Honduras." *Revista Extra*, no. 13 (August 1966): 11–13.

——. "Aspectos Sociales del Desarrollo Económico de Honduras." *Economía Política*, no. 15 (1966): 50–65.
——. "Diagnóstico de la Industria Manufacturera Hondureña." Thesis, UNAH, 1964.
——. "El Plan Nacional de Desarrollo y la Alianza para el Progreso." *El Día*, 24 March 1963.
Rivas Chacon, Catarino. *Bananas: Bosquejo Histórico de Su Desarrollo Industrial*. San Pedro Sula: Imprenta Antúnez, 1951.
Rivera y Morillo, Humberto. *San Pedro Usula: Génesis Histórica*. San Pedro Sula: Central Impresora, 1978.
Ropp, Steve C. "The Honduran Army in the Sociopolitical Evolution of the Honduran State." *The Americas* 30, no. 4 (April 1974): 504–28.
Ropp, Steve C., and James A. Morris. "Corporatism and Dependent Development: A Honduran Case Study." *Latin American Research Review* 12, no. 2 (1977): 27–68.
Rosenberg, Mark B. "Can Democracy Survive the Democrats? From Transition to Consolidation in Honduras." In *Elections and Democracy in Central America*, edited by John Booth and Mitchell Seligson, pp. 40–59. Chapel Hill: University of North Carolina Press, 1989.
Ross, Delmer G. *Visionaries and Swindlers: The Development of the Railways of Honduras*. Mobile, Ala.: Institute for Research in Latin America, 1975.
Rouquie, Alain. "Honduras–El Salvador, the War of One Hundred Hours: A Case of Regional Disintegration." *International Journal of Politics* 3, no. 3 (Fall 1973): 17–51.
Rovelo Landa, Pedro. "Nuestra Situación Económica: Concesiones II." *El Economista Hondureño*, no. 3 (30 April 1937): 8–10.
——. "Nuestra Situación Económica: Concesiones I." *El Economista Hondureño*, no. 2 (3/30/37): 20–23.
Rowles, James. *El Conflicto Honduras–El Salvador, 1969*. San José: EDUCA, 1980.
Ruhl, J. Mark. "Agrarian Structure and Political Stability in Honduras." *Journal of Interamerican Studies and World Affairs* 26, no. 1 (February 1984): 33–68.
Ruíz, José T. *Apuntes Biográficos Hondureños e Informaciones para el Turista*. Tegucigalpa: Imprenta Hernández, 1943.
Saavedra, David. *Bananas, Oro y Plata*. Tegucigalpa: Talleres Nacionales, 1936.
Sabillón García, and Orbelina Avila. "Enfoque Social y Económico de 'Cementos de Honduras, S. A.'" Thesis, UNAH, 1968.
Salgado, Félix. "Noticia Biográfica del Gral. don Luis Bográn." *Revista del Archivo y Biblioteca Nacional* 24, nos. 1–2 (July–August 1945): 2–5.
——. *Compendio de Historia de Honduras*. Comayagua: Imprenta "El Sol," 1928.
Salomón, Leticia. *Militarismo y Reformismo en Honduras*. Tegucigalpa: Editorial Guaymuras, 1982.
Santos M., Benjamín. *Díez Años de Lucha: Partido Democrata Cristiano de Honduras*. Guatemala: Editorial INCEP, 1980.
Schulz, Donald, and Deborah Sundloff Schulz. *The United States, Honduras, and the Crisis in Central America*. Boulder, Colo.: Westview Press, 1994.
Shepherd, Robert. "Honduras: A Land of Promise." *Industrial Development*. A reference study by Conway Research, Inc., November 1964, pp. 22–52.

Sieder, Rachel. "Honduras: The Politics of Exception and Military Reformism, 1972–1978." *Journal of Latin American Studies* 27 (1995): 99–127.
Slutsky, Daniel. "La Agroindustria de la Carne en Honduras." *Estudios Sociales Centroamericanos*, no. 22 (January–April 1979): 101–25.
Solorzano de Quesada, A. Julia. "Análisis de la Producción de Azucar en Honduras y Su Incidencia en la Economía Nacional durante el Quinquenio, 1969–1973." Thesis, UNAH, 1974.
Sorto Batres, Max. *Ramón Amaya Amador: Vida y Obra, Ensayo Biográfico*. Tegucigalpa: Ministerio de Cultura, 1989.
Stansifer, Charles L. "E. George Squier and the Honduras Interoceanic Railroad Project." *Hispanic American Historical Review* 46, no. 1 (1966): 1–27.
Stokes, William S. *Honduras: An Area Study in Government*. Madison: University of Wisconsin Press, 1950.
Stonich, Susan C. *"I Am Destroying the Land!" The Political Ecology of Poverty and Environmental Destruction in Honduras*. Boulder. Colo.: Westview Press, 1993.
Suazo, Filadélfo. *Una Vida en Nuestra Historia: Roque J. Rivera*. Tegucigalpa: RYCO, 1983.
——. "Suplemento Especial Dedicado al Desarrollo Histórico de San Pedro Sula." *Diario Tiempo*, 29 June 1973.
Suazo Rubí, Sergio. *Auge y Crisis Ideológica del Partido Liberal*. Tegucigalpa: Alin Editora, 1991.
Swedberg, Richard. "The Honduran Trade Union Movement, 1920–1982." Paper, Central American Information Office, Boston, March 1983.
Tenenbaum, Edward A. *Helping Honduran Industry: A Diagnostic Study*. Washington, D.C.: Continental-Allied Co., Inc., 1961.
Tosco, Manuel, Gabriel A. Mejía, Ernesto Sánchez, Míriam Napky, and V. Mejía. *Ingresos del Gobierno Central, 1924–1925/1951–1952*. Tegucigalpa: BCH, 1953.
Tosco, Manuel, and Rubén Mondragón Carrasco. *Primera Investigación Industrial: 1950, Honduras, Centroamerica*. Tegucigalpa: BCH, 1951.
Turcios, Froylán. *Memorias*. Tegucigalpa: Editorial Universitaria, 1980.
Turcios Rodriguez, Israel. *Movimiento Militar del 12 de Julio de 1959*. Tegucigalpa: Imprenta Calderón, 1990.
Valladares, Paulino. "Paradojas del Progreso Industrial." *Foro Hondureño*, no. 3 (October 1916): 80–81.
Valle, Rafael H., ed. *Oro de Honduras: Antología de Ramón Rosa*. Tegucigalpa: N.p., 1948.
Vallejo, Antonio R. *Primer Anuario Estadístico, 1889*. Tegucigalpa: Imprenta Nacional, 1893.
——. *Compendio de la Historia Social y Política de Honduras*. Tegucigalpa: TIPN, 1882.
Velásquez Cerrato, Col. Armando. *Las Fuerzas Armadas en una Democracia*. Tegucigalpa: TIPN, 1954.
Velásquez Díaz, Max. *Reorganización Liberal: Nuevas Bases para el Partido*. Tegucigalpa: Imprenta Calderón, 1972.
Vélez O., Annarela, and Iván Herrera. "Historia de la Municipalidad de Tegucigalpa, Años 1870–1903." Thesis, UNAH, 1982.
Villars, Rina. *Porque Quiero Seguir Viviendo. . . . Habla Graciela García*. Tegucigalpa: Editorial Guaymuras, 1991.

Villeda Morales, Ramón. *El Pensamiento Vivo de Villeda Morales*. Tegucigalpa: Tipografía Ariston, [1964?].

——. "La Natalidad Ilegítima." *Vanguardia*, no. 5 (5 July 1946).

Vinelli, Paul. "The Currency and Exchange System of Honduras." *IMF Staff Papers*. Vol. 1, no. 3, pp. 420–31, 1950–51.

Waiselfisz, Jacobo. "El Comercio Exterior, el Mercado Común y la Industrialización en Relación al Conflicto." In Carías and Slutsky, *La Guerra Inutil: Análisis Socio-económico del Conflicto entre Honduras y El Salvador*, pp. 165–240. San José: EDUCA, 1971.

Wild Foote, William. *Folklore Ceibeño: Un Siglo de Historia*. La Ceiba: Tipografía Renacimiento. 1982.

Wright, Theodore P., Jr. "Honduras: A Case Study of United States Support of Free Elections in Central America." *Hispanic American Historical Review* 40, no. 2 (May 1960): 212–23.

Young, Arthur N. "Reforma Financiera en Honduras, [1921]." In *Historia financiera de Honduras*, compiled by Banco de Central de Honduras, pp. 7–61. Tegucigalpa: Banco Central de Honduras, 1957.

Yu Shan Salinas, Adriana. "Historia y Desarrollo de la Banca Privada en Honduras." Thesis, UNAH, 1968.

Zaldívar Guzmán, Raúl. *Liberalismo en Honduras*. Tegucigalpa: Asociación Liberal de Profesionales, 1964.

Zelaya, Oscar. "Tipificación del Grupo Social Dominante en el Antiguo Departamento de Tegucigalpa, 1839–1875." Thesis, UNAH, 1992.

Zerón, José. *Roosevelt y Carías Andino*. Tegucigalpa: TIPN, 1942.

Zúñiga Huete, Angel. *Cartas: Una Actitud y Una Senda*. Mexico: N.p., 1949.

——. *Un Cacicázgo Centroamericano*. Mexico: Imprenta Victoria, 1938.

——. *Idolo Desnudo*. Mexico: Acción Moderna Mercantil, 1939.

Zúñiga Figueroa, Carlos. *Estadísticas Demográficas, 1926–1951*. Tegucigalpa: TIPN, 1953.

## Secondary Works on Latin America

Acuña, Victor H. "Las Repúblicas Agroexportadoras, 1870–1945." In *Historia General de Centro América*, vol. 4, edited by Edelberto Torres-Rivas, pp. 255–323. Madrid: Quinto Centenario-FLACSO, 1993.

Adams, Frederick U. *Conquest of the Tropics*. New York: Doubleday, Page and Co., 1914.

Ameringer, Charles D. *The Democratic Left in Exile: The Antidictatorial Struggle in the Caribbean, 1945–1959*. Coral Gables: University of Miami Press, 1974.

Anderson, Charles W. "Central American Political Parties." *Western Political Quarterly* 15, no. 1 (March 1962): 125–39.

Araya Pochet, Carlos. "El Enclave Minero en Centroamérica, 1880–1945: Un Estudio de los Casos de Honduras, Nicaragua y Costa Rica." *Revista de Ciencias Sociales* 17–18 (1979): 13–59.

Baloyra, José. "Reactionary Despotism in Central America." *Journal of Latin American Studies* 15 (November 1983): 295–315.
Barber, Willard F., and C. Neale Ronning. *Internal Security and Military Power: Counterinsurgency and Civic Action in Latin America*. Columbus: Ohio State University Press, 1966.
Bergquist, Charles. *Labor in Latin America: Comparative Essays on Chile, Argentina, Venezuela, and Colombia*. Stanford, Calif.: Stanford University Press, 1986.
Bernstein, Marvin D., ed. *Foreign Investment in Latin America: Cases and Attitudes*. New York: Alfred A. Knopf, 1966.
Best, Michael H. "Political Power and Tax Revenues in Central America." *Journal of Development Economics*, no. 3 (1976): 49–82.
Black, Jan Knippers. *Sentinels of Empire: The United States and Latin American Militarism*. New York: Greenwood Press, 1986.
Blandón, Jesús Miguel. *Entre Sandino y Fonseca Amador*. Managua: Talleres de Impresiones Troquela, 1980.
Booth, John A., and Thomas W. Walker. *Understanding Central America*. Boulder, Colo.: Westview Press, 1989.
Borge, Tómas. *La Paciente Impaciencia*. Managua: Editorial Vanguardia, 1989.
Bulmer-Thomas, Victor. *The Political Economy of Central America since 1920*. Cambridge: Cambridge University Press, 1987.
Burns, E. Bradford. *The Poverty of Progress: Latin America in the Nineteenth Century*. Berkeley: University of California Press, 1983.
Cable, Vincent. "The 'Football War' and the Central American Common Market." *International Affairs*, no. 45 (October 1969): 658–71.
Cardoso, Ciro F. S. "The Liberal Era, ca. 1870–1930." In *Central America since Independence*, edited by Leslie Bethell, pp. 37–67. Cambridge: Cambridge University Press, 1991.
——. "Historia Económica del Café en Centroamerica (Siglo xix): Estudio Comparativo." *Estudios Sociales Centroamericanos*, no. 10 (January–April 1975): 9–55.
Carlson, Reynold E. "Economic Development in Central America." *Inter-American Economic Affairs* 11, no. 2 (Autumn 1948): 3–29.
Casaus Arzú, Marta E. "La Metamorfosis de las Oligarquías Centroamericanas." In *Centroamérica: Balance de la Década de los 80*, compiled by M. E. Casaus Arzú and Rolando Castillo Quintana, pp. 265–322. Madrid: Fundación CEDEAL, 1993.
Castillo Rivas, Donaldo. *Acumulación de Capital y Empresas Transnacionales en Centroamerica*. Mexico: Siglo XXI, 1980.
Christou, G., and W. T. Wilford. "Trade Intensification in the Central American Common Market." *Journal of Interamerican Studies and World Affairs* 15, no. 2 (May 1973): 249–63.
Cline, William R., and Enrique Delgado, eds. *Economic Integration in Central America*. Washington, D.C.: Brookings Institute, 1978.
Collier, Ruth Berins, and David Collier. *Shaping the Political Arena: Critical Cunjunctures, the Labor Movement, and Regime Dynamics in Latin America*. Princeton: Princeton University Press, 1991.
Cooper, Frederick, Steve J. Stern, and Florencía E. Mallon. *Confronting Historical Para-*

*digms: Peasants, Labor, and the Capitalist World System in Africa and Latin America.* Madison: University of Wisconsin Press, 1993.
Crowther, Samuel. *The Romance and Rise of the American Tropics.* 1929. Reprint. New York: Arno Press, 1976.
Dada Hirezi, H. *La Economía de El Salvador y la Integración Centroamericana.* San José: EDUCA, 1983.
Davis, Sheldon. "Agrarian Structure and Ethnic Resistance: The Indian in Guatemalan and Salvadoran National Politics." In *Ethnicities and Nations,* by Remo Guidieri et al., pp. 78–106. Houston: Rothko Chapel, 1988.
Delgado, Enrique. *Evolución del Mercado Común Centroamericano y Desarrollo Equilibrado.* San José: EDUCA, 1981.
Dunkerley, James. *Power in the Isthmus: A Political History of Modern Central America.* London: Verso Press, 1988.
——. *The Long War: Dictatorship and Revolution in El Salvador.* London: Verso Press, 1982.
Ellis, Frank. *Las Transnacionales del Banano en Centroamerica.* San José: EDUCA, 1983.
Escobar, Arturo, and Sonia E. Alvarez, eds. *The Making of Social Movements in Latin America: Identity, Strategy, and Democracy.* Boulder, Colo.: Westview Press, 1992.
Escobar Bethancourt, Rómulo. *Torrijos: Espada y Pensamiento.* Panama: N.p., 1982.
Etchison, Don L. *The United States and Militarism in Central America.* New York: Praeger Press, 1975.
Foster, David W., ed. *Latin American Government Leaders.* 2d ed. Tempe: Arizona State University Press, 1975.
Furtado, Celso. *Economic Development of Latin America.* Cambridge: Cambridge University Press, 1976.
Gleijeses, Piero. "La Aldea de Ubico: Guatemala, 1931–1944." *Mesoamérica* 17 (June 1989): 25–59.
——. "Juan José Arévalo and the Caribbean Legion." *Journal of Latin American Studies,* no. 21 (February 1989): 133–45.
Gould, Jeffrey L. " 'For an Organized Nicaragua': Somoza and the Labour Movement, 1944–1948." *Journal of Latin American Studies* 19 (November 1987): 354–87.
Grieb, Kenneth J. *Guatemalan Caudillo: The Regime of Jorge Ubico.* Athens: Ohio University Press, 1979.
Gudmundson, Lowell. "Lord and Peasant in the Making of Modern Central America." In *Agrarian Structures and Political Power in Latin America,* edited by Evelyn Huber-Stephens and Frank Safford, pp. 153–78. Pittsburgh: University of Pittsburgh Press, 1995.
Haggard, Stephen. "The Political Economy of Direct Foreign Investment in Latin America." *Latin American Research Review* 4, no. 1 (1989): 184–208.
Hamill, Hugh M., ed. *Caudillos: Dictators in Spanish America.* Norman: Oklahoma University Press, 1992.
Handy, Jim. " 'The Most Precious Fruit of the Revolution': The Guatemalan Agrarian Reform, 1952–54." *Hispanic American Historical Review* 68, no. 4 (November 1988): 675–705.
Hill, Roscoe R. "Economic Factors in Central America." In *The Caribbean Area,* edited by A. Curtis Wilgus, pp. 228–46. Seattle: Washington University Press, 1934.

Hilton, Ronald H., comp. "Honduras." In *Who's Who In Latin America, 1945–1951*. Stanford University. 3d ed., pp. 53–66. Reprint. Detroit: Blaine Ethridge Books, 1971.
Humphreys, R. H. *Latin America and the Second World War*. Vol. 1, *1939–1942*. London: Athlone Press, 1981.
Immerman, Richard G. *The CIA in Guatemala: The Foreign Policy of Intervention*. Austin: University of Texas Press, 1982.
James, Daniel. *Red Design for the Americas*. New York: John Day, 1954.
Jenkins, Rhys. *Transnational Corporations and Industrial Transformation in Latin America*. Cambridge: Cambridge University Press, 1984.
Johnson, John J. *The Military and Society in Latin America*. Stanford, Calif.: Stanford University Press, 1964.
Jonas Bodenheimer, Susanne. "El Mercomún y la Ayuda Norteamericana." In *Inversiones Extranjeras en Centroamerica*, edited by Rafael Menjivar, pp. 124–66. San José: EDUCA, 1975.
——. "Poder a Control Remoto: La Ayuda de AID al Mercado Común Centroamericano." *Economía Política*, no. 10 (May–October 1975): 102–57.
Kantor, Harry. *Patterns of Politics and Political Systems in Latin America*. Chicago: Rand McNally, 1969.
Karnes, Thomas L. *The Tropical Enterprise: The Standard Fruit and Steamship Company in Latin America*. Baton Rouge: Louisiana State University, 1978.
——. *The Failure of Union: Central America, 1824–1960*. Chapel Hill: University of North Carolina Press, 1961.
Klaren, Peter F., and Thomas J. Bossert, eds. *Promise of Development: Theories of Change in Latin America*. Boulder, Colo.: Westview Press, 1986.
Koebel, W. H. *Central America*. New York: Charles Scribner's Sons, 1927.
Krehm, William. *Democracies and Tyrannies of the Caribbean*. Westport, Conn.: Greenwood Press, 1984.
Langley, Lester, and Thomas Schoonover. *The Banana Men: American Mercenaries and Entrepreneurs in Central America, 1880–1930*. Lexington: University of Kentucky Press, 1995.
Levine, Meldon E. *El Sector Privado y el Mercado Común*. Guatemala: Instituto Nacional de Administración para el Desarrollo, 1968.
Lieuwen, Edwin. *Generals versus Presidents: Neomilitarism in Latin America*. New York: Praeger Press, 1964.
——. *Arms and Politics in Latin America*. New York: Praeger Press, 1960.
Liss, Sheldon B. *Radical Thought in Central America*. Boulder, Colo.: Westview Press, 1991.
Lockley, Lawrence C. *A Guide to Market Data in Central America*. Tegucigalpa: Central American Bank for Economic Integration, 1964.
Long, William Rodney. *Railways of Central America and West Indies*. Washington, D.C.: GPO, 1925.
McCamant, John F. *Development Assistance in Central America*. New York: Praeger Press, 1968.
McClintock, Cynthia, and Abraham F. Lowenthal, eds. *The Peruvian Experiment Reconsidered*. Princeton: Princeton University Press, 1983.

Marichal, Carlos. *A Century of Debt Crises in Latin America: From Independence to the Great Depression, 1820–1930*. Princeton: Princeton University Press, 1989.

Martin, Percy A. *Who's Who in Latin America*. Stanford, Calif.: Stanford University Press, 1935.

Martz, John D. *Central America: The Crisis and the Challenge*. Chapel Hill: University of North Carolina Press, 1959.

May, Stacy, and Galo Plaza. *The United Fruit Company in Latin America*. Washington, D.C.: National Planning Association, 1958.

Mörner, Magnus. *Region and State in Latin America's Past*. Baltimore: Johns Hopkins University Press, 1993.

Naylor, Robert A. *Penny Ante Imperialism: The Mosquito Shore and the Bay of Honduras, 1600–1914: A Case Study in British Informal Empire*. London: Fairleigh Dickinson University Press, 1989.

Ochoa, Enrique C. "The Rapid Expansion of Voter Participation in Latin America: Presidential Elections, 1845–1986." In *Statistical Abstracts of Latin America*, vol. 25, edited by Richard Wilkie and David Lorey, pp. 862–910. Los Angeles: UCLA Publications, 1987.

O'Connor, James. "Agrarian Reform in Cuba, 1959–1963." *Science and Society* 12 (Spring 1968): 169–217.

Pan American Union. *Economic Survey of Latin America, 1962*. Baltimore: Johns Hopkins University Press, 1964.

Parkman, Patricia. *Nonviolent Insurrection in El Salvador: The Fall of Maximiliano Hernández Martínez*. Tucson: University of Arizona Press, 1987.

Pérez Brignoli, Héctor. *A Brief History of Central America*. Berkeley: University of California Press, 1989.

Pincus, Joseph. *The Central American Common Market*. Washington, D.C.: AID, 1962.

——. *Industrial Development Laws of Central America*. Washington, D.C.: International Cooperation Administration, 1961.

Poitevin, René. *El Proceso de Industrialización en Guatemala*. San José: EDUCA, 1977.

Ramírez, Sergio, comp. *Augusto C. Sandino: El Pensamiento Vivo*. Vols. 1–2. Managua: Editorial Nueva Nicaragua, 1981.

Robles, Farah C. "Los Empresarios Deben Influir para que la Política la Manejen los Honestos." An interview with Jorge Bueso Arias enclosed in a special edition of *Diario Tiempo*, 2 May 1995, dedicated to "Jorge Bueso Arias: Empresario del Año, 1994."

Romualdi, Serafíno. *Presidents and Peons: Recollections of a Labor Ambassador in Latin America*. New York: Funk and Wagnalls, 1967.

——. "A Report on Central America Today." *American Federationist* 62 (1955): 18–20.

Ropp, Steve C. "Teorías sobre el Comportamiento de los Militares Centroamericanos." *Estudios Centroamericanos* (San Salvador) (May–June 1986): 411–30.

——. *Panama Politics: From Guarded Nation to National Guard*. New York: Praeger Press, 1982.

Roseberry, William. "Beyond the Agrarian Question in Latin America." In *Confronting Historical Paradigms: Peasants, Labor, and the Capitalist World System in Africa and Latin America*, edited by Frederick Cooper, Allen F. Isaacman, Florencía E. Mal-

lon, William Roseberry, and Steve J. Stern, pp. 318–68. Madison: University of Wisconsin Press, 1993.
Roxborough, Ian. "Labor Control and the Postwar Growth Model in Latin America." In *Latin American in the 1940s: War and Postwar Transitions*, edited by David Rock, pp. 248–64. Berkeley: University of California Press, 1994.
Samper, Mario, and Héctor Peréz Brignoli, eds. *Tierra, Café y Sociedad: Ensayos sobre la Historia Agraria Centroamericana*. San José: FLACSO, 1994.
Sánchez-Albornoz, Nicolas. "The Population of Latin America, 1850–1930." In *The Cambridge History of Latin America*, vol. 4, edited by Leslie Bethell, pp. 121–52. Cambridge: Cambridge University Press, 1986.
——. "The Population of Colonial Spanish America." In *The Cambridge History of Latin American*, vol. 2, edited by Leslie Bethell, pp. 3–35. Cambridge: Cambridge University Press, 1984.
Schoonover, Thomas, and Ebba Schoonover. "Statistics for an Understanding of Foreign Intrusions into Central America from the 1820s to 1930." *Anuario de Estudios Centroamericanos* 15, no. 1 (1989): 93–117.
Smith, Robert S. "Financing the Central American Federation, 1821–1838." *Hispanic American Historical Review* 43 (November 1963): 483–510.
Stern, Steve J. "Feudalism, Capitalism, and the World-System in the Perspective of Latin America and the Caribbean." *American Historical Review* 93, no. 4 (October 1988): 829–72.
Torres-Rivas, Edelberto. *Repression and Resistance: The Struggle for Democracy in Central America*. Boulder, Colo.: Westview Press, 1989.
——. "The Nature of the Central American Crisis." In *Towards an Alternative for Central America and the Caribbean*, edited by G. Irvin and Xabier Gorostiaga, pp. 38–53. London: George Allen and Unwin, 1985.
——. "Notas para Comprender la Crisis Política Centroamericana." In *Centroamerica: Crisis y Política Internacional*, edited by T. Martínez Tarrago and M. Campillo Illanes, pp. 39–69. Mexico: Siglo XXI, 1982.
——. "Notas sobre la Crisis de la Dominación Burguesa en America Latina." In *Clases Sociales y Crisis Política en America Latina*, edited by R. Benítez Zenteno, pp. 13–70. Mexico: Siglo XXI, 1977.
——. "Naturaleza y Crisis del Poder en Centroamérica." *Estudios Sociales Centroamericanos*, no. 3 (September–December 1972): 37–81.
——. *Interpretación del Desarrollo Social Centroamericano: Procesos y Estructuras de una Sociedad Dependiente*. 3d ed. San José: EDUCA, 1973.
Towsend Ezcurra, Andrés. *Las Provincias Unidas de Centro América: Fundación de la República*. San José: EDUCA, 1973.
Vilas, Carlos. "Revolutionary Unevenness in Central America." *New Left Review*, no. 175 (May–June 1989): 111–25.
Weaver, Frederick Stirton. *Inside the Volcano: The History and Political Economy of Central America*. Boulder, Colo.: Westview Press, 1994.
Weeks, John. "An Interpretation of the Central American Crisis." *Latin American Research Review* 21, no. 3 (1986): 31–53.
——. *The Economies of Central America*. New York: Holmes and Meier, 1985.

Wilkie, Richard W. *Latin American Population and Urbanization Analysis: Maps and Statistics, 1950–1982*. Los Angeles: UCLA, 1984.
Williams, Robert G. *States and Social Evolution: Coffee and the Rise of National Governments in Central America*. Chapel Hill: University of North Carolina Press, 1994.
——. *Export Agriculture and the Crisis in Central America*. Chapel Hill: University of North Carolina Press, 1986.
Wilmore, Larry. "Direct Foreign Investment in Central American Manufacturing." *World Development* 4, no. 6 (1976): 499–517.
Wilson, Charles M. *Empire in Green and Gold: The Story of the American Banana Trade*. New York: Henry Holt, 1947.
Woodward, Ralph L., Jr. "The Historiography of Modern Central America since 1960." *Hispanic American Historical Review* 67, no. 3 (August 1987): 461–96.
Wynia, Gary W. *Politics and Planners: Economic Development Policy in Central America*. Madison: University of Wisconsin Press, 1972.
Young, John P. *Central American Currency and Finance*. Princeton: Princeton University Press, 1925.

## Works on U.S. Foreign Policy

Agee, Philip. *On the Run*. Secaucus, N.J.: Lyle Stuart, 1987.
——. *Inside the Company: CIA Diary*. 6th ed. New York: Bantam Books, 1976.
Beaulac, Willard B. *The Fractured Continent: Latin America in Close-Up*. Stanford, Calif.: Hoover Institution Press, 1980.
——. *A Diplomat Looks at Aid to Latin America*. Carbondale: Southern Illinois University, 1970.
Bishop Berle, Beatrice, and Travis Beal Jacobs, eds. *Navigating the Rapids, 1918–1971: From the Papers of Adolf A. Berle*. New York: Harcourt Brace Jovanovich, 1973.
Erb, Claude E. "Prelude to Point Four: The Institute of Inter-American Affairs." *Diplomatic History*, no. 9 (Summer 1985): 249–69.
LaFeber, Walter. *Inevitable Revolutions: The United States in Central America*. New York: W. W. Norton, 1983.
——. "Latin American Policy." In *Exploring the Johnson Years*, edited by Robert D. Divine, pp. 63–90. Austin: University of Texas Press, 1981.
——. *America, Russia, and the Cold War, 1945–1966*. New York: John Wiley and Sons, 1967.
Leonard, Thomas M. *The United States and Central America, 1944–1949*. Mobile: University of Alabama, 1984.
Levinson, Jerome, and Juan de Onís. *The Alliance That Lost Its Way*. Chicago: Quadrangle Press, 1970.
Paterson, Thomas G. "Fixation with Cuba: The Bay of Pigs, Missile Crisis, and Covert War against Castro." In *Kennedy's Quest for Victory: American Foreign Policy, 1961–1963*, edited by T. G. Paterson, pp. 123–55. New York: Oxford University Press, 1989.
Rabe, Stephen G. *Eisenhower and Latin America: The Foreign Policy of Anticommunism*. Chapel Hill: University of North Carolina Press, 1988.

———. “Inter-American Military Cooperation, 1944–1954.” *World Affairs*, no. 137 (Fall 1974): 132–49.
Schwarz, Jordan A. *Adolf A. Berle and the Vision of an American Era*. New York: Free Press, Collier, Macmillan, 1987.
Tulchin, Joseph L. “The United States and Latin America in the 1960s.” *Journal of Interamerican Studies and World Affairs* 30, no. 1 (Spring 1988): 1–36.
White, Richard A. *The Morass: United States Intervention in Central America*. New York: Harper and Row, 1984.

## DISSERTATIONS AND THESES WRITTEN IN THE UNITED STATES

Anderson, Charles W. “Political Ideology and the Revolution of Rising Expectations in Central America, 1944–1958.” Ph.D. diss., University of Wisconsin, 1960.
Baer, Donald E. “Taxation and the Economic Development of Costa Rica and Honduras with Emphasis upon Consumption and Agricultural Based Taxes.” Ph.D. diss., University of Illinois at Urbana-Champaign, 1971.
Bengston, Nels A. “Studies in the Geography of Honduras.” Ph.D. diss., Clark University, 1927.
Bishop, Jeff M. “Arévalo and Central American Unification.” Ph.D. diss., Louisiana State University, 1971.
Brand, Charles A. “The Background of Capitalist Underdevelopment: Honduras to 1913.” Ph.D. diss., University of Pittsburgh, 1972.
Bruhn, Kathleen. “Elections and Democracy in Honduras: Kissing Cousins or Feuding Kin?” Master’s thesis, Stanford University, 1988.
Crowley, William K. “San Pedro Sula, Honduras: The Order and Disorder of the Pubescent Period in Central America’s Most Rapidly Growing City.” Ph.D. diss., University of Oregon, 1972.
Echeverri-Gent, Elisavinda. “Labor, Class, and Political Representation: A Comparative Analysis of Honduras and Costa Rica.” 2 vols. Ph.D. diss., University of Chicago, 1988.
Euraque, Darío A. “Merchants and Industrialists in Northern Honduras: The Making of a National Bourgeoisie in Peripheral Capitalism, 1870s–1972.” Ph.D. diss., University of Wisconsin-Madison, 1990.
———. “Social Structure and the Emergence of the Bourgeois Press in Honduras: A Historical Perspective.” Master’s thesis, University of Wisconsin-Madison, 1986.
Fernández Molina, José A. “Coloring the World in Blue: The Indigo Boom and the Central America Market, 1750–1810.” Ph.D. diss., University of Texas-Austin, 1992.
Finney, Kenneth V. “Precious Metals Mining and the Modernization of Honduras: In Quest of El Dorado, 1880–1900.” Ph.D. diss., Tulane University, 1973.
———. “The Central Americans’ Reaction to Herbert Hoover’s Foreign Policy.” Master’s thesis, Tulane University, 1969.
Gálvez, Laura. “Honduras and the United States, 1890–1903.” Master’s thesis, University of Florida, 1984.
Gibson, Jeffrey R. “A Demographic Analysis of Urbanization: Evolution of a System

of Cities in Honduras, El Salvador, and Costa Rica." Ph.D. diss., Cornell University, 1970.
Guevara-Escudero, Francisco. "Nineteenth-Century Honduras: A Regional Approach to the Economic History of Central America, 1839–1914." Ph.D. diss., New York University, 1983.
LaBarge, Richard A. "A Study of United Fruit Company Operations in Isthmian America, 1946–1956." Ph.D. diss., Duke University, 1960.
Lommel, Anne W. "U.S. Efforts to Foster Peace and Stability in Central America, 1923–1954." Ph.D. diss., University of Minnesota, 1967.
Martinson, Tommy. "Selected Changes in Agricultural Production and Economic Rent along the Western Highway of Honduras." Ph.D. diss., University of Kansas, 1970.
Millorn, Mark. "The Loan War: The Honduran Revolution of 1910–1911 and Its Causes." Master's thesis, New Mexico State University, 1993.
Morris, James A. "Interest Groups and Politics in Honduras." Ph.D. diss., University of New Mexico, 1974.
Navarrete, George. "The Latin American Policy of Charles Evans Hughes, 1921–1925." Ph.D. diss., University of California-Berkeley, 1965.
Naylor, Robert. "British Commercial Relations with Central America, 1821–1851." Ph.D. diss., Tulane University, 1958.
Noé Pino, Hugo R. "The Structural Roots of Crisis: Economic Growth and Decline in Honduras, 1950–1984." Ph.D diss., University of Texas at Austin, 1988.
Padula, Alfred L., Jr. "The Fall of the Bourgeoisie: Cuba, 1959–1961." Ph.D. diss., University of New Mexico, 1974.
Palmer, Steven. "A Liberal Discipline: Inventing Nations in Guatemala and Costa Rica, 1870–1900." Ph.D. diss. Columbia University, 1990.
Rietti, Mario V. "Industrialization and Economic Integration: The Case of Honduras." Master's thesis, Stanford University, 1965.
Ropp, Steve C. "In Search of the New Soldier: Junior Officers and the Prospects of Social Reform in Panama, Honduras, and Nicaragua." Ph.D. diss., University of California, Riverside, 1971.
Ross, Daniel J. "The Honduras Revolution of 1924 and American Intervention." Master's thesis, University of Florida, 1969.
Ross, David F. "The Economic Development of Honduras." Ph.D. diss., Harvard University, 1955.
Ross, Delmer G. "The Construction of the Railroads of Central America." Ph.D. diss., University of California, Santa Barbara, 1970.
Shirey, Ruth I. "An Analysis of the Location of Manufacturing: Tegucigalpa and San Pedro Sula." Ph.D. diss., University of Tennessee, 1970.
Thompson, Joseph R. "An Economic Analysis of Public Expenditure in Honduras, 1925–1963." Ph.D. diss., University of Florida, 1968.
Villanueva, Benjamin. "Institutional Innovation and Economic Development: Honduras: A Case Study." Ph.D. diss., University of Wisconsin, 1968.
Williams, Robert G. "The Central American Common Market: Unequal Benefits and Uneven Development." Ph.D. diss., Stanford University, 1978.

Yeager, Gene S. "The Honduran Foreign Debt, 1825–1953." Ph.D. diss., Tulane University, 1975.
———. "Honduras Transportation and Communication Development: The Rise of Tegucigalpa, 1878–1900." Master's thesis, Tulane University, 1972.

## Other Works Consulted

Alford, Robert R., and Roger Friedland. *Powers of Theory: Capitalism, the State, and Democracy*. Cambridge: Cambridge University Press, 1985.
Anderson, Benedict. *Imagined Communities: Reflections on the Origins and Spread of Nationalism*. London: Verso Press, 1983.
Chilcote, Ronald H. *Theories of Comparative Politics: The Search for a Paradigm*. Boulder, Colo.: Westview Press, 1981.
Hobsbawm, Eric J. *Nations and Nationalism since 1780: Programme, Myth, and Reality*. Cambridge: Cambridge University Press, 1990.
Johnson, Dale L. "Dialectics and Determination in the Theory of Social Classes." In *Class and Social Development: A New Theory of the Middle Class*, edited by D. L. Johnson, pp. 49–84. Beverly Hills, Calif.: Sage Publications, 1982.
Kay, Cristóbal. *Latin American Theories of Development and Underdevelopment*. London: Routledge, 1989.
Love, Joseph L. "Raul Prebisch and the Origin of the Doctrine of Unequal Exchange." *Latin American Research Review* 15, no. 3 (1980): 45–72.
Offe, Clause, and Helmut Wiesenthal. "Two Logics of Collective Action: Theoretical Notes on Social Class and Organizational Form." In *Political Power and Social Theory*, vol. 1, edited by Maurice Zeitlin, pp. 67–115. Greenwich, Conn: JAI Press, 1980.
McCann, Thomas P. *On the Inside*. Boston: Quinlan Press, 1987.
Schleit, Philip. *Shelton's Barefoot Airlines*. Annapolis, Md.: Fishergate Publishing Co., 1982.
Smith, Alan K. "Where Was the Periphery?: The Wider World and the Core of the World-Economy." *Radical History Review*, no. 3 (1987): 28–48.
Therborn, Goran. *Science, Class, and Society*. London: Verso Press, 1980.
———. "The Rule of Capital and the Rise of Bourgeois Democracy." *New Left Review*, no. 103 (May–June 1977): 3–41.
Wallerstein, Immanuel. "The Bourgeois [*sic*] as Concept and Reality." *New Left Review*, no. 162 (January–February 1988): 91–106.
Whitfield, Stephen J. "Strange Fruit: The Career of Samuel Zemurray." *American Jewish History* 82, no. 3 (March 1984): 307–23.
Wright, Erik O. *Classes*. London: Verso Press, 1985.

# INDEX